T0320882

Capitalisms

Capitalisms

Towards a Global History

Edited by
Kaveh Yazdani
and
Dilip M. Menon

OXFORD
UNIVERSITY PRESS

OXFORD
UNIVERSITY PRESS

Oxford University Press is a department of the University of Oxford.
It furthers the University's objective of excellence in research, scholarship,
and education by publishing worldwide. Oxford is a registered trademark of
Oxford University Press in the UK and in certain other countries.

Published in India by
Oxford University Press
22 Workspace, 2nd Floor, 1/22 Asaf Ali Road, New Delhi 110002, India

© Oxford University Press 2020

The moral rights of the authors have been asserted.

First Edition published in 2020

ISBN-13 (print edition): 978-0-19-949971-7
ISBN-10 (print edition): 0-19-949971-3

ISBN-13 (eBook): 978-0-19-909925-2
ISBN-10 (eBook): 0-19-909925-1

Typeset in Adobe Garamond Pro 11/13
by The Graphics Solution, New Delhi 110 092
Printed in India by Replika Press Pvt. Ltd

Contents

II CASE STUDIES IN THE HISTORIES OF CAPITALISMS

Figures and Tables

Figure

Tables

Acknowledgements

This project came into being through lively discussions that took place November 2015 onwards between the editors over Kaveh's own work as well as the developing field on the various histories of capitalism and the idea of the 'Great Divergence'. We started to think about a major workshop regarding these issues and an array of institutions to secure funding. We also reflected upon possible contributors for the workshop.

The Centre for Indian Studies in Africa was congenial to the enterprise of examining historical capitalism from a global perspective. Founded in 2010 with funding from the Andrew W. Mellon Foundation, it was set up as a research centre that would study the connected histories of Africa and India through narratives of the Indian Ocean. The intellectual remit expanded over time from studying the movement of material and people to the circulation and genealogy of ideas. This coincided with the moment when there was a popular student demand to decolonize knowledge in South African universities. From thinking about transnational and global history, we moved to engaging with knowledge from the Global South—Latin America, the Caribbean, Africa, and Asia. This demanded that we search for newer ways of theorizing existing concepts like capitalism, modernity, migration, and their histories. This volume arises from the desire to engage with wider geographies and longer temporalities, while at the same time questioning inherited categories and historical trajectories.

Being in South Africa and in the exciting intellectual climate of the University of the Witwatersrand has shaped this book. We would like to thank the vice chancellor, Professor Adam Habib; the former vice principal, Professor Tawana Kupe; and the Dean of Humanities,

Professor Ruksana Osman, for their unstinting support for the intellectual work of the Centre. Professor Isabel Hofmeyr, with her wide-ranging engagement with the history of the Indian Ocean, was the spur for our initial engagements with wider histories and geographies. Professor Imraan Valodia, dean of commerce, law and management, and Professor Eric Worby, director of Humanities Graduate Centre, generously assisted with the airfare for two participants. Adéle Prins, artist and graphic designer, conceptualized the brilliant poster for the conference; we would also like to extend our gratitude to her and Givan Lötz from PR/NA (www.prinsdesign.co.za) for the cover illustration.

In the making of this volume, we would like to express our gratitude to the Rosa Luxemburg Foundation (in particular, Jan Leidecker, Fredson Guillengue, and Tafadzwa Mlambo) for their generous funding and support. We would also like to thank our collaborator and co-host Professor Peter Vale, founding director of the Johannesburg Institute for Advanced Study (JIAS). Riaan de Villiers painstakingly and accurately transcribed the proceedings of the conference so that not a single observation or aside was lost.

We would further like to acknowledge Professor Bill Freund, Professor Gillian Heart, and Professor Pedro Machado for their active and committed participation in the conference. While conceptualizing and preparing this volume, we sought advice from a number of historians and economists across the world to introduce us to academics and new voices who have studied the subject and have important things to say. The scholars we consulted include Nasser Mohajer, Professor Osamu Saito, Professor Jeffrey Wasserstrom, Professor Dale Tomich, Professor Seth Rockman, Professor Victor Lieberman, Professor Kaoru Sugihara, Professor Suraiya Faroqhi, Professor Timur Kuran, Professor Sanjay Subramanyam, Dr Kerem Nişancıoğlu, Professor Jared Rubin, and Professor Metin Cosgel. We are grateful to them for their precious support and assistance. We would also like to express our sincere appreciation to the anonymous reviewers who provided us with helpful comments and suggestions.

We are further grateful to a number of colleagues who supported us in proofreading parts of the manuscript (Naima and Kimberly Bright), as well as helping us in doing the obligatory paperwork, in correcting typographical errors, and formatting the manuscript

(Lerato Sekele, Anh-Susann Pham Thi, Ezge Sezgin, and Frederic Kunkel). We would like also to thank Murat Çizakça, who engaged in discussions with us on 'Islamic capitalism'. Last but not least, the editorial team at Oxford University Press deserves an abundance of gratitude for their support and valuable suggestions.

Above all, we would like to thank the contributors to the volume, both those who attended the conference in Johannesburg in June 2016 as well as those who contributed later, drawn in by the intellectual enterprise of writing the history of diverse capitalisms globally.

We hope that this volume can make a humble contribution to the existing literature on the histories of capitalism(s). It will hopefully encourage more profound studies from the vantage point of both similar as well as other spaces and periods.

Introduction

Kaveh Yazdani and *Dilip M. Menon*[1]

In writing the history of both pre-capitalist and capitalist socio-economic development prior to 1850, that is, before capitalism emerged as a full-fledged system, only few studies include core regions of the globe in Asia, Africa, Latin America, and the Caribbean in the general framework. Hence, it is imperative that we ask what historical roles different world regions played in the making of *capitalism*(s). Addressing this question may help to shed new light on contemporary aspects of industrial and finance capitalism, particularly the reasons underlying socio-economic development and underdevelopment.

The question of history is also important if we are not to make trans-historical arguments in which capitalism has existed for time immemorial, wherein all history becomes the history of the unfolding of capitalism. Such a view falls victim to the problem of teleology and questions of different trajectories, of plurality, and of stillborn pathways, which cannot be accounted for. Accepting capitalism as an

[1] We would like to thank Nasser Mohajer for his valuable comments on parts of this 'Introduction'.

all-encompassing way of understanding all human history and socio-economic formations may lead to the adoption of minimal definitions of the phenomenon, which leech it of specificity and historicity. For example, Larry Neal, in his introduction to *The Cambridge History of Capitalism*, states that 'four elements … are common in each variant of capitalism' and goes on to specify: private property rights, contracts enforceable by third parties, markets with responsive prices, and supportive governments (Neal and Williamson 2014: 2). This allows the Cambridge volume to begin with Babylonia in the first millennium BCE, and arguably much is lost in historical explanations that do not account for geographical and temporal conjunctures and specificities, nor the important issue of transition between forms.[2]

Entangled Histories in the Making of Capitalism(s)

Historians still sharply disagree amongst themselves as to the origins of capitalism, the Industrial Revolution, and the 'rise of West'. In order to explain these phenomena, most historians and social scientists from both the Eurocentric and non-Eurocentric spectrums have put forward rather monocausal explanations, merely focusing on a few factors that potentially triggered Western Europe's take-off. Holistic explanations remain rare, even though a totalizing approach could help shed light on the complexity of the matter. What caused the 'Great Divergence' was a combination of factors: a *global dialectical conjuncture* based on a concatenation of intra-European, extra-European, and entangled processes; and long-term, short-term, continuous, as well as contingent factors (Mohajer and Yazdani 2020; Yazdani 2017).

The ways in which the West shaped the global emergence and expansion of capitalism is a well-established fact. Internal factors were crucial and complementary preconditions for Britain's and Western Europe's industrial breakthrough: They include a multiplicity of aspects such as: (1) favourable geo-climatic conditions; (2)

---

[2] We will not delve into these issues in the 'Introduction' as we have elsewhere examined questions of periodization, the semantics, and definition of capitalism. See Yazdani (2020a, b).

social watersheds (the European peasant wars, the Reformation and the emergence of capitalist social relations); (3) economic factors (agricultural, commercial, and industrious revolutions; the level of production and labour productivity; market integration; wages and living standards); (4) techno-scientific advancements (for example, invention of mechanical instruments, the spread of printing and improvements in mechanical engineering); (5) political developments (especially the bourgeois revolutions and mercantilist state policies); (6) institutional changes (for example, emergence of universities, central banks, the modern tax system, joint-stock companies, stock exchange); (7) force and warfare (for example, the sixteenth and seventeenth century European religious wars, the British involvement in numerous wars and military conflicts throughout the eighteenth and early nineteenth century in the struggle for European and global supremacy, and the so-called original accumulation leading to pro-letarianization and the capital relation); (8) culture and intellectual developments (most notably during the Age of Enlightenment); (9) competition (inter-state rivalry); and (10) education and 'human capital' formation. However, much less is known and too little emphasis has been put on how the non-Western world influenced developments in Europe and framed the unfolding of global capitalism and modernity. Global conjunctures and dimensions—that is, the importance of Asian, African, and American resource portfolios (ideas, institutions, goods, science, and technologies); African slave labour; Asian–African consumer demands; Asian dynamism; and competitiveness in global markets—in the making of commercial and industrial capitalism are often neglected in accounts, narrations, and historical studies on this socio-economic formation.

This is much more apparent in the case of capitalism's development than with studies on the rise of the West, the roots of modernity, and the Industrial Revolution. Marshall Hodgson (1974: 198) already pointed out that: 'Without the cumulative history of the whole Afro-Eurasian Oikoumene, of which the Occident had been an integral part, the Western Transmutation would be almost unthinkable.' If we consider the underlying causes of the European colonization of the New World, for instance, André Gunder Frank (1978: 257) argued that the expanding Ottoman Empire was 'instrumental in the long-distance Oriental and African trade, and this trade encouraged the expansion of the Ottoman Empire, which, in the 15th century, led to the discovery of America; and both were intimately related to the transition from feudalism to capitalism in Western Europe' (see also Mielants 2007: 85). New World silver was in high demand in Asia and to a large extent ended up in China and India. Silver bullion flows were backed by the colonization of the Americas and spurred the demand for luxuries and everyday consumer goods in Europe, permitting the Europeans to be competitive in Asian and African markets. It also stimulated the domestic economies of Western Europe, as well as the economies of Asia (especially China and India) (Barrett 1990; Flynn and Giráldez 2008: 359–87; Frank 1998; Pomeranz 2000: 193, 274; see also Chapters 1 and 2 in this volume). In short, Europe took advantage of the fact that China and India had insatiable demands for silver, which, in turn, provided an outlet for plundered American bullion—largely extracted through indigenous and African forced labour. The extensive Western European exploitation of slave labour in the sphere of production was absent in the advanced economies of Asia. This relieved Europe's trade deficit with Asia and consequently supplied European markets with numerous exotic goods. It is equally significant to note that profits derived from the Atlantic slave trade stimulated investment in new industries. Even more important is the contribution of export markets and profits from slave labour to financial institutions (marine insurance, the national debt, the bill of exchange, bill discounting, and the development of banking) and to those industries that pioneered the use of industrial methods (textile, mining, metal) (Blackburn 1997: 520–32, 542–54, 563, 572).[3] Indeed, the New World—apart from being a British population outlet—along with Africa and Asia, provided an important market for finished goods. As Patrick O'Brien (2006: 16) has recently reaffirmed, 'at least half of the increment to industrial production which came on stream over a long 18th century (1688–1815) was sold overseas.... Already by the close of the Seven Years War, something like half of the nation's workforce

[3] As John Lord (2006) has argued: 'It was with money gained from the West India trade that capital was eventually found to finance Watt' (quoted in Blackburn 1997: 551). For financial institutions, see Inikori (2002: 81–8, 475–82), Acemoglu, Johnson, and Robinson (2005: 546–79).

(de-linked from agriculture) depended directly and indirectly on markets overseas for its livelihood'.[4]

In addition, New World bullion, crops (for example, potatoes and maize); timber; meat; and sugar; American, Indian, and Egyptian cotton; African palm oil; cocoa; gold; rubber; Eastern resources like tea and coffee; and Australian wool became indispensable in the rise of caloric intake and factory employment in Europe. Indeed, land-saving products from the Americas such as cheap guano, cotton, sugar, wood, and the like relieved Europe's 'eco-system' and stimulated further specialization in manufactures (Barbier 2011; Hersh and Voth 2011; Mintz 1985; Nunn and Qian 2011; Pomeranz 2000; Richards 2003). In addition, the enormous cotton imports from the colonies enhanced the technical refinements of the all-important textile industry. It is only logical to argue that without cheap American cotton, higher purchase prices might have made the mechanization of textile production more difficult (Pomeranz 2000). Maxine Berg (2004) highlights the geographical extension of the frontiers through colonies, especially Britain's eighteenth-century empire, which provided a crucial connection between consumption and production, resulting in a British consumer industry.

Christopher Bayly further attests that wealth generated in the wider world (for example, slave and sugar trade, activities of the East India Company) added to Britain's capital stock for investment; while African consumer demand and taste helped to sustain the British Industrial Revolution. He adds that even throughout the nineteenth century, 'non-European knowledge and techniques continued to play an important part in the development of European science, philosophy, and industrial change' (Bayly 2004: 471). Indeed, as late as the eighteenth and early nineteenth century, Indian technologies had important ramifications in Europe, enhancing Britain's economic, scientific, and military developments. Fernand Braudel ([1979] 1992: 377), for example, pointed out: 'During the early decades of the nineteenth century, many Western scientists and Russian metallurgists endeavoured to discover the secrets of damask steel [Indian wootz steel]: the results of their research marked the birth of metallography.' In the seventeenth and eighteenth centuries,

---

[4] For a different view, see Vries (2013: 104–9, 234–62, 419–22).

Indian cloth printing, as well as South Asian, West Asian, and North African textile production and methods of dyeing inspired British, French, and Swiss artisans who tried to imitate these Asian and North African techniques (Beckert 2014: 49–50; Hanna 2014: 95–125; Raveux 2008; Riello 2010; Siebenhüner 2019; Smith 2016). With respect to plants and the use of drugs, Europeans and Indians cross-fertilized each other. Europeans were also fascinated by Indian rhinoplasty (the precursor to plastic surgery). The birth of modern rhinoplasty in nineteenth-century Europe was mainly influenced by Indian methods of plastic surgery that were observed and spread by British colonists and scientific journals. Furthermore, in the 1750s, Europeans adopted blue lights, which they first encountered in India and, last but not the least, rockets that were produced in late eighteenth-century Mysore served as a model for the nascent European rocket industry of the nineteenth century (Yazdani 2017: 101–2, 251–4, 275; Yazdani 2020: 31–3).[5] Although these techno-scientific transfers were not all connected to the development of capitalism, they helped in revolutionizing and reproducing the capitalist mode of production.

As for intellectual history and political economy, it is noteworthy that both Quesnay and Turgot are said to have been influenced by Chinese thought. Confucianism, Daoism, and idealized Chinese practices arguably influenced the Physiocrats' refutation of mercantilism and the conceptualization of laissez-faire, which later also influenced Adam Smith (Citton 2007; Gerlach 2005; Maverick 1946; Pinot 1906/7; Schorer 1938). Various seventeenth- and eighteenth-century European, especially German and French, thinkers (for example, Leibniz, Wolff, and Voltaire) were imbued with 'sinophilia', and often regarded China as a model society that had much to offer to the world. Especially 1600 onwards, European theoreticians were influenced by Jesuit missionaries like Du Halde who reported favourably on many Chinese institutions, technologies, economic ideas, philosophical schools, and attitudes. Before the late eighteenth century, 'sinophile' sentiments had not yet been replaced

---

[5] For the fascination with Indian medical practices, see, for example, the account of the Scottish minister, historian, and writer William Thomson (1746–1817), *Memoirs of the Late War* (1780: 77–8).

by a growing wave of 'sinophobia' (Osterhammel 1998: 300–4, 325–30; 2002: 75). Quesnay ([1767] 2005), who was known as the 'European Confucius' amongst his followers, advocated the alleged Chinese lack of government interference and regulation of the economy. He was in favour of imitating the 'Chinese model' in order to increase agricultural productivity and tax revenues. He not only appreciated China's agricultural productivity but also its supposedly well-functioning revenue system and meritocratic administration in contrast to hereditary succession. He suggested the introduction of the Chinese examination system in France and believed that China was the only kingdom in the world that had established institutions where the 'science of making laws' (*la science de faire des loix*) could be studied (Quesnay [1767] 2005, Vol. 2: 1014).[6] However, similar to Montesquieu (*Lettres Persanes* 1721), he used China as a foil and pretext to advance his ideas and avoid censorship. In turn, Turgot's *Reflections*, arguably one of the most important treatises on economics prior to Smith's *Wealth of Nations*, was written due to the following:

> Two [Christian] Chinese youths, who had been sent by the Jesuits to France to pursue their studies, were about to return home. ... Turgot not only gave them many books and scientific instruments, but wrote for them a set of 'Questions on China,' fifty-two in number; and, to help them in their replies, drew up this system of economic doctrine. (Hodgson 1870: 65)

Exactly 60 years earlier, the *Critical Review* had already mentioned '[a] list of questions respecting China addressed to two learned Chinese who resided at Paris for the sake of instruction in European sciences' (Smollett 1810: 522; see also Cordier 1909: 151–8). In the words of P.D. Groenewegen (1977: xvii–xviii), 'economics appears to owe the existence of the *Reflections* to the accident of a visit to Paris of MM. Ko [Louis Ko] and Yang [Étienne Yang] as guests of the

---

[6] He developed his ideas through reading Rouselot de Surgy's transcription of Du Halde and other Jesuit sources (Jacobsen 2013: 372). For the Chinese influence on the eighteenth- and nineteenth-century French and British examination systems and the meritocratic civil examinations, see Têng (1943).

Jesuits.' Indeed, in his letters to colleagues, Turgot repeatedly (at least three times) wrote that the *Reflections* was written 'without a plan and with no other object than to explain the questions which I put to some Chinese about their country' (Groenewegen 1977: xviii).[7]

All this suggests that, at least to some degree, the emergence of political economy in Western Europe cannot be disentangled from developments in and encounters with Asia and Asians. The possible transmission of economic ideas from West Asia to Europe added to this. Although these could also have been staggered independent developments without being the result of knowledge transfer, it is worth noting that the ways in which the Persian polymaths Abu Hamid Muhammad Ghazali (c. 1058–1111) and Nassereddin Tusi (1201–1274) discussed the division of labour was not unlike the deliberations expressed by some British and French political economists and philosophers since William Petty. Indeed, similar to Adam Smith and to an article on pins by Delaire, written in Diderot's *Encyclopédie*, Ghazali 'elaborated the concept of division of labour using the example of a needle factory (instead of a pin factory)' (Hosseini 1998: 655). Jean-Louis Peaucelle (2006: 489–512) points out that Smith based his analysis on the descriptions published in Diderot's *Encyclopédie* and other publications such as those by the Paris Academy of Science.[8] Be that as it may, Tusi, in turn, 'emphasized that exchange (and also division of labour) is a necessary consequence of the faculties of reason and speech. Both of these writers [Tusi and Smith] charge that animals such as dogs do not exchange one bone for another' (Hosseini 1998: 672). Although there is no proof for any direct transmission, it is worth noting that in the seventeenth and eighteenth centuries, there was a thorough interest in

---

[7] Cordier's research confirmed that 'pour permettre à Ko et Yang de répondre à ces questions, le grand économiste [Turgot] écrivit ce chef d'oeuvre [*Réflexions*].' [In order to permit Ko and Yang to respond to these queries, the great economist (Turgot) wrote this masterpiece (Réflexions)] (Cordier 1909: 151).

[8] The German political economist and politician Ernst Ludwig Carl (1682–1742) was 'the first to introduce the pin factory as an example to illustrate the division of labour' in Europe (1722–3) (Reinert et al. 2017: 61).

Arabic learning in England and other European countries; a move-ment Alexander Bevilacqua has most recently termed 'The Republic of Arabic Letters' (Bevilacqua 2018; Russel 1994). Incidentally, 'toward the end of the seventeenth century, English economic lit-erature rediscovered the concept of division of labour and began to analyse the more modern manufacturing forms' (Groenewegen 1987: 901, quoted in Hosseini 1998: 673).

What is intriguing here is that these writings seem to be responses to similar challenges and socio-economic conditions. Nonetheless, to some extent, the occupation with these matters in Europe at later points in time might well be a result of processes of uneven develop-ment that had little to do with the circulation of knowledge. During the 'early modern' period (c. tenth to fifteenth centuries CE), West and Central Asian polymaths were already addressing problems such as cost of production, division of labour, and cooperation (Islahi 2014: 22).[9] By contrast, Europe was only beginning to fully recover from disintegrated markets, demonetization, and de-urbanization of the early Middle Ages, the so-called Dark Ages between the fifth and eighth, ninth, or tenth century, depending on the particular region at hand (Wickham 2005). Maybe the last great figure of the intellectual and scientific 'golden age' (eighth to fifteenth century) of North Africa, Central and West Asia, as well as Arabic Spain, before the European latecomers resumed supremacy in the production of knowledge sometime between the sixteenth and eighteenth centuries, was Ibn Khaldun (1332–1406)—who developed a labour theory of surplus production. As Ernest Mandel (1968: 697–8) pointed out, his conception of social history 'comes close—four-and-a-half centu-ries before Marx!—to historical materialism'.[10] However, we should be cautious not to conflate Ibn Khaldun's argument with a Ricardian or Marxian labour theory of value. Ibn Khaldun did not mean accu-mulation for the sake of accumulation as the following quotation

[9] For the idiosyncratic periodization into 'early', *middle* (c. sixteenth to eighteenth century), and *late* (c. nineteenth to mid-twentieth century) modernity, see Yazdani (2017: Introduction).

[10] A number of scholars are of the opinion that Ibn Khaldun is the father or at least the precursor of modern historiography, sociology, and eco-nomics. See, for example, Gates (1967); Boulakia (1971); Haddad (1977).

illustrates: 'All the additional labour serves luxury and wealth, in contrast to the original labour that served (the necessities of) life' (Ibn Khaldun [1967] 1989: 274). Nonetheless, in his *Muqaddima*, he precociously argued that:

> human labor is necessary for every profit and capital accumulation. When (the source of profit) is work as such, as, for instance, (the exercise of) a craft, this is obvious. When the source of gain is animals, plants, or minerals, human labor is still necessary. Without it, no gain will be obtained, and there will be no useful (result) ... the capital a person earns and acquires, if resulting from a craft, is the value realized from his labour. ... The share of labour may be concealed. This is the case, for instance, with the price of foodstuffs. The labour expenditure that have gone into them show themselves in the price of grain ... gains and profits, in their entirety or for the most part, are value realized from human labour. (Ibn Khaldun 1989 [1967]: 298)

Ibn Khaldun's views are close to Adam Smith's when he writes that 'commerce means the attempt to make a profit by increasing capital, through buying goods at a low price and selling them at a high price' (Ibn Khaldun [1967] 1989: 309). Last but not least, he also emphasized the correlation between the rise of tax and the security of property:

> The finances of a ruler can be increased, and his financial resources improved, only through the revenue from taxes. This can be improved only through the equitable treatment of people with property and regard for them, so that their hopes rise, and they have the incentive to start making their capital bear fruit and grow. This, in turn, increases the ruler's revenues in taxes. (Ibn Khaldun [1967] 1989: 234)

Thus, in order to better understand the transition to and the history of capitalisms, developments in East, Central, West, South, and Southeast Asia between the eighth and nineteenth centuries should be included in the narrative. Furthermore, it may be argued that even the coming of age of industrial capitalism in Britain and Western Europe was highly dependent on non-Western demands, labour power, resources, ideas, institutions, commodities, and techno-scientific developments, as has been argued by Marx and other nineteenth- and early twentieth-century scholars (for example, Hobson, Lenin, Luxemburg, and so on). This has also been reiterated by recent scholarship (Acemoglu, Johnson, and Robinson 2005; Arrighi 1994; Allen 2009; Amin 2011; Anievas and Nişancıoğlu 2015; Bala and Duara 2016; Beckert 2014; Blackburn 1997; Braudel 1949–79; Darwin 2007; Davis 2002; Frank 1998; Goldstone 2008; Goody 2006; Hanna 2014; Hobsbawm [1968] 1986; Hobson 2004; Hodgson 1974, 1993; Inikori 2002; Marks 2007; Needham 1969; Parthasarathi 2011; Pomeranz 2000; Riello 2013; Wallerstein 1980–9; Washbrook 1990; Williams 1944; Yazdani 2017). European import substitution in textiles, pottery, and porcelain, for example, was to some extent a result of the supremacy of Asian goods in global markets. England's lack of competitiveness in global markets vis-à-vis Indian products, in conjunction with her higher wages, prices, and production costs, partly explains why it was beneficial to invest in the mechanization of textile production in Britain. In the Indian context, a transition towards mechanization would not have made much sense given her leading competitive position and the low returns that would have been scored by mechanized textile production. As K.N. Chaudhuri (1978: 273) argues:

> The development and application of a whole range of machinery, from mechanical carding and cleaning of cotton to spinning and weaving, were intended to create an import-substituting industry. … Without the cost-reducing function of machinery, it would have been impossible to overcome the comparative advantage possessed by India.

British inventors and contemporaries of the seventeenth and eighteenth centuries were aware that innovations in textile production were intimately connected to the imitation of Indian cloth manufacture. However, many historians of the nineteenth and especially twentieth century rather ignored the Indian connection (Parthasarathi 2011: 89–114). Braudel ([1979] 1984: 572) was also among the first scholars to re-emphasize that, in England, the 'aim was to produce fabrics of comparable quality at cheaper prices. The only way to do so was to introduce machines—which alone could effectively compete with Indian textile workers'.[11] Significantly, Robert Allen points out that 'the spinning jenny was not used in France or India; it brought no economic benefit in those countries in view of their low wages. Hence, it would not have been worth-while to spend the time to develop the jenny' (Allen 2009: 194). Furthermore, in the 1780s

> the rate of return to building an Arkwright mill was 40% in England, 9% in France, and less than 1% in India. With investors expect-ing a 15% return on fixed capital, it is no surprise that about 150 Arkwright mills were erected in Britain in the 1780s, 4 in France, and none in India. (Allen 2011)

However, 'by the 1850s, it proved profitable to install even more improved machinery in low-wage economies such as Mexico and India' (Allen 2011: 35).[12] Similar to Braudel, the late economist, Angus Maddison, reaffirmed that:

> Asian trade stimulated expansion of the European shipping industry and improvement of navigation techniques. It created new employ-ment opportunities and provided new consumer goods for which demand was highly elastic. Tea and coffee improved social life. To the degree that they displaced gin and beer, they increased life expecta-tion. Asian textiles and porcelain created new fashions in clothing, domestic utensils, decorative fabrics, and wallpaper. Familiarity with these new goods eventually sparked European import-substitution particularly in textiles, pottery, and porcelain. (Maddison 2007: 115; see also Berg 2004)

Indeed, Findlay and O'Rourke (2009: 344) confirm that, 'it seems clear that any sensible model would yield the result that if

---

[11] For a comprehensive study on this line of argumentation, see Parthasarathi (2011).

[12] Allen's low-wage thesis has been subjected to criticisms for underesti-mating the significance of low-paid labourers (for example, London build-ing workers) and the low wages of women and children. See the critiques by Judy Z. Stephenson, Jane Humphries, and Benjamin Schneider and Allen's responses to his critics.

Britain had been closed to trade, the Industrial Revolution could not have been sustained.'

Contributions to This Volume

The present volume is the outcome of a workshop on capitalism that took place in June 2016 and was organized by the Centre for Indian Studies in Africa, University of the Witwatersrand.[13] It was conceived initially as a response to the recent two-volume *Cambridge History of Capitalism* (2014). Despite its many merits, we were troubled by the definition of capitalism given in its first volume as being too broad and ahistorical.[14] Furthermore, the Cambridge volumes do not have chapters on tenth- to fourteenth-century West and East Asia, or sixteenth- to nineteenth-century Southeast Asia, Japan, Persia, Egypt, and Russia. (However, some individual chapters of the volumes touch upon Song China, West and Southeast Asia, Egypt, Japan, and Russia.) There is little attention to Atlantic slavery and global entanglements in the emergence and development of capitalism are not sufficiently emphasized either. To fill this gap, we invited scholars from Asia (China, Japan), Europe (England and France), North America (USA and Canada), South America (Brazil), and Africa (Egypt and Nigeria) to examine the aforementioned regions and themes. Needless to say, the present volume comprises different and sometimes contradictory approaches towards capitalism, and, also far exceeds the remit with which we began. But this is hardly avoidable in an anthology on one of the most complex and controversial issues in the fields of history, the social sciences, and economics.

---

[13] Edited proceedings of Revisiting the History of Capitalism Workshop, organized by the Centre for Indian Studies in Africa (CISA) and the Johannesburg Institute for Advanced Study (JIAS), held at the University of the Witwatersrand, Johannesburg, South Africa, 14–15 June 2016: See 'Revisiting the History of Capitalism'. Available at http://jias.joburg/wp-content/uploads/2016/10/Revisiting-the-History-of-Capitalism-full-length-report.pdf; accessed on 1 July 2018.

[14] For a critique and alternative definition, see Yazdani (2020a).

Historical narratives, as Hayden White showed, rest on a series of plots and devices that help the story along. Capitalism, as much as modernity, have often produced self-regarding accounts of their evolution characterized by linearity, telos, and a resultant homogeneity. Many accounts are marked by the idea of ineluctable points of origin (Europe and England); of the special characteristics of nations (ranging from superior rationality to resources); and the positing of spaces of backwardness that serve as limit arguments (Russia in Europe). All of these are wrapped up in a version of fulfilment theology (economic growth may have happened elsewhere but only in Europe did it culminate in capitalism). Singular features like the role of the state, the existence of contracts, free markets, and availability, as well as organization of labour are specified. However, the exclusive emphasis on these factors does not sufficiently allow for the recognition of a number of those diverse immanent developments in different socio-economic contexts that are not necessarily derogatory to capitalist or industrial expansion. All characterizations of capitalisms are alike, but economic growth in countries is different, each in its own way, to paraphrase Tolstoy (2014). This volume stresses the diversity of economic development across space and time and attends to the specificity of regions and processes—refusing to wrap varying stories into a unified narrative. At the same time, the authors argue that commodities (silver, gold, cotton); labour forms (slavery); varying forms of the state (Czarist or Chinese); institutional forms (merchant families); and spaces (the New World as much as Indian Ocean trade) all interact within global connections and circulations in a way that resists purely national histories and implicit teleologies. The thrust of this volume on historical capitalism(s) is less to create a genealogy of 'antediluvian forms of capitalism' (Marx), and more to lay out a map of possibilities for comparison and interconnections. Each story may be unique in its own way, but the intercontinental connections that began to emerge twelfth century onwards meant that the non-Western regions examined in this volume were not simply autarchic spaces awaiting European expansion before they were integrated into an idea of the world.

The chapters are organized into two sections: the first on major debates and controversies, and the second, which looks at case studies.

Major Debates and Controversies

In Chapter 1 in this volume, Dennis Flynn takes up the issue of globalization: a term that, like capitalism, has acquired great imprecision in terms of its temporality. He brings a degree of specificity to it through a history of the impact of engagement with the New World and the consequent circulation of commodities, particularly silver. Moving beyond a narrative confined by national histories, he knits together the story of the ecological consequences of the massive burning of forests for the harnessing of labour in plantations and mines in the Americas, and the movement of agricultural products across the world with multiple consequences. Rubber from the Americas undergirded the Industrial Revolution, just as much as Chinese agricultural expansion and population growth depended on the introduction of crops like peanuts and sweet potato. The Chinese demand for silver, which Japan had supplied, was now met by Mexico, involving a chain of intermediaries and the linking of the world economy from the Americas to Asia. Japan turned inwards and the accumulation and deployment of silver internally may have been one of the impetuses towards the establishment of the Tokugawa shogunate in the seventeenth century. He suggests that the relation between silver mining and capitalism in the New World may have been more complex than is usually suggested. Recent works have shown not only a range of labour arrangements from slavery to wage payments, but also forms of organization of capital involving the issuing of shares and corporations. The movement of gold and silver (from the Americas to Asia and in the other direction as well) underlie the growth of capitalism.

Chapter 2 in this volume takes up the relation of slavery to capitalism: a contentious issue ever since Eric Williams made his classic argument of the intimate connection between the two. Here again, nationally or regionally located histories—slavery in the United States or the Caribbean—or studies that do not consider changes in forms of slavery over time and present it as an immutable phenomenon do not allow us to progress beyond polemical positions. Leonardo Marques emphasizes that slavery 'was part of the total ensemble of global relations that formed the capitalist world economy between the sixteenth and the nineteenth centuries. It is a history of *slavery in capitalism*. If capitalism is about the production and circulation of commodities, the histories of cotton, sugar, silver, and their circulation across vast geographies is undergirded by the trade in slaves as much as the regimes of production that involved their labour. The history of slavery cannot be confined to national borders. The early Iberian empires were built on slavery, inasmuch as the Spanish colonies between 1501 and 1640 received 335,000 slaves who were involved in grain production, silver mining, wine making, and textile production. Portuguese access to Peruvian silver allowed them to acquire slaves, with Angola emerging as a hub for the movement of silver from America to Asia through Europe. Marques argues that the plantation complex (in Madeira, Sao Tome, and Canaries) and the use of gang labour by the British in the Caribbean in the seventeenth century should be seen as a series of agricultural revolutions prior to the eighteenth-century British agricultural revolution. He emphasizes that a conventional understanding of 'industrious revolution' needs to be glossed too, since it was driven by a desire for sugar and tobacco. There is an intimate connection between 'superfluous consumption and coercive labour'. Again, the settling of trade deficits between European powers in gold (mined from Brazil) was one of the significant monetary sources that lay behind the availability of public credit in Europe. The competition between three slave societies—Brazil, Cuba, and the United States of America—producing coffee, sugar, and cotton was a feature of economic dynamism, and political processes of the nineteenth century and the history of slavery cannot be abstracted from these.

Alessandro Stanziani in Chapter 3 of this volume takes up the standard tropes of unfree labour and economic backwardness that characterize Russia, which has allowed for studying the region as always an exception—the Russian road, as it were. He raises the question of whether forced labour is compatible with capitalism, given that contemporary capitalism itself is characterized by such a diverse range of labour practices, ranging from the free to the unfree. With the rise in agricultural prices in the eighteenth century, both landlords and peasants began to engage in rural markets riding the rise in exports both locally and to Europe. From 1750, profits from rural production and trade saw landlords enter the industrial sector as also the emergence of serf entrepreneurs—in cotton and silk weaving—with a rise in wage relations. As markets developed, one counter-intuitive development was the rebirth of *barshchina* or corvée labour. By the nineteenth century, there was an improvement in agricultural production and living standards with integration of markets; the wheat market was fully integrated by 1900. Between 1881 and 1913, the share of industry in national income had risen to 32 per cent, and over 93 per cent of factory workers were peasant migrants. Stanziani's redrawing of the Russian economy requires a reframing of the arguments that structure an understanding of capitalism. Russian capitalism was accompanied by labour coercion; landed aristocracies and peasantry participating in industrial investment; peasant workers and proto-industrialization as 'estates and peasants took part in the development of local and national markets'; privatization was not a necessary condition for the emergence of capitalism; and finally, the historical cliché of the 'international division of labour between advanced industrial regions and "backward" agricultural regions' is proposed to be radically revised. This chapter also suggests that the trope of 'exceptions' does little historical work except to subordinate variation across space and time to an ideal argument.

David Washbrook and Kaveh Yazdani, in Chapters 4 and 5, respectively, further the argument about cumulative, interlocked, yet disparate histories of economic growth, which need a transnational lens for analysis. While many scholars may accept an argument about different paths of development, which do not privilege one trajectory towards capitalism, there is less consensus about the impact of colonialism on economies in Asia and Africa. Most arguments work within a framework that emphasizes the disruption of evolutionary tendencies by colonialism, which stymied a natural progression towards the historically desirable telos of capitalism. Institutionalist perspectives on India, like that of Tirthankar Roy, work with the idea of already existing capitalism (inland and coastal), which was, however, fragile in nature, and therefore, succumbed easily to superior forms of organization possessed by the Europeans. More to the point may be the fact that nodes of growth were regional, disaggregated, and incapable of bringing about a large-scale structural transformation of the South Asian economy as a whole. Moreover, as Washbrook pithily puts it, wealth may have been easily acquired, but was not sustained from generation to generation and little was invested in fixed assets; both private and public capital were risk-averse and spread across dispersed portfolios, as in a number of other regions of the world prior to the assertion of industrial capitalism. Merchant capital was institutionally weak, and property rights were vested not in individuals but in corporate or community groups, making capital less supple and less available for entrepreneurial deployment.

For a brief while in the eighteenth century, some Indian states seemed to be following policies of mercantilism and moving in a direction that could have led to the emergence of sustained economic growth in the long run (as Yazdani shows in the case of Mysore), but it was too little, too late. They were reacting to an 'emergent global system of capital' in which the British were already dominant. Washbrook suggests another line of enquiry that puts a different spin on an older argument about the drain of wealth from India. Regardless of the quantum of the drain, the consequences for Britain were profound. Inflows from India were crucial in sustaining Britain's international position from the Napoleonic wars till 1914. Arguably, having captive markets in India could well have acted as the disincentive for further investment in technology, 'presaging Britain's economic decline later on'. India also provided huge advantages in supplying goods to support 'everything from the West African slave trade to the China trades' and in supplying cheap labour from Southeast Asia to the Caribbean. A 'peculiar species of capitalism' did develop, a process of 'petty bourgeoisification' where the ownership of small property in land and manufacture proliferated, and artisanal production became a 'leading motor-force of the industrial economy' into the present. Another specific feature was the survival of the 'family firm' model—the Tatas being a notable example—as community institutions became embedded in the structure of new laws seeking to regulate capital. As Washbrook provocatively suggests, with India now one of the fastest growing economies in the world, many of the seeming peculiarities of Indian society need to be evaluated differently for an understanding of twenty-first-century capitalism.

Chapter 5 in this volume is a case study of Mysore exploring the pre-colonial potentialities of capitalist development and industrialization in the second half of the eighteenth century, under the reigns of the Muslim rulers Haidar Ali and Tipu Sultan. Yazdani argues that the South Indian sultanate was in a transitory stage that would have potentially allowed for a process of catching-up industrialization in the absence of British subjugation. The state of Mysore was crucial in fostering a process of semi-modernization: Tipu enhanced textile production and introduced technical innovations, especially in mechanical engineering and arms production. He understood the importance of coal, invited foreign merchants and artisans, and established trading houses in South Asia as well as the Persian Gulf region. Haidar and Tipu also envisaged state ownership of the means of production, the reorganization of the administration (including the military establishment), centralization via the decimation of the landlords, the substitution of hereditary positions with state officials, and, consequently, managed to increase public revenues. However, Yazdani also indicates that this process was not based on pure imitation or a mere reactive step of the state trying to modernize the country in the wake of the British threat. There were relations of production in the private sector (for example, in textile, iron, and glass manufacture) and local traditions of employing machinery (for watering fields, raising and removing water, oil and sugar mills) that indicated indigenous potentialities of capitalist development. While Mysore possessed potentialities for both capitalist development and industrialization, a process of non-capitalist, forced industrialization from above was the most viable alternative that would have been available in the absence of colonial rule.

While South Asia was at the heart of the world economy seventeenth century onwards through the export of diverse commodities such as textiles, cotton, and opium, Southeast Asia is strangely absent from these (or the) narratives of the history of capitalism. In many senses, this is the result of a historical bias that writes history outwards from Europe, but this exclusion becomes even more puzzling when we consider that the Asian economies have been at the centre of stories of economic dynamism from the late twentieth century to the present. Eric Tagliacozzo argues in Chapter 6 in this volume that it would be logical to include the 11 odd countries that make up the region of Southeast Asia, if only because it was the search for spices that started the eastward movement out of Europe from the Iberian Peninsula. Western notions of territorial control took root very slowly in this region and the logic of trade and commerce was based on an upriver/downriver dynamic, in which forest produce came down and goods like muskets and porcelain went up. The region was characterized by fluid boundaries—whether overland into South and Central Asia or across the ocean where the Indian Ocean and the Bay of Bengal formed distinct zones of movement of people, goods, and ideas. International capitalism was only slowly grafted on to these inchoate spaces where agricultural regions were themselves transregional. Between the fifteenth and eighteenth centuries, the flow of commerce had led to the emergence of the centralized states of Burma, Siam, and Vietnam alongside the presence of 'great families' (of Persian, Arab, and Chinese origin). Southeast Asia alerts us to the histories of maritime trade and mercantile activity; of spaces not amenable to the idea of bounded national territories; and of commodities traded through a space characterized by its entrepôt nature. This was a space where custom enforced contract; states were one among many players in a protean economy; property rights were fluid; and markets consisted of several overlapping domains on ocean and land, calling for a revision of minimal definitions in an understanding of historical capitalism(s).

In Chapter 7, Henry Heller revisits the older debates about the temporality, location, and trajectories of capitalism in the classic works of Brenner and Wallerstein, and looks at whether they hold up in the face of emerging research. He looks at the relative place of markets, the state and the expropriation of peasantry in these arguments, and, also, the assumption of England as 'the terminal point of capitalism'. The proletarianization of labour as a crucial transformative, he argues, is not as important now with an increasing recognition of a 'spectrum of labour'—from wage labour to serfdom to slavery, that is, the coexistence of free and unfree labour rather than a teleology of labour forms. Heller agrees with Hobsbawm's interpretation of the idea of uneven development, which posited that European advancement was at the cost of Asia and Africa. Along with Anievas and Nişancıoğlu, he further stresses 'uneven and combined development'—a concept developed by Marx and theorized by Trotsky—which is located in conflicts between states and empires, as also a global geographical reorientation; to new spaces (the Americas) and new forms of labour (plantations and slavery). As with Flynn, he recognizes the radical emergence of silver as a commodity that transformed the creation of value across the globe through the 'emergence of capitalist world money'. There is an attempt to move away from Europe as the motor and the telos of capitalist development, but Heller is clear that we need to politically and pragmatically recognize that the core of the capitalist system is in Europe and the USA: 'the headquarters of capitalism'. This affirmation of a contemporary reality does not, however, detract from the multiple trajectories and possibilities, as well as the sites of economic growth over the period from the tenth to the eighteenth century.

Case Studies in the Histories of Capitalism(s)

Kent Deng (Chapter 8 in this volume) emphasizes the conjunctural in what he evocatively calls 'one-off capitalism' in Song China between the tenth and thirteenth centuries CE. As he says, 'discontinuity is the key' to understanding the transformations from the Tang to the Song period, contrary to the terms of existing Western (but not Chinese) historiography. He points to the conjuncture of a 'little Ice Age' in East Asia during the tenth century and the threat of invasions along the northern borders of the Song territory that set into motion social and political processes with major economic consequences. They first pushed China's rice-growing belt southwards, while resulting in an overall decline of farmland. However, a 'mini green revolution' was inaugurated by the introduction of a double cropping regime by migrant farmers, and a secure food supply had knock-on effects on mining and manufacturing. The demand for copper, tin, and lead was fuelled by the need for bronze coins and the development of sea-going ships led to a huge demand for iron. As Deng points out, the response of Song China to climate change was to divert land capital and labour to 'non-food sectors'. The second conjuncture was the threat from nomads (the Jurchen and the Mongols) along the northern border. A preference for a strategy of appeasement and tribute led to an increase in silk production in relation to the Khitans and the invention of paper currency to meet the unprecedented demand for gold and silver from the Jurchens. Taxes started to be paid in cash: the cash component of the Song tax revenue went up 226 per cent in the early eleventh century. Finally, there was a turn outwards to the sea since the Silk Route was held by the nomadic tribes, leading to shipbuilding and, at its peak, the Song fleet had 3,000 seagoing ships equipped with sails, compasses, and sea charts. The new sea routes extended to the Arabian Peninsula and the east African coast. Even though 'openness replaced autarchy, mercantilism replaced physiocracy, monetization/marketization/profiteering replaced self-sufficiency' in this critical moment, Mongol rule from the thirteenth century ended this 'one-off' efflorescence of growth in the Chinese economy and 'China went back to its old growth pattern for another half millennium from 1368 to 1911' (Chapter 8 in this volume).

Joseph E. Inikori (Chapter 9 in this volume) takes on the shibboleth of England as the 'first capitalist nation' and emphasizes population growth and international trade over the long term as the drivers of economic development. Between 1086 and 1660, three counties of East Anglia were the main beneficiaries, but from 1660 to 1850, the counties that dominated production for export to Atlantic markets—Lancashire, West Riding, and West Midlands—launched the Industrial Revolution. This chapter moves away from a nation-centred, internal, and myopic history towards emphasizing a much wider geography of trade and connected histories. He also cautions us that capitalism cannot be the horizon for the writing of history: '[T]he history of capitalism is not the history of everything'. Again, an emphasis on conjuncture and on a differently articulated geography—the connections of parts of England with an intercontinental economy take precedence over endogenous factors such as enclosure, agricultural revolution, and so on. From 1086 to 1600, there was a long-drawn-out process of commercialization of the economy and a move from subsistence production to self-employed labour. Prolonged low agricultural prices made wage incomes in the capitalist sector attractive to small cultivators. The growth of manufacturing and commerce resulted in population growth as young men and women were incentivized to marry and raise children even before they inherited land. Inikori argues that industrialization in England in the eighteenth and nineteenth centuries 'largely created its own labour through [a] demographic response'; population growth rather than expropriation contributed to the industrial workforce. He also emphasizes the 'regional distribution of capitalist industry' as mercantilist policies in Europe led to the decline of English exports in the eighteenth century. Exports to the Atlantic markets of West

Africa and the Americas grew phenomenally benefiting West Riding of Yorkshire for wool and Lancashire for cotton textile, which, by the late eighteenth century, had one-half of the mills and over two-thirds of the handloom weavers in the country. The Industrial Revolution was the result of this decisive shift to an engagement with the Atlantic world and, for Inikori, had less to do with anything 'uniquely English'.

Masaki Nakabayashi (Chapter 10 in this volume) argues that a strong state was able to emphasize social stability in Japan between the twelfth and nineteenth centuries (from Kamakura through Muromachi and Edo into Meiji times) without stymieing economic growth. From a subordination to the Chinese economy in the twelfth century, Japan had surpassed China by the eighteenth century and caught up with peripheral regions in Central and Eastern Europe. By the late 1880s, Japan had emerged as one of the most advanced economies, able to compete with the British Empire after the reforms of the Meiji Restoration. The Kamakura shogunate saw the increased involvement of the samurai with financiers in a monetized economy and increasing indebtedness, which resulted in attempts to regulate the financial sector. In the succeeding Muromachi period, the financial sector came to be seen as essential for economic growth, deepening the farmers' reliance on them, resulting in coerced labour forms in order to pay off debts. A balance was maintained between indebtedness and the maintenance of free financial markets through periodic debt write-offs by way of ordinances for virtuous governance. Under the Tokugawa shogunate, ownership of land was registered and protected, creating a large mass of small-property owners. Lords were absorbed into the administration, and slavery and forms of indentured labour were prohibited in contrast to Europe. Besides these structural safeguards, the shogunate worked with financiers in Osaka to create a sophisticated security market and futures trading at the Dojima exchange, the 'world's oldest market of futures'. Financial markets in rural areas were heavily regulated, as were labour markets to maintain rural stability in land and labour. Between the mid-seventeenth and mid-eighteenth century, the shogunate vacillated on preventing farm foreclosure for non-payment of loans before, finally, formally legalizing foreclosure so as to make agricultural finance available. Nakabayashi argues that *middle modern* Japan took a deliberate route of 'regulating land collateral loan markets to prevent an increase in wealth inequality, while maintaining the principle of free product and factor markets'. In the mid-nineteenth century, the relative income of the samurai, merchant, and farmer classes amounted to 1.2:1.1:1.0, suggesting that a rise in inequality and mass impoverishment need not accompany a transition to capitalism as in Britain. The strict protection of property rights was enabled by one of the highest rates of taxation for a *middle modern* state, reaching 30 per cent of total output. As late as the end of the nineteenth century, 60 per cent of the state revenue came from the land tax enabling the financing of all the civil and military modernization after the Meiji Restoration. In Japan, a strong interventionist state played a positive role in striking a balance between market dynamism and social stability, and ensuring a transition to capitalism without too much of a social churn.

Anne Gerritsen (Chapter 11 in this volume) explores a case study of ceramics manufacture and the Jingdezhen porcelain production system to suggest a form of capitalism in *middle modern* China. Given a historiography that sees porcelain production as being subordinated to imperial needs and hindered from a transition to capitalist relations, Gerritsen asks whether we must accept ideal trajectories of the evolution of capitalism. She suggests that a nuanced definition 'can encompass the divergent paths we might encounter in extra-European historical development' and, in the spirit of this volume, 'consider[s] different chronologies and geographies'. Jingdezhen, with its thin, white porcelain decorated with cobalt blue pigment (brought by merchants from the Muslim world), was the biggest ceramics producing site of the Ming dynasty and held this position till well into the twentieth century. Ceramic goods from here travelled within the Empire but also to Central and West Asia, to Europe, and via the Philippines to the Americas. While the imperial court made demands of ceramic wares from official kilns (*guanyao*), the vast majority of kilns outside of this system (*minyao*) produced for markets beyond the Empire. The total production for the imperial court may have amounted to less than 1 per cent of the overall output, and the extent of production was on a 'proto-industrial scale'. Such a scale of production required a workforce on a vast scale, and from the late sixteenth century, a major proportion of the labour force was paid in copper or silver. Jingdezhen was known for its assembly-line style of production: the required entry level of skill was low, and the transmission of knowledge was through 'osmosis and proximity'. Labour was variegated and included those drawn from locally based battalions, those providing corvée service, and supplementary kiln workers. The shift to making payments in lieu of corvée service is intimately connected with the silverization of the late Ming economy through the influx of Spanish silver. Gerritsen argues that it is in this transition from conscripted to hired labour that we see 'the emergence of capitalism'. The example of Jingdezhen with its waged labour force, its involvement in global markets and circuits of silver, and the location of the product itself within a discourse of culture and self-cultivation makes it less than surprising that 'the late Ming period is described as capitalist'.

Nelly Hanna (Chapter 12 in this volume) looks at artisans and capitalist development in Egypt between 1600 and 1800 and, like Washbrook, argues that it was artisanal production (in cloth, leather, and oil) that allowed participation in a widening international market. World demand was met through expansion of workshops and more efficient management techniques, which in the end became the victim of its own success and culminated in the state capitalism of Muhammad Ali in the mid-nineteenth century. Hanna emphasizes, 'a capitalist trend emerging from within (rather than coming from Europe) and from below (guilds and craft production)' in Egypt. This chapter too stresses the interconnectedness of goods and their trade across the world, which does not allow for merely national narratives of economy. Textiles from Egypt were shipped to Marseilles and then distributed from there to the colonies. Egyptian cloth was sent to the Caribbean to clothe the slave population and cloth from the Levant was used by European merchants to purchase slaves in West Africa. In response to the growing demand, new textile guilds emerged that dealt with the specialized demand, as for Indian-style designs. Workshops expanded from the traditional 4–5 looms to between 17 and 21 looms, and newer methods of division of labour and distribution of profit emerged. Contracts started to be drawn up by *qadi*s, guilds producing similar products were grouped together, and were consolidated through concentration of capital by setting up pious foundations (*waqf*s). In the early nineteenth century, as

Muhammad Ali took over these burgeoning economic processes, the increasing tensions between merchant guilds and craft guilds, and between merchants and political actors like the emirs allowed for the state to intervene. Local craftsmen lost their autonomy, but as Hanna argues, 'the organization of artisans and guilds ... left its mark' on Muhammad Ali's state capitalism.

Rudi Matthee (Chapter 13 in this volume) takes up the case of the dog that did not bark, as it were. Safavid Persia does not 'qualify as capitalist or even proto-capitalist (even though it possessed some merchant capitalist elements)', and, until the early twentieth century, no capital-intensive industry with a substantial wage labour force emerged. Of the great triad of Islamicate empires—Ottoman, Mughal, and Safavid—arguments for the seeds of capitalism have been made only for the' first two. As Matthee suggests, the case of Persia allows a nuancing of the master narrative of the inevitability of the emergence of capitalism and forces us to reflect on a mark-sheet style historiography that speaks of failure and success, of absences, and of potentiality unfulfilled. The Persian state under Shah Abbas I was interventionist and managed to put together a strong army; provide security for caravan trade; showed a curiosity for European innovations in knowledge and arms; and supported the mercantile activity of the Armenians of New Julfa. However, it was not an integrated national economy—more a multitude of oasis cities—and the harsh physical geography of deserts, the mountains, and the absence of navigable waterways meant that alongside limited agricultural output was an 'equally limited export portfolio'. While the state attempted to promote trade and manufacturing, Matthee argues that the most consequential impediment to the development of capitalism was that the intellectual ferment that did happen 'remained speculative and metaphysical in orientation' and showed a lack of interest in applied science. Given the low levels of economic growth, the state relied on squeezing the merchants, forcing them to offer 'loans', and confiscating the movable wealth of real estate of high functionaries upon dismissal or death. There was a flight of capital from the New Julfa entrepreneurs to India, Russia, and Italy. Even as maritime trade was becoming the hinge of the world economy, Persia suffered for being landlocked. In the early nineteenth century, when Persia reconnected with the larger world, it fell under the economic sway of Britain and

Russia, which diverted trade and also imposed preferential tariffs; the textile industry in particular was hit hard. Cotton-weaving workshops in Kashan and Isfahan plummeted by 90 per cent in the 1830s and 1840s. Persia's involvement in the world economy did lead to growth in the production of tobacco, cotton, and opium but this benefited large landowners and merchants who did not reinvest in the economy and this development helped only to create private wealth. However, at the heart of Persia's failed economic growth was the fact that in addition to ecological and attitudinal matters, there was 'little systemic, sustained and self-reinforcing state support for commercial and artisanal activity and expansion'. It was the simultaneous 'disengagement' of the state and its exactions of subjects that resulted in Persia's 'exceptionalist' development in global economic history.

In summary, this volume emphasizes both the internal socio-economic dynamics of a number of regions outside of Europe, as well as the global interconnections, entangled histories, and interwoven processes that went into the making of historical capitalism(s). The pre-industrial world was polycentric while different regions, resources, and knowledge contributed to an encounter we may term a *global dialectical conjuncture*—ultimately ushering in a novel socio-economic formation known as industrial capitalism.

Bibliography

Acemoglu, Daron, Simon Johnson, and James Robinson. 2005. 'The Rise of Europe: Atlantic Trade, Institutional Change, and Economic Growth.' *The American Economic Review* 95(3): 546–79.

Allen, Robert C. 2009. *The British Industrial Revolution in Global Perspective*. Cambridge: Cambridge University Press.

———. 2011. *Global Economic History: A Very Short Introduction*. Oxford: Oxford University Press.

Amin, Samir. 2011. *Global History: A View from the South*. Cape Town: Pambazuka Press.

Anievas, Alexander and Kerem Nişancıoğlu. 2015. *How the West Came to Rule: The Geopolitical Origins of Capitalism*. London: Pluto.

Arrighi, Giovanni. 1994. *The Long Twentieth Century: Money, Power, and the Origins of Our Times*. London: Verso.

Bala, Arun and Prasenjit Duara. 2016. *The Bright Dark Ages: Comparative and Connective Perspectives*. Leiden and Boston: Brill.

Barbier, Edward. 2011. *Scarcity and Frontiers. How Economies have Developed through Natural Resource Exploitation.* Cambridge: Cambridge University Press.

Barrett, Ward. 1990. 'World Bullion Flows, 1500–1800.' In *The Rise of Merchant Empires: Long-Distance Trade in the Early Modern World, 1350–1750,* edited by James D. Tracey. Cambridge: Cambridge University Press.

Bayly, Christopher Alan. 2004. *The Birth of the Modern World, 1780–1914: Global Connections and Comparisons.* Oxford: Blackwell.

Beckert, Sven. 2014. *Empire of Cotton. A Global History.* New York: Alfred A. Knopf.

Berg, Maxine. 2004. 'In Pursuit of Luxury: Global History and British Consumer Goods in the Eighteenth Century.' *Past and Present* 182(1): 85–142.

Bevilacqua, Alexander. 2018. *The Republic of Arabic Letters: Islam and the European Enlightenment.* Cambridge and London: Harvard University Press.

Blackburn, Robin. 1997. *The Making of New World Slavery. From the Baroque to the Modern, 1492–1800.* London: Verso.

Boulakia, Jean David C. 1971. 'Ibn Khaldûn: A Fourteenth-Century Economist.' *Journal of Political Economy* 79(5): 1105–18.

Braudel, Fernand. (1979) 1984. *Civilization and Capitalism, 15th–18th Century Vol. 3: The Perspective of the World.* London: Harper & Row.

———. (1979) 1992. *The Structures of Everyday Life: The Limits of the Possible.* Berkeley: University of California Press.

———. (1979) 1992. *Civilization and Capitalism, 15th–18th Century, Vol. 1: The Structures of Everyday Life: The Limits of the Possible.* Berkeley: University of California Press.

———. (1949) 1995. *The Mediterranean and the Mediterranean World in the Age of Philip II.* 2 Vols. Berkeley: University of California Press.

Carl, Ernst Ludwig. 1722–3. *Traité de la Richesse des Princes, et de leurs etats: et des moyens simples et naturels pur y parvenir.* 3 Vols. Paris: Theodore Legras.

Chaudhuri, Kirti Narayan. 1978. *The Trading World of Asia and the English East India Company: 1660–1760.* Cambridge: Cambridge University Press.

Citton, Yves. 2007. 'L'Ordre économique de la mondialisation libérale: une importation chinoise dans la France des Lumières?' *Revue internationale de philosophie* 239(1): 9–32.

Cordier, Henri. 1909. 'Les Chinois de Turgot.' In *Florilegium…Melchior de Vogüé….,* edited by G. Maspero. Paris: Imprimerie Nationale.

Darwin, John. 2007. *After Tamerlane: The Rise & Fall of Global Empires, 1400–2000.* London: Penguin.

Davis, Mike. 2002. *Late Victorian Holocausts: El Nino Famines and the Making of the Third World.* London: Verso.

Findlay, Ronald and Kevin H. O'Rourke 2009. *Power and Plenty: Trade, War, and the World Economy in the Second Millennium.* Princeton: Princeton University Press.

Flynn, Dennis O. and Arturo Giráldez. 2008. 'Born Again: Globalization's Sixteenth-Century Origins.' *Pacific Economic Review* 13(3): 359–87.

Frank, André Gunder. 1978. *World Accumulation. 1492–1789.* New York: Monthly Review Press.

———. 1998. *ReOrient: Global Economy in the Asian Age.* Berkeley: University of California Press.

Gates, Warren E. 1967. 'The Spread of Ibn Khaldûn's Ideas on Climate and Culture.' *Journal of the History of Ideas* 28(3): 415–22.

Gerlach, Christian. 2005. 'Wu-Wei in Europe—A Study of Eurasian Thought.' Available at http://hsozkult.geschichte.hu-berlin.de/daten/2005/gerlach_christian_wu-wei.pdf; accessed on 13 February 2019.

Goldstone, Jack A. 2008. *Why Europe? The Rise of the West in World History, 1500–1800.* Boston: McGraw-Hill Higher Education.

Goody, Jack. 2006. *The Theft of History.* Cambridge: Cambridge University Press.

Groenewegen, Peter D., ed. 1977. *The Economics of A.R.J. Turgot.* The Hague: Martinus Nijhoff.

———. 1987. 'Division of Labor.' Vol. 1. *The New Palgrave: A Dictionary of Economics.* New York: Stockton Press.

Haddad, L. 1977. 'A Fourteenth-Century Theory of Economic Growth and Development.' *Kyklos* 30(2): 195–213.

Hanna, Nelly. 2014. *Ottoman Egypt and the Emergence of the Modern World, 1500–1800.* Cairo: The American University in Cairo Press.

Hersh, Jonathan and Joachim Voth. 2011. 'Sweet Diversity: Colonial Goods and the Rise of European Living Standards after 1492.' *Economics Working Papers*, 1163. Department of Economics and Business, Universitat Pompeu Fabra.

Hobsbawm, Eric J. (1968) 1986. *Industry and Empire: From 1750 to the Present Day.* Harmondsworth: Penguin.

Hobson, John M. 2004. *The Eastern Origins of Western Civilisation.* Cambridge: Cambridge University Press.

Hodgson, Marshall G.S. 1974. *The Venture of Islam, Vol. 3: The Gunpowder Empires and Modern Times.* Chicago: University of Chicago Press.

———. 1993. *Rethinking World History: Essays on Europe, Islam and World History.* Cambridge: Cambridge University Press.

Hodgson, William Ballantyne. 1870. *Turgot: His Life, Times, and Opinions: Two Lectures*. London: Trübner & Co.

Hosseini, Hamid. 1998. 'Seeking the Roots of Adam Smith's Division of Labor in Medieval Persia.' *History of Political Economy* 30(4): 653–81.

Inikori, Joseph. 2002. *Africans and the Industrial Revolution in England: A Study in International Trade and Economic Development*. Cambridge: Cambridge University Press.

Islahi, Abdul Azim. 2014. *History of Islamic Economic Thought Contributions of Muslim Scholars to Economic Thought and Analysis*. Cheltenham: Edward Elgar.

Jacobsen, Stefan Gaarsmand. 2013. 'Limits to Despotism: Idealizations of Chinese Governance and Legitimizations of Absolutist Europe.' *Journal of Early Modern History* 17(4): 347–89.

Khaldun, Ibn. (1967) 1989. *The Muqaddimah: An Introduction to History*. Translated from Arabic by Franz Rosenthal. New Jersey: Princeton University Press.

Lord, John. (1923) 2006. *Capital and Steam Power: 1750–1800*, p. 13. Oxon: Routledge.

Maddison, Angus. 2007. *Contours of the World Economy, I-2030 AD, Essays in Macro-Economic History*. Oxford: Oxford University Press.

Mandel, Ernest. 1968. *Marxist Economic Theory*. Vol. 2. London: Merlin.

Marks, Robert. 2007. *The Origins of the Modern World: Fate and Fortune in the Rise of the West*. Lanham: Rowman & Littlefield.

Maverick, Lewis A. 1946. *China: A Model for Europe*. San Antonio: Paul Anderson Company.

Mielants, Eric. 2007. *The Origins of Capitalism and the 'Rise of the West'*. Philadelphia: Temple University Press.

Mintz, Sidney. 1985. *Sweetness and Power. The Place of Sugar in Modern History*. New York: Penguin.

Mohajer, Nasser and Kaveh Yazdani. 2020. 'Reading Marx in the Divergence Debate.' In *What Is Left of Marxism?*, edited by Benjamin Zachariah and Lutz Raphael. Oldenbourg: De Gruyter.

Neal, Larry and Jeffrey G. Williamson, eds. 2014. *The Cambridge History of Capitalism*. Vol. 1. Cambridge: Cambridge University Press.

Needham, Joseph. 1969. *The Grand Titration. Science and Society in East and West*. London: Allen & Unwin.

Nunn, Nathan and Nancy Qian. 2011. 'The Potato's Contribution to Population and Urbanization: Evidence from an Historical Experiment.' *The Quarterly Journal of Economics* 126: 593–650.

O'Brien, Patrick. 2006. 'Provincializing the First Industrial Revolution.' *Working Papers of the Global Economic History Network (GEHN)* 17(6):

1–40. Available at http://eprints.lse.ac.uk/22474/1/wp17.pdf; accessed on 13 February 2019.

Osterhammel, Jürgen. 1998. *Die Entzauberung Asiens*. München: C.H. Beck.

———. 2002. 'Gesellschaftsgeschichtliche Parameter chinesischer Modernität.' *Geschichte und Gesellschaft* 28: 71–108.

Parthasarathi, Prasannan. 2011. *Why Europe Grew Rich and Asia Did Not: Global Economic Divergence, 1600–1850*. Cambridge: Cambridge University Press.

Peaucelle, Jean-Louis. 2006. 'Adam Smith's Use of Multiple References for His Pin Making Example.' *The European Journal of the History of Economic Thought* 13(4): 489–512.

Pinot, Virgil. 1906/7. 'Les physiocrates et la Chine au XVIIIe siècle.' *Revue d'Histoirie Moderne et Contemporaine* 8: 200–14.

Pomeranz, Kenneth. 2000. *The Great Divergence: China, Europe and the Making of the Modern World*. Princeton: Princeton University Press.

Quesnay, François. (1767) 2005. *Le Despotisme de la Chine*. In *Oeuvres Économiques Complètes et Autres Textes*, edited by Christine Théré, Loïc Charles, and Jean-Claude Perrot. 2 Vols. Paris: L'Institut National D' Études Démographiques.

Raveux, Olivier. 2008. 'A la façon du Levant et de Perse': Marseille et la naissance de l'indiennage européen (1648–1689).' *Rives Méditerranéennes* 29: 37–51.

Reinert, Erik S., Kenneth E. Carpenter, Fernanda A. Reinert, and Sophus A. Reinert. 2017. '80 Economic Bestsellers before 1850: A Fresh Look at the History of Economic Thought.' *Working Papers in Technology Governance and Economic Dynamics* 74: 1–105.

Richards, John. 2003. *The Unending Frontier. An Environmental History of the Early Modern World*. Berkeley: University of California Press.

Riello, Giorgio. 2010. 'Asian Knowledge and the Development of Calico Printing in Europe in the Seventeenth and Eighteenth Centuries.' *Journal of Global History* 5(1): 1–28.

———. 2013. *Cotton: The Fabric That Made the Modern World*. Cambridge: Cambridge University Press.

Russel, G.A., ed. 1994. *The 'Arabick' Interest of the Natural Philosophers in Seventeenth Century England*. Leiden: Brill.

Schorer, Edgar. 1938. *L'influence de la Chine sur la genèse et le développement de la doctrine physiocratique*. Paris: F. Loviton.

Siebenhüner, Kim, ed. 2019.*Cotton in Context. Manufacturing, Marketing, and Consuming Textiles in the German-Speaking World (1500 – 1900)*. Köln/Wien: Böhlau.

Smith, Blake. 2016. 'Myths of South Asian Stasis. Trade with India in Late-Eighteenth-Century French Thought.' *Journal of the Economic and Social History of the Orient* 59(4): 499–530.

Smollett, Tobias George. 1810. *The Critical Review, Or, Annals of Literature.* Vol. XVIII. London: J. Mawman.

Têng, Ssu-yü. 1943. 'Chinese Influence on the Western Examination System.' *Harvard Journal of Asiatic Studies* 7(4): 267–312.

Thomson, William. 1780. *Memoirs of the Late War.* Vol. 2. London: J. Murray.

Tolstoy, Leo. 2014 [1878]. *Anna Karenina.* New Haven and London: Yale University Press, p. 3.

Vries, Peer. 2013. *Escaping Poverty: The Origins of Modern Economic Growth.* Vienna: Vienna University Press.

Wallerstein, Immanuel. 1980–9. *The Modern World-System.* Vols 1–3. New York/London/San Diego: Academic Press.

Washbrook, David. 1990. 'South Asia, the World System, and World Capitalism.' *The Journal of Asian Studies* 49(3): 479–508.

Wickham, Chris. 2005. *Framing the Early Middle Ages Europe and the Mediterranean 400–800.* Oxford: Oxford University Press.

Williams, Eric. 1944. *Capitalism and Slavery.* Chapel Hill: University of North Carolina Press.

Yazdani, Kaveh. 2017. *India, Modernity and the Great Divergence. Mysore and Gujarat (17th and 18th C.).* Leiden and Boston: Brill.

———. 2019. 'South Asia in the Great Divergence Debate'. In *Oxford Research Encyclopedia of Asian History,* edited by David Ludden et al. [online publication].

———. 2020. 'Mysore at War. The Military Structure during the Reigns of Haidar Ali and Tipu Sultan.' In *A Great War in South India. German Accounts of the Mysore Wars, 1766–1799,* edited by Ravi Ahuja and Martin Christof-Füchsle. Oldenbourg: De Gruyter.

———. In preparation (a). 'Capitalism—Begriffsgeschichte and Definition of a Concept'.

———. In preparation (b). 'The Biography of Capitalism'.

I

MAJOR DEBATES AND CONTROVERSIES

1

Silver, Globalization, and Capitalism

Dennis O. Flynn

A Sketch of Arguments and Propositions

Academic publishers claimed decades ago that 'globalization' was the most ubiquitous term used worldwide, yet Arturo Giráldez and I could find no operational definition of 'globalization' in European or American dictionaries. Authors seemed to use the term for any purpose that suited them. We sought to determine beginnings of the Globalization Age without resort to ideology. Everyone agrees on birthdates of the Aviation Age and Nuclear Age irrespective of political judgments. Similarly, an objective birthdate for the Age of Globalization should exist. We looked to physical geography to create this definition: [1]

---

[1] Literatures surrounding the words 'global history' contain a cacophony of ideological propositions, frequently containing Eurocentric components. See Perez (2014) for an overview of European vis-à-vis Chinese conceptions of 'global history'. In this chapter, globalization refers to physical connections around the globe, *not* ideology.

Globalization began when all heavily populated landmasses initiated sustained interaction—both directly with each other and indirectly through other landmasses—in a manner that deeply and permanently linked them. (Flynn and Giráldez 2008: 360)

According to '1/3, 1/3, 1/3 logic', Earth's surface can be divided into three segments (Flynn and Giráldez 2002). The Pacific Ocean: one-third of Earth's surface. The Americas (Atlantic Ocean included): another one-third. Thus, 'Old World' Afro-Eurasia (Indian Ocean included) must comprise the remaining one-third of Earth's surface. Humans had migrated to all populated landmasses before the last ice age ended. When ice caps melted due to global warming, sea levels rose 300–400 feet, leading to mutual isolation of 'New World' and 'Old World' for more than 10,000 years. When the Americas reconnected with Afro-Eurasia—across the Atlantic and Pacific Oceans—modern globalization was born around 450 years ago.

Access to lucrative Asian products motivated European 'voyages of discovery'. New trade routes were designed to circumvent traditional maritime/overland trade circuits, such as Italian city–state trade connections across the Ottoman Empire and Eurasia generally. The diaries of Columbus attest that Europeans also sought Asian gold, since the price of gold in Europe was double its price in China. European merchants subsequently focused upon incredibly rich Spanish-American silver mines, however, because the price of silver in China was also double its European price. Consequently, European traders acquired silver to re-sell eastward, not to accumulate silver within Europe. The Spanish Crown controlled most American silver shipped across the Atlantic, but lost control once silver exited Spain. Spanish-American silver comprised 70 per cent to more than 90 per cent of cargo value shipped eastward via the Cape Route by European maritime powers up to the middle of the eighteenth century (de Vries 2003: 75–7),[2] which makes sense given the 100 per cent price premium in Chinese markets for silver. Spain's only direct access to Chinese merchants

---

[2] Jan de Vries notes that the Verenigde Oost-indische Compagnie (VOC), like other European traders, increasingly obtained silver from Persia and elsewhere within Asia; 'Persian' silver, however, was also overwhelmingly of Spanish-American origin.

was westward via the Pacific and Manila Bay. Silks and other Chinese products were exchanged eastward through Manila and Acapulco. Vast quantities of Japanese silver also entered China via Portuguese and Dutch (from 1639) middlemen. In short, profits associated with worldwide silver markets motivated the sixteenth-century birth of global trade.

Biological Exchanges

Low-profit items were also carried aboard maritime vessels fixated upon silver-trade profits. New World/Old World impacts are known collectively as the 'Columbian Exchange', thanks to pioneering investigations by Alfred Crosby:

> Tradition has limited historians in their search for the true significance of the renewed contact between the Old and New Worlds. Even the economic historian may occasionally miss what any ecologist or geographer would find glaringly obvious after a cursory reading of the basic original sources of the sixteenth century: the most important changes brought on by the Columbian voyages were biological in nature. (Crosby 1972: xiv)

More than 10,000 years of mutual isolation bequeathed profoundly divergent physical environments within each hemisphere; whereupon sixteenth-century maritime connections generated ecological and social transformations so profound that Crosby (1986: 271) depicted exchange of flora, fauna, and diseases as 'a revolution more extreme than any seen on this planet since the extinction at the end of the Pleistocene'.

Lacking immunity to Afro-Eurasian diseases, 75 per cent to 90 per cent of the New World population died soon after contact. However, exploitation of American natural resources required labourers, prompting the importation of millions of African slaves for centuries.

> Blacks were with Balboa when he claimed the Pacific, with Pedrarias Davila when he colonized Panama, with Cortés when he marched to Tenochtitlan, with Alvarado when he entered Guatemala. Almagro apparently had twice as many blacks as Spaniards serving with him,

and Gonzalo Pizarro at the time of his rebellion had up to 400 blacks in his force.... The principal role of Black Africans in the Spanish Empire was as mainstay of the economy.... In no small measure, the black man created the empire that Spain directed in the New World. (Kamen 2003: 139, 141)

Reforestation, Global Cooling, and Global Crisis in the Seventeenth Century

New World demographic collapse led to reforestation across the Americas, due to curtailment of intentional forest burnings. In turn, New World reforestation may have led to massive sequestration of carbon dioxide, contributing substantially to the seventeenth-century Little Ice Age. Utilizing stratigraphic records, Lewis and Maslin (2015) argue that decline in global carbon dioxide emissions initiated the Anthropocene era—human domination of the global environment—early in the seventeenth century.

Irrespective of decisions by geologists regarding official dating of the Anthropocene era, the impacts of the seventeenth-century Little Ice Age across Earth are undeniable.[3] Eminent historian Geoffrey Parker (2013: xxx) documents global impacts as: 'The [Little Ice Age] crisis increased an imbalance between supply and demand for resources—an imbalance that would eventually reduce the global population by perhaps one-third.'

In China, the cultivated area of land decreased by about one-third during the Ming-Qing transition, while 'demographic losses were nearly the same'.... Ireland's population fell by at least one-fifth during the mid-seventeenth century. In Germany, 'about 40 per cent of the rural population fell victim to war and epidemics [while] in the cities, losses may be estimated at about 33 per cent' between 1618 and 1648. Many villages in the Ile-de-France suffered their worst demographic crisis of the entire Ancien Régime in 1648–53. Census data from Poland, Russia and the Ottoman empire suggest a population fall in the mid-seventeenth century of at least one-third.... These

---

[3] See Hamilton (2015) for rejection of this proposition by Lewis and Maslin; the outcome of their Anthropocene controversy is distinct from the argument of this chapter.

staggering losses were not caused by the Little Ice Age alone, however, it required the misguided policies by religious and political leaders to turn the crisis caused by sudden climate change into catastrophe. (Parker 2013: 25)

Given the extreme worldwide transformations of physical environments traceable to the sixteenth-century linkage of hemispheres, it is clear that 'globalization' debates cannot be confined to narrow economic considerations alone.[4]

From Depopulation to Population Explosions

Introduction of Old World plants and animals permanently transformed the physical landscapes across the Western Hemisphere. Try to imagine North, Central, or South American histories without horses, cattle, donkeys, mules, sheep, goats, pigs, large dogs, bees, coffee, wheat, sugar, rice, grapes, oranges, and other foundational building blocks of American societies (see Crosby 1972, for details). Charles Mann's two volumes alone demonstrate that post-1492, histories of the Americas must be portrayed in a global context (Mann 2006, 2011).

American plants/seeds previously unknown in the Old World—including corn/maize, potato, sweet potato, peanut, tomato, most beans, peppers, tobacco, and numerous others—also physically transformed Afro-Eurasia. One-third to one-half of the calories consumed worldwide by humans and domesticated animals today are attributable to the New World plants previously unknown in the Old World. Eighteenth-century population explosions worldwide resulted largely from dissemination of American plants and seeds, in stark reversal of the global demographic collapse during the seventeenth-century Little Ice Age. Additionally, the Industrial Revolution is difficult to imagine without the New World rubber for gaskets, tires, and other applications (Mann 2011: Chapter 7). In sum, the physical geography of Earth was fundamentally and permanently altered as a result of the integration of global landmasses initiated during the sixteenth century.

---

[4] For impacts of New World plants worldwide, including European natural philosophy, see multiple essays in Aram and Yun-Casalilla (2014).

Conventional Economic History versus Global History

Despite the global interconnections outlined earlier, economic historians argue that long-distance trade comprised an insignificant percentage of gross domestic products (GDPs), hence contributing little to the economic growth of West European powers that allegedly flourished on the basis of domestic considerations alone (for instance, see O'Brien 1982 for England). Long-distance trade is also alleged to have involved exchange of mere luxuries for elites, thus implying that impacts upon lives of ordinary people were negligible. In short, thin global linkages prevailed until certain global prices converged in the 1820s, which 'really mattered to the economic lives of the vast majority' (O'Rourke and Williamson 2002: 28).[5] Both percentage GDP and luxuries-for-elites arguments (*a*) emphasize domestic *economic* factors independent of worldwide developments, (*b*) assume nation-state units of analysis correct, and (*c*) deny global effects upon the masses. Yet, were not tens of millions of indigenous Americans eliminated by Old World diseases regular people? Were not more than 10 million trans-Atlantic slaves ordinary people? Was not one-third of humanity, extirpated due to seventeenth-century global cooling, composed of regular people? Eighteenth-century population explosions included hundreds of millions of ordinary Africans, Asians, and Europeans kept alive by plants grown locally, *yet of New World origin*.[6] Global connections have, in fact, impacted ordinary people everywhere since the sixteenth century, even in the highlands of New Guinea.

> In former times New Guinea's available root crops were limiting for calories as well as for protein, because they do not grow well at

---

[5] This argument is repeated in O'Rourke and Williamson (2004). For criticism of O'Rourke and Williamson on empirical grounds, see de Zwart and van Zanden (2018).

[6] Pomeranz (2000: 274–8) argues that England escaped its ecological cul-de-sac due to imported calories in the form of New World sugar, grains, and other land-intensive imports (unavailable to Asian societies). Calories from plants of American origin grown within China, however, surely must have exceeded (many times over) the *total* calories produced within England. See Flynn and Giráldez (2008: 379–81).

high elevations.... Many centuries ago, however, a new root crop of ultimately South American origin, the sweet potato, reached New Guinea, probably by way of the Philippines.... Compared with taro and other presumably older New Guinea root crops, the sweet potato can be grown up to higher elevations, grew more quickly, and gives higher yields per acre cultivated and per hour of labor. The result of the sweet potato's arrival was a highland population explosion [*sic*]. (Diamond 1997: 149)

Even though Indigenous New Guineans arrived 40,000 years ago, it was the introduction of the sweet potato (and European firearms) that fundamentally restructured the highland societies.

Globalization and the Novel

Ning Ma challenges the conventional depictions of the novel as European in origin. Analysis of British, Chinese, Japanese, and Spanish novels reveals that sixteenth-century global trade generated deep cultural impacts worldwide.

The ... realistic inventions of these texts rest in the foregrounding of the force of materiality as a historical agent of social and cultural mobility. In attending to changes in both social life and the political economy under conditions of commercial circulations, furthermore, these narratives become nationally allegorical and express modes of critical political consciousness. Other than the somewhat exceptional case of *Robinson Crusoe*, the narrative works we have examined treat the material domain as a lived, desublimated realm, in the absence of a reified capitalist ideology ... these narrative worlds ... reflect multilocal cultural displacements during the Age of Silver ... we are one step closer to reimagining 'world literature' as a 'global civil society,' which is characterized by diversity, but also commonality and interconnections. (Ma 2017: 180–1)

Written in sixteenth-century China, *The Plum in the Golden Vase* was the world's 'first modern novel ... [and] utilizes the motif of silver money for narrating a nation in decay and ... new individual images foregrounded by such a historical crisis' (Ma 2017: 62). Ma also documents materialistic disruptions in Spain depicted in Cervantes' *Don Quixote*, and undermining of Japanese cultural traditions due to global trade networks presented in Saikaku's seventeenth-century 'floating world' novels. In sharp contrast, Daniel Defoe's eighteenth-century novel *Robinson Crusoe* gained extraordinary popularity among nineteenth-century economists as 'a powerful origin tale of the "starting point of history", in theorizations of an Anglocentric narrative of modernity' (Ma 2017: 158–9). Ning Ma argues that the subject matter of the earliest novels—East and West—reflected global sixteenth-century material connections during *The Age of Silver*.[7]

Global Silver History: Short Version

The Chinese invented paper and paper monies centuries prior to European usage. China maintained a silver exchange standard—paper monies convertible into silver—at least as early as the eleventh century, although copper-based cash prevailed for ordinary retail purchases (von Glahn 1996: 51). A decisive step towards a silver-based economy occurred when the Mongol conquest of China led to a repudiation of (copper-based) coin early in the thirteenth century CE, leading to domination by silver and silver-backed paper monies. Taxes came to be collected in silver. The Mongols confiscated immense quantities of stored silver upon the collapse of the Song Dynasty (960–1279), and silver was *exported from China* to Western Asia and the Mediterranean during the thirteenth century. Muslim states from Spain to Persia had returned to a silver standard; strong demand to hold silver raised its westward market value to double its value within China. Thus, unification of Islamic merchant communities across Eurasia facilitated silver's East-to-West relocation.

Reversal of Eurasian Silver Flows

Excessive issuance of paper monies generated hyperinflation that destroyed China's silver exchange standard by the 1430s. Private parties refused worthless paper monies and demanded payment in silver.

---

[7] Islamic influences (from North Africa and West Asia to Spain) on Cervantes fit into this pattern of global influences. Thanks to Kaveh Yazdani for calling my attention to López-Baralt (2006).

Repeated attempts by Ming authorities to thwart 'silverization' across China failed. Demand for silver mounted and local/regional governments increasingly specified tax payments in silver. Domestic mine production satisfied perhaps 10 per cent of the burgeoning demand, escalating the price of silver in China. Thus, silver became *overvalued* in China relative to the rest of Afro-Eurasia, the opposite of prior *undervaluation* of Chinese silver during the Mongol era.

Presumably boosted by buoyant Chinese demand, silver's price in Europe rose concurrently. Mid-fifteenth-century Central European silver production quintupled in response. Coin production in trade centres such as Antwerp rose. Venetian silver exports to the Levant alone were double the combined mint output of England and the Habsburg Low Countries. Ever-higher silver values existed eastward (Munro 2007: 924–5). Silver demand in China continued to surge in the private sector, and highly decentralized regional Ming tax systems followed suit. Tax collections in silver were not 'planned but merely resorted to out of necessity in the failure of all other currencies' (Fairbank 1992: 135).

Sixteenth-Century Silver Discoveries

Unprecedented Japanese and Spanish-American silver mine production beginning in the sixteenth century must be viewed in context of the extensive and expanding Chinese demand to hold silver. Chinese markets simply offered premium silver prices: From 1592 to the early seventeenth century gold was exchanged for silver in Canton at the rate of 1:5.5 to 1:7, while in Spain the exchange rate was 1:12.5 to 1:14, thus indicating that the value of silver was twice as high in China as in Spain (Chuan 1969: 2).

Silver worldwide was attracted by premium silver prices in Chinese markets due to arbitrage: Buy where price is low, and sell where price is high (Geiss 1979: 165). Simultaneously, arbitrage also existed for gold exported from China to Japanese, European, and American markets that offered premium gold prices.

China contained 25 per cent of the world's population (perhaps 40 per cent including tributary states) at globalization's dawn. Massive imports caused silver to accumulate ('inventory supply') faster than the inventory demand, slowly depressing silver prices in

China. China's silver price premium vanished entirely by 1640, when bimetallic ratios equilibrated worldwide. Elimination of silver super-profits crippled the economic foundation of the Spanish Crown, and contributed mightily to a global trade crisis. The Potosi/Japan Cycle of Silver had ended.

Ecological and Demographic Revolutions: The Mexican Cycle of Silver

Stowaway American plants and seeds—aboard maritime vessels focused on global trade profit—were commercially insignificant, yet the unintended worldwide impacts were profound. Just three American plants—maize/corn, peanut, and sweet potato—trans-formed physical and social landscapes throughout China.

Traditional depictions of China as backward/stagnant contradict historical evidence. China's landmass doubled, for instance, while population more than doubled during the eighteenth century. China's 'population growth in the eighteenth century was speeded up by massive ecological change: the introduction of new crops into China from the New World' (sweet potato, peanut, and maize) (Spence 1990: 95).[8] Bray stressed the 'rapidity with which the sweet potato spread throughout China in the seventeenth and eighteenth centuries.... By the eighteenth century it was grown in all the Yangzi provinces, and Sichuan had become the leading producer; by 1800 it accounted for almost half the year's food supply of poor Shantung' (Bray 1984: 532). Trans-Pacific dispersion of American crops/seeds receives scant attention, although notable exceptions exist: 'Most [American plants] were introduced first to the eastern coast provinces, especially Fukien, probably through the intermediary of Chinese settlers in the Philippines and other Pacific islands, and spread rapidly inland from the coast.... Peanuts were already listed as a local product of Chang-shu county near Suchou in the mid-sixteenth century' (Bray 1984: 427–8).

---

[8] New World crop impacts on Chinese agriculture have long been acknowledged by Ho (1959: 268) and Naquin and Rawski (1987: 23). See Mazumdar (1999) for contrast between New World crop introductions into China vis-à-vis India.

New World crops spread into northern Fujian before 1700, again via the Pacific: 'As this area [northern Fujian] was in contact with Manila ... the Pacific seems the most likely course for it to have followed. Where maize grew on sunny hillsides, sweet potatoes on shady, and peanuts on sandy bottomland...' (Adshead 1988: 284) Labelled 'Magellan Exchange' by John McNeill (2001: xix–xx), eco-logical transfers across the Pacific deserve co-billing alongside Alfred Crosby's Atlantic 'Columbian Exchange'.

The Chinese population surged simultaneously with inter-regional migration on a grand scale, spurred by cultivation in new regions like Sichuan, the Yangzi highlands, the Han River, and elsewhere (Ho 1959: 268). Han Chinese moved into areas previously inca-pable of sustaining large and growing populations: 'Between 1400 and 1800, China's Southwest Frontier ... was transformed from a poorly understood and seldom visited periphery into an integral part of the Chinese empire.... [that] changed in dramatic and fundamen-tal ways, from an economically underdeveloped and sparsely settled rural frontier inhabited almost exclusively by indigenous non-Han peoples to an increasingly commercialized region populated pre-dominantly by Han in-migrants' (Herman 2006: 135).

At least 10 million mostly freehold farmers or freehold tenants, more than the total population of England, migrated internally to underdeveloped parts of China during the late seventeenth and eigh-teenth centuries (Pomeranz 2000: 84). The millions of Han Chinese migrants who moved to cold, hilly, rainy, and rocky areas could not have survived without American plants.

Environmental Degradation and Eventual Collapse

American plants rendered intensive exploitation of resources in former Chinese hinterlands possible. Resource sustainability was practised in some regions, but environmental tragedy evolved in others. 'Ming ... population increase spurred consolidation of a broader marketing system.... But especially important for the movement of larger numbers of Han people from the lowlands into the highlands was the availability of new kinds of foods from the Americas that were especially adapted for those environments' (Marks 2017: 229).

High prices in lowland markets induced expansion into frontier regions. Upon exhaustion of soil, Han immigrants moved to nearby lands with American plants (von Glahn 2016: 329), leading to erosion and widespread environmental collapse during the nineteenth century (Marks 2017: Chapter 5, especially 228–47).

China's Population Explosion and the Eighteenth-Century Cycle of Silver

Given the firm establishment of 'silverization' within China, widespread demographic and economic expansion augmented the inventory demand for silver, causing silver prices to soar 50 per cent above non-Chinese silver prices by 1700. Eighteenth-century Chinese expansion induced a surge in Spanish-American silver production (Japanese silver mines were exhausted by the late seventeenth century). Eighteenth-century Spanish-American silver production, largely from New Spain/Mexico this time, exceeded the combined silver output of the sixteenth-century and seventeenth-century New World.[9] The 'Mexican Cycle of Silver' (1700–50) lasted only half as long as its 'Potosi-Japan Cycle of Silver' (1540s–1640) predecessor, since increasingly sophisticated maritime networks facilitated silver flows. Silver prices fell as silver accumulated globally, eliminating silver super-profits in a mere 50 years this time around. Bimetallic ratios converged globally by 1750. As happened at the end of the 1540s–1640 silver cycle, a general global trade crisis emerged again at the end of the 1700–50 cycle.

Taking advantage of the next lucrative market opportunity, the British were the first to seize meaningful mainland Asian real estate, conquering Bengal in 1757 as opium replaced silver as the most profitable Chinese import. In effect, expanding Chinese tea exports exchanged for Chinese opium and silver imports.[10] Trade in

---

[9] Drawing upon geology, chemistry, and archives, Guerrero (2017) argues that key New World mining innovations were home-grown (not introduced from Europe), and also that a legacy of environmental damage resulted from smelting of silver ores, *not* the mercury amalgam process.

[10] Chinese opium consumption was intimately linked to American tobacco plants introduced via the Philippines. See Spence (1992: 231).

opium generated at least 100 per cent clear profit for the East India Company, even on sales to the Dutch in Calcutta (now Kolkata) (Troki 1999: 54). While Chinese silver imports were twice as large as opium imports in *market value* terms, opium-trade *profits* no doubt dominated. Profits build wealth, and high market share can accompany low (or zero) profit rates.

Interdisciplinary scholarship is necessary for the advancement of global history. Exceptionally high Chinese silver prices from the mid-fifteenth century, coupled with fabulous sixteenth-century Japanese and American silver mine discoveries, generated the birth of global trade. Afro-Eurasian diseases decimated indigenous New World populations in the sixteenth century, leading to reforestation and demographic collapse worldwide (except Japan and Spanish America itself) during the seventeenth century.[11] Unprecedented population explosions worldwide followed during the eighteenth century, fuelled by New World plants and seeds. Histories of agriculture, culture, economics, environment, epidemiology, demography, geography, labour, medicine, and technology should be viewed as components of global history. Modern globalization began when new, deep connections spanned Earth beginning in the sixteenth century.

Global Silver: Winners and Losers

Two Silver-Based Empires in a Global Setting

Profits from mines in South America and New Spain/Mexico funded Imperial Spain's sixteenth-century rise as a military powerhouse. How else could Spain fight simultaneous wars against European powers, Ottomans in the Mediterranean, Europeans in the Americas, and the Dutch in Asian waters? Sixteenth-century Spain contained only six or seven million inhabitants, having experienced neither agricultural nor industrial revolutions. Fuelled by external profits, Spain's empire depended upon Chinese silver customers (Flynn and

---

[11] On Spanish American growth during the seventeenth century, see Klein and Serrano Hernández (2019). For Japanese markets, see Hayami, Saitô, and Toby (2004).

Giráldez 1996). Indeed, silver dominated all Asia-bound European maritime shipments.

Extraordinary profits from Japanese and Spanish-American silver mines could not persist indefinitely because silver stocks accumulated faster than the demand to hold silver stocks. Thus, worldwide silver market values fell by a few per cent annually. Above-normal silver trade profits fell to zero around 1640. Silver-related profits in 1540s–1640, however, had funded imperial Spain's exorbitant worldwide military expenditures, and nothing remained for funding large-scale domestic infrastructure projects (Flynn 1991).

Japan forged a different path. The Shogun controlled all silver mines, profits from which funded subjugation of more than 250 powerful daimyos (lords). When silver profits vanished in the 1630s, Dutch merchants (replacing the Portuguese) were confined to a small man-made island in Nagasaki Bay, Deshima, a World Heritage Site today. The Tokugawa shoguns invested heavily in land reclamation and other domestic infrastructure projects. The shogun intentionally weakened and held samurai families hostage in Edo (Tokyo), while collaborating with business interests. 'Closure' of Japan from the late 1630s involved regulation of trade and curtailment of international migration. Portrayal of Tokugawa policy as anti-trade, however, is misleading. Japan subsequently became an important exporter of gold, and also the world's leading exporter of copper (mainly to China, but also to Europe).[12]

Pax Tokugawa generated prosperity. Unthreatened by foreigners, the shogun forbade domestic access to critical military technology.[13] A wayward Portuguese ship had introduced European firearms to the Japanese in 1543. The adoption and improvement of guns in Japan was remarkable: 'The number of guns produced in Japan in the latter part of the 16th century, according to one source, was 300,000. This exceeded the total number of guns in Europe at that time' (Sakae 2001: 48).

A Dutch envoy compared Tokugawa castle in Edo (Tokyo) 'to one of the largest walled cities in Europe, and it contained enough

---

[12] See Shimada (2006: 47) for comparison of Japanese and Swedish copper production. Silver mines also switched to copper production.

[13] For classic treatment of this topic, see Perrin (1980).

weapons to equip 100,000 soldiers' (quoted in Parker 2013: 498). After a disastrous attempt to conquer Ming China (via a 160,000-troop invasion of Korea) during the 1590s, shoguns subsequently abandoned overseas wars. Pax Tokugawa yielded profound economic benefits. 'Whereas Europe knew only four years of peace during the seventeenth century, and China knew none, Tokugawa Japan knew only four years of war (and none at all after 1638). By avoiding war, the sink that drained the revenues of most other early modern states, the shoguns managed to keep tax rates relatively low and yet still accumulate resources' (Parker 2013: 497).

Japan's population more than doubled and its urban population quintupled during the seventeenth century. Pro-market Japanese prosperity stemmed from low taxes, heavy infrastructure investment, and the most literate population in the world (Waswo 1986; Yasuba 1986).

Claim That Foreign Silver Stimulated Ming–Qing China[14]

Prominent scholars Earl J. Hamilton and John Maynard Keynes (1920s and 1930s) invoked 'quantity theory of money' mechanisms while arguing that American silver stimulated European capitalism beginning in the sixteenth century. Many others also maintained that the influx of silver stimulated European nations and regions (see, for example, Wallerstein 1974).

In stark reversal of the quantity theory of money logic of Hamilton and Keynes (applied to European price inflation), Andre Gunder Frank (1998) argued the opposite: influx of silver stimulated China because Chinese price inflation *failed to occur*. Invoking Irving Fisher's $MV = PQ$ equation of exchange, Frank claimed that Chinese prices (P) failed to rise when money (M) increased (via silver imports), and therefore output (Q) rose dramatically. Frank's argument is incorrect. First, Chinese price inflation mirrored European price inflations, once Chinese 'cash' prices are converted to silver-content prices (standard practice in European price history since

---

[14] This section summarizes conclusions treated in more detail in Flynn and Giráldez (2000). For earlier criticism of Fisher's flow-theory, see Flynn (1984).

the 1920s). Second, no monetary economist today invokes MV = PQ mechanisms to explain anything. Fisher's antiquated model was rejected in favour of a superior monetary model from Cambridge, England, a century ago. Cambridge-style monetary theory focuses on *inventory* demand and *inventory* supply concepts.[15]

Silver Imports Stimulated Growth, Yet Impeded Economic Development

Contradicting Frank's silver-stimulus view, Flynn and Giráldez (2000) contend that the influx of silver represented a massive drain of wealth for Chinese society. Had the Ming paper-money system continued to function properly since the 1430s, gargantuan Chinese importation of foreign silver would have been unnecessary, and Chinese economic wealth would have been higher.

Influx of silver did indeed stimulate Chinese domestic production and exports, as reflected in Richard von Glahn's classic Chinese monetary history: 'The influx of foreign silver coincided with rapid advances in the commercialization of China's domestic economy.... Current scholarly opinion tends to view silver imports as the key stimulus to commercialization in the late Ming' (von Glahn 1996: 142).

Silks and ceramics were especially notable Chinese exports. Souza ([1986] 2004: 46) cites seventeenth-century Portuguese historian Bocarro's estimate of annual Chinese silk production at 2,500 tons, 800 tons of which was exported, mostly to Japan, to the New World via Manila, and also to India. Manila-Acapulco trade alone carried enough raw Chinese silk that 'silk manufacturers in Mexico City, Puebla, and Oaxaca gave work to more than 14,000 people' (Borah 1943: 90). Chinese silk exports via the Portuguese increased eightfold between 1600 and 1637, when silks comprised 89.9 per cent of cargo value (Souza [1986] 2004: 50–1). Japanese imports of raw silk by the 1630s, mostly from China, totalled 280 tons per year (Atwell 1998: 396). Silk production was decentralized and exceedingly labour-intensive, so employment impacts were

---

[15] See Flynn (2015, 2018) for further criticisms of modern monetary theory.

significant. In addition, up to 60,000 pieces of Chinese porcelain arrived annually in Lisbon by the 1530s, and 'by 1614, Ming blue and white wares are said to have been "in daily use" among the ordinary citizens of Amsterdam' (Atwell 1998). All 'indications are that Ming porcelain was in common use in Peru as well' (Atwell 1998: 401).

Given such economic stimulation, why claim that silver imports and Chinese exports nevertheless led to massive *economic costs* to Chinese society over centuries? Consider 'money-and-growth' arguments by theorists who examined nearly costless paper monies that replaced gold and silver coins during the nineteenth century. Theorists noted significant land, labour, and capital resources necessary to produce coins. Substitution of zero-cost paper monies in place of resource-intensive mining, refining, and minting of coins liberated resources previously tied up in the production of commodity monies. No longer needed for mining, refining, and minting of precious-metal coins, land, labour, and capital therefore became available for the production of non-monetary goods. Similar to the discovery of new resources, social wealth rose because pre-existing resource stocks were redirected to the production of non-monetary items. Paper monies liberated existing resources, and social wealth rose.

Beginning in the 1430s, commodity silver replaced Chinese paper monies, the exact opposite of nineteenth-century replacement of silver and gold coins with paper monies. Money-and-growth logic mandates the conclusion that substitution of high-cost silver in place of (almost) costless paper monies must have involved huge loss of Chinese wealth. Mining, refining, and transport of hundreds of tons of silver annually imported into Chinese markets *bound up vast resources* (used to produce export goods) previously liberated under the paper-money regime.

> By the nineteenth century, commodity money was almost exclusively limited to metals like silver and gold.... Because money had intrinsic value, there was no need for the government to guarantee its value, as the quantity of money was regulated by the market through the supply and demand for gold and silver. But metallic money has shortcomings because scarce resources are required to dig it out of the ground. (Samuelson and Nordhaus 1995: 480)

Massive resources embedded in the production of Chinese silks, ceramics, and other exports should be viewed as *costs* absorbed due to the high-resource-cost silver imports that substituted for nearly resource-free paper monies. These social costs must be viewed indirectly, in that resource-heavy Chinese exports had to be exchanged for resource-heavy silver imports. Nonetheless, vast Chinese resources were surrendered during acquisition of silver, irrespective of whether silver was mined domestically or imported. Losses mounted over centuries of silver importation, even though Chinese decision-makers were as rational as decision-makers elsewhere. Social costs stemmed from the fifteenth-century collapse of China's paper-money system, not from the rational response to that collapse. Massive silver imports required equally massive non-silver Chinese exports, thereby binding the domestic resources otherwise available for fortification of Chinese wealth.

The Birth of Capitalism

European Silver Mining and European Capitalism

Marxists and non-Marxists alike tend to depict medieval mining as rooted in feudal tradition, isolated in mountain hinterlands, and therefore lacking the dynamism associated with industry or agriculture. Graulau (2019) offers archival evidence that contradicts traditional depictions of mining backwardness. It is true that feudal lands with silver mines could not be operated efficiently by lords, who lacked (*a*) mining expertise, (*b*) linkages to widespread market distribution centres, and (*c*) sufficient liquidity for capital-intensive mining projects. This is why discovery of silver ores on a lord's lands led to elimination of obsolete feudal-vassal contractual rights and obligations. Instead, share-issuing corporations were formed and laws altered in favour of private mining works, while entrepreneurs, merchants, and miners routinely travelled great distances across boundaries throughout the mountainous Europe. Accounting methods were updated. In a nutshell, Graulau argues that European capitalism emerged from dynamic mining enterprises prior to New World mine discoveries.

American Metals and European Capitalism: A Classic View Debunked

Earl J. Hamilton formulated a classic account of sixteenth-century capitalistic stimulation. Precious metals from Spanish America raised Spain's money supply, and stoked Spanish price inflation via 'quantity theory of money' reasoning. Once New World metals reached other European countries, they too experienced protracted inflations collectively called the 'Price Revolution'.[16] Prices rose faster than wages, according to Hamilton, creating wage-lag profits that enhanced capital accumulation by entrepreneurs. Spanish wages, however, failed to lag prices sufficiently to yield permanent Iberian capitalism (Hamilton 1929: 357, repeated in Hamilton 1952: 337). John Maynard Keynes endorsed Hamilton's 'profit thesis'. Keynes contended that Spain's early profit inflation (1520–1600) was offset by profit deflation (1600–30). Arrival of American precious metals in England, on the other hand, generated momentous British profit inflation from 1585 to 1630: 'Never in the annals of the modern world has there existed so prolonged and so rich an opportunity for the businessman, the speculator and the profiteer. In those golden years modern capitalism was born' (Keynes 1930: Vol. II, 159).

However, Nef (1936) soon criticized this Hamilton/Keynes profit thesis as 'a demolition exercise completed in 1956 by David Felix' (Outhwaite 1969: 40). Historical evidence showed that wages lagged behind agricultural prices, yet wages lagged industrial prices slightly or not at all. As for Spain, Nadal (1959: 523–4) countered that Spanish real wages fell as rapidly as elsewhere. Empirical evidence ultimately doomed Hamilton's 'profit thesis'.

American Silver and the Birth of Capitalism via European Trade with Asia

Hamilton (1929: 348–9) was on firmer ground when tying capital accumulation to trade between Europe and East Asia (a secondary

---

[16] Flynn (1978) discusses reasons for defeat of Hamilton's Price Revolution argument.

argument): 'From the very beginning of the modern era trade with the East Indies by the Cape route was almost incredibly lucrative ... enormous profits obtained from the East India trade doubtless contributed powerfully to capital formation and thus to the rise of modern capitalism.'

Given that European exports of Spanish-American silver dominated trade with East Asian markets, Hamilton implicitly argued that exportation of silver—that is, *non-accumulation* of silver in Europe—stimulated European entrepreneurial wealth.[17] This Asian side-argument echoes Adam Smith's ([1776] 1965: 408) anti-Bullionist insistence that encouragement of national accumulations of precious metals is foolish: 'Attempt to increase the wealth of any country, either by introducing or detaining in it an unnecessary quantity of gold and silver, is as absurd as it would be to attempt to increase the good cheer of private families, by obligating them to keep an unnecessary number of kitchen utensils.'

Re-exportation of most imported silver—specifically *not* accumulating silver—enhanced national wealth. In effect, Smith saw benefits in re-exportation of silver:[18] 'The discovery of America ... certainly made a most essential [change in the state of Europe].... By opening a new and inexhaustible market to all the commodities of Europe, it gave occasion to new divisions of labour and improvements of art, which ... could never have taken place for want of a market to take off the greater part of their produce' (Smith [1776] 1965: 416).

Thinking globally, Smith realized that the extraction of massive quantities of American minerals required (profitable) European exports in exchange for New World silver. Moreover, subsequent European re-export of silver in exchange for Asian products generated

---

[17] Hamilton's profit-inflation argument required *accumulation* of silver (and gold) in order to augment money supplies (and price levels), whereas his Asian-trade argument hinged upon *non-accumulation* of silver. Hamilton somehow maintained contradictory positions regarding stimulation of European capitalism.

[18] Much of the older literature spoke of 'American treasure' in the sense of 'gold and silver' combined. Metals and monies must be disaggregated, however, because they moved in diverse directions over extended time periods. See Flynn (1986) and Flynn and Giráldez (1997) on this point.

further profits. In short, European merchants and supporting governments reaped prodigious gains as global middlemen: silver produced
in Spanish America was destined for endmarkets in China (and to a
lesser extent, in India).[19] Portuguese and Dutch merchants played
parallel middleman roles as re-exporters of Spanish-American silver
to East Asia, and also as exporters of Japanese silver (in exchange for
Chinese silks) via Nagasaki Bay.

Two points deserve emphasis. First, all facets of the silver trade—
including non-silver trade goods linked (directly and indirectly) to
silver—must be viewed globally. Second, there exists no evidence
that European global-trade profits were greater than non-European
global-trade profits. If non-European global-trade profits were
roughly on par with European global-trade profits, then why focus
on *European* capitalism?

Wallerstein on Silver and Capitalism

Wallerstein's initial world-systems volume essentially boils down to
two alleged sources of surplus extraction from peripheries to West
European core nations: (*a*) Spanish-American bullion and (*b*) East
European grains. The dynamic European world-system core captured
surplus value from both sources (Wallerstein 1974: 100). Moreover,
this 'modern world-economy is, and only can be, a capitalist world-
economy' (Wallerstein 1974: 350).

Brenner protested that Wallerstein's import-of-surplus-value
argument contradicts the Marxist interpretations of East European
agriculture (Brenner 1977). Wallerstein claimed that cheap East
European grain underwrote capitalistic development in West Europe
via east-to-west transfer of economic surplus. Brenner insisted that
the dramatic rise in West European agriculture (especially the Low
Countries), on the contrary, ruined high-cost feudalistic agricultural
competitors in East Europe. The economy of Poland was completely
export-oriented, yet inefficiency permitted export of a mere 5–7 per
cent of Polish grain production (Brenner 1977: 69–70). 'Indeed,
precisely because it [Polish agriculture] was not (despite Wallerstein's

---

[19] See Smith ([1776] 1965: 174–247) for his global 'Digression on
Silver'.

assertion) "capitalist", it could not develop the productive potential successfully to underwrite the long-term development of the "core"' (Brenner 1977: 60)

Wallerstein's 'core' generated and regenerated surplus internally, countered Brenner, and therefore neither needed nor received Marxian surplus from the East European periphery.

Having eliminated East European sources of Marxian surplus transmitted to West European 'core' countries, only 'surplus' via Spanish-American bullion remained to support Wallerstein's overall argument. The New World metals leg of his world-systems scheme, however, contains theoretical misconceptions and contradicts historical evidence. Whereas Brenner denied the existence of Marxian surplus value within the East European grain periphery, Flynn (1984) argued that the New World silver-mining 'periphery' generated enormous economic profit/surplus. Indeed, surplus/profits linked to American silver underwrote Spain's global empire, and initiated global trade in the process (Flynn and Giráldez 1995).

The Spanish Crown extracted New World profits through direct taxation of silver (for example, 20 per cent *quinto*), and multiple levies on economic activities directly and indirectly linked to underlying mine production. Silver super-profits underwrote Habsburg Spain's 80-year war in the Netherlands, and wars against England and other European 'core' nations that Wallerstein claims benefited from New World mining. Spain also fought continuously in the Mediterranean, especially against the Ottomans, against European powers in the New World, and against the Dutch in Asian waters. American mine profits were marshalled in Spanish attempts to subdue the 'core' of northwest Europe.

Wallerstein fails to recognize the theoretical Marxist distinction between sphere of production vis-à-vis sphere of circulation. Marx stated explicitly that surplus value is generated in the sphere of production only, *not* in the sphere of circulation. Imagine a slave-produced table having production cost of $100 but a market value of $200—the slave owner captures $100 in surplus value. The slave owner later exchanges the table for a $200 jacket produced entirely by a neighbour's own labour. Surplus value is not attached to the slave-produced table now owned by the neighbour. The slave owner retains $100 in surplus value, even though the slave owner now possesses the jacket produced voluntarily. The neighbour now owns the slave-produced table, but no surplus value is attached to that table. Marx maintained that surplus value is neither created nor transferred via sphere of circulation exchange; rather, surplus value can only be created in the sphere of production.[20] Hence, when Wallerstein argues that the flow of Spanish-American silver through 'semi-periphery' Spain to the northwest European 'core' involved transfer of surplus value to the 'core' of northwest Europe, he contradicts basic Marxist theory. Massive surplus extraction based upon Spanish-American silver production underwrote Spanish wars worldwide, including efforts to crush Wallerstein's 'core' in northwest Europe.

Since Adam Smith's *Wealth of Nations*, classical economists have consistently denounced bullionist reasoning like that expressed by Wallerstein (1974: 46): 'And hence without it [bullion], Europe would have lacked the collective confidence to develop a capitalist system, wherein profit is based on various deferrals of realized value ... bullion must be seen as an essential crop for a prospering world-economy.'

Troubles deepened when Wallerstein (1974: 57) attempted to integrate Asian powers into his narrative: 'Asia, or even Indian Ocean border regions, did not become part of the European world-economy in the sixteenth century. Asia was an external arena with which Europe traded.' China is an insular world-empire: 'China is a vast empire ... Europe is not.' An empire cannot be conceived of as an entrepreneur as can a state in a world-economy. For an empire pretends to be the whole. It cannot enrich its economy by draining from other economies, since it is the only economy (Wallerstein 1974: 60).

Wallerstein (1974: 332) discusses world-systems (plural)—as opposed to a singular interconnected global system—because he judges interactions between European core states and Asian powers insignificant: 'Asia's inner life remained basically unchanged by the contact. Surely it would be hard to argue that Asian primary production was an integral part of this time of the European division of

---

[20] See Marx ([1894] 1967, Vol. 3: 279) for explicit statement of this key distinction.

labor.' Geographical boundaries of the 'European world-economy' are chosen: 'Hungary inside, but the Ottoman Empire outside ... Russia outside ... the Americas inside, and the East Indies outside' (Wallerstein 1974: 301). Meanwhile, Poland and the Americas were 'peripheries' in service of the 'core':

> The periphery of a world-economy is that geographical sector of it wherein production is primarily of lower-ranking goods (that is, goods whose labor is less well rewarded) but which is an integral part of the overall system of the division of labor, because the commodities involved are essential for daily use. The external arena of a world-economy has some kind of trade relationship, based primarily on the exchange of preciosities, what is sometimes called the 'rich trades'.
>
> Had the bullion of the Americas *all* flowed out to Asia, the Americas would have been just another external arena (i.e. not periphery) and Europe would have been merely an axis of three arenas—America, Europe, and Asia—obtaining its Asian luxuries at the price of goods sent to the Americas. (Wallerstein 1980: 109)

The capitalistic European world-system of Wallerstein contradicts Marxist theory and historical evidence. Japanese silver (which he failed to acknowledge) and Spanish-American silver engaged in global, not European, settings. Hundreds of thousands of workers extracted and refined silver. Millions transported silver, as well as goods exchanged for silver, in a fully global system. Silver was exchanged for countless products, not simply luxuries. Chinese peasants were required to pay taxes in silver. The global economy was on a silver standard. China contained the most dynamic silver end-markets in the world. If Wallerstein believes that surplus value is somehow physically attached to silver, then he should have logically proposed a Chinese capitalistic world-system rather than his European capitalistic world-system:

> In the most crowded of all—China—the share of the harvest that was marketed over long distances seems to have been considerably higher than in Europe. Wu Chengming has conservatively estimated that 30,000,000 *shi* of grain entered long-distance trade in the 18th century, or enough to feed about 14,000,000 people. This would be more than five times a generous estimate of Europe's long-distance

grain trade in a normal year during its heyday.... Eighteenth-century China (and perhaps Japan as well) actually came closer to resembling the neoclassical ideal of a market economy than did western Europe. (Pomeranz 2000: 34, 70)

***

Scholars attach a dizzying variety of modifiers to the word 'capitalism', a small sample of which includes: merchant capitalism, financial capitalism, industrial capitalism, agrarian capitalism, monopoly capitalism, state capitalism, borderland capitalism, crony capitalism, racialized capitalism, Dutch capitalism, European capitalism, global capitalism, incipient capitalism, modern capitalism, capitalist modernity, historical capitalism, capitalist world ecology, rampant capitalism, Western capitalism, and so on.

Confronted with so many capitalisms, Larry Neal (2014, Vol. 1: 2) proposed four elements common to all capitalistic variants: (*a*) private property rights, (*b*) contracts enforceable by third parties, (*c*) markets with responsive prices, and (*d*) supportive governments. Immediately following Neal's 'Introduction', Jursa (2014: 27) argues persuasively that in 'northern Mesopotamian, i.e. Assyrian, data from around 1850 BCE document profit-oriented commerce in textiles and in base and precious metals that can be classified as "capitalist" according to the definitions set out in the [Neal] introduction'.[21] Similarly, Bresson (2014: 69) follows with citations of low taxation, contract law, vibrant long-distance trade, enlarged ships, issuance of precious metal coins, rise of finance, complex bookkeeping, and mass production for markets in ancient Greece: 'a new-institutional analysis allows us to make better sense of the complex history of the ancient classical world, of its unprecedented growth of specific "capitalist" type, but also of its limitations and of its final failure.'

Criticism that Neal's definition of 'capitalism' is too inclusive is predictable, but then critics are obliged to provide an alternative definition that (*a*) identifies specific characteristics of capitalism, (*b*)

---

[21] Skepticism surrounding Jursa's claim is likely to dissipate upon consideration of extensive evidence provided in Jursa (2010).

permits identification of a start date for the Age of Capitalism, and (c) allows discussion of relationships between capitalism and globalization. No such definition of capitalism exists, to my knowledge, which is why I avoid the word 'capitalism' when discussing globalization history. When pressed to identify globalization's specific birthdate, Arturo Giráldez and I propose 1571, when Manila became the key Spanish entrepôt that connected hemispheres via the Pacific Ocean.[22] Earth became permanently and deeply interlinked during the sixteenth century, according to 1/3, 1/3, 1/3 logic, but how does capitalism fit into this five-century narrative?

'Capitalism' has been traditionally defined according to specific characteristics—social relations of production, wage labour, proletariat, surplus value, extreme concentrations of wealth, bourgeoisie, capture of governments, and so on. The vision of Marx was based upon Eurocentric-nation-state units of analysis, however, not on a globally connected system. Nonetheless, capitalism debates highlight key issues that must be integrated into discussions of globalization history. Wage labour today, for instance, is much more prevalent than what existed globally five centuries ago. Tracking the multi-century transition from diverse types of labour payment to predominance of wage labour during the twenty-first century should be a priority.

Silver mining and refining involved slave labour, forced labour, wage labour, and own labour during early globalization. For instance, the *mita* system at Potosí was more complicated than common stereotypes suggest. Mine exploitation was initially (1545–74) based upon sharecropping whereby workers owned portions of mined silver. Implementation of the mita system (1574–75) initially involved 14,000 indigenous forced labourers annually, but no more than 4,000 by 1700, and 3,000 later in the eighteenth century. The entire labour system evolved, as *mitayo*s coexisted with free *minga* workers; moreover, the same person was frequently a free minga and an un-free mitayo. Self-employed *kajcha*s ('weekend thieves' to mine owners) utilized rudimentary ore-grinding *trapiche* mills (rented or owned) in the eighteenth century. Some workers paid cash to escape mita obligations (Barragan 2016: 3–8, 15).

---

[22] Nagasaki Bay became the key entrepôt for Japanese silver exports, also in 1571.

The existence of the *kajchas* meant therefore that neither ownership of the mines, nor the exclusive property rights of the Spanish mine owners were entirely accepted by the workers, who, for their part, insisted on their own rights of access to the silver mines, such as they had had since early times. Similarly, although deprived of actual ownership of the mines, as *kajchas* the *mita* and [free] *minga* workers nevertheless maintained control over a substantial portion of the ore. (Barragan 2016: 15)

Classification of Chinese miner compensation is no less complicated. Golas divides Chinese miners into four groups: (*a*) farmers who mined seasonally; (*b*) day labourers available for any work; (*c*) compulsive labour by soldiers, convicts, debtors, and corvée, and (*d*) full-time miners with various skill levels. Landowners normally leased mine sites, receiving a share of ore, as did those with capital and mining experience. Mines were sub-leased. Mining shares were often divided among headmen, landowners, labour contractors, and miners. Chinese miners were largely paid wages, and Chinese markets flourished during the seventeenth- and eighteenth-centuries (Golas 1999: 387–403): private enterprise was the dynamic force fostering market growth in the late imperial era. Unfettered development of private commerce promoted a pattern of 'Smithian growth' in which greater economic efficiency was achieved through market expansion and specialization of labour (von Glahn 2016: 346).

How should one describe worldwide social relations of production over these centuries: slavery, feudalism, share cropping, capitalism, a composite? At what point does the drift towards wage labour and market activity deserve to be labelled 'capitalism'?

The situation might be clarified by abandonment of the term 'capitalism' altogether, since its use will always tend to suggest some kind of long-term, privileged position for the west … we can speak of the increasing scope of industrialization, even of an Industrial Revolution, without denying the beginnings of this process to Asian and other societies, without regarding it as a purely European development. (Goody 2006: 305–6)

Wealth Creation and Distribution

Wealth creation and wealth distribution, mostly ignored by mainstream economists today, is another central theme of the feudalism-to-capitalism literature. Note that silver, silk, and other commodities have intentionally been described as 'wealth components' throughout this chapter. Wealth (that is, net worth) is defined as the sum of wealth components owned, minus liabilities (that is, claims on wealth) owed. Forbes and other business publications obsess over rankings of the wealthiest 'capitalists' on Earth. Economists should likewise obsess with wealth creation and wealth distributions worldwide, but few do so.[23] None has tackled centuries of global wealth levels and wealth distribution, to my knowledge.[24] Lack of focus on wealth studies is at least partially attributable to inadequate mainstream economic theory. Foundational building blocks of modern economic theory steer attention away from wealth studies.

Combining Stock and Flow Concepts

Introductory economics textbooks begin with bedrock laws of supply and demand. Microeconomic supply involves profit-maximizing production rates; microeconomic demand involves optimal consumption rates. Market price and market-clearing quantity ('units/time') are said to result from a combination of these laws. Macroeconomic theory also involves 'units/time' quantity flows. Gross domestic product refers to combined production rates over time, as does aggregate demand. In sum, both micro-analyses and macro-analyses focus 99.9 per cent on 'units/time'.

The (unconventional) laws of supplies and demands referenced in this chapter differ fundamentally from conventional economic theories: focus shifts to *inventory quantities* of goods (wealth components). Inventories are denominated in 'units' at a particular instance in time, unlike 'units/time' flows that dominate standard models. Three supply functions (rather than simply 'supply') are specified: production supply ('units/time' increase in inventory 'units'), inventory

[23] Piketty (2014) is a notable exception, as are Saez and Zucman (2018) at UC Berkeley's Center for Equitable Growth.

[24] Although Alfani (2019) provides an excellent survey of empirical wealth (and income) distribution studies in the economic history literature, especially over the past decade.

supply (inventory 'units' held), and sales supply ('units/time' reduction in inventory 'units').[25] Three demand functions are specified: purchase demand ('units/time' addition to inventory 'units'), inventory demand (*desired* inventory 'units'), and consumption demand ('units/time' subtraction from inventory 'units'). Wealth components (that is, inventories) correspond to assets on balance sheets and accumulate through time. Thus, the model is inherently historical.

In contrast, conventional economic theory is ahistorical because 'units/time' quantities refer to a single period of time. Accumulated inventories are assumed 'given' or entirely ignored. Economists neglect analysis of inventory accumulations because mathematical limitations preclude integrating them. Strange as it may seem to readers, conventional supply and demand analysis applies only to (non-stockable) services, not (stockable) goods, despite the fact that textbooks routinely portray goods in supply–demand examples.[26]

Traditional explanation for flows of 'precious metals' from Europe to Asia illustrates the misunderstanding inherent in 'flows-only thinking'. Many historians emphasize European preferences for Asian silks, ceramics, and teas. Vigorous European imports of Asian products is said to have confronted weak Asian purchases of European goods. Inward-looking Asian customers are therefore responsible, in a sense, for substantial European trade deficits vis-à-vis Asia. Precious metals had to *flow* from Europe to Asia in response to Europe's trade deficit with Asia. Imbalance in the 'real sector' required response from the 'monetary sector'. This traditional European *trade deficit* view makes no sense. First, silver flowed to China, not to 'Asia'. Second, Japanese

---

[25] Since production supply augments inventories while sales supply depletes inventories, conventional microeconomics conflates them as 'supply'. See Flynn (2019) for further discussion.

[26] Inventory supply and inventory demand functions vanish for services, which cannot be stocked by definition. Production supply (PS) and sales supply (SS) for any service merge into conventional 'supply' (PS = SS = S) because inequality (PS ≠ SS) requires inventories. Purchase demand (PD) and consumption demand (CD) merge into conventional 'demand' (PD = CD = D) because inequality (PD ≠ CD) requires inventories. Since conventional 'supply' and 'demand' ignore inventories, they apply solely to services, thereby neglecting the tangible world.

silver also flowed to China. Third, ('precious metal') gold flowed in the opposite direction of silver, from China to Japan, to Europe, and to Acapulco in the 1540s–1640 and 1700–50. Fourth, *causation* emanated from global silver markets; silver never flowed as a 'passive balancing item' anywhere throughout world history. Demand-side dynamism/causation emanated from Chinese demand to hold silver (coupled with non-Chinese demand-side attraction for Chinese exports). European merchants were middlemen in the global silver trade. Elimination of distortions caused by *flows-only* reasoning requires a model that disaggregates—including separation of gold, silver, and other monetized goods—and also re-focuses analysis upon inventory considerations in global settings (Flynn 1986).

As discussed earlier, *inventory demand (desired holdings)* for silver surged due to collapse of China's paper-money system 1430s onwards. Surge in *inventory demand* for silver holdings yielded unusually high Chinese silver prices. Silver production and sale/purchase *flows* were necessary for proper functioning of this global market system, of course, but the driving force emanated from inventory (that is, wealth) considerations. All goods are wealth components. The world's wealthiest people today often build wealth by choosing to minimize (not maximize) income. Common people cannot avoid taxable income because negligible, zero, or negative net worth precludes this option. Modern economic theory focuses on time-dimensioned *flows*, which render it ahistorical in that it downplays/ignores wealth, wealth distribution, as well as individual wealth components.

Bibliography

Adshead, S.A.M. 1988. *China in World History*. London: Macmillan.

Alfani, G. 2019. 'Wealth and Income Inequality in the Long Run of History.' In *Handbook of Cliometrics*, edited by C. Diebolt, M. Haupert, pp. 1–30. Germany: Springer Verlag GmbH. Available at https://doi.org/10.1007/978-3-642-40458-0-_29-1.

Aram, B. and B. Yun-Casalilla, eds. 2014. *Global Goods and the Spanish Empire, 1492–1824: Circulation, Resistance and Diversity*. Basingstoke and New York: Palgrave Macmillan.

Atwell, W. 1988. 'Ming Observers of Ming Decline: Some Chinese Views on the "Seventeenth-Century Crisis" in Comparative Perspective.' *Journal of the Royal Asiatic Society of Great Britain and Ireland* 2: 316–48.

————. 1998. 'Ming China and the Emerging World Economy, c. 1470–1650.' In *The Cambridge History of China*, Vol. 7, edited by D. Twitchett and F.W. Mote, pp. 585–640. Cambridge: Cambridge University Press.

Barragan, R. 2016. 'Dynamics of Continuity and Change: Shifts in Labour Relations in the Potosí Mines (1680–1812).' *International Review of Social History* 61(S24): 93–114.

Borah, W. 1943. *Silk Raising in Colonial Mexico*. Berkeley: University of California Press.

Boulding, K. (1950) 1967. *A Reconstruction of Economics*. New York: John Wiley & Sons.

Bray, F., ed. 1984. *Agriculture*. Part 2 of *Biology and Biological Technology. Science and Civilization in China*. Vol. 6, edited by Joseph Needham. Cambridge: Cambridge University Press.

————. 1984. *Agriculture* . Vol. 6, edited by Joseph Needham. Cambridge: Cambridge University Press.

Brenner, R. 1977. 'The Origins of Capitalist Development: A Critique of Neo-Smithian Marxism.' *New Left Review* 104: 25–92.

Bray, F. 1984. *Agriculture*. Vol. 6, edited by Joseph Needham. Cambridge: Cambridge University Press.

Bresson, A. 2014. 'Capitalism and the Ancient Greek Economy.' In *The Cambridge History of Capitalism Volume I: The Rise of Capitalism: From Ancient Origins to 1848*, edited by L. Neal and J.G. Williamson, pp. 43–74. Cambridge: Cambridge University Press.

Chuan H.S. 1969. 'The Inflow of American Silver into China from the Late Ming to Mid-Ch'ing Period.' *The Journal of the Institute of Chinese Studies of the Chinese University of Hong Kong* 2: 61–75.

Crosby, A. 1972. *The Columbian Exchange: Biological and Cultural Consequences of 1492*. Westport, CN: Greenwood Press.

————. 1986. *Ecological Imperialism: The Biological Expansion of Europe, 900–1900*. Cambridge: Cambridge University Press.

de Vries, J. 2003. 'Connecting Europe and Asia: A Quantitative Analysis of the Cape-Route Trade, 1497–1795.' In *Global Connections and Monetary History, 1470–1800*, edited by D.O. Flynn, A. Giráldez, and R. von Glahn. Aldershot: Ashgate Publishing.

De Zwart, P. and J.L. van Zanden. 2018. *The Origins of Globalization: World Trade in the Making of the Global Economy, 1500–1800*. Cambridge: Cambridge University Press.

Diamond, J. 1997. *Guns, Germs, and Steel: The Fates of Human Societies*. New York: W.W. Norton and Company.

Fairbank, J.K. 1992. *China: A New History*. Cambridge: Harvard University Press.

Flynn, D.O. 1978. 'A New Perspective on the Spanish Price Revolution: The Monetary Approach to the Balance of Payments.' *Explorations in Economic History* 15: 388–406.

———. 1984. 'El desarollo del primer capitalismo a pesar de los metales preciosos de Nuevo Mundo: Una Interpretation Anti-Wallerstein de la Espana Imperial.' *Revista de Historia Economica* 2(2): 29–58. [Reprinted in English as 1996. 'Early Capitalism Despite New World Bullion: An Anti-Wallerstein Interpretation of Imperial Spain.' In *World Silver and Monetary History in the Sixteenth and Seventeenth Centuries*, pp. 29–58. Aldershot: Ashgate/Variorum.]

———. 1986. 'The Microeconomics of Silver and East-West Trade in the Early Modern Period.' In *The Emergence of a World Economy 1500–1914. Papers of the IX International Congress of Economic History. Part I: 1500–1850*, edited by W. Fisher, R.M. McInnis, and J. Schneider, pp. 37–60. Stuttgart: Steiner-Verlag-Weisbaden-GmbH.

———. 1991. 'Comparing the Tokugawa Shogunate with Hapsburg Spain: Two Silver-Based Empires in a Global Setting.' In *The Political Economy of Merchant Empires*, edited by J.D. Tracy, pp. 332–59. Cambridge: Cambridge University Press.

———. 2015. 'Tangible and Intangible Monies: Theory and Global History.' In *Documents and Studies on 19th c. Monetary History: Mints, Technology and Coin Production*, edited by G. Depeyrot and M. Marcher, pp. 61–92. Wetteren, Belgium: Moneta.

———. 2018. 'Six Monetary Functions over Five Millennia: A Price Theory of Monies.' In *Money, Currency and Crisis: In Search of Trust, 2000 BC to AD 2000*, edited by R.J. van der Spek and B. van Leeuwen, pp. 13–36. London and New York: Routledge.

———. 2019. 'Big, History, Geological Accumulations, Physical Economics, and Wealth.' *Asian Review of World Histories* 7: 80–106.

Flynn, D.O. and A. Giráldez. 1995. 'Born with a "Silver Spoon"; World Trade's Origin in 1571.' *Journal of World History* 6(2): 201–21.

———. 1996. 'China and the Spanish Empire.' *Revista de Historia Economica* 14(2): 309–38.

———. 1997. 'Introduction: Monetary Substances in Global Perspective.' In *Metals and Monies in an Emerging Global Economy*, edited by D.O. Flynn and A. Giráldez, pp. xv–xl. Aldershot: Ashgate/Variorum.

———. 2000. 'Money and Growth without Development: The Case of Ming China.' In *Asia-Pacific Dynamism, 1550–2000*, edited by A.J.H. Latham and H. Kawakatsu, pp. 199–215. London: Routledge Press.

———. 2002. 'Cycles of Silver: Global Economic Unity through the Mid-Eighteenth Century'. *Journal of World History* 13(2): 391–427.

————. 2004. 'Path Dependence, Time Lags and the Birth of Globalization: A Critique of O'Rourke and Williamson.' *European Review of Economic History* 8: 81–108.

————. 2008. 'Born Again: Globalization's Sixteenth-Century Origins.' *Pacific Economic Review* 3(13): 359–87.

Frank, A.G. 1998. *ReOrient: Global Economy in the Asian Age*. Berkeley: University of California Press.

Geiss, J. 1979. 'Peking under the Ming (1368–1644).' PhD Dissertation, Princeton University.

Gernet, J. 1982. *A History of Chinese Civilization*. Cambridge: Cambridge University Press.

Golas, P.J. 1999. *Mining. Science and Civilization in China*, Joseph Needham, Vol. 13, edited by Joseph Needham. Cambridge: Cambridge University Press.

Goody, J. 2006. *The Theft of History*. Cambridge: Cambridge University Press.

Graulau, J. 2019. *The Underground Wealth of Nations: On the Capitalist Origins of Silver Mining, A.D. 1150–1450*. New Haven: Yale University Press.

Guerrero, S. 2017. *Silver by Fire, Silver by Mercury: A Chemical History of Silver Refining in New Spain and Mexico, 16th to 19th Centuries*. Leiden: Brill.

Hamashita, T. 1988. *The Tribute System and Modern Asia*. Tokyo: The Toyo Bunko.

Hamilton, C. 2015. 'Getting the Anthropocene so Wrong.' *The Anthropocene Review* 2(2): 102–7.

Hamilton, E.J. 1929. 'American Treasure and the Rise of Capitalism (1500–1700).' *Economica* 9: 338–57.

————. 1952. 'Prices as a Factor in Business Growth.' *Journal of Economic History* 12(4): 325–49.

Hayami, A., O. Saitó, and R. Toby 2004. *The Economic History of Japan: 1600–1990*. Vol 1. New York: Oxford University Press.

Herman, J. 2006. 'The Cant of Conquest: Tusi Offices and China's Political Incorporation of the Southwest Frontier.' *Empire at the Margins: Culture, Ethnicity and Frontier in Early Modern China*, edited by P. Crossley, D. Sutton, and H. Siu, pp. 135–68. Berkeley: University of California Press.

Ho, P.-T. 1959. *Studies in the Population of China, 1368–1933*. Cambridge: Harvard University Press.

Jursa, M. 2010. *Aspects of the Economic History of Babylonia in the First Millennium BC: Economic Geography, Economic Mentalities, Agriculture, the Use of Money and the Problem of Economic Growth*. Münster: Ugarit-Verlag.

————. 2014. 'Babylonia in the First Millennium BCE—Economic Growth in Times of Empire.' In *The Cambridge History of Capitalism, Volume I: The Rise of Capitalism: From Ancient Origins to 1848*, edited by L. Neal and J.G. Williamson, pp. 24–42. Cambridge: Cambridge University Press.

Kamen, H. 2003. *Empire: How Spain Became a World Power 1492–1763*. New York: Harper Collins.

Keynes, J.M. 1930. *A Treatise on Money, Volume II: The Applied Theory of Money*. New York: Harcourt Brace Company.

Klein H. and Serrano Hernández, S. 2019. 'Was There a 17th Century Crisis in Spanish America?' *Revista de Historia Económica, Journal of Iberian and Latin American Economic History* 37(1): 43–80.

Lewis, S. and M. Maslin. 2015. 'Defining the Anthropocene.' *Nature* 519: 171–80.

López-Baralt, L. 2006. 'Islamic Influence on Spanish Literature: Benengeli's Pen in *Don Quixote*.' *Islamic Studies* 45(4): 579–93.

Ma, N. 2017. *The Age of Silver: The Rise of the Novel East and West*. New York: Oxford University Press.

Mann, C.C. 2006. *1491: New Revelations of the Americas before Columbus*. New York: Vintage Books.

————. 2011. *1493: Uncovering the New World Columbus Created*. New York: Alfred A. Knopf.

Marks, R.B. 1997. *Tigers, Rice, Silk, and Silt: Environment and Economy in Late Imperial South China*. New York and London: Cambridge University Press.

————. 2017. *China: An Environmental History*. Lanham, Boulder, New York, London: Rowman and Littlefield.

Marx, K. (1894) 1967. *Capital: A Critique of Political Economy. Volume III. The Process of Capitalist Production as a Whole*. New York: International Publishers.

Mazumdar, S. 1999. 'The Impact of New World Food Crops on the Diet and Economy of China and India, 1600–1900.' In *Food in Global History*, edited by R. Grew, pp. 58–78. Boulder: Westview Press.

McNeill, J.R. 2001. 'Introduction.' In *Environmental History in the Pacific World*, edited by J.R. McNeill, pp. xiii–xxix. Aldershot: Ashgate/Variorum.

Munro, J. 2007. 'South German Silver, European Textiles, and Venetian Trade with the Levant and Ottoman Empire, c. 1370 to c. 1720: A Non-Mercantilist Approach to the Balance of Payments Problem.' In *Relazione economiche tra Europa e mondo islamico, seccoli XIII–XVIII, Atti delle 'Settimana di Studi' e altri convegni*, edited by S. Cavaciocchi, pp. 907–62. Florence: Le Monnier.

Nadal Oller, J. 1959. 'La Revolution de los Precios Españoles en el Siglo XVI.' *Hispania* 19: 503–29.

Naquin, S. and E.S. Rawski. 1987. *Chinese Society in the Eighteenth Century.* New Haven: Yale University Press.

Neal, L. 2014. 'Introduction.' In *The Cambridge History of Capitalism, Volume I: The Rise of Capitalism: From Ancient Origins to 1848*, edited by L. Neal and J.G. Williamson, pp. 1–23. Cambridge: Cambridge University Press.

Nef, J.U. 1936. 'Prices and Industrial Capitalism in France and England, 1540–1640.' *Economic History Review* 7(2): 155–85.

O'Brien, P. 1982. 'European Economic Development: The Contribution of the Periphery.' *Economic History Review* 35(1): 1–18.

O'Rourke, K. and J. Williamson. 2002. 'When Did Globalization Begin?' *European Review of Economic History* 6(1): 23–50.

———. 2004. 'Once More: When Did Globalization Begin?' *European Review of Economic History* 8(1): 109–17.

Outhwaite, R.B. 1969. *Inflation in Tudor and Early Stuart England.* London: Macmillan.

Parker, G. 2013. *Global Crisis: War Climate Change, & Catastrophe in the Seventeenth Century.* New Haven and London: Yale University Press.

Perez, M. 2014. 'From Eurocentrism to Sinocentrism: The New Challenges in Global History.' *European Journal of Scientific Research* 119(3): 337–52.

Perrin, N. 1980. *Giving Up the Gun: Japan's Reversion to the Sword, 1543–1879.* Boulder: Shambhala Publications.

Piketty, T. 2014. *Capital in the Twenty-First Century*, translated from French by Arthur Goldhammer. Cambridge: The Belknap Press of Harvard University Press.

Pomeranz, K. 2000. *The Great Divergence: China, Europe, and the Making of the Modern World Economy.* Princeton: Princeton University Press.

Saez, E. and G. Zucman. 2018. *World Inequality Report 2018.* Cambridge: Harvard University Press.

Sakae, T. 2001. 'Sakai, East Asia's Largest Trading City: Where Did All the Riches Go.' *Journal of Japanese Trade and Industry*: 46–9. [Reprinted as Chapter 3 in M. Caprio and Matsuda Koichirō, eds. 2006. *Japan and the Pacific, 1540–1920*. Aldershot: Ashgate/Variorum.]

Samuelson, P.A. and W.D Nordhaus. 1995. *Economics.* New York: McGraw-Hill.

Shih, M-h. 1976. *The Silk Industry in Ch'ing China.* Ann Arbor: Center for Chinese Studies, University of Michigan.

Shimada, R. 2006. *The Intra-Asian Trade in Japanese Copper by the Dutch East India Company during the Eighteenth Century.* Leiden and Boston: Brill.

Smith, A. (1776) 1965. *An Inquiry into the Nature and Causes of the Wealth of Nations*. New York: The Modern Library.

Souza, G. (1986) 2004. *The Survival of Empire: Portuguese Trade and Society in China and the South China Sea 1630–1754*. Cambridge: Cambridge University Press.

Spence, J.D. 1990. *The Search for Modern China*. New York and London: W.W. Norton.

———. 1992. *Chinese Roundabout: Essays in History and Culture*. New York and London: W.W. Norton.

Troki, C.A. 1999. *Opium, Empire and the Global Political Economy: A Study of the Asian Opium Trade, 1750–1950, Asia's Transformations*. London and New York: Routledge.

von Glahn, R. 1996. *Fountain of Fortune: Money and Monetary Policy in China, 1000–1700*. Berkeley: University of California Press.

———. 2016. *The Economic History of China: From Antiquity to the Nineteenth Century*. Cambridge: Cambridge University Press.

Wallerstein, I. 1974. *The Modern World-System: Capitalist Agriculture and the Origins of the European World-Economy in the Sixteenth Century*. New York: Academic Press.

———. 1980. *The Modern World-System II: Mercantilism and the Consolidation of the European World-Economy, 1600–1750*. New York: Academic Press.

Waswo, A. 1986. 'Innovation and Growth in Japanese Agriculture, 1600–1868.' In *Pre-Conditions to Industrialization in Japan*, edited by A. Hayami, pp. 1–9. Bern, Switzerland.

Yasuba, Y. 1986. 'The Tokugawa Legacy: A Survey.' In *Pre-Conditions to Industrialization in Japan*, edited by A. Hayami. Bern, Switzerland.

2

New World Slavery in the Capitalist World Economy

Leonardo Marques[*]

The relationship between capitalism and slavery in the Americas was the subject of a voluminous literature throughout the twentieth century, starting with precursors such as Eric Williams, Caio Prado Jr., and Sergio Bagú in the 1930s and 1940s to the more empirical and theoretical debates of the 1960s and 1970s among Marxists, economic historians, historical sociologists, and others. These debates faded by the end of the century, as the concept of capitalism was largely abandoned by scholars in the social sciences. Slavery continued to be a hot topic, but by then was devoid of the larger contexts that had inspired the earlier scholarship. Issues of agency and subjectivity became the focus of most labour studies. Recent historiographical contributions, however, have revived some of the questions that animated the earlier debates, ranging from the contribution of

[*] The author would like to thank Rafael Marquese, Tâmis Parron, Thiago Krause, and the editors of this book for their suggestions.

slavery to European development to the nature of labour relations in colonial Latin America (Marquese 2013).[1]

Very few of these issues appear in the first volume of *The Cambridge History of Capitalism*, organized by Larry Neal and first published in 2014. In what follows, I explore, first, how New World slavery and other forms of coerced labour appear in that volume. In the second section, I offer a brief alternative interpretation of the history of slavery in the Americas as a constitutive part of historical capitalism. In this way, I hope to tackle a central problem in *The Cambridge History of Capitalism*: its static representation of slavery, which, abstracted from the broader world structures of which it was part, appears as a single immutable institution throughout the modern era. My main goal here is to emphasize, first, how slavery changed over time and, second, how it was part of the total ensemble of global relations that formed the capitalist world economy between the sixteenth and the nineteenth centuries. It is a history of *slavery in capitalism*.[2]

New World Slavery in *The Cambridge History of Capitalism*

In the introduction to the first volume of *The Cambridge History of Capitalism*, Larry Neal provides a description of the concept of capitalism and a general methodological approach that is shared by the authors. According to him, they 'search for characteristics that may have been present in different historical settings when economic growth was achieved for a significant period'. This approach has the merit of abandoning old images of pre-modern societies as invariably stagnant, but it also extends the concept of capitalism into the beginnings of human history, completely de-historicizing it. On the subject of modern slavery, such an approach could hardly allow for a thorough investigation of its role in the development of capitalism as a historical system. Thus, it is not surprising that the vast literature

---

[1] For a useful overview of the new history of capitalism, see Clegg (2015). For Latin America, see Tutino (2011). For a trenchant diagnosis of the discipline, see Wilder (2012).

[2] The use of the idea of slavery in capitalism throughout this chapter is inspired by McMichael (1991).

on the contribution (or lack thereof) of the transatlantic slave trade and slavery in the New World to the development of Europe is nearly ignored in the volume (Neal 2014: 4).

The subject appears in a few paragraphs in Roy Bin Wong's comparison of Europe and China and in Knick Harley's account of British and European industrialization, in both cases to dismiss its importance. Harley recognizes that an enslaved Caribbean was a crucial component of the successful history of colonization in North America, since the success of northern colonies depended on the selling of goods to the plantation colonies. Still, according to him, the Englishmen 'probably would have settled and population grown rapidly even if the West Indian slave colonies had not existed' (Harley 2014: 504). Thus, Harley explicitly points to the connections between the enslaved Caribbean and the mainland colonies, but concludes with a counterfactual question that gives due weight to the colonies but not to Caribbean slavery. Besides these few references, essays that deal with New World slavery more extensively are those on the United States (Jeremy Atack) and Latin America (Richard Salvucci).[3]

For Jeremy Atack (2014: 537), farms in colonial America could be more or less capitalist—understood as 'market-focussed and market-driven'—since the early days of colonization. According to this definition, those producing tobacco in the colonial era were the most capitalist, focusing on a single staple and depending on the market for foodstuffs and other goods. In the nineteenth century, slavery further expanded along with cotton production into the Southwest, as the soil got exhausted quickly. In a second moment, he deals with the thornier issue of the compatibility between slavery and industrialization in the long run, arguing that slaves were not directly market consumers themselves and that the South had a larger number of poor whites than the Midwest. 'As a result', he argues, 'the mass southern market was weak and failed to support a

---

[3] A more careful overview of the slavery and capitalism debate appears in Gareth Austin's chapter in the second volume of the *Cambridge History of Capitalism*. Austin, however, focuses mostly on Africa and Asia in the second half of the nineteenth century, which is beyond the scope of the present chapter. See Austin (2014).

local domestic industry' (Atack 2014: 554). Here, he touches on an important subject that has been explored by a few other historians, and that goes a long way towards explaining the results of the US Civil War, but has been generally ignored by the new US historians of capitalism (Atack 2014: 554).

In sharp contrast to Atack's essay, the assumption that free labour is the key feature of capitalism is a major thread in Richard Salvucci's essay on Latin America. In his discussion of mining, the author goes back to the classic comparison between free labour in Mexico and coerced labour in Peru. Free labour in the Mexican mines 'produced greater competition for labor, and, therefore, higher wages and better working conditions', which explains how they eventually surpassed their Peruvian counterparts over the eighteenth century (Salvucci 2014: 409). The freer labour that could be found in Mexican mines, however, was an exception. Mining in Peru was marked by institutions such as the mita (responsible for annually drafting thousands of labourers to work in Peruvian mines) in Peru. The following section demonstrates how labour in the *haciendas* (large rural estate) and *obraje*s (textile workshop) was also very far from anything resembling free labour in the modern sense, with both establishing restrictions on labour mobility that could go from the direct enslavement of labourers to the so-called debt *peonaje* (debt labour). This vast array of mechanisms to extract labour—including slavery in Brazil and the Caribbean—made colonial Latin America non-capitalist in Salvucci's view (Salvucci 2014: 409). The author has moved away from some of the ideas of his earlier book on colonial obrajes in New Spain. In that work, he notices the presence of non-market mechanisms in the obrajes but concludes that 'the result was capitalistic—obrajes were conducted as profit-making enterprises—even though self-regulating labor markets did not exist. But they hardly existed in Western Europe until the nineteenth century, and no one seriously doubts that economic activity there was capitalistic' (Salvucci 1987: 42). Now, a few decades later, by reading the Brenner Debate through neo-institutionalist glasses, Salvucci has reached the very different conclusion that free labour is important not only in an 'ideological sense', as part of a working definition of capitalism, but also in an 'economic sense' because a functioning labour market is the sine qua non of economic growth and development (Salvucci 2010: 630).

The main problem here is that the kind of approach developed by Salvucci and most other authors in *The Cambridge History of Capitalism* is based on the abstraction of specific areas from the bundle of global capitalist relations that form and are formed by them. This problem can be seen on multiple levels and explains why modern slavery has such a marginal role in the book. The problem is not only one of showing the role of slavery in the development of Europe, but also of showing its importance for non-slave parts of the Americas as well. The formal separation between Spanish America, the Caribbean, Brazil, and the United States leave important chunks of this story out. A broader, systemic approach can not only reconnect the history of slavery in the Americas to its global dimensions, but also transcend rigid separations between different forms of labour in the colonial Americas themselves. Such an approach can avoid some of the conceptual traps that marked the earlier debates. Instead of the violent abstractions that separate different spheres of capitalism in order to elect one of them as the defining feature of the system, one should search for 'production, distribution, exchange, and consumption as a unified field of relational concepts linked by the commodity form' (Tomich 2003: 29).

Three Cycles of Slavery in Capitalism

Immanuel Wallerstein's (1995: 13–4) broader characterization of capitalism as a historical system in which capital 'came to be used with the primary objective or intent of self-expansion' is a useful starting point. Such a world depended on the transformation, in the words of Giovanni Arrighi (1994: 86), 'from a system in which networks of accumulation were wholly embedded in and subordinate to networks of power into a system in which networks of power are wholly embedded in and subordinate to networks of accumulation'. The networks of accumulation that supported the self-expansion of value, in turn, seem to have been not only indifferent to the forms of labour they dominate, but, more importantly, have historically explored *combinations* of these multiple forms on various scales and in shifting ways over time. Arrighi offers a good model for understanding these historical developments with the concept of *systemic cycle of accumulation*. Using Marx's famous 'MCM' formula (money converted into commodities to be converted into more money) in a completely original way, he describes the development of capitalism as a world historical system that alternates 'epochs of material expansion (MC phases of capital accumulation) with phases of financial rebirth and expansion (CM' phases)'. In the first phase, money capital launches 'an increasing mass of commodities (including commoditized labor-power and gifts of nature)', while in the second, 'money capital "sets itself free" from its commodity form, and accumulation proceeds through financial deals' (Arrighi 1994: 6–7). Together, the two phases form a systemic cycle of accumulation. According to Arrighi, there were four of these cycles in the history of capitalism: the Genoese cycle, during the long sixteenth century; the Dutch cycle, in a long seventeenth century; the British cycle, in the long nineteenth century; and the US cycle, in the long twentieth century (Arrighi 1994: 6–7, 86; Wallerstein 1995: 13–14).

The first three systemic cycles of accumulation roughly coincided with three overlapping moments in the history of Atlantic slavery. As Berbel, Marquese, and Parron (2016) have shown, the Genoese cycle corresponded to the construction of an Iberian Atlantic system, which largely depended on Genoese capital in its initial phase; the Dutch cycle was marked by the emergence of the Northwestern European Atlantic system, in which the Dutch themselves played an important role; and the British cycle led to the expansion of new slave frontiers in Brazil, Cuba, and the United States, in what Dale Tomich (2003: 56–8) has called the *second slavery*. While one may disagree with the characteristics outlined by the authors for each of these systems, the organization of their model around three different moments in the history of New World slavery is supported by other studies from very different theoretical perspectives as discussed later in the chapter (Marquese, Parron, and Berbel 2016).

The Genoese Systemic Cycle of Accumulation and the Iberian Atlantic System

The production of a mass of commodities in the phases of material expansion described by Arrighi also 'set in motion' the commodification of labourers. In the long sixteenth century, the Atlantic islands

(Madeira, Canaries, and São Tomé) experienced a series of developments that paved the way for the rise of the plantation complex in the Americas. As the sugar frontier expanded into each of these islands, landscapes were transformed, productivity increased, and the role of slavery became more central. In Madeira and the Canary Islands, the labour force that produced sugar was very heterogeneous, ranging from European free labourers to African and Guanche (the native population from the Canaries) slaves. The organization of production was divided between a few mills (which were owned by wealthy merchants of different origins, including Genoa) and a larger number of colonists who planted sugarcane and established contracts with mill-owners to process it. It was in São Tomé that the labour force came to be composed mainly of African slaves. Here, the main characteristics of the sugar plantation complex were finally present: an enslaved African labour force producing large volumes of sugar to be sold in European markets (Blackburn 1997: 108–12).

It was this plantation complex that was transferred to the Spanish Caribbean and, especially, Brazil, although important changes also took place on the other side of the Atlantic. Between 1583 and 1629, the number of sugar mills in Brazil went from 120 to 346, most of them concentrated in the northeast provinces of Bahia and Pernambuco. In the 1620s, the colony was producing something between 15,000 and 22,000 metric tons of sugar per year. Part of this rising productivity came from technological innovations, especially the introduction of the vertical three-roller mill. As Antônio Barros de Castro (1980: 701) has shown, this innovation was a direct transference from Peru, where it had been used to grind the ores that were extracted from Potosí and other silver mines. In terms of labour organization, the system was similar to that in the old Atlantic islands, with a small number of wealthy mill owners and a vast number of *lavradores* (the less wealthy individuals who planted sugarcane and established contracts for milling the cane). The labour force in the second half of the sixteenth century consisted mainly of Indians, free and enslaved. By the second quarter of the following century, most Indians had been replaced by enslaved Africans and their descendants (Castro 1980; Schwartz 2004: 161–2, 188–9).

Despite the rapid ascent of Brazilian sugar production, most slaves carried across the Atlantic in the long sixteenth century went to the

Spanish Americas. Estimates are that between 1501 and 1640, the Spanish colonies received approximately 335,000 enslaved Africans. The main commodity behind this coerced migration was silver, even though only a small percentage of those individuals worked directly in its extraction. A report from the late sixteenth century for New Spain mines shows that enslaved Africans comprised only 14 per cent of the labour force. In Peru, that percentage was even smaller. The key factor, as Peter Bakewell (1984: 109) shows, was that silver generated vast economic circuits that set in motion a large number of ancillary activities: 'Grain cultivation in the Bajío and Michoacán, wine making on the Peruvian coast and in Chile, cattle and mule raising in the Río de la Plata provinces, textiles in Peru and Quito; and everywhere freighting and craftwork. Very few large regions escaped the influence of the bullion flows.' A large number of enslaved Africans could be found in many of these enterprises, from the obraje production of bags used by Indians to carry the silver out of the mines to the supply of foodstuffs and animals from *chacara*s and *estancia*s in different parts of Spanish America (Bakewell 1984: 109; Bowser 1974).

Most of these captives were supplied by Portuguese slave traders. The fifteenth-century treaties between Castile and Portugal had long-term implications for the Spanish empire, which would not have direct access to Africa until the end of the transatlantic slave trade in the 1860s, thus depending on the supply of captives by foreign traders. The solution was to establish the *asiento*, a contract in which the Spanish Crown allowed the introduction of slaves into its domains by non-Spanish merchants during an established period of time. After the union of the Iberian Crowns in 1580, the Portuguese successively became asiento holders. The Iberian Union facilitated Portuguese access to Peruvian silver in exchange for African slaves (along with other goods in both directions). This trade, in turn, strengthened Portuguese presence in Angola, where wars against the Kingdom of Ndongo had been producing a large number of captives since 1575. The number of Africans carried out of West Central Africa in the last two decades of the sixteenth century (101,574) was more than six times the total number of individuals embarked in the previous eight decades (16,304). By then, Angola had become the main region of slave embarkation, a status that it would maintain until the end of the traffic in the nineteenth century. Also, it was the traffic to Spanish America that, to a large extent, financed the consolidation of Portuguese rule in the region. João Rodrigues Coutinho, who was sent by the Portuguese king with the mission of conquering Angola, for example, became both *asientista* and governor of Angola in the early seventeenth century, fighting wars against local populations soon after his arrival. Silver production in Potosí and the construction of the Portuguese branch of the transatlantic slave trade were part of a single integrated process (Alencastro 2000: 80–2).

On the other side of the Atlantic, the construction of the structures of the silver trade depended on the arrival of slaves. Enslaved Africans, along with engineers and other skilled labourers from Europe, were among the main ones responsible for the construction of the entire fortification system of the Spanish empire in the Americas. In the 1580s, while the Portuguese slave trade intensified as a result of the wars of conquest in Angola, Philip II sent the Italian military engineer Antonelli to coordinate an enormous project of fortifications in the Spanish Caribbean that included Santo Domingo, Cartagena, San Juan, Veracruz, St. Augustine, and Havana (Fuente 2008: 73). As Manuel Moreno Fraginals (2005: 102) shows, the various forts in Cuba demanded an extraordinary volume of labour, with stones being carried from distances of over 25 km in order to provide the approximately two million blocks that were used in those buildings. In some years, there were more workers in the forts than in Cuban plantations. As the Dutch and other interlopers started to threaten the empire, enslaved Africans were also employed in the construction of fortifications in Cartagena, on the coast of Peru, and other parts of the Americas. Similarly, Havana shipyards demanded a great volume of enslaved labour, not only for the direct construction of ships, but also for the cutting, preparation, and transportation of timber, with the sources becoming increasingly distant from the coast. The royal shipyards at Callao and Guayaquil also had a growing number of enslaved Africans among their labour force (along with a minority of free black artisans). As this labour intensified, so did the demand for slaves. From these shipyards came many of the vessels of the *Armada de Barlovento* (responsible for policing the Caribbean) and the *Armada del Mar del Sur* (responsible for protecting trade in Peru and the Pacific coast). All this investment on fortifications and the navy paid off: very few pirate attacks against shipments of silver leaving Spanish America succeeded (Bowser 1974: 128; Wing 2015: 103).

While part of the silver stayed in America and financed these internal developments, most of it flowed to the Old World, stimulating the emergence of a world economy (as trade between Europe and Asia intensified) and the development of different parts of Europe. While the role of silver in global dynamics has been at the centre of recent global history debates, many of these studies tend to neglect the older discussions on the impact of silver on Europe. Still, some of the most reliable estimates show that most silver went to Europe, not Asia (Findlay and O' Rourke 2009: 218).[4] Among the many roads that took silver from Spain to the rest of Europe, usually under Genoese banking supervision, were those to the Low Countries, France, northern Italy, and England. During much of the sixteenth century, Antwerp would be a major financial, commercial, and manufacturing centre, with silver playing an important role, for example, in the commercial circuits that provided Baltic grain for a society that was becoming highly urbanized (Mielants 2017). In the following two centuries, the flows of New World silver and gold became a fundamental component of financial developments and the construction of fiscal-military states in northwest Europe.

The Dutch Systemic Cycle of Accumulation and the Northwestern European Atlantic System

By the late sixteenth century, Amsterdam had replaced Antwerp as the major financial, commercial, and manufacturing centre of Europe in the context of the Dutch war against the Spanish empire. New World bullion, which had financed the imperial adventures of Philip II, went in ever large quantities to the Netherlands. By the seventeenth century, Amsterdam became the financial centre of the world, an entrepôt for most of the precious metals that were extracted from Africa and the Americas. As in Antwerp, New World silver entered the Baltic trade and gave the Dutch access to grain,

---

[4] On silver and the price revolution in Europe, see Stein and Stein (2000).

timber, and other essential products from the other side of the Elbe (Moore 2010). With a powerful navy and a series of financial innovations that included the creation of the famous East and West Indies Companies, the Dutch were soon fighting the Iberian Union on the global stage. During this period, the Dutch conquered Portuguese territories and forts in Brazil and Africa, learning various aspects of slave trading and sugar production in the Atlantic and playing an important role in the construction of a renewed plantation complex in the Caribbean. By the mid-1650s, they had been expelled from all the old Portuguese possessions except for the fort of Elmina, on the Gold Coast, where they would remain until the nineteenth century (Alencastro 2000: 188–246; Emmer 1991). The traditional view that the Dutch were mainly responsible for transferring sugar-producing technologies, know-how, slaves, tools, and capital for the development of sugar production in the British Antilles may have been exaggerated, but it does hold true for the French case, as Wim Klooster has recently shown (Menard 2006; Klooster 2016).

The emergence of Barbados and other sugar-producing islands in the Caribbean was not merely the product of a geographical transition, but part of a deeper structural reconfiguration. Despite the arguments that tend to emphasize the continuities between Mediterranean and Brazilian slavery, the dramatic growth in slave productivity in Barbados in the late seventeenth century does seem to indicate some important structural transformations. Key to this change was the incorporation of the growth of sugarcane into integrated large estates and the use of gang labour, which was probably first introduced by the British in their Caribbean colonies in the seventeenth century (but first theorized by Jean Baptiste Labat in the early eighteenth century) (Eltis 2000: 221).[5] Figures such as the lavradores disappeared from the British and French Caribbean. In a recent article, Ralph Austen nicely summarizes the significance of these changes. After emphasizing that the British and French colonies in the Caribbean incorporated the Brazilian three-roller mill into an integrated plantation using gang labour, he concludes that 'the entire plantation system represents a series of early modern "agricultural

[5] On Labat, see Marquese (2004: 70–5).

revolutions," whose major innovations occurred somewhat prior to the changes in eighteenth-century British agriculture with which it is often invidiously compared' (Austen 2017: 169).

A number of other broad changes accompanied this growth in productivity, especially the fall in shipping costs and the emergence of new consumption patterns in Europe. The consumption of products such as slave-produced sugar and tobacco, whose prices decreased as productivity in the Americas increased (along with other factors such as a larger offer and more intense competition), stimulated what Jan de Vries has called an 'industrious revolution'. Families in northwest Europe and the northern United States started to work for longer periods of time in order to have access to those goods (de Vries 2008).[6] Leaving aside the role of this transformation for European industrialization (and de Vries makes a good case for it), these developments clearly point to the articulation through the world economy of wage and slave labour, with both becoming more intense on the opposite sides of the Atlantic. Much of the debate on the contribution of slavery to European development has concentrated on economic issues: profits, new markets for industrial goods, and the expansion of ancillary industries such as shipbuilding. However, there is a sociocultural dimension in the history of this industrious revolution that must be more fully acknowledged. The connections between superfluous consumption and labour (including its coercive forms) have been a central part of the capitalist world system until today. From this perspective, the counterfactual questions on whether individuals could live without sugar or other tropical goods seem less important.

During the eighteenth century, the plantation complex of the northwestern European Atlantic system reached its peak. Jamaica and Saint Domingue produced an unprecedented volume of tropical goods for a rising number of European consumers. Together the British and French Caribbean colonies received 2,808,000 enslaved Africans between 1701 and 1800, or half the total number of captives taken to the Americas during that century. A much smaller number

---

[6] The balance between desires and necessities that accounts for this transformation, however, still needs to be more carefully discussed in the historiography.

of slaves, less than 300,000, were sold in the North American mainland, where tobacco, indigo, and rice plantations had also expanded on the basis of slave labour. These slaves were mostly supplied by British merchants, who became the main Atlantic slave traders over the course of the eighteenth century. This traffic had important global dimensions, as recent works on India and the history of cotton have emphasized. A large percentage of the goods traded for slaves in Africa came from Asia, especially Indian cotton textiles (Beckert 2014; Parthasarathi 2011; Riello 2013).

This recent research offers the opportunity to reassess the importance of the Iberian Atlantic system to the global history of the long eighteenth century. After all, the main commodity that gave Europeans access to Asian goods continued to be precious metals. New World silver was one of the main reasons why the British, the Dutch, and the French competed so avidly for the Spanish asiento. It was also the main motor behind the emergence of a vast contraband slave trade to the Spanish colonies. As Greg O'Malley has shown, a number of conflicts emerged in Jamaica between planters, who wanted slaves to work in their plantations, and slave traders, who frequently tried to sell their captives in Spanish America, where they could have easier access to silver in exchange for their human cargoes (Borucki, Eltis, and Wheat 2015; O'Malley 2014).

Less attention has been given to the place of the Portuguese empire in the global history of capitalism, an absence that is reinforced by the excessive focus of Portuguese and Brazilian historians on imperial and colonial developments. Almost two-million enslaved Africans were carried to Brazil during the eighteenth century, the largest single colony to receive slaves in the Americas during that period. The key factor here was gold. During the first half of the eighteenth century, an unprecedented volume of gold entered the world economy. Its main source was Minas Gerais, a region in Southeast Brazil. As in New Granada, the labour force was composed mainly of enslaved Africans and their descendants. Moreover, the rise of gold mining set in motion a series of ancillary sectors, as had been the case with the earlier developments of silver mining in neighbouring Spanish America (Boxer 1962).

Northwestern European powers tried to access the riches of the Brazilian golden era, but the contraband slave trade was not an option. The Portuguese had been some of the greatest slave smugglers themselves (Canabrava 1984; Prado 2015). Thus, most of the access to Brazilian gold by other powers seems to have taken place outside Brazil. In Lisbon, European merchants had access to gold in exchange for manufactures, a trade that was formally illegal but largely tolerated by the Portuguese Crown. Portuguese trade deficit with Britain reached £25,000,000, most of which was paid with gold (Ebert 2011: 116). A second important and much less studied location for contraband gold outside Brazil was Africa. The greatest London slave trader of the first half of the eighteenth century, as well as member of Parliament and director of the Bank of England in the 1720s, Humphry Morice frequently instructed his captains to purchase slaves as they arrived on the Windward Coast. But instead of sending them to the other side of the Atlantic, in most letters, Morice insisted that the captain should sell all the captives on the Gold Coast to the Portuguese in exchange for gold (Marques 2017). Similar strategies were pursued by the Royal African Company and other merchants. It seems likely that much of the gold taken to Africa went to the Dutch, who continued to control the Elmina castle (Acioli and Menz 2008; Ferreira 2014: 96).

There are no estimates of the global routes of Brazilian gold comparable to those for Spanish-American silver, but much of it probably went to India, which, unlike China, had a great demand for the yellow metal (Parthasarathi 2011: 46–9). A larger part of this gold, however, certainly went to Europe, where it played a fundamental role in eighteenth-century developments. At least one-third of the Brazilian gold output may have gone to Britain (Marshall 1998: 22). The construction of the British fiscal-military state depended on the creation of a series of financial innovations such as bills of exchange, company bonds (of companies such as the aforementioned Royal African Company), and government securities. The financing of war expenditures came mostly from the selling of government bonds, most of which were purchased by the Dutch. Thus, the symbiosis of Dutch and British capital played a key role in the financing of British war victories in most of the eighteenth century, a situation that changed only after the British conquest of Bengal provided the resources that allowed for the indigenization of the national debt. A full account of the construction of the system of public credit in

Northwest Europe should include its connections to international trade, plantation slavery, and the slave trade, as Joseph Inikori has done, along with the various labour systems that produced silver and gold in Potosí, the Gold Coast, and Minas Gerais, among other minor producers. It was this ensemble of relations that allowed the series of financial transformations that would ultimately pave the way for the British systemic cycle of accumulation (Cain and Hopkins 1993: 95; Inikori 2002; Wallerstein 2011: 108–12, 276–89).

The British Systemic Cycle of Accumulation and the Second Slavery

In the British systemic cycle of accumulation, the role of Asia in global dynamics was radically transformed. The expansion of British hegemony in the aftermath of the Napoleonic wars, with London as the financial hub of the world and its push towards freer trade, depended on the enormous amount of resources that were siphoned off from the Indian subcontinent by the empire. Asia, in the words of Findlay and O'Rourke (2009: 406), 'played a crucial role in the international trading system, in that the United Kingdom's unilateral commitment to free trade, which underpinned the system as a whole, would have been difficult to sustain had it not been able to offset its growing deficits vis-à-vis the other industrial economies by means of its surpluses with the East'. On the Western hemisphere, the inclusion of the new independent nations of Latin America expanded the interstate system, a process punctuated by the establishment of bilateral commercial agreements with Britain. These diplomatic negotiations also included treaties for the abolition of slave trade, which had become part of British imperial policy since the end of the Napoleonic Wars. Britain itself had formally abolished the traffic in 1807. Thus, the world of free trade and free labour envisioned by liberal political economists was becoming entrenched in imperial politics. The policies inspired by this ideology in turn depended on British formal imperialism in Asia.[7]

---

[7] If the *Cambridge History of Capitalism* has little to say about slavery, it has even less on abolition. For a recent attempt at a more global history of abolition, see Parron (2018).

The liberal creed was warmly embraced by slaveholders in Brazil, Cuba, and the United States, who quickly adapted to the new world that was being created. By 1850, Western Cuba, Southeast Brazil, and the US South had, respectively, become the main world producers of sugar, coffee, and cotton. British demand for primary products had been on the rise since the late eighteenth century, as industrialization and consumption intensified along with demographic growth. In the context of this rising British demand, the Haitian Revolution significantly enlarged the opportunities for sugar, coffee, and cotton producers in the Atlantic world. The British Caribbean could have occupied the space left by the end of Saint Domingue, but the abolition of the slave trade in 1807 and slavery in the 1830s made such a possibility more difficult (in addition to the fact that production in the British Caribbean could be reaching its ecological limits) (Tomich 2003: 56–71).

Another important consequence of the Haitian Revolution was that it shattered Napoleon's plans for a renewed French Atlantic empire, leading to the sale of Louisiana to the United States in 1803, a process that had the active participation of European banking firms such as Baring and Hope (and was paid with silver coming directly from Mexico) (Marichal 2007: 171–6). The acquisition of Louisiana in turn led to the expansion of cotton cultivation in the United States, with an extremely dynamic influx of people and capital transforming the southwestern territories in the following decades. In 1810, the United States was responsible for 16.3 per cent of the total volume of raw cotton produced in the world. Four decades later, this participation rose to 67 per cent. By the late 1850s, more than two-thirds of all the raw cotton that entered Britain came from the United States. At the same time, coffee and sugar in Brazil and Cuba also went through dramatic expansions into formerly peripheral areas, with the incorporation of new technologies, new forms of labour organization, and increasing specialization. Unlike the United States, however, the main destination of Cuban and Brazilian sugar and coffee was not Britain, but the United States itself. As the United States developed its national identity in opposition to the old tea-drinking British, coffee became the country's drink of choice. With it came sugar (Marquese 2015b). 'Challenged by both increasing slave resistance and abolitionist politics', Daniel

Rood (2017: 3) argues, 'Cuban sugar planters, US cotton planters, and Brazilian coffee planters were not merely filling a hole in Atlantic markets left by British and French West Indian elites. With the help of plantation experts immersed in the Industrial Revolution, they actively reinvented slavery in response to a different moment in the history of world capitalism.'

Unlike previous restructurings of Atlantic slavery, the expansion of slave frontiers in Cuba, Brazil, and the US took place within the context of growing anti-slavery forces in the North Atlantic. In the case of the United States, the country passed anti-slave trade legislation between 1808 and 1820 that effectively dismantled the US branch of the business (Marques 2016). The slave trade in the US, however, did not disappear; it was domesticated. Between 1820 and 1860, approximately 875,000 slaves from old slave states such as Virginia and Maryland were carried and sold in the new slave frontiers of the Southwest, in what Ira Berlin (2003) has called a 'Second Middle Passage'. It is this domestic slave trade that is at the centre of a great number of studies of the so-called new history of capitalism. The transformation of the slave south and the construction of a vast machinery for the selling of human beings were in turn directly connected to the great financial centres of the world. 'Enslavers in the lower South were increasingly reliant on foreign capital to finance the expanding U.S. cotton economy', as Calvin Schermerhorn (2015: 22) argues. 'Consequently, some of the money that reached New York or Baltimore in the form of bills of exchange from London or Liverpool financiers became dollars invested in cotton production in Mississippi or Alabama, a portion of which ended up in the pockets of Rives, the Masons, and their colleagues', all of them great slave traders of the antebellum period.

The new history of capitalism has generated a vast debate that is beyond the limits of the present essay. One point worth mentioning, however, is that most of these works (as well as their critics) are excessively US-centred, remaining within the boundaries of a deeply entrenched methodological nationalism. The main global references in most of these works are to British finance or to the failed expansionist plans of southern slaveholders who were eager to create a broader slaveholding empire in the Caribbean. Slavery in other parts of the Americas appears in formal comparisons, but the dynamics of US history are determined almost exclusively by events taking place within national (or Anglo-American) borders. Such a problem is exacerbated by grandiose claims on the centrality of US slavery to the development of the West. While slave-produced cotton was indeed a fundamental aspect of the Industrial Revolution, the development of historical capitalism depended on an ensemble of labour relations of global scope. Not only has the significance of these different production sites shifted as the system evolved over time, but they also mutually conditioned each other in this process.[8]

Unlike the United States, Brazil and Cuba continued to rely on the supply of slaves from the outside. In the context of international pressure against the transatlantic slave trade, the business went through significant changes. Financial innovations and an expanding set of manufactured commodities for exchanges in Africa were incorporated. 'A major source of financing in the nineteenth-century slave trade', David Eltis (1987: 155) argues, 'was credit advanced by the merchants (mainly British) who provided the slave dealers with their trade goods'. At the same time, slave-trading strategies increasingly involved US resources. The use of US-built ships, the US flag, and eventually US ports became central because the country was one of the few to persistently refuse the passing of any kind of treaty with Britain that included the mutual right of search between their navies and the creation of mixed commission courts. A number of slave traders explored citizenship issues—and crews became even more internationalized during this period—in order to escape authorities in different parts of the Atlantic. They also explored the growing legitimate commerce with Africa as a cover to their illegal activities. By the last decades of the traffic, a growing number of British steamships entered the traffic. In sum, the illegal slave trade became entrenched in the main institutions and technologies of a reconfigured nineteenth-century capitalism under British hegemony (Marques 2016).

With new technologies and forms of labour exploitation, favourable environmental conditions, and a continuous supply of enslaved labourers, second slavery planters managed to successfully compete

---

[8] Two recent excellent accounts of US history that escape the limits of methodological nationalism are Rugemer (2009) and Rood (2017).

in the more or less self-regulating world market of the nineteenth century. Brazilian coffee planters, for example, had to compete not only with slave producers in Cuba and Jamaica, but also with enterprises (that used alternative forms of labour) in Haiti and Dutch Java. Cuban sugar competed not only with plantations in the United States, Brazil, India, East Africa, and the Pacific Islands, but also with the expanding beet-sugar production in Europe. US cotton also faced competition from Brazilian, British Caribbean, Egyptian, and a few other producers, with the British putting into practice a number of experiments to improve cotton production in India, including the creation of experimental farms run by US-born planters (Beckert 2014: Chapter 5; Bosma and Curry-Machado 2012; Marquese 2015a; Tomich 2003: 80–6).

In all these cases, Brazil, Cuba, and the United States managed to surpass their competitors. Competition was nonetheless intense, especially between the three slave societies themselves. This competition imposed a true limit to any possible formal pro-slavery articulation between the three powers, an incapacity that can be interpreted as another evidence of the dynamics of second slavery *in* capitalism. Some of the greatest critics of US participation in the illegal slave trade were southern slaveholders, who feared that the continuance of the contraband slave trade to Cuba and Brazil could leave the United States behind in the competition for world markets. During the US Civil War, Brazilian cotton producers furnished raw cotton to the northern United States, ultimately contributing to the Union victory. The great irony was that the destruction of US slavery by the war threw a shadow over the institution across the rest of the Americas, stimulating the processes that would ultimately lead to abolition in Brazil and Cuba (Marquese, Parron, and Berbel 2016).

***

Arrangements with various degrees of dependence and coercion in the Atlantic (which included wage workers in northern European fields and Spanish-American mines, enslaved Africans in Caribbean, Brazilian, and North American plantations, as well as in the gold mines of Brazil and New Granada, and a wide range of other labourers in export-related sectors) were all part of a wide web of relations of production, exchange, and consumption that also connected labourers in Africa and Asia. Wage labour on both sides of the Atlantic were part of an ensemble of relations that included a number of other labour forms, among which was New World slavery.

It is this wide set of relations that disappear from view in approaches that tend to conflate their units of observation (which can be a county, a country, or a continent) with their units of analysis (which should be the system as a whole). *The Cambridge History of Capitalism* contains a number of invaluable contributions on the history of economic growth in various parts of the world that can certainly be further explored in the scholarship but those parts are completely isolated from each other. This approach inevitably leads to the near absence of debates on the place of slavery in capitalism as a historical world system. Whenever the theme appears, it is from an institutionalist perspective that tends to abstract one of its aspects (for example, relations of production) as the defining feature of the system. In most cases, the conclusion is that slavery is not capitalist. Instead of discussing whether a region is capitalist or not, a more interesting approach is to look at the capitalist system as a whole. But, for this, approaches marked by an enduring methodological nationalism will not do.

A more rigorous and systemic conceptualization of capitalism can allow us to explore the role of New World slavery *in* capitalism, looking at the broader relations that formed and were formed through it. In this way, we can move beyond the kind of counterfactual questions that have marked so much of the debate on the relationship between capitalism and slavery. The main problem in the approaches that animate a large part of this historiography is that they are usually based on ahistorical concepts of both capitalism and slavery. Not only did slavery change over time, but the system of which it was part—the capitalist world system—did as well. A more fruitful approach therefore should track the totality of labour relations that formed the capitalist world economy, and how this whole and its parts dynamically changed over time.

Bibliography

Acioli, Gustavo and Maximiliano M. Menz. 2008. 'Resgate e mercadorias: uma análise comparada do tráfico luso-brasileiro de escravos em Angola e na Costa da Mina (século XVIII).' *Afro-Ásia* 37: 43–73.

Alencastro, Luiz Felipe de. 2000. *O Trato Dos Viventes: Formação Do Brasil No AtlâNtico Sul, Séculos XVI e XVII*. São Paulo: Companhia das Letras.

Arrighi, Giovanni. 1994. *The Long Twentieth Century: Money, Power, and the Origins of Our Times*. London; New York: Verso.

Atack, Jeremy. 2014. 'America: Capitalism's Promised Land.' In *The Cambridge History of Capitalism*, edited by Jeffrey G. Williamson and Larry Neal. Cambridge; New York: Cambridge University Press.

Austen, Ralph A. 2017. 'Monsters of Protocolonial Economic Enterprise: East India Companies and Slave Plantations.' *Critical Historical Studies* 4(2): 139–77.

Austin, Gareth. 2014. 'Capitalism and the Colonies.' In *The Cambridge History of Capitalism: Volume 2, The Spread of Capitalism: From 1848 to the Present*, edited by Jeffrey G. Williamson and Larry Neal. Cambridge; New York: Cambridge University Press.

Bakewell, P.J. 1984. 'Mining in Colonial Spanish America.' In *The Cambridge History of Latin America*, edited by Leslie Bethell. Cambridge; New York: Cambridge University Press.

Beckert, Sven. 2014. *Empire of Cotton: A Global History*. New York: Knopf.

Berlin, Ira. 2003. *Generations of Captivity: A History of African-American Slaves*. Cambridge, MA: Belknap Press of Harvard University Press.

Blackburn, Robin. 1997. *The Making of New World Slavery: From the Baroque to the Modern, 1482–1800*. London: Verso.

Borucki, Alex, David Eltis, and David Wheat. 2015. 'Atlantic History and the Slave Trade to Spanish America.' *The American Historical Review* 120(2): 433–61.

Bosma, Ulbe and Jonathan Curry-Machado. 2012. 'Two Islands, One Commodity: Cuba, Java, and the Global Sugar Trade (1790–1930).' *New West Indian Guide/Nieuwe West-Indische Gids* 86(3–4): 237–62.

Bowser, Frederick P. 1974. *The African Slave in Colonial Peru, 1524–1650*. Stanford, CA: Stanford University Press.

Boxer, C.R. 1962. *The Golden Age of Brazil, 1695–1750: Growing Pains of a Colonial Society*. Berkeley: University of California Press.

Cain, P.J. and A.G. Hopkins. 1993. *British Imperialism: Innovation and Expansion, 1688–1914*. London; New York: Longman.

Canabrava, Alice Piffer. 1984. *O comércio português no Rio da Prata (1580–1640)*. Belo Horizonte; São Paulo: Itatiaia; EdUSP.

Castro, Antonio Barros de. 1980. 'Brasil, 1610: mudanças técnicas e conflitos sociais.' *Pesquisa e Planejamento Econômico* 10(3): 679–712.

Clegg, John J. 2015. 'Capitalism and Slavery.' *Critical Historical Studies* 2(2): 281–304.

Ebert, Christopher. 2011. 'From Gold to Manioc: Contraband Trade in Brazil during the Golden Age, 1700–1750.' *Colonial Latin American Review* 20(1): 109–30.

Eltis, David. 1987. *Economic Growth and the Ending of the Transatlantic Slave Trade*. New York: Oxford University Press.

———. 2000. *The Rise of African Slavery in the Americas*. Cambridge: Cambridge University Press.

Emmer, P.C. 1991. 'The Dutch and the Making of the Second Atlantic System.' In *Slavery and the Rise of the Atlantic System*, edited by Barbara L. Solow. Cambridge; New York: Cambridge University Press.

Ferreira, Roquinaldo. 2014. 'From Brazil to West Africa: Dutch–Portuguese Rivalry, Gold-Smuggling, and African Politics in the Bight of Benin.' In *The Legacy of Dutch Brazil*, edited by Michiel van Groesen. New York, NY: Cambridge University Press.

Findlay, Ronald, and Kevin H. O'Rourke. 2009. *Power and Plenty: Trade, War, and the World Economy in the Second Millennium*. Princeton: Princeton University Press.

Fraginals, Manuel Moreno. 2005. *Cuba/Espanha, Espanha/Cuba: uma história comum*. História. Bauru: EDUSC.

Fuente, Alejandro de la. 2008. *Havana and the Atlantic in the Sixteenth Century*. Chapel Hill: University of North Carolina Press.

Harley, C. Knick. 2014. 'British and European Industrialization.' In *The Cambridge History of Capitalism*, edited by Jeffrey G. Williamson and Larry Neal. Cambridge; New York: Cambridge University Press.

Klooster, William. 2016. *The Dutch Moment: War, Trade, and Settlement in the Seventeenth-Century Atlantic World*. Ithaca: Cornell University Press.

Inikori, J.E. 2002. *Africans and the Industrial Revolution in England: A Study in International Trade and Economic Development*. Cambridge; New York: Cambridge University Press.

Marichal, Carlos. 2007. *Bankruptcy of Empire: Mexican Silver and the Wars between Spain, Britain, and France, 1760–1810*. New York: Cambridge University Press.

Marques, Leonardo. 2016. *The United States and the Transatlantic Slave Trade to the Americas, 1776–1867*. New Haven; London: Yale University Press.

———. 2017. 'Um Banqueiro-Traficante Inglês e a História Global Do Tráfico de Escravos Para as Américas Ibéricas (1688-1732).' In *Ramificações Ultramarinas: Sociedades Comerciais No âMbito Do AtlâNtico Luso - Século XVIII.*, edited by C.L. Kelmer Mathias, A.V. Ribeiro, A.C.J. Sampaio, and C.G. Guimarães. Rio de Janeiro: Mauad.

Marquese, Rafael de Bivar. 2004. *Feitores do corpo, missionários da mente: senhores, letrados e o controle dos escravos nas Américas, 1660–1860*. São Paulo: Companhia das Letras.

———. 2013. 'As Desventuras de Um Conceito: Capitalismo Histórico e Historiografia Sobre a Escravidão Brasileira.' *Revista de História* 169: 223–53.

———. 2015a. 'As Origens de Brasil e Java: Trabalho Compulsório e a Reconfiguração Da Economia Mundial Do Café Na Era Das Revoluções, c.1760-1840.' *História (São Paulo)* 34(2): 108–27.

———. 2015b. 'Capitalism, Slavery and the Brazilian Coffee Economy.' In *The Legacy of Eric Williams: Caribbean Scholar and Statesman*, edited by Colin A. Palmer. Kingston, Jamaica: University of the West Indies Press.

Marquese, Rafael B. and Tâmis P. Parron. 2016. 'International Proslavery: The Politics of the Second Slavery.' In *The Politics of the Second Slavery*, edited by Dale W. Tomich. Albany: State University of New York Press.

Marquese, Rafael, Tâmis Parron, and Márcia Berbel. 2016. *Slavery and Politics: Brazil and Cuba, 1790–1850*. Albuquerque: University of New Mexico Press.

Marshall, Peter James. 1998. 'Introduction.' In *The Oxford History of the British Empire: The Eighteenth Century*. Oxford: Oxford University Press.

McMichael, Philip. 1991. 'Slavery in Capitalism: The Rise and Demise of the U.S. Ante-Bellum Cotton Culture.' *Theory and Society* 20(3): 321–49.

Menard, Russell R. 2006. *Sweet Negotiations: Sugar, Slavery, and Plantation Agriculture in Early Barbados*. Charlottesville: University of Virginia Press.

Mielants, Eric. 2017. 'Early Modern Antwerp: The First "World City"?' *Journal of Historical Sociology* 30(2): 262–83.

Moore, Jason W. 2010. '"Amsterdam Is Standing on Norway" Part I: The Alchemy of Capital, Empire and Nature in the Diaspora of Silver, 1545–1648.' *Journal of Agrarian Change* 10(1): 33–68.

Neal, Larry. 2014. 'Introduction.' In *The Cambridge History of Capitalism*, edited by Jeffrey G. Williamson and Larry Neal. Cambridge; New York: Cambridge University Press.

O'Malley, Gregory E. 2014. *Final Passages: The Intercolonial Slave Trade of British America, 1619–1807*. Chapel Hill: University of North Carolina Press.

Parron, Tâmis P. 2018. 'The British Empire and the Suppression of the Slave Trade to Brazil: A Global History Analysis.' *Journal of World History* 29(1): 1–36.

Parthasarathi, Prasannan. 2011. *Why Europe Grew Rich and Asia Did Not: Global Economic Divergence, 1600–1850*. Cambridge; New York: Cambridge University Press.

Prado, Fabrício Pereira. 2015. *Edge of Empire: Atlantic Networks and Revolution in Bourbon Rio de La Plata*. Oakland, CA: University of California Press.

Riello, Giorgio. 2013. *Cotton: The Fabric That Made the Modern World.* Cambridge: Cambridge University Press.

Rood, Daniel. 2017. *The Reinvention of Atlantic Slavery: Technology, Labor, Race, and Capitalism in the Greater Caribbean.* New York, NY: Oxford University Press.

Rugemer, Edward Bartlett. 2009. *The Problem of Emancipation: The Caribbean Roots of the American Civil War.* Louisiana State University Press.

Salvucci, Richard J. 1987. *Textiles and Capitalism in Mexico: An Economic History of the Obrajes, 1539–1840.* Princeton, NJ: Princeton University Press.

———. 2010. 'Some Thoughts on the Economic History of Early Colonial Mexico.' *History Compass* 8/7: 626–35.

———. 2014. 'Capitalism and Dependency in Latin America.' In *The Cambridge History of Capitalism*, edited by Jeffrey G. Williamson and Larry Neal. Cambridge; New York: Cambridge University Press.

Schermerhorn, Calvin. 2015. *The Business of Slavery and the Rise of American Capitalism, 1815–1860.* New Haven Connecticut: Yale University Press.

Schwartz, Stuart B., ed. 2004. 'A Commonwealth within Itself: The Early Brazilian Sugar Industry, 1550–1670.' In *Tropical Babylons: Sugar and the Making of the Atlantic World, 1450–1680.* Chapel Hill: University of North Carolina Press.

Stein, Stanley J. and Barbara H. Stein. 2000. *Silver, Trade, and War: Spain and America in the Making of Early Modern Europe.* Baltimore, MD: The Johns Hopkins University Press.

Tomich, Dale W. 2003. *Through the Prism of Slavery: Labor, Capital, and World Economy.* Lanham, MD: Rowman & Littlefield Publishers, Inc.

Tutino, John. 2011. *Making a New World: Founding Capitalism in the Bajío and Spanish North America.* Durham, NC: Duke University Press.

Vries, Jan de. 2008. *The Industrious Revolution: Consumer Behavior and the Household Economy, 1650 to the Present.* Cambridge: Cambridge University Press.

Wallerstein, Immanuel M. 1983. *Historical Capitalism; with Capitalist Civilization.* New. London; New York: Verso, 13–14.

———. 1995. *Historical Capitalism: With Capitalist Civilization.* London; New York: Verso.

———. 2011. *The Modern World-System II: Mercantilism and the Consolidation of the European World-Economy, 1600–1750.* Berkeley: University of California Press.

Wilder, Gary. 2012. 'From Optic to Topic: The Foreclosure Effect of Historiographic Turns.' *The American Historical Review* 117(3): 723–45.

Wing, John T. 2015. *Roots of Empire: Forests and State Power in Early Modern Spain, c. 1500–1750.* Leiden, the Netherlands; Boston: Brill.

3

Russian Capitalism

Exceptionalism versus Global Labour-Intensive Path, 1700–1914

Alessandro Stanziani

Authors as different as Immanuel Wallerstein and Douglass North agree that in early modern times, Russia and Eastern Europe responded to the commercial, agrarian, and then industrial expansion of the West by binding the peasantries to the land and its lords (Kula 1976; North 1981; Wallerstein 1974, 1976). More surprisingly, new approaches to world history such as Kenneth Pomeranz's 'Great Divergence', while contesting Chinese backwardness and European eurocentrism, still consider Russia the paradigm of unfree labour and lack of markets and, as such, opposed to both the Lower Yangtze and Britain (Pomeranz 2000). Jürgen Osterhammel as well, in his magisterial book, qualified Russia as an 'exception' in Europe in terms of its inability to end famines, introduce private property and democratic rules (Osterhammel 2014). In all these approaches, the 'Russian case' systematically expresses either the boundary or the negation of Western economic growth and capitalism. Where Russia is concerned, decentralizing perspectives fall apart. Why is that? Why is it so difficult to include Russia in a critical (and not normative and teleological) global perspective similar to those advanced for China, India, Africa, or Latin America during recent years?

This chapter seeks to answer these questions. After reviewing the historiography of the Russian economic path, I will discuss the period running from the early eighteenth century to the abolition of serfdom (1861) and World War I (WWI), in order to argue that Russian economic dynamics were more important than usually held in terms of rate of growth, that they were labour-intensive and mostly based on modernizing peasants and landlords. The problem was that these solutions were eventually compatible with the first industrial revolution but not the second.

The Historiography of the Russian Economy: A Festival of *lieux communs*?

From the eighteenth century to the present, comparisons between Russia and the major European countries have formed part of a wider debate about 'backwardness'. The invention of backwardness in Western economic and philosophical thought owes a great deal to the attention given to Russia and Poland after the start of the eighteenth century (Diderot 1963: 365). French philosophers and economists (physiocrats) strongly contributed to this view (Stanziani 2008b). These approaches had an important impact on Russia itself where Catherine II encouraged her collaborators and young economists to familiarize themselves with and disseminate the ideas of the physiocrats (Moriakov 1981), together with those of the German cameralists (Raeff 1983). Those were well known in Russia thanks to the activities of a few German economists recruited at the Academy of Sciences and at Moscow University (Hasek 1925; Small 1909; Tribe 1988).

During much of the nineteenth century, and particularly after the 1850s, the question arose in the main countries of Europe as to whether or not the 'historical laws of development' were the same everywhere. Like Russia's political and intellectual elites, its nobility was ultimately less afraid of the peasants' emancipation than of their proletarianization. The idea that wage labour was the worst form of slavery was accepted by much of the Russian elite. That is why, in the 20 years preceding the emancipation, the debate on serfdom intersected with that about the commune and then about Russia's 'uniqueness' vis-à-vis the West (Kingston-Mann 1999; Stanziani 1998; Walicki 1975). In Russia, this comparison between the West and the East and their economies became the keystone in the tensions between Slavophiles and Westernizers and later between populists and Marxists (Chicherin [1882–3] 2005; Emmons 1968). The issue was precisely whether there was a global tendency at work in economies and societies or whether historical singularities could shape its direction (Belinskii 1953–5: Vol. 12, 444–68). This debate was at once ideological (the role of the peasantry under capitalism), empirical (how to prove the arguments used), and methodological (how to make comparisons).

As it is well known, Marx admitted that Russia could take a different route from the one in the West. In a letter to Vera Zasulich, he wrote that the peasant commune could become the basis for the social regeneration of Russia (Shanin 1983). At the turn of the century, Lenin still sought to preserve Marxist orthodoxy against so-called revisionists who instead referred to the late Marx. He claimed the universality of Marx's scheme: there was no place for the Asian mode of production and still less for a direct passage from the commune to socialism (Lenin 1899). Instead, he defended the insertion of Russia into the universal transition to capitalism and sought to prove this statement with figures and empirical analysis. A huge debate followed, several authors confirming and others denying Lenin's argument (Stanziani 1998).

After 1917, the problem changed to how to reconcile the October Revolution with this scheme. Until the mid-1920s, the debate was relatively open. The identification of capitalism in tsarist Russia was the crucial point in this debate: Trotsky as well as Menshevik authors considered the revolution as a deviation from the 'normal' historical path insofar as capitalism had not really developed in tsarist Russia (Barber 1981; Baron and Heer 1977). Instead, despite his argument at the turn of the century more or less in line with this reasoning, Lenin advanced—at the eve of WWI and mostly after 1917—an alternative approach, according to which the limitations of capitalism in tsarist Russia actually exemplified a 'different path' compared to the West, where the transformation of the peasant economy contributed to the process of industrialization.[1] During the years following Lenin's death, the debates continued until when, at the end of the 1920s and the 1930s, a new turn took place (Yilmaz 2015): the so-called 'contradictions' of the tsarist economy were said to have produced the revolution and, then, socialism. Historical necessity, the role of the leader, and the Soviet path were bound together in the Stalinist interpretation of history.

Debates on tsarist Russian economic history and capitalism officially reopened in the late 1950s. Some Soviet authors returned to Marx and his idea of the Asiatic mode of production, while some others insisted on the historical possibility of alternative forms of socialism. Comparative history and economic history went far beyond the basic vulgate of Marxism (Markwick 2001). There was a huge increase of studies on the Russian economy during the late tsarist period and eventually during the New Economic Policy (Anfimov 1962; Dubrovskii 1963; Koval'chenko 1967; Koval'chenko and Milov 1974). This is where the dialogue with Western economists and historians worked the best. Alexander Gerschenkron is justly famous for his work *Economic Backwardness in Historical Perspective*. This was a very clever solution to the problem raised by the need to reconcile particular features, historical specificities, and general dynamics (Gerschenkron 1962). He did not seek to impose one single economic path on all historical experiences, but he advanced different solutions according, on the one hand, to the state of the country at the beginning of the 'modernization' process, and on the other hand, to its gap with the most advanced countries.

This work was part of a broad debate in the 1950s and 1960s; with decolonization, economists raised the problem of (under)development and what should be done to remedy it. In the context of the Cold War, this issue was inseparable from the question regarding which economic and political form the new states would take: capitalism or socialism. Several economists emphasized the need to put

[1] RGASPI (Russian State Archive of Socio-political History) fond 5 (Lenin), Opis' 1.

these debates in 'historical perspective'. The debate over modernization, in fact the very use of this concept, implied a strongly deter-
minist philosophy of history, Eurocentric categories and postulates
and, ultimately, circular explanatory arguments (Cooper et al. 1993;
Tipps 1973).

Since the 1990s, the 'transition' to capitalism in the former
Soviet-bloc countries was seen as the inevitable outcome of an economic model considered to be valid everywhere. Neo-institutional
economics, developed in the 1970s by Douglass North among
others, became the dominant paradigm in comparative economic
history when discussing contemporary and earlier Russian capitalism (Dennison 2011; Nafziger 2010; North and Thomas 1973).
A new economic and demographic history stressed the economic
development of late tsarist Russia, between 1861 (abolition of serfdom) and WWI (Gatrell 2005; Hoch 1994, 1998; Kingston-Mann
1981, 1999; Kotsonis 2014; Pallot 1999; Wilbur 1983). Debates
focused either on the eventual 'contradiction' of this development,
in terms of inter-sectoral equilibrium, or on the gap between market development and political constraints (Simms 1977, 1982;
Wheatcroft 1991). More recently, discussions have moved to the
so-called economic attitudes of the peasantry: were they capitalist
or cooperative oriented? Depending on the answer given, authors
put the finger either on the institutional constraints on optimiz-
ing peasants or on the alternative they provided to capitalist values
(Markevich and Zhuravskaya 2015). These debates found only a
partial echo in Russia, where the end of socialism brought a general lack of interest in economic and social history (considered as a
Marxist-oriented domain), except a few studies adopting neo-institutionalist approaches (Anan'ich 2001; Andriushin 1998; Baranov
and Dmitriev 2000; Khristoforov 2011).

In the following pages, I will try to reverse this approach: instead
of looking for the 'missing factors' in Russia—compared to an ideal
Western capitalism—I will first detail the economic dynamics in
tsarist Russia and their strength and weakness. Following on from
this, I will examine the main features of Russian historical economics to question the current Eurocentric notions of capitalism and
'modernization'.

The Origin of Serfdom: Russia as the Quasi-Periphery of Europe and Asia?

Landlords could ask peasants either for quit-rent[2] or for labour services (corvée). Western, Russian, and Soviet historiography all traditionally argue that quit-rent encourages trade and economic growth, whereas labour services restrict both (Aston and Philpin 1985). Of course, many others maintain that trade and economic growth can also take place under a system of corvée labour or even slavery in the strict sense (Blanchard 1989; Dennison 2011). Any satisfactory answer to this question requires an assessment of labour productivity and the overall efficiency of the demesne; some consider that corvée entails high supervision costs while reducing labour productivity and peasants' interest in increasing both productivity and market production. Some others have objected that labour supervision is not necessarily stricter under corvée than under quit-rent. In particular, Hoch (1984) has shown that serf owners were able to exploit serf labour with minimum supervisory costs by harnessing the patriarchal authority structure of the peasant household.

The question underlying this debate is important: Were historical forms of forced labour compatible with the market, innovation, and capitalism (Stanziani 2008a, 2014b)?

According to the traditional analysis of serfdom, the rapid development of labour service was linked to a drop in commodity sales, causing the estates to fall back on their own resources and exert greater pressure on the peasants. The dynamics of Russian estates at the time does not confirm this argument. Most microeconomic studies focus on large estates (Czap 1982; Dennison 2011); data reveals reasonably good outcomes for the Russian economy as compared to most Western economies (Leonard 2011; Stanziani 2014a), and this despite the well-known tendencies of statistics to underestimate products, yields, and revenues. In eighteenth-century Russia, agricultural prices continued to climb, rising by a factor of two and a half, which no doubt made service labour more profitable than quit-rent (Mironov 1999). At the same time, this solution was possible only

---

[2] Quit-rent is a tax in kind or in money paid to the landlord by the peasant.

if the estates were efficiently supervised, and landowners began to stress the necessity for supervisors. The supervisor was supposed to adopt good working methods, carry out an inventory of goods, land, and harvests, and keep the landowner informed about the running of the estate.

In this context, there is no evidence of an increasing autarchy of the demesne coupled with increasing wheat exports from 'backward' Russia to the benefit of 'advanced' Europe, as Wallerstein and Kula have argued. Exports undoubtedly rose, and Russian markets were integrated more and more into the international and European markets. At the same time, the growth of exports did not take place at the expense of local and national markets. Indeed, by 1760, the demand for grain in the heartland created a rise in grain prices. Russian local markets were therefore increasingly integrated into a national market during the second half of the eighteenth century (Mironov 1981; Mironov and Leonard 1985). The nobility's role in the expansion of rural trade is reflected in the fact that much of the rural expansion took place on the gentry's estates. While, in 1760, nobles' estates were the sites of 413 out of 1,143 rural fairs (36 per cent), in 1800 they had 1,615 out of 3,180 (51 per cent). This data clearly shows that not only landlords but also their peasants firmly entered the rural agrarian markets. Peasants' activity in rural markets surpassed that of merchants and small urban traders (Mironov 1981: 153–4). Therefore, contrary to traditional arguments, trade under estate production increased with barshchina (corvée), which was compatible not only with exportation and long distances, but also with the rise of local and national markets (Koval'chenko 1967). Peasants had been buying important shares of proto-industrial products while benefiting from increasing incomes. For example, the larger accessible labour market of peasants, already familiar with linen weaving, gave Moscow-based and Ivanovo-based firms a greater competitive viability than St. Petersburg (Gestwa 1999; Serbina 1978).[3] To control this market, noble landowners were taking back control of the sale of products from their estates and entering into urban trade circuits with a certain degree of firmness (Izmes'eva 1991). Proto-industry

---

[3] For the Demydov estate in Tula: RGADA, fond 271, delo 1061.

became ruralized (Indova 1975: 248–345; 1964; Strumilin 1966: 330–3).[4] The urban population dropped from 12 per cent to 8 per cent of the total population between 1742 and 1801 (Mironov 1992). Thus, agricultural and industrial rural areas were sometimes differentiated and sometimes overlapped.

Thus, while 5 per cent of all private factories belonged to nobles in the 1720s (the rest being in the hands of merchants, eventually the state), the percentage rose to 20 in 1773. In 1725, 78 per cent of industrial activity was located in cities; that percentage dropped to 60 in 1775–8 and 58 in 1803 and encouraged labour-intensive organizations (Mironov 1992: 465). On the whole, during the second half of the eighteenth century, landlords massively entered the proto-industrial sector; the 'ruralization' of proto-industry was not a symptom of demesne autarchy, but, quite the contrary, testified to the demesne's increasing commercialization. Both peasants and landlords entered the market in cereals as well as going in for proto-industrial activities and trade and transportation activities. Numerous 'serf-entrepreneurs' registered, on behalf of the land-owner or sometimes quite independently, to start businesses or even proto-industrial and industrial activities (Prokov'eva 1981; Tikhonov 1974).[5] Serf-entrepreneurs often employed workers in their proto-industrial activity. They came from the same villages or from neighbouring districts (Serbina 1978: 37). During and after the mid-eighteenth century, peasants bought an important share of proto-industrial products while benefiting from increasing incomes.

All this increased the need for labour and exacerbated competition for goods and proto-industrial and labour markets. Competition rose not only between nobles and merchants, but also among nobles; even more than in the first half of the eighteenth century, landlords

[4] RGADA, fond 199 (G.F. Miller).
[5] On the urban activity of private peasants: RGADA, fond 294, opis' 2 and 3; fond 1287, opis' 3. TsGIAM, opis' 2, dela 31, 40, 82, 124, 146; RGADA, fond 210: razriadnyi prikaz; fond 248, Senat I senatskie uchrezh-deniia; fond 350: revizkie skazki po nizhegorodskoi gubernii, opis' 2, dela 1975 and 2056; fonds 615, krepostnye knigi, dela 526, 528, 529, 4753, 6654; fond 1209 (pomestnyi prikaz), opis' 1, delo 292; fond 1287 (Sheremetev), opis' 5 and 6; RGIA, fond 1088 (Sheremetev, opis' 3, 5, 10).

were in competition with each other to keep the best master peasants who trained other artisans. Many estate owners sought to keep their peasant workers on the estate instead of sending them to town. As in the case of the sale of products, it would be reductive to see the landowners' orientation towards factories merely as a desire for estate autarchy and market closing, and hence as a regression of the Russian economy. In reality, what the landowners wanted was to take over the proto-industrial and manufacturing sector, once dominated by peasants and merchants. This accounts for their request, which Catherine granted, to prohibit any form of serfdom in factories owned by non-nobles (Melton 1987). Estate archives show that landlords had every interest to develop a sort of 'protectionist' politics beneficial to the estate's peasants and craftsmen.[6] Peasant masters also demanded the exclusive right to sell their products in Nizhegorod.[7] Sheremetev's estate-law court regulated conflicts between peasants and merchants, and the decisions were often favourable to the former.[8] In other words, peasants and landlords made arrangements to shape markets and competition rules to their own advantage and to exclude urban merchants and producers.

Labour relations were therefore extremely complex. In Nizhny-Novgorod province (250-miles east of Moscow), on the Demidov estate in particular, there was a mix of both forced and hired labour. The latter was used for processing of products and as supervisory personnel in the mills and brickworks; forced labour was used to mill rye and wheat and for cottage industry, including spinning yarn and making linen cloth (Rudolph 1985). Relations of 'dependence' among peasants, merchants, and manufacturers have to be included in this context. One of the key factors was the control of raw materials. As long as every stage in the production process took place within the peasant household, the producer remained more or less an independent craftsman. The fact that flax cultivation was so widespread in the non-black-soil provinces helped make linen production especially resistant to change. But in sectors like cotton and

[6] RGIA, fond 1088, opis' 10, dela 616 and 618.

[7] RGIA, fond 1088, opis' 10, delo 611.

[8] Sheremetev published *instruktsiia* (estate regulation) in 1802 and 1832. RGIA, fond 1088, opis' 10, delo 607.

silk weaving, where the cottage weavers depended on outside sources for their materials, wage relations grew more rapidly. For the supply of raw materials for metalworking, the development of production in the Ural region modified the networks and the hierarchies. This was true in particular after the 1760s, when the Demidov estate in the Ural region 'exported' 'raw materials for metallurgy to the proto-industrial districts of Tula, Nizhny Novgorod, and Moscow (Gestwa 1999; Serbina 1978: 100–1).

Peasants could buy materials themselves, but sometimes landlords provided raw materials and gave advances to their peasant master (Kashin 1935: Vol. 1, 215, 347–9). In such cases, too, after the end of the eighteenth century, landlords developed a clear strategy to enter and control networks that had been previously dominated by traders and merchants. It is interesting that nobles adopted the same strategies as merchants in order to control the output system (that is, advancing money and/or raw materials).[9] Again, this confirms that legal limitations to mobility alone did not suffice; otherwise estate owners would have not developed this system of advances to keep peasant-workers bound to them.

To sum up, the rebirth of barshchina (corvée) during the second half of the eighteenth century was accompanied neither by increased exploitation of peasants solely with a view to export trade, nor by a crisis in manufacturing business and markets in general, as predicted by Witold Kula's model. The demesne economy and the Russian economy as a whole were more efficient, flexible, and market-oriented than he stated. Agriculture and proto-industrial markets developed intensively, and so did national income and per capita income. Agriculture and proto-industry expanded, and the competition between noble landowners and merchants was institutional before it became economic. The former wanted to enter into trade and industry at the expense of the latter and succeeded, thanks to the support of institutional measures such as the exclusion of 'serfs' from factories managed by merchants. Thus, labour services raised commercial produce, and proto-industrial activity became strongly integrated into the demesne activity.

---

[9] RGIA, fond 1088, opis' 10, delo 524.

The decreasing impact of bad harvests on the standard of living and the increasing integration of the peasantry and the landlords into market networks testify to this increasing coordination among the involved actors. Evidence suggests that the output of both agricultural produce and proto-industrial products increased throughout the eighteenth and nineteenth century; in turn, this sustained the demand for manufactured goods, which was mostly satisfied by local proto-industrial activity that utilized labour-intensive technology (Domar and Machina 1984).

The coexistence of service labour and quit-rent enabled the peasant economy and that of the noble landowners to cope with the fluctuations of the economy by limiting their impact on the level of activity, standard of living, and investments. Even if the collected data are not corrected (some considered the underestimation to be about 20 per cent), the final picture still shows increasing productivity, well-being, and commercialization eighteenth-century onwards. Between 1718 and 1788, Russian aggregate national income increased fivefold, raising per capita income by 85 per cent. After 1788, the annexation of rich southern provinces further intensified this growth.[10]

New Trends during the First Half of the Nineteenth Century

The first half of the nineteenth century has usually been described as the deepening 'crisis of serfdom' in terms of income growth, demographic trends, and social unrest. However, in the last two decades, these views have been seriously challenged, and historians have revised upwards the rate of growth in agriculture and industry as well as overall economic activity (Gregory 1994). Recent analyses had sought to take into account the underestimation of birth rates in eighteenth-century and nineteenth-century censuses as well as the annexation of new territories and the resettlement (legal and illegal) of the peasantry. Once these biases were corrected, the natural rate of population growth proved to be considerable: on peasant estates,

[10] For a full discussion of these materials, see Blanchard (1989: Chapter 5, Appendix 2).

it was about 0.70 per cent between 1678 and 1719, 0.62 per cent between 1719 and 1744, 0.97 between 1744 and 1762, and 0.96 per cent over the next 20 years. It fell to 0.60 between 1782 and 1795 and rose again to 0.86 between 1795 and 1811, but collapsed during the Napoleonic Wars to –0.42 per cent. During the first half of the nineteenth century, the natural rate of growth of Russia's peasant population increased again to 0.94 in 1815–33, 0.59 between 1833 and 1850, and 0.54 per cent between 1850 and 1857 (Moon 1999: 27). In the decades before the abolition of serfdom, the population in some areas increased mainly because the rate of mortality dropped and children's exposure to disease also fell (Hoch 1998). Both reflect increasing well-being and better hygienic practices.

Price fluctuations were more pronounced than during the second half of the eighteenth century and this led again, as during the first half of the previous century, to mixing corvée and quit-rent.[11] At the same time, noble estates were concentrated; the number of small estates declined while large properties became the rule, to such an extent that in 1857 noble estates with less than 21 peasants accounted for barely 3.2 per cent of all estates; those with between 21 and 100 peasants made up 15.9 per cent, and the great majority of estates had between 100 and 500 peasants (37.2 per cent); 500 and 1,000 peasants (14.9 per cent); or even more than 1,000 peasants (28.7 per cent) (Troinitskii 1861: 45). This trend was linked to the increasing indebtedness of the estate owners and the limited capital markets available to them; the growing institutional pressure of a tsarist state favouring peasants' emancipation and merchants' development also contributed to the concentration of estates.

Quit-rent declined on state estates and on some private estates as well while rising in the heartland (although this rise was generally moderate). Regional specialization also increased, with central and other industrial and proto-industrial areas tending to specialize while agricultural areas lost non-agrarian activities. In particular, in steppe and central black earth areas, while factories shut down and

---

[11] RGADA, fond 1252, opis' 1: Abamelek-Lazarevy's estate, province of Tula; fond 1282, Tolstye-Kristi's estate, province of Riazan; fond 1262, opis' 1, Prince Gagarin's estates in Saratov and Tambov provinces; fond 1287, Sheremetev's estate.

proto-industrial activity was reduced (Ledovskaia 1974: 240–5), the surface area of cultivated land expanded in the territory as a whole and inside the main estates. This process corresponded to an increase in agricultural production and, most importantly, a growth in marketed production and market integration. Grain prices in Russia showed a clear tendency towards homogenization and correlation on the national level (Koval'chenko and Milov 1974; Mironov and Leonard 1985).

In the central industrial regions, the main difference from the previous century was that noble landowners no longer restricted peasant movements between city and country. This was for reasons of choice and constraint—in part, more volatile prices led some landlords to diversify their economic strategies; in part, industrial and tsarist elites pushed for increasing liberalization of the labour market. The main issue was the levying of *obrok* (quit-rent) and the movements of peasants in the city and in neighbouring estates had intensified (Gorshkov 2000). During the 1840s, in the northwestern and western agricultural and industrial regions of European Russia, domestic passports granted to peasants affected between 25 and 32 per cent of the male population. By 1850, almost all the state peasants of these areas were involved in proto-industrial activities (Druzhinin 1974: Vol. 2, 296–390). However, the way back to proto-industry from countryside to town was not synonymous with a decline of the putting-out system (that is, subcontracting while supplying raw materials). With a flexible network of knowledgeable peasant weavers, cotton-printing firms had little incentive to expend capital on centralized weaving establishments; in general, only high-end grades of cloth were factory-produced. In Vladimir province in the early 1850s, 18,000 factory looms merely supplemented the 80,000 peasant looms filling factory orders (Crisp 1978: 308–415, 337–9).

As the putting-out system grew through the early 1800s, many independent domestic weavers found themselves increasingly tied to particular factories or particular putting-out middlemen because they had accepted loans or advances to buy yarn or more advanced looms. A law of 1835 stipulated that the employment of all workers be based upon the conclusion of a personal contract between employer and employee that specified the responsibilities of both sides. Since most workers were peasants whose period of residence in the city was determined by their passports, the period of the contract's validity was usually limited by the term of the passport. Workers were not supposed to leave their places of work until expiration of their contracts. This regulation, however, was difficult to enforce. Many entrepreneurs and managers complained that workers left their enterprises for the countryside or better employment opportunities before their contracts had expired.[12] Yet all this was a symptom of economic and social dynamics, not of stagnation.

The Russian agrarian market developed further during the first half of the nineteenth century, and the convergence of prices testifies to the formation of a real national market. At the same time, regional specialization progressed: central and eastern agricultural areas increased productivity and marketable production, while proto-industrial areas created a denser network of urban towns and intensified product specialization. Russian growth took place on the basis of the coexistence of these different organizations and on the basis of a long-term trend in which proto-industry and manufacture units moved from the town to the countryside and vice versa.

The functioning of serfdom was founded upon these multiple institutions, actors, and rules. There were no classes in the Marxist sense, but rather porous estates. Russian peasants were not 'serfs de la glebe' but strongly dependent people with extremely limited legal rights. These rights, however, increased over time. They were not chattel slaves like American slaves; since the early nineteenth century, private peasants increasingly moved to other legal and social categories, and as a consequence, their rights increased before the general abolition of serfdom in 1861. This is why labour services and strong legal constraints on labour mobility were not opposed to market development. Landlords and the demesne economy were not devoted to unproductive tasks and supporting monopolistic and parasitic attitudes, but instead sought to exploit imperfect competition to increase their profits. The peasant economy under 'serfdom' corresponded neither to the Chayanovian model of a peasant willing to satisfy his family's needs and entering the market only when

---

[12] RGIA fond 18, opis' 2, delo 1927, ll. 1, 3, 212–13; TsGIAM fond 14, opis' 1, delo 3266, ll. 2–38 and TsGIAM fond 2354, opis' 1, delo 41, ll. 197a–99, 228.

obliged, nor to Kula's model of peasants pushed to produce by the landlord, who took the entire product and sold it on the market. Peasants were already integrated into market activity, and proto-industry was not necessarily 'residual' (that is, an activity engaged in only after time and opportunities in agriculture had been fully exploited). Peasants' and nobles' integration into the market does not confirm the link between labour service and poor market development. 'Anti-economic' cultural values are used to oppose imaginary peasantries to proletarians, landlords to capitalists. In reality, Russian landlords and peasants were interested in profits and they were integrated into markets in various degrees. That they did not transform in accordance with some Western model does not mean that they were backward, but only that historical transformations of markets and societies may take different forms.

Yet, in political terms, European peasants lived under very different conditions. French peasants were formally free after the Revolution, although most of them participated in the labour market as seasonal workers and had far fewer rights than their masters and employers. This leads us to pose two main questions: first, to what extent did institutions affect the economic activity? Second, from a political standpoint, the long-term strength of the European nobility and peasantry and their integration in market activity raises the questions of when and how the 'old regime' ended in Europe: in the eighteenth century; with the rise of markets; after the French Revolution; or following on from WWI. To answer these questions, we have to study the continuities and changes in Russia after the official abolition of serfdom.

Impact of the Abolition of Serfdom

Conventional historiography stressed the limits of reforms, the increasing poverty of the peasantry, and the persistent backwardness of Russia (Gerschenkron 1962). More recent historiography has provided a completely different picture. Russia experienced significant social transformation and economic growth between 1861 and 1914; revised population trends show that mortality and birth rates were lower than was previously thought (Hoch 1982). There was a decline in the pauperization of the peasantry and the number and severity of large-scale famines (Wheatcroft 1991); the period from 1861 to 1914 was an era of steady improvement in both agricultural production and living standards (Kingston-Mann 1981; Simms 1977; Wilbur 1983).

We know that, in practice, the size of peasant land allotments in the local statutes varied greatly depending on soil fertility, population density, and agricultural practices (Saunders 1992). More land was assigned in the steppe and non-black earth lands than in black earth areas, where the land was more fertile and there was greater pressure from the population. Indeed, instead of a fixed amount of land per capita (or per family or per commune), each statute identified an interval within which the final amount of land should be determined (Hoch 1991).

The amount of labour was set at 40 days a year for men and 30 for women, and it had to be performed primarily during the summer and other periods of heavy agricultural work. There was a complex arrangement that varied the amount of labour according to the area, fertility of land, size of the allotment, and so on. Rules for cash dues were even more complicated, depending on the distance from St. Petersburg, major towns and markets, and the size of the allotment. As peasants were considered indebted until they had completed their redemption, the state and the estate owners retained their rights to restrict mobility and require formal consent for any market operation (selling, offering labour, and the like). In practice, in many localities, nobles abused their position and imposed unfair terms on the peasants; in many cases, landlords gave away their worst land and the peasants had to redeem it at the highest price (Litvak 1972). But how high was it?

Peasant land possessions more than doubled between the 1870s and WWI, and acquisitions were made not only by land communes but also increasingly by individual households. Between 1863 and 1872, Russian peasants bought lands to add to their communal allotments. Over three-quarters of all peasant acquisitions on the open market were made by individuals. This trend accelerated with the foundation of the Peasant State Bank, intended to encourage loans to peasants seeking to buy land. There was a twofold increase in peasant land properties between 1877 and 1905. In 80 per cent of the cases, the transactions were made by the peasant commune or by peasant associations. During the following years, between 1906 and 1914, the state sold 1.5 million *desiatine*s (1 desiatine = 1.10 hectares) to peasants; landlords sold them one-fifth of their land, that is, 10.2 million out of 49.7 desiatines. Two-thirds of the purchases were made by peasant associations and land communes and one-third by individual households (GUZiZ 1908–16). The dynamics of land acquisition thus further substantiate the assertion that peasant well-being increased between 1861 and 1914.

At the same time, *zemleustroistva* (land settlement) operations were a major factor in strengthening the peasant economy while preserving the commune. They were carried out as part of Stolypin's reforms (1906–11). Those reforms have usually been associated with 'privatization' of common lands, partly owing to tsarist propaganda, partly because of the interpretations of the intelligentsia. However, the reality was far more complex (Dubrovskii 1963; Pallot 1999; Yaney 1982). Peasants could, in fact, ask to leave the commune and privatize lands, but they could also simply apply for a consolidation of their lands (which, as we have seen, were scattered in several strips), without leaving the commune.[13] These practices had already been in use since the 1880s (Pallot 1999: 87–8). Despite official propaganda and the efforts of top-ranking officials, almost all peasant requests were for this latter form of consolidation, which was achieved by dividing up large villages, whereas the division of common lands— the real equivalent of English enclosures—seldom took place. This was accomplished through the cooperation of local and low-ranking state officials responsible for these operations. In other words, the 'privatization' of agriculture, as announced by tsarist officials, actually did not play much of a role in the pre-War Russian countryside. Overall, between 1906 and 1914, about 11 per cent of peasant land in European Russia was in one form or another subject to settlements (GUZiZ 1908–16). Comparatively speaking, land settlement was requested and practiced in industrial and proto-industrial areas more than in rural regions. Even more important: this intermediate solution—land settlement while formally keeping the commune—was

---

[13] RGIA, fond 1291, opis 1, 54 (1907), delo 16; opis' 120 (1909), delo 79.

far from being exceptional. The Russian version of the open fields was one variant of a system of mixed grain and livestock farming common to many areas of Europe. Formal title and final decisions over the use of open-field plots were vested in the commune, not the individual household. In Western Europe, peasant households typically held private and perpetual rights to well-defined plots of land within the open fields. This encouraged soil maintenance and other substantial land improvements. These property rights also supported active sales and rental markets for arable strips (Mironov 1985). In Russia, the commune decided each household's land endowment, as well as exactly where this land was located in the village's holdings. As a result, communes could and evidently did occasionally redistribute usufruct rights to individual strips among member households.

At the same time, these differences lessened in early twentieth century when the Stolypin's reforms, as interpreted and practised by local communities, led to a sharp transfer of decision power from the commune to the household.

The rate of growth and commercialization of Russian agriculture also accelerated (Gatrell 1986; Gregory 1982). Between the 1880s and 1900, through the grain trade, capitalism spread to the most remote corners of the empire (Koval'chenko and Milov 1974) and Russia's wheat market was fully integrated into global markets (Goodwin and Grennes 1998). The contribution of agriculture to the national income rose at a rapid pace, comparable to that of contemporary western European economies. In Paul Gregory's assessment, Russia experienced growth rates similar to those of Germany, France, America, Japan, Norway, Canada, and the United Kingdom—1.35 per cent average annual productivity growth in agriculture between 1883–7 and 1909–13, which was three-quarters of the rate of industrial productivity growth and nearly equal to the 1.5 per cent rate of the economy as a whole (Gregory 1982: 126–30; 168–94).

Net grain production rose to 3.1 per cent annually between 1885 and 1913; Russia produced more grain than any other country in 1861, and, in 1913, was second only to the United States. The average annual growth rate of wholesale grain and potato production in European Russia from 1870 to 1913 was 2.5 per cent: 1.6 per cent for the first 30 years and 4.4 per cent after the turn of the century.

Gregory estimated the rate of economic growth in the entire Russian empire including frontier regions from 1883 to 1887 through 1909–13 at 2.8 per cent, with some fluctuations within the intervals of that period (Gregory 1982: Table 6.3). The value of labour input between 1861 and 1913 increased by 42.6 per cent, or an average annual rate of 1.7 per cent.

Economic growth relied on the evolution of core Russian social institutions such as the peasant commune. It is no accident that over the past few decades, when the history of enclosures in Britain and agriculture in Europe was being re-examined (McCloskey 1989: 5–51), the image of the Russian commune has been called into question as well (Zyrianov 1992). Recent estimates for Russia confirm that there was no correlation between land redistribution practices and economic productivity (Nafziger 2006). Periodic redistributions had far less influence on productivity than endogenous investment decisions. When redistributing land plots, communes often took into account as key factors the quality of the soil and any improvements in its quality made by the previous tenant. Repartitions allowed land communes to respond to sudden, unexpected changes in their size brought about by epidemics or migrations, to recast the shape of the open fields and to bring order to field strips by reducing their number (Pallot 1999: 81).

Among agrarian forms of capital, livestock requires special attention: the abundance of livestock has been usually considered as one of the crucial specificities of the 'West' over other continents, while within Europe and in the same vein, Britain's advance in agricultural development over other countries has been equally explained with reference to livestock. On the contrary, Asian and African backwardness is attributed, among other crucial variables, to the lack of livestock. This view has been progressively contested. As regards Russia, since Gregory, who followed Vainshtein, livestock appear to be not only quite widespread but also growing at around 2 per cent per year in late tsarist Russian agriculture (Gregory 1982). Deflated net investments in agriculture grew at about 10–13 per cent per year during the same period (1885–1913) (Vainshtein 1960). Even if most of the advanced machines were still imported, tools and new equipment were more and more widespread in rural Russia, also thanks to the growing role of credit and peasant cooperatives and state peasant banks (Anfimov 1962; Bartlett 1990; Minin 1925; Vainshtein 1969).

This revised view of Russian agriculture corresponds to the new assessments of Russia's industrialization. According to recent estimates, between 1881 and 1913, the share of industry in national income rose from 25 per cent to 32 per cent. The productivity of industrial labour was 28 per cent higher than agricultural labour (Gregory 1982: 132). The rate of urbanization was considerable (Gatrell 1986), largely attributable to the influx of peasant migrants who accounted for 93 per cent of all factory workers in Moscow in 1902 (Pretty 1997), most of whom worked in textiles. By the time of the emancipation of the serfs in 1861, Russia possessed the sixth-largest cotton-spinning industry in the world (Pazhitnov 1958). However, mechanization only slowly took hold in the 1860s and 1870s; in 1866, probably only 36.6 per cent of cotton cloth was produced on mechanical looms. By 1879, 58.4 per cent of Russian cotton was produced on mechanical looms (Pazhitnov 1958: 81). The real victory of the mechanized loom took place in the 1880s and 1890s: in the Ivanovo region in 1860, 10 per cent of the weavers carried out 20 per cent of cloth production on mechanical looms; the respective figures grew to 28 per cent and 44 per cent in 1868, 57 per cent and 84 per cent in 1879, 67 and 92 per cent in 1884, 77 and 94 per cent in 1890, and 96 and 98 per cent in 1896. If the production share of mechanical looms had become overwhelming by the 1880s, the hand weavers remained an important part of the workforce until the industrialization drive of the 1890s and a small putting-out industry remained right up to the end of the empire. This also explains why, throughout the post-emancipation period, large firms intentionally jacked up the price of yarn or withheld it altogether from small producers to intentionally drive them away from the market, both to stifle competition and exert more control over the production process. Rather than a widespread diffusion of mechanical power, machines became the feature of a few firms, denoting an increasing polarization of the Russian industry. Of the 588 Russian factories that employed more than 6 workers in 1902, 98 with over 1,000 workers had a collective labour force of 257,353; the other 490 employed only 90,118. Thus, one-sixth of the firms employed three-quarters of the workers. The industry remained geographically concentrated in the central provinces of Moscow and Vladimir, as well as in and around the imperial capital. In 1890, 255 of 344 finishing factories were concentrated in these three provinces, responsible for more than 90 per cent of the workers and 97 per cent of the value of production. Only eight of these were in St. Petersburg province, but they were by far the largest and the most productive on average. By 1902, one quarter of cotton textile firms, accounting for 75 per cent of workers, were located in the Central Industrial Region. If Russian Poland is excluded, these figures rise to one-third of the firms, that is, 85 per cent of workers (Pretty 1997).

According to the 1897 census, 23.3 per cent of the active population was employed in non-agricultural sectors, half of them in proto-industrial and craft activities and the rest in industry and services. Proto-industry and especially rural cottage industry were still serious competitors for urban industry, not only in terms of production but also in the size of the labour market (Gatrell 1986). Thus, the relatively low numbers of the industrial labour force were not due to internal passports or legal constraints on mobility (Borodkin, Granville, and Leonard 2008) but due to the strength of agriculture, its profitability, and people's interest in staying in rural areas and leaving only for seasonal urban employment (Leonard 2011). In proto-industrial and industrial areas, between 1870 and 1906, passports were delivered to about a quarter of the population (Burds 1998). Even after 1906, when internal passports were suppressed, change was slow to occur. Sixty-nine per cent of St. Petersburg's population in 1910, and certainly a far greater percentage of the factory labour force, were peasants, and less than 10 per cent of those over the age of 20 had been born in the capital (McKean 1990: 17). This means that despite an increasing rate of urbanization and regional specialization, the peasant worker was still the leading figure in the Russian economy (Burds 1998).

The credit system developed equally strongly: at the central level, the State Bank, the Peasant Bank, and the Nobility Bank sustained the overall monetary and credit system, in particular on the land market. At the immediate lower level, commercial banks and urban banks added to a third circle, including cooperative banks and mutual aid institutions. According to several interpretations, one of the weaknesses of this system was the second level, the commercial banks, that were barely developed and not really supporting productive economic activities while being involved in speculation (Andriushin 1998).

To this, one has to add the relatively weak development of the stock exchange. Conventional interpretations systematically stressed the major difference between the 'West' and Russia in this respect (Owen 1991). In fact, these interpretations reflect a conventional mythology on the role of capital and stocks in the West. Numerous recent works confirmed that this role became relevant only at the turn of the nineteenth and twentieth centuries. Until then, corporations and the stock exchange were extremely limited in Western countries, including Britain (Cheffins 2001; Fohlin 1997; Harris 2000; Lamoreaux and Rosenthal 2006: 125–52). Instead, it is true that in the early twentieth century, the stock exchanges and the corporation strongly developed in the West, while they still lagged behind in Russia (Baranov and Dmitriev 2000; Shepeliov 1973).

In short, late tsarist Russia experienced relatively high rates of growth, mostly based upon proto-industry and agriculture. It lacked capital and institutions that protected investments and property, not to mention the extremely weak political representative institutions. As a result, Russia lagged behind most Western countries, particularly after the rise of the second industrial revolution, the stock exchange, and global capitalism.

Russian Capitalism in Reciprocal Comparison

Was Tsarist Russia Capitalist?

In a recent article, Gareth Austin took up the proposal put forward a few years ago by Kenneth Pomeranz and Roy Bin Wong to develop a form of 'reciprocal comparison' in which Africa (Austin's case) and China (Pomeranz and Wong) would not be compared exclusively to the Western model as an exemplary scenario and exclusive yardstick (Austin 2007: 1–28; Bin Wong 1997; Pomeranz 2000: 8). The fundamental aim of these proposals was to break free from the 'Eurocentrism' underlying most economic history analyses and show African (or Asian) peasants' market-oriented behaviour.

We adopted a different definition of reciprocal comparison: the goal is not to develop a new 'general model' and qualify tsarist Russia as 'capitalist' or not according to our general definition of capitalism. Quite the contrary, we use a revisited Russian history to reframe our conventional definition of capitalism in the West as well. In particular, labour coercion and capitalism are fully compatible, as it is confirmed not only in late tsarist Russia, but also in the American South, in several other historical contexts (Nazi Germany), and even nowadays in so many areas such as South and Southeast Asia, the 'Middle East', as well as some African areas. Thus, the relevant question is not to explain why Russia maintained coercive labour relations, but rather why, in some specific historical contexts, labour coercion was done away with under market and capitalism, while in many other capitalist contexts it was not.

Historians have claimed that peasants and land aristocracies were the opposite of English entrepreneurs and American farmers. Recent studies have shown, however, that presumed absentee landlords in Russia, Poland, and German areas did not always make use of compulsory labour and directly took part in the management of their estate.

Peasant workers and proto-industrialization played a crucial role in tsarist Russia. Estate relations sometimes opposed proto-industry but in some cases were favourable to it, which did not necessarily enhance or retard the proletarization of peasants and craftsmen (as asserted in Franklin Mendel's model in which proto-industrialization slowed the growth of towns, which was also confirmed by Jan de Vries) (de Vries 1984). Not only in Central and Eastern Europe and Russia (Hagen 1988), but also to a certain extent in Western Europe (Ogilvie and Cerman 1996; Sabel and Zeitlin 1997) and Asia (Lee 1999; Sugihara 2007), the success of proto-industry, in particular of rural proto-industry, was at the root of a labour-intensive path of growth (Franck 2006). In all these areas, as in most Russian regions, agriculture did not turn into a simple supplier of produce and labour force for industry; quite the contrary, estates and peasants took part in the development of local and national markets, for both wheat and proto-industrial products. Not only in Russia, Japan, and France (Postel-Vinay 1994: 64–83), but also in Britain (Lindert and Williamson 1982, 1983), until the mid-nineteenth century, double employment (mostly in rural and urban areas) was the rule rather than the exception. If this is true, then the massive proletarization of the peasantry belongs to the second, not the first industrial revolution, and took place mostly in the twentieth century. In this context, only the United States expressed a precocious capital intensification and highly specialized path. We need therefore to explain these cases instead of the presumed Russian exceptionality. This became a problem only at the turn of the nineteenth and twentieth centuries, when most of the West turned to the second industrial revolution while Russia preserved a labour-intensive path of growth.

Contrary to neo-institutional and traditional Marxist arguments, privatization was not a necessary and sufficient condition for the rise of capitalism. The legal defence of private property was still subject to caution in the nineteenth century, particularly in the face of arguments in favour of 'public utility', not only in France and Germany, but even in Great Britain and the United States (Stanziani 2012). The examples of Russia in the nineteenth century and China today show that very particular notions of property are not opposed to market development.

The international division of labour between advanced industrial regions and 'backward' agricultural regions—the former resorting to wage labour, the others to continuing forms of service in husbandry or even bondage (in Russia) and slavery (in the colonies and much of Asia, Africa, and Latin America)—has to be qualified and carefully defined. It is thus possible to rethink the theories of (under)development, the division of labour, and international trade and its effects. If this is so, then, unlike Osterhammel's argument (Russia as an exception in Europe), Russia expressed an extreme variation of eighteenth-century and nineteenth-century Western solutions, that is, capitalism based on small units and making use of unequal rights and eventually coercion. Russia diverged from the West only under the second industrial revolution and, even more, under the Soviet rule, seeking to move to the second industrial revolution while preserving labour coercion.

Bibliography

Archives

RGADA (Russian State Archives of Ancient Acts)

fond 199 (G. F. Miller)
fond 210: razriadnyi prikaz; fond 248, Senat I senatskie uchrezhdeniia.

fond 271, delo 1061
fond 294, opis' 2 and 3; fond 1287, opis' 3.
fond 350: revizkie skazki po nizhegorodskoi gubernii, opis' 2, dela 1975 and 2056.
fonds 615, krepostnye knigi, dela 526, 528, 529, 4753, 6654.
fond 1209 (pomestnyi prikaz), opis' 1, delo 292; fond 1287 (Sheremetev), opis' 5 and 6.
fond 1252, opis' 1: Abamelek-Lazarevy's estate, province of Tula; fond 1282, Tolstye-Kristi's estate, province of Riazan.
fond 1262, opis' 1, Prince Gagarin's estates in Saratov and Tambov provinces.

RGASPI (Russian State Archive of Socio-political History)

fond 5 (Lenin), Opis' 1.

RGIA (Russian National Imperial Archives),

fond 18, opis' 2, delo 1927, ll. 1, 3, 212–13;
fond 1088 (Sheremetev, opis' 3, 5, 10).
fond 1291, opis 1, 54 (1907), delo 16; opis' 120 (1909), delo 79
TsGIAM (State Archives of Moscow)
fond 14, opis' 1, delo 3266, ll. 2–38
fond 1287, opis' 2, dela 31, 40, 82, 124, 146;
fond 2354, opis' 1, delo 41.

Printed Sources

Anan'ich Boris V., ed. 2001. *Puti poznaniia Rossii: Novye podkhody i interpretatsii* [Path of Growth in Russia: New Approaches and Interpretations]. St. Petersburg: Liki Rossii.

Andriushin, Serguei A. 1998. *Bankovskaia Sistema Rossii: osobennosti evoliutsii i kontseptsiia razvitiia* [The Bank System in Russia: Features of Its Evolution and the Notion of Development]. Moscow: Knorus.

Anfimov, Andrei Matsevich. 1962. *Rossiiskaia dereveniia v gody pervoi mirovoi voiny* [The Russian Countryside during World War I]. Moscow: Nauka.

Aston, Timothy and Charles Philpin, eds. 1985. *The Brenner Debate: Agrarian Class Structure and Economic Development in Preindustrial Europe*. Cambridge: Cambridge University Press.

Austin, Gareth. 2007. 'Reciprocal Comparison and African History: Tackling Conceptual Eurocentrism in the Study of Africa's Economic Past.' *African Studies Review* 50(3): 1–28.

Baranov Ivan N. and A.L. Dmitriev. 2000. *Istoriia finansovoi politiki v Rossii* [History of Financial Policies in Russia]. St. Petersburg: Izdanie Politeknicheskogo Universiteta.

Barber John. 1981. *Soviet Historians in Crisis, 1928–1932.* New York: Holmes and Meier.

Baron, Samuel H. and Nancy W. Heer, eds. 1977. *Windows on the Russian Past: Essays on Soviet Historiography Since Stalin.* Columbus, OH: Anchor Press.

Bartlett, Roger, ed. 1990. *Land Commune and Peasant Community in Russia.* London: Macmillan.

Belinskii, Vissarion G. 1953–5. *Polnoe sobranie sochinenii* [Complete Works]. 13 Vols. Moscow: Akademia Nauk SSSR.

Bin Wong, Roy. 1997. *China Transformed.* Ithaca: Cornell University Press.

Blanchard Ian. 1989. *Russia's Age of Silver: Precious Metal Production and Economic Growth in the Eighteenth Century.* London and New York: Routledge.

Borodkin, Leonid, Brigitte Granville, and Carol Scott Leonard. 2008. 'The Rural/Urban Wage Gap in the Industrialization of Russia, 1884–1910.' *European Review of Economic History* 12(1): 67–95.

Burds, Jeffrey. 1998. *Peasant Dreams and Market Politics: Labour Migration and the Russian Village, 1861–1905.* Pittsburgh: University of Pittsburgh Press.

Cheffins, Bruno. 2001. 'History and the Global Corporate Governance Revolution: the UK Perspective.' *Business History* 43(4): 87–118.

Chicherin, Boris N. (1882–3) 2005. *Sobstvennost' i gosudarstvo* [Property and the State]. 2 Vols. St. Petersburg: Izdatel'stvo Russkoi Khristianskoi gumanitarnoi akademii.

Cooper Frederick, Allen Isaacman, Florencia Mallon, William Roseberry, and Steve Stern. 1993. *Confronting Historical Paradigms: Peasants, Labor, and the Capitalist World System in Africa and Latin America.* Madison: University of Wisconsin Press.

Crisp, Olga. 1978. 'Labour and Industrialization in Russia.' In *The Cambridge Economic History of Europe*, Vol. 7, Part 2, edited by Peter Mathias and Michael Postan, pp. 308–415. Cambridge: Cambridge University Press

Czap, Peter. 1982. 'The Perennial Multiple-Family Household. Mishino, Russia, 1782–1856.' *Journal of Family History* 7(1): 5–26.

Danilov, Viktor P. 1961. 'O kharaktere sotsioal'no-ekonomiceskikh otnoshenii sovetskogo krest'ianstva do kollektivizatsii sel'skogo khozjaistva' [On the Nature of the Socio-Economic Relations among the Russian Peasantry before the Collectivization]. In *Istoriia sovetskogo kret'ianstva i kolhoznogo stroitel'stva v SSSR*, [History of the Soviet Peasantry and Collective Farms in the USSR], edited by Viktor Danilov. Moscow: Nauka.

de Vries, Jan. 1984. *European Urbanization, 1500–1800*. London: Meuthen.

Dennison, Tracy. 2011. *The Institutional Framework of Russian Serfdom*. Cambridge: Cambridge University Press.

Diderot, Denis. (1774) 1963. 'Observations sur le Nakaz de Catherine II' [Observations on the Edit of Catherine II], edited by Paul Vernière. In *Oeuvres politiques*. Paris: Garnier.

Domar, Evsey and Michael Machina. 1984. 'On the Profitability of Russian Serfdom.' *The Journal of Economic History* 44: 919–55.

Druzhinin, Nikolai M. 1974. *Gosudarstvennye krest'iane i reforma P.D. Kiseleva* [The State Peasants and the Reforms of Kiselev]. Moscow: AN SSSR.

Dubrovskii, Serguei M. 1963. *Stolypinskaia zemel'naia reforma. Iz istorii sel'skogo khoziaistva i krest'ianstva Rossii v nachale XX veka* [The Stolypin's Agrarian Reform. The History of Agriculture and Peasantry of Russia at the Beginning of the Twentieth Century]. Moscow: Akademiia nauk.

Emmons, Terence. 1968. *The Russian Landed Gentry and the Peasant Emancipation of 1861*. Berkeley: University of California Press.

Fohlin, Claude. 1997. 'Bank Securities Holdings and Industrial Finance before World War I: Britain and Germany Compared.' *Business and Economic History* 26(2): 463–75.

Franck, Penelope. 2006. *Rural Economic Development in Japan: from the Nineteenth Century to the Pacific War*. London, New York: Routledge.

Gatrell, Peter. 1986. *The Tsarist Economy, 1850–1917*. New York, St Martin's Press.

———. 2005. *Russia's First World War: A Social and Economic History*. London: Pearson-Longman.

Gerschenkron Alexander. 1962. *Economic Backwardness in Historical Perspective*. Cambridge, MA: Harvard University Press.

Gestwa Klaus. 1999. *Protoindustrialisierung in Russland*. Göttingen: Vandenhoeck and Ruprecht.

Goodwin, Barry K. and Thomas J. Grennes. 1998. 'Tsarist Russia and the World Wheat Market.' *Explorations in Economic History* 35(4): 405–30.

Gorshkov, Boris. 2000. 'Serfs on the Move: Peasant Seasonal Migration in Pre-reform Russia, 1800–1860.' *Kritika. Explorations in Russian History* 1(4): 627–56.

Gregory, Paul. 1982. *Russian National Income 1885–1913*. Cambridge: Cambridge University Press.

———. 1994. Before Command: The Russian Economy FROM Emancipation to Stalin. Princeton: Princeton University Press.

GUZiZ. 1908–16. *Ezhegodnik GUZiZ, 1906–16* (Yearbook of the Land Commission of the Ministry of Agriculture). St. Petersburg: Gosizdat.

Hagen, William. 1988. 'Capitalism in the Countryside in Early Modern Europe: Interpretations, Models, Debates.' *Agricultural History* 62(1): 13–47.

Harris, Ron. 2000. *Industrializing English Law*. Cambridge: Cambridge University Press.

Hasek, Carl William. 1925. *The Introduction of Adam Smith's Doctrine into Germany*. New York: Columbia University Press.

Hoch, Steven. 1982. 'Serfs in Imperial Russia: Demographic Insights.' *The Journal of Interdisciplinary History* 13(2): 221–46.

———. 1991. 'The Banking Crisis, Peasant Reforms, and Economic Development in Russia, 1857–1861.' *American Historical Review* 96(3): 795–820.

———. 1994. 'On Good Numbers and Bad: Malthus, Population Trend and Peasant Standard of Living in Late Imperial Russia.' *Slavic Review* 53(1): 41–75.

———. 1998. 'Famine, Disease and Mortality Patterns in the Parish of Boshervka, Russia, 1830–1932.' *Population Studies* 52(3): 357–68.

Indova, Emilia I. 1964. *Dvortsovoe khoziaistvo v Rossii* [The Palace Economy in Russia)]. Moscow: Nauka.

———. 1975. 'O rossiskikh manufakturakh vtoroi poloviny XVIII v.' [On the Russian Manufactures during the Second Half of the Eighteenth Century]. *Istoricheskaia geografiia Rossii: XIX-nachalo XX v*, pp. 248–345. Moscow: Nauka.

Izmes'eva, Tatiana F. 1991. *Rossiia v sisteme evropeiskogo rynka. Konets XIXe-nachalo XX v.* [Russia in the System of the European Market. End of the Nineteenth to the Early Twentieth Century]. Moscow: Nauka.

Kashchenko, Serguei. 1995. *Reforma 19 Fevralia 1861 goda na severo-zapade Rossii* [The Reforms of 1861 in North-Western Russia]. Moscow: Mosgoarchiv.

Kashin, Boris N. 1935. *Kres'ianskaia promyshlennost'* [The Peasant Rural Industry]. 2 Vols. Moscow and Leningrad.

Khristoforov, Igor. 2011. *Sud'ba reformy: Russkoe krest'ianstvo v pravitel'stvennoi politike do i posle otmeny krepostnogo prava (1830–1890 gg.)* [The Issue of Reform: Russian Peasantry and State Policies Before and After the Abolition of Serfdom]. Moscow: Sobranie.

Kingston-Mann, Esther. 1981. 'Marxism and Russian Rural Development: Problems of Evidence, Experience and Culture.' *American Historical Review* 86(4): 731–52.

————. 1999. *In Search of the True West*. Princeton: Princeton University Press.

Kotsonis, Yanni. 2014. *States of Obligation: Taxes and Citizenship in the Russian Empire and Early Soviet Republic*. Toronto: Toronto University Press.

Koval'chenko, Ivan D. 1967. *Russkoe krepostnoe krest'ianstvo v pervoi polovine XIX v.* [Russian Serfdom during the First Half of the Nineteenth Century]. Moscow: Nauka.

Koval'chenko, Ivan D. and L. Milov. 1974. *Vserossiiskii agrarnyi rynok, XVIII-nachalo XX v.* [The All-Russian Agrarian Market, Eighteenth-Early Twentieth Centuries]. Moscow: Nauka.

Kula, Witold. 1976. *An Economic Theory of the Feudal System*. London: New Left Books.

Lamoreaux, Naomi and Jean-Laurent Rosenthal. 2006. 'Corporate Governance and the Plight of Minority Shareholders in the United States before the Great Depression.' In *Corruption and Reform: Lessons from America's Economic History*, edited by E. Glaeser and Claudia Goldin. Chicago: University of Chicago Press.

Ledovskaia, Irina V. 1974. 'Biudzhet russkogo pomeshchika v 40–60kh godakh XIX v' [Estate Owners' Budgets in the 1840s–60s]. In *Materialy po istorii sel'skogo khoziaistva i krest'ianstva SSSR*, Vol. 8. Moscow: Nauka.

Lee, John. 1999. 'Trade and Economy in Preindustrial East Asia, c. 1500–1800: East Asia in the Age of Global Integration.' *The Journal of Asian Studies* 58(1): 2–26.

Lenin, Vladimir Ilich. 1899. *Razvitie kapitalizma v Rossii* [The Development of Capitalism in Russia]. Saint-Petersburg: A. leifert.

Leonard, Carol, 2011. *Agrarian Reforms in Russia*. Cambridge: Cambridge University Press.

Lindert, Paul and Geoffrey Williamson. 1982. 'Revising England's Social Tables, 1688–1812.' *Explorations in Economic History* 19(4): 385–408.

————. 1983. 'English Workers' Living Standards during the Industrial Revolution: a New Look.' *Economic History Review* 36(2): 1–25.

Litvak, Boris. 1972. *Russkaia derevniia v reforme 1861 goda: Chernozemnyi tsentr 1861–1895 gg* [The Russian Countryside in the Reform of 1861: The Central Blacklands, 1861–1895]. Moscow: Nauka.

Markevich, Andrei and Ekaterina Zhuravskaya. 2015. 'Economic Effects of the Abolition of Serfdom: Evidence from the Russian Empire'. CEPR Discussion Paper No. DP10398, Center for Economic Policy Research, London.

Markwick, Roger D. 2001. *Rewriting History in Soviet Russia: The Politics of Revisionist Historiography, 1956–1974*. New York: Palgrave.

McCloskey, Donald. 1989. 'The Open Fields of England: Rent, Risk, and the Rate of Interest, 1300–1815.' In *Markets in History: Economic Studies of the Past*, edited by David Galenson. Cambridge: Cambridge University Press.

McKean, Robert B. 1990. *St. Petersburg between the Revolutions*. New Haven: Yale University Press.

Melton, Edgar. 1987. 'Proto-industrialization, Serf Agriculture and Agrarian Social Structure. Two Estates in Nineteenth-Century Russia.' *Past and Present* 115(1): 73–81.

Minin, Aleksanr'. 1925. *Sel'sko-khoziaistvennaia kooperatsiia SSSR* [Agrarian Cooperation in the USSR]. Moscow: Gosizdat.

Mironov, Boris. 1981. *Vnytrennii rynok Rossii vo vtoroi polovine XVIII-pervoi po- lovine XIX v.* [The Domestic Market in Russia during the Second Half of the Eighteenth-First Half of the Nineteenth Century]. Leningrad: Nauka.

———. 1985. 'The Russian Peasant Commune after the Reforms of the 1860.' *Slavic Review* 44(3): 438–67.

———. 1992. 'Consequences of the Price Revolution in Eighteenth-Century Russia.' *The Economic History Review* 45(2): 457–78.

———. 1999. *The Social History of the Russian Empire*, 2 Vols. Boulder, CO: Westview.

Mironov, Boris and Carol S. Leonard. 1985. 'In Search of Hidden Information: Some Issues in the Socio-Economic History of Russia in the Eighteenth and Nineteenth Centuries.' *Social Science History* 9: 339–59.

Moon, David. 1999. *The Russian Peasantry, 1630–1930*. London: Longman.

Moriakov, Vladimir I. 1981. *Iz istorii evoliutsii obshchestvenno-politicheskikh vzgliadov prosvetitelei kontsa XVIII veka: Reinal' i Radishchev* [On the History of the Evolution of the Sociopolitical Orientations of Institutors during the Eighteenth Century: Raynal and Radishchev]. Moscow: Izdatel'stvo Moskovskogo Universiteta.

Nafziger Steven. 2010. 'Peasant Communes and Factor Markets in Late Nineteenth-Century Russia.' *Explorations in Economic History* 47(4): 381–402.

———. 2006. 'Communal Institutions, Resource Allocation, and Russian Economic Development'. PhD dissertation, Yale University.

North, Douglass. 1981. *Structure and Change in Economic History*. New York: Norton.

North, Douglass and Robert Thomas. 1973. *The Rise of Western Civilization: A New Economic History*. Cambridge: Cambridge University Press.

Ogilvie, Sheilag and Markus Cerman, eds. 1996. *European Proto-Industrialization*. Cambridge: Cambridge University Press.

Osterhammel, Jürgen. 2014. *The Transformation of the World: A Global History of the Nineteenth Century*. Princeton: Princeton University Press.

Owen, Thomas. 1991. *The Corporation under Russian Law, 1800–1917*. Cambridge: Cambridge University Press.

Pallot, Judith. 1999. *Land Reforms in Russian 1906–1917*. Oxford: Clarendon Press.

Pazhitnov, K.A. 1958. *Ocherki istorii tekstil'noi promyshlennosti dorevoliutsionnoi Rossii* [Studies on the Textile Proto-industry in Pre-revolutionary Russia. Moscow: Gosizdat.

Pomeranz, Kenneth. 2000. *The Great Divergence*. Princeton: Princeton University Press.

Postel-Vinay, Gilles. 1994. 'The Di-integration of Traditional Labour Markets in France. From Agriculture and Industry to Agriculture or Industry.' In *Labour Market Evolution: The Economic History of Market Integration, Wage Flexibility and the Employment Relation*, edited by George Grantham and Mary MacKinnon, pp. 64–83. London and New York: Routledge.

Pretty, David. 1997. 'Neither Peasant nor Proletarian. The Workers of the Ivanovo-Voznesensk Region.' PhD dissertation, Brown University.

Prokov'eva, Lidia S. 1981. *Krest'ianskaia obshchina v Rossii vo vtoroi polovine XVIII-pervoi polovine XIX v* [The Peasant Commune in Russia during the Second Half of the Eighteenth to the First Half of the Nineteenth Centuries]. Leningrad: Nauka.

Raeff, Marc. 1983. *The Well-Ordered Police State: Social and Institutional Change Through Law in the Germanies and Russia, 1600–1800*. New Haven: Yale University Press.

Rudolph, Robert. 1985. 'Agricultural Structure and Proto-industrialization in Russia: Economic Development with Unfree Labour.' *The Journal of Economic History* 45(1): 47–69.

Sabel, Charles and Jonathan Zeitlin, eds. 1997. *Worlds of Possibilities. Flexibility and Mass Production in Western Industrialization*. Cambridge, Paris: Maison des Sciences de l'Homme, Cambridge University Press.

Saunders, Daniel. 1992. *Russia in the Age of Reaction and Reform, 1801–1881*. London and New York: Longman.

Serbina, Ksenia N. 1978. *Krest'ianskaia zhelezodelatel'naia promyshlennost' tsentral'noi Rossii XVI-pervoi poloviny XIXe vekoi* [The Peasant Metallurgic Home Industry in Central Russia, from the Sixteenth to the First Half of the Nineteenth Century]. Leningrad: Nauka.

Shanin, Teodor, ed. 1983. *Late Marx and the Russian Road, Marx and the 'Peripheries of Capitalism'*. New York: Monthly Review Press.

Shepeliov, Leonid E. 1973. *Aktsionernye kompanii v Rossii* [The Corporation in Russia]. Leningrad: Nauka.

Simms, James. 1977. 'The Crisis in Russian Agriculture at the End of the Nineteenth Century: A Different View.' *Slavic Review* 36(3): 377–98.

———. 1982. 'The Crop Failure of 1891: Soil Exhaustion, Technological Backwardness, and Russia's Agrarian Crisis.' *Slavic Review* 41(2): 236–50.

Small, Albion. 1909. *The Cameralists: Pioneers of German Social Policy*. New York: Burt Franklin.

Stanziani, Alessandro. 1998. *L'économie en revolution. Le cas russe, 1870–1930* [Revolutionary Economics. The Russian Case, 1870–1930]. Paris: A. Michel.

———. 2008a. 'Free Labour-Forced Labour: An Uncertain Boundary? The Circulation of Economic Ideas between Russia and Europe from the 18th to the Mid-19th Century.' *Kritika. Explorations in Russian and Eurasian History* 9(1): 1–27.

———. 2008b. 'Serfs, Slaves, or Wage Earners? The Legal Statute of Labour in Russia from a Comparative Perspective, from the 16th to the 19th Century.' *Journal of Global History* 3(2): 183–202.

———. 2012. *Rules of Exchange. French Capitalism in Comparative Perspective, 18th–20th Centuries*. Cambridge: Cambridge University Press.

———. 2014a. *After Oriental Despotism. Eurasian Growth in Global Perspective, 17th–Early 20th Century*. London: Bloomsbury.

———. 2014b. *Bondage. Labor and Rights in Eurasia, 17th–20th centuries*. New York: Berghahn.

Strumilin, Sergei. 1966. *Ocherki ekonomicheskoi istorii Rossii i SSSR* [Studies in the Economic History of Russia and the USSR]. Moscow: Nauka.

Sugihara, Kaouro. 2007. 'Labour-Intensive Industrialisation in Global History.' *Australian Economic History* 47(2): 121–54.

Tikhonov, Iurii A. 1974. *Pomeshchic'i krest'iane v Rossii: feodal'naia renta v XVII-nachale XVIII v* [The Private Estates' Peasants in Russia: the Feudal Rent in the Seventeenth to Early Eighteenth Century]. Moscow: Nauka.

Tipps, Dearn. 1973. 'Modernization Theory and the Comparative Study of Societies: A Critical Perspective.' *Comparative Studies in Society and History* 15(2): 199–226.

Tribe, Keith. 1988. *Governing Economy: The Reformation of German Economic Discourse, 1760–1840*. Cambridge: Cambridge University Press.

Troinitskii, Aleksandr. 1861. *Krepostnoe naselenie v Rossii po 10 narodnoi perepisi* [The Russian Serf Population According to the Tenth Census]. Saint Petersburg: Wulf.

Vainshtein, Albert L. 1960. *Narodnoe bogatstvo I narodnokhoziaistvonnoe nakoplenie predrevoliutsionnoi Rossii* [National Wealth and Accumulation in Pre-revolutionary Russia]. Moscow: Gosizdat.

————. 1969. *Nardonyi dokhod Rossiii I SSSR* [The National Income of Russia and the USSR]. Moscow: Ekonomika.

Walicki, Andrzej. 1975. *The Slavophile Controversy: History of a Conservative Utopia in Nineteenth Century Russia*. New York: Oxford University Press.

Wallerstein, Immanuel. 1974–6. *The Modern World-System: Capitalist Agriculture and the Origins of the European World-Economy in the Sixteenth Century*. 2 Vols. New York, London: Atheneum.

Wheatcroft, Stephen. 1991. 'Crisis and Condition of the Peasantry in Late Imperial Russia.' In *Peasant Economy, Culture and Politics of European Russia, 1800–1921*, edited by Esther Kingston-Mann and Timothy Mixter, pp. 101–27. Princeton: Princeton University Press.

Wilbur Elvira M. 1983. 'Was Russian Peasant Agriculture Really That Impoverished? New Evidence from a Case Study from the "Impoverished Center" at the End of the Nineteenth Century.' *Journal of Economic History* 43(1): 137–44.

Yaney, George. 1982. *The Urge to Mobilize. Agrarian Reform in Russia, 1861–1930*. Urbana: University of Illinois Press.

Yilmaz, Harun. 2015. *National Identities in Soviet Historiography*. London: Routledge.

Zyrianov, P. 1992. *Krest'ianskaia obshchina Evropeiskoi Rossii 1907–1914 gg.* [The Peasant Commune in the European Russia, 1907–1914]. Moscow: Nauka.

4

The Cambridge History of Capitalism
India

David Washbrook[1]

To make an obvious point, the major problem for any 'history of capitalism' is to agree on a definition of the concept and phenomenon that it is meant to elucidate. Larry Neal (2014), the editor of *The Cambridge History of Capitalism*, offers a very broad definition related to four 'institutional' criteria: private property rights, enforceable contracts, markets with responsive prices, and supportive governments. Yet, as the other essays in Volume 1 indicate, these might be found—in some measure or another—in many societies from ancient Mesopotamia onwards, and it is not immediately clear what historical point a focus on them is meant to clarify. Rather, by hint

[1] I am very grateful to Professor Dilip M. Menon, Dr Kaveh Yazdani, and the staff at the Centre for Indian Studies in Africa at University of the Witwatersrand for organizing the conference on the Cambridge History of Capitalism at which this paper was originally presented. I am also grateful for the comments received both from them and from other participants.

and assumption, it emerges that Neal takes these criteria to be key to the phenomenon of economic growth and to play a critical role in understanding, particularly, the emergence of *modern* economic growth (MEG), which itself is hardly separable from industrialization. In effect, Neal equates capitalism with MEG—reflecting a definition famously associated with the 'institutional' economic theories of Douglass North (1990) and drawn largely from the experience of 'Anglo-America'.

However, by no means all the contributors to *The Cambridge History of Capitalism* I and II seem to share the same definition and assumptions. Bin Wong (2014), for example, presents the history of China as a case of economic growth and even industrialization without capitalism. Patrick O'Brien (2014) seeks to subsume the history of capitalism under the history of the state, making the organization of state power rather than of market institutions its primary focus.

Other definitions of capitalism and assumed theories of economic growth lead in other directions. World-System Theory takes the 'outbreak' of MEG to be unique to the 'West' and non-replicable elsewhere. Its global history consists of studying how (the exploitation of) other parts of the world contributed to, and helped support, this singular geographical outcome (Frank 1967; Wallerstein 2011). Here, the history of capitalism is equated with (and subsumed under) the history of global inequality.

Parallel to this, there are several different histories of capitalism derivable from the ideas of Karl Marx, such as Asiatic modes of production, primitive accumulation, universal proletarianization, and colonial monopoly capitalism (Brown 1972). Here, again, it seems to be socio-economic inequality that is the real problem being addressed, but expressed in class rather than geographic terms and with a view to forge political strategies for its transcendence.

Different definitions lead to different conclusions and may make for very different histories. To complicate matters, these histories are not necessarily incompatible. As we know from very recent times, faster GDP growth and deepening social inequality can go together (at least for some time); the rise of one 'national' economy can be at the expense of another. The history of capitalism looks very different depending on the vantage point from, and the ideological spectacles through, which it is viewed.

Intriguingly, such differences show up even between Tirthankar Roy's chapter on India and Larry Neal's summary of it. Neal (2014: 10) tells us that Roy concludes with: 'The disastrous economic consequences of political rule by a profit-seeking corporation, which Adam Smith had derided in the case of the Dutch East India Company's rule over the Spice Islands and Indonesian archipelago in the eighteenth century, [which] became even more evident with the rule of the English East India Company in nineteenth-century India.'

But Roy's (2014: 190) last words on the subject read:

> The British empire, formed of a diverse collection of world regions with a shared official language and mutually compatible legal regimes, brought down transaction costs in exchanges between parts of the empire. The empire, therefore, was crucial to expanding the axes of interaction from commodity to capital, labor and technology. Economic laws, especially in the sphere of commercial exchanges, broadened the scope of contracts....New currency regimes reduced the risks of overseas investment. The abolition of slavery encouraged the tropical plantations to import Asian labor.

In this light, it may be most useful to operate in (at least) three dimensions and briefly look at the history of capitalism in India from the perspectives of 'institutionalist', world system, and Marxist theories, and the interesting questions raised by this history to each of them.

Tirthankar Roy's chapter in *The Cambridge History of Capitalism* I is largely 'institutionalist' and, in effect, offers a broad overview of India's economic history from medieval times with specific address to the four criteria highlighted by Neal. To summarize: Roy sees the Indian economy, at least prior to the sixteenth century, as essentially dualistic. It was divided between, on the one side, an interior economy dominated by the extractive policies of rulers operating largely within local confines; and, on the other, a coastal economy long involved in seaborne trade (and acting as the 'workshop of the world', especially for textiles, in this era). He describes these two systems as different 'capitalisms' with different organizational rules and features. He sees India's economic history between the sixteenth and eighteenth centuries largely in terms of the coming together of these previously separate systems, with the capitalism of the coasts increasingly taking the lead under European direction. He fights shy of making any statistical estimate of economic growth because of the paucity of reliable statistics (correctly, in my view). However, I think that his inferences suggest the possibility of modest, pre-modern growth in some places and over some periods, including the eighteenth century. Yet it was a very fragile growth, easily 'arrested' or even reversed. Roy (2014) is very clear that there were no signs of a shift towards mechanized/industrialized forms of manufacture before the onset of colonial rule.

In institutional terms, Roy sees both inland and coastal 'capitalisms' having long-established forms of private property right. However, difficulties arose over the performance of markets, the enforceability of contracts, and the support supplied by the state. Inland transport facilities were primitive, making it hard to integrate commodity markets for all but luxury goods. Labour and capital markets also suffered from distortions: spare land and rival employers made labour difficult to regulate and mercantile wealth was at risk from predatory rulers and poor information networks. With regard to contract, while there is evidence in earlier periods of supra-kin commercial organizations, Roy takes these to have declined by the sixteenth century. Enforcement of contract was highly precarious and based on varying contexts of negotiation, with trust largely circumscribed within sectarian, kinship, and caste groups. With regard to the state, very few rulers invested heavily in public goods (beyond, for example, the Mughal provision of roads). However, some were interested in the profits of commerce and did invest in trade—although not always to the benefit of other merchant capitalists. In the eighteenth century, some of the successor regional states to the Mughals pursued what Bayly (1989a) termed 'Asian mercantilist' policies but inconsistently and in a context of perennial warfare.

In almost all areas except property rights, Roy takes the incoming Europeans to have had superior forms of institutional organization. However, even these were not without serious flaws: for example, in terms of the relationship between principals and agents (where control from Europe could be weak). At least at first, the expansion of European political authority (under Company auspices) by no means led to institutions necessarily supportive of the market and economic growth (Roy and Swami 2016). Yet Roy (2014) does see colonialism, eventually, maturing into an institutional system progressively more adequate to Douglass North's notion, and underpinning a future moving in the long term towards MEG: his chapter is subtitled 'Capitalism in India in the Very Long Run'.

Roy (2013) has developed his 'dualism' thesis at greater length in other work where it has also drawn criticism from Shami Ghosh (2015) on two grounds: first, that it underestimates the commercialization of the interior economy generated, especially, out of elite consumption; and, second, that its all-India focus misses the potential of certain regional economies with stronger growth trajectories of their own (such as Gujarat and Mysore). In a recent work, Kaveh Yazdani (2017) has further endorsed this latter point. I think that there is some substance to these criticisms. Roy's own evidence of deepening monetization (via cash tax-collection) and high levels of labour mobility suggest greater dynamism in the interior economy than his argument is prepared to allow. Mughal India, at its height in the seventeenth century, created a series of major inland consumption centres—whose traditions at least some of the interior successor states of the eighteenth century carried on. These centres supported large markets for foodstuffs and attracted artisanal industries to supply courts and armies (Bayly 1983, 1989b). A few of them generated strong local histories of economic growth.

At the same time, caution may need to be exercised. There is a tendency in the historiography to link positive histories of pre-modern growth to suppositions about possibilities of an autochthonous transition to MEG, outside Western Europe, had colonialism not supervened. However, the status of this supposition depends on which theory of MEG is adopted. Ghosh appeals to Jan de Vries (2008) and the theory of an 'industrious' rather than 'industrial' revolution, with MEG understood as 'evolving' out of long-term changes in work patterns, habits, and consumption rather than springing from a sudden 'revolution' in technology and production. Not only de Vries but even Nick Crafts (1985) made such 'evolutionary' understandings popular 30 years ago. But lately, the pendulum appears to have swung back in favour of at least a moderate 'revolution', which is reflected in Knick Harley's (2014) essay on the British case in *The Cambridge History of Capitalism* I. Even strong pre-modern growth may not just have 'evolved' into MEG without the catalyst of sharp disruption: in effect, however strongly or weakly the Indian economy may have grown before 1800 may not be relevant to the place it came to occupy subsequently in a global economy dominated by MEG.

Also, the rise of Mughal consumption and the growth strategies of some of the eighteenth-century successor states can scarcely be divorced from the deepening impact of the coasts and, increasingly, the Europeans. It was largely American silver that enabled Akbar to unify the monetary system of North India around the silver rupee and greatly reduce the transaction costs of commerce (Richards 1987); successor states, like the famous Mysore of Hyder Ali and Tipu Sultan, were reacting to the growing mercantilist threat of the European companies by trying to forge Asian mercantilisms of their own (Stein 1985; Washbrook 1988). Hyder and Tipu may at best be seen generating strategies of 'reactive' modernization, of which Asia subsequently produced many, but only one with any long-term success—that of Japan. It need not be said that if we are comparing the economies of late Tokugawa and early Meiji Japan and eighteenth-century Mysore, the differences may be more striking than the similarities.

A further consideration, which Roy (2015) himself raises elsewhere, is that regional nodes of growth were actually quite small—scarcely capable of transforming vast hinterlands—and themselves inclined to be fragile. In Gujarat, more than a century of strong growth was virtually wiped out by the devastating famines of the 1630s; in Tamil Nadu, the rich economy built up around the Kaveri delta was severely damaged by the wars of the later eighteenth century and the volume of paddy production fell by possibly two-thirds. Famously, Chris Bayly (1983) commented on the recuperative powers of the north Indian economy during the 'troubles' of the eighteenth century when labour and capital moved from wartime 'hot spots' to regenerate lands and towns elsewhere. However, recuperation means getting back to … not moving forward.

My own view of pre-modern India in the history of capitalism would begin with an assessment of the character of capital itself: the sustained accumulation of material wealth and its investment in the creation of further wealth. By comparative Eurasian standards, wealth in early modern India may have been easily acquired but was very difficult to keep from generation to generation; and very little of it was ever invested in *fixed* assets. In Roy's interior economy, it was largely gained by acquiring liens on the land revenue and taxes—which meant a close dependence on state power and politics (Subrahmanyam and Bayly 1988). Indian empires and kingdoms were not necessarily marked by longevity and courtiers came and went even faster.

In the coastal economy (and in the interstices of commerce inland), wealth was largely gained through buying and selling in bazaars where prices (including the price of money/bullion) were vagarious and contracts difficult to enforce. John Richards questioned of Karen Leonard whether the great bankers with whom the European companies dealt in the eighteenth century had existed much earlier (Leonard 1979; Richards 1981). Even where they rose very high, they could also fall (literally) very far: as did Jagath Seth, who once commanded two-thirds of the revenues of Bengal, but was thrown off a clifftop by the nawab of Bengal (Marshall 1987). Greater security could be achieved by investing via a series of 'community' institutions often associated with religion and enjoying both state immunities and market privileges, such as temples. Indeed, temples (especially in South India) provide rare examples of fixed-asset investment too (Stein 1960). However, complex issues of ownership, management, and appropriation of this wealth could also lead it to atrophy (for example, in large stores of 'useless' gold ornaments).

Equally, by comparative Eurasian standards, ratios of fixed to liquid capital in productive operations were very low. Beyond the southern river deltas, India had little by way of public goods provision to match that of the Chinese imperial state. Also, it had little by way of private investment goods to match the land-drainage schemes of the Netherlands and the English Fens. Classically, merchant capital 'contracted' for goods with independent groups of artisanal and peasant producers. Advances were principally of cash rather than tools or goods (such as thread) and contracts could be cancelled at any point by mere return of the advance. In this context, capital not only remained liquid but was obliged to pursue complex risk-averting strategies (Parthasarathi 2001).

Sanjay Subrahmanyam and Chris Bayly (1988) have noted the 'portfolio' character of business operations with investors splitting their activities across multiple trades and ventures—different commodity markets, liens on land and other revenues, and manufacture of various goods. The strategy was based on hope that potential short-term super-profits in one activity could offset near-certain losses in others. It made India, quintessentially, the home of a merchant capitalism marked by complex and highly sophisticated financial institutions. But, in terms of industrial capitalism, it meant that India (before the colonial transition) never quite achieved the 'proto-' condition represented even by 'putting out' (pace Frank Perlin[2]).

Why India should have exhibited these characteristics is open to speculation on several fronts. Elsewhere, I have drawn attention particularly to ecological issues (Washbrook 2007). With tropical heat and long hours of sunlight, many parts of India were capable of very high levels of agricultural production, provided water could be found. However, water was a key problem: brought by vagarious and short-term monsoon winds and a Himalayan snow-melt of uncontrollable power. The issue was, in the main, not resolved by fixed investment in water-regulating and storage facilities, which may not have been technologically feasible in any event. (Even today, India has less than one-fifth the per capita water-storage capacity of China). Rather, in a context where new lands were still plentiful, it was resolved by mobility and exchange. Significant segments of the population were always on the move (taking their labour and 'light' capital with them), looking for water, work, and opportunities wherever they were found. Also, surplus production in one place was exchanged to supply deficit production in others—leading on to a logic of diversification and specialization in commodity production and skills (exemplified by the caste system). Here, I would disagree with Roy's characterization of the 'interior' economy as implicitly static: he may underestimate, for example, both the scale and the logic of the *banjara* caravan traffic, which discounted fixed costs against time.

Mobility and exchange undoubtedly gave capital opportunity for profit, not least from the dearth and famines created by climatic

---

2 While arguing strenuously for a 'proto-industrializing' model of early modern India, Perlin does not consider fully the crucial distinction between 'contracting' for finished goods and 'putting out' thread and tools (Perlin 1983).

instabilities. But the 'system' was not geared to nor dominated by the logic of profit and accumulation. Rather, it served the needs of subsistence and social reproduction in difficult circumstances. In effect, while there was a great deal of exchange, it was—in Polanyi's terms—less market than non-market exchange, governed by the principles of the 'community', on the one side, and the 'state', on the other (Polanyi 1944). This meant that capital had to bear very high risks in return for its profits. Not only did it face the familiar 'gamble on the monsoon', but it could be sequestered by the demands of the community to underwrite subsistence, and of the state to underwrite power. Such high risks further enhanced preferences for short-term and liquid over long-term and fixed forms of investment.

Nonetheless, and if not very adequate to the notion of capitalism, the 'system' served its primary goals quite well. Quantitative estimates of population and production for this era are precarious, and some (notably, those of Irfan Habib) have suggested virtual stasis and very low Malthusian 'ceilings' (as, of course, did Karl Marx with this Asiatic mode of production) (Habib 1985). But the most recent attempts at quantification suggest steady growth through the sixteenth and, especially, the seventeenth century, which was turned back by the disruptions of the early eighteenth century but starting to recover again by its end (Guha 2001). India may have supported a population 40–60 per cent higher in 1800 than it had in 1500.

Whether the ecological case is accepted or not, the evidence seems clear that merchant capital was institutionally weak. Roy notes this in terms of the difficulties of enforcing contract. He might also have noted it in relation to the character of property right. While, no doubt, it is true that private property right was recognized outside the authority of the state, it was not invested, in the first instance, in legal 'individuals'. Predominantly, it was vested in corporate or community groups of one kind or another (caste, clan, sect) who then 'shared' it among their members. At least over the course of the eighteenth century, these corporations did become partially penetrated by principles of commercial exchange and the shares partially made alienable and transferable for cash. However, this process was very partial: participants were still restricted by various forms of ascription and access to rights did not become universal. Moreover, all rights of this kind also brought obligations to invest in corporate activities (such as worship) and to maintain corporate assets. They were not unilaterally emancipated from community constraints (Roy and Swamy 2016; Washbrook 2007).

This reflected, in effect, a very distinctive type of state structure, which Frank Perlin (1985) once described as 'dualist'. Private rights over resources derived both from rulers' prerogatives above (classically as liens on the revenues) and from community prerogatives below (classically, as entitlements to 'share' in joint-property). Hopefully, the two came together in a compact to reinforce 'private' possession from both sides. However, this could be very 'hopefully'. The great Emperor Akbar, who brought the Mughal imperium to its apogee, himself faced no fewer than 278 revolts led by zamindars at the head of community organizations. Friction was endemic and *fitna* (division) built into the system (Wink 1986). In the course of the eighteenth century, this friction may have facilitated the strengthening of a claim to right that was more properly 'individual'. Habib (1965), for example, noted the tendency of holders of royal rights to try to make their possessions hereditary. (In South India, there was an expansion in forms of *inam* [tax immunity] right held not subject to the ability of either ruler or community to take back [Washbrook 1988]). Yet, very often, such rights were couched in terms of religious privileges, which scarcely made them easily transferable or alienable. The marketing of private property rights remained attenuated into the Company period—and, as Roy (2014) notes himself, actually for a considerable time afterwards.

What all this might be taken to suggest, as Patrick O'Brien strenuously argues in his *The Cambridge History of Capitalism* I chapter, is that market 'institutions' cannot be isolated from their contexts in wider political and state formations. He posits that Britain's premier role in pioneering the transition to MEG is inseparable from the aggressive policies that its state pursued in institutionalizing the dominance of capital (by crushing labour and community rights) at home and expanding the power of emergent national capital abroad through ruthless policies of mercantilism (O'Brien 2014). In a way (if elliptically), Parthasarathi's *Why Europe Grew Rich* would agree with him, in that, after rehearsing the many ways (in trade, technology, finance, and the like) in which the Indian economy at least matched Western European precociousness, he nonetheless accepts that the naval, military, and fiscal power of the imperial European state overcame an India whose indigenous versions could never match it in these dimensions (Parthasarathi 2011).

Admittedly, in the eighteenth century, there were signs that the Indian state was beginning to move in a similar direction itself. Whether derived endogenously from its politically induced collapse or exogenously from the pressure applied by the Europeans, the old Mughal imperium devolved towards the formation of regional states, much more compact and, in some cases, much better able to harness capital to the reproduction of state power. For a time, the likes of Mysore, the Peshwa's Maratha confederacy, and Ranjit Singh's Punjab gave the English East India Company a real fright. Internally, they sought to crush certain forms of 'community' privilege and constitute more universal forms of property right and capital under their own authority. Externally, they adopted strategies of Asian mercantilism (Bayly 1983; Sen 1977; Washbrook 1988; Perlin 1983; Yazdani 2017). Yet, having already given away to the Europeans the sea—the prime source of trade and specie metal—their efforts can be regarded as too little, too late. In many ways, they were reacting to, and imbricated in, an emergent global system of capital within which the Europeans, and especially the British, were already dominant (Washbrook 2004). For political reasons as much as anything else, India was never going to be an alternative to Britain as the founding location of MEG.

However, looked at from another angle, this does not mean that it played no role in that British-centred transition. The 'World-Systems' and 'Underdevelopment' theories of Wallerstein and Frank have not fared very well over the last 20 years (Frank 1967; Wallerstein 2011). Their insistence that the geographical distribution of wealth directed by the 'expansion of Europe' between the sixteenth and nineteenth centuries became structurally immoveable (except by revolution) appears undermined by the hyper-development of parts of Asia in more recent times. Nonetheless, these theories may still retain historical value in pointing out that, while industrialization and MEG may have 'broken out' originally only in a few small locations, they represented events of global significance not only in terms of their consequences, but also their causes. They happened in the context of long-term histories of contact, conflict, and exchange with other

parts of the world, which vitally shaped their possibilities and outcomes (Bayly 2004).

Viewed from this perspective, another way to understand India's
place in the history of capitalism is to consider its impact and influence on the development of Europe, and most obviously Britain,
between the sixteenth and nineteenth centuries. In *The Cambridge
History of Capitalism* II, Gareth Austin (2014) attempts this in a
chapter on 'Capitalism and the Colonies'. However, his eye mainly
falls on the post-1850 period (to which I shall return presently) and
he gives only a few hints about earlier trajectories. Yet these may be
worth spelling out because they suggest that the role of India may
have been strategically vital at various points.

Indian historiography, under nationalist prompting, generated
its own world-system/underdevelopment thesis, a century before
Wallerstein and Frank, in the venerable theory of 'The Drain'. Here,
it was surmised that Britain consistently drained India of its resources
through various payment mechanisms and that this contributed substantially to both British wealth and Indian poverty. Yet there have
always been a number of problems to specifying the thesis, precisely,
and calculating its effects. One such problem concerns separating out
the positive services which India may have received from investments/
policies/structures associated with the British Empire from payments
that reflected 'unrequited' flows and simple tribute extraction. The
very high figure for the drain given by Habib (1985) in an earlier
Cambridge Economic History of India (6–9 per cent of Indian GDP
annually across the bulk of the colonial period) is based on assuming
all payments and transfers to Britain to be negative costs without any
positive returns. Yet, economically, this would imply that India had
some kind of extra-market right to British-made goods and services
without having to pay at least a market price for them. Balachandran
(2003) has attempted a more considered re-calculation and puts the
element of (unrequited) drain at around 0.5–1 per cent of Indian
GDP—a considerable sum but hardly likely to make a key difference
between modernity and backwardness.

Nonetheless, if not in aggregate terms, the drain (and even 'legitimate' returns) from India may have played an important role, at certain key times, in sustaining British economic growth. There can be
little doubt, for example, that 'unrequited' payments from India were

at their height in the late eighteenth and early nineteenth centuries when Company power and private trade interests came together to create not only an empire but an orgy of looting. Indeed, the creation of a trade flow unrequited by shipments of bullion (and anything else) from Europe was an explicit goal of the Company from the seventeenth century and one reason for its driving interest in the Indian tax system (Marshall 1976).

Due to the hidden nature of private trade, we can only imagine the amount of 'loot' that came back to Britain. But the timing of its arrival is interesting: as Cuenca-Estaban has argued, it coincided with the 'crisis' in Britain's balance of payments caused by the Revolutionary and Napoleonic wars. According to Cuenca-Estaban (2007), inflows from India were crucial in sustaining Britain's international trading position through these difficulties—and, arguably, helping it defeat Napoleon with all that followed for the global economy. Also, it has long been held that, from the 1870s to the First World War, it was the surplus that Britain claimed from its trade with India that helped it balance a deteriorating deficit in trade with the rest of the world (Tomlinson 1979).

What impact any of this had on the history of capitalism as MEG is more difficult to assess. Many British historians would see the era of the Revolutionary and Napoleonic wars as also the era of the first Industrial Revolution. But how much the wealth of the 'Nabobs' contributed to it is largely conjectural: most of them were more interested in land and titles and, at least by the second generation, helped sponsor that 'gentlemanly capitalist' ethos that stultified Britain's ongoing industrialization (Cain and Hopkins 1986, 1987a, 1987b). No less, as Austin reflects, the trade surpluses that Britain gained from India in the later period were generated from near-captive markets for British industrial goods (notably textiles) sustained by imperial rule. In 1913, India took 25 per cent of Britain's total textile production. Yet it was precisely the possession of such near-captive markets that acted as a disincentive for further investment in technology, presaging Britain's economic decline later on. The role of empire in capitalism-as-MEG is not without ambiguities (Austin 2014).

However, in the case of India, there were also some very positive points of impact. In the seventeenth century, Indian textiles were part of that inruption of tropical crops and Asian manufactured goods that promoted the formation of the first national markets in Britain and sponsored the commercial revolution that some historians have seen as a precondition for later industrialization (McKendrick, Brewer, and Plumb 1982). Also, and more directly, fierce competition with Indian textiles, especially in markets such as that for West African slaves, led to early experiments in technology, such as the spinning jenny, to overcome superior Indian products (Austin 2014; Washbrook 1997). Britain's first industrially manufactured goods, of course, were imitation Indian textiles (and fake Chinese pots). It goes without saying that it took a great deal more by way of domestic economic, state, and political change in Britain to turn this competition to productive ends—and not see it either blunted by stronger protectionism or promoting 'de-industrialization', as happened in reverse to India in the mid-nineteenth century. Nonetheless, without the spark fired by the collision between India's then-advanced and Britain's then-backward textile industries, one wonders whether the 'revolution' introduced by technological innovation at this time would necessarily have happened.

It needs less speculation, however, to see the role played by India more generally in sustaining capitalism-as-wealth-accumulation in Britain in the nineteenth century. Davis and Huttenback (2009), somewhat notoriously, have performed an extended accountancy operation on the British Empire to show that its costs outweighed its benefits—especially because of the price of maintaining British naval supremacy. However, this scarcely applies to the Indian section of the Empire. Half of India's tax revenues were diverted into supporting an imperial army that sustained *Pax Britannica* east of the Mediterranean as a complement to the British navy, where the two fought together from Egypt in 1799 to Canton in 1839 to (if disastrously) Singapore in 1942. Britain maintained only a small land army and its military 'clout' outside Europe came largely from India (Washbrook 2012).

Also, India provided huge benefits by way of multilateral trades that do not show up on bilateral accountancy sheets. Even in the eighteenth century, India's key role was in supplying goods (preferably by unrequited means) to support everything from the West African slave to the China trades (where Indian opium, silver, and cotton were prime trade goods). Over the course of the nineteenth century, an estimated five million Indians migrated abroad: most as labourers to work in labour-deficit plantations and mines from the Caribbean to the Pacific, but some as key intermediary personnel in imperial governments and bazaars, from East Africa to Hong Kong. As India's trade with the rest of the world recovered in the later nineteenth century, most of its exports also went to areas outside the British Empire (for example, cotton to central Europe, leather to southern Europe), earning surpluses that then were 'creamed' by Britain with whom India ran a permanent (and artificially inflated) deficit. While precise figures can scarcely be calculated, India's reputation at the time as 'the jewel in the British crown' was not mistaken, and the British imperial economy itself would have been very poor without its many forms of support (Washbrook 2012).

It may well be that Wallerstein and Frank were wrong that the distribution of wealth in the global economy became fixed with the 'expansion of Europe'; and that Roy is correct in surmising that India in the 'long run' (that is, by today) has become a beneficiary of its sometime colonial connection. But it has been a very, very long run with much greater benefits on one side than the other; and the costs incurred by India along the way have not been inconsiderable.

Those costs also may show up in clearer form if, finally, we consider India in a history of capitalism cast in Marxist conceptual terms. Admittedly, a large part of the existing Marxist canon on India appears interesting more for its theological than its historical content: from discourses on an Asiatic mode of production, that bear little relation to anything empirically demonstrable about the past, to prognoses of a universal proletarianization that has plainly failed to happen. Marx's writings on India in his own time were also largely polemical. Nonetheless, Marx's conceptual tools may offer others ways into the subject, which look more promising. Here, the relationship between labour and capital is posited as the core of the capitalist process, its struggle the key to understanding possibilities and outcomes. That struggle, of course, is not 'merely' economic; rather, it is political and focused on labour's ability to retain a measure of control over its own reproduction—its sociability and even humanity—and prevent itself from meeting capital's objective of turning into a 'mere' factor of production.

In this light, what is striking about the pre-colonial Indian situation is not only the weakness of capital (as noted earlier), but also the strength of labour. Units of production, both in agriculture and manufacturing, were primarily organized around the household, which bound itself into larger corporate groupings through social ties of kinship, caste, and/or religious sect. Such corporate groupings protected access to land, the distribution of productive resources, and, crucially, the transmission of skills. The ruler's state and merchant capital could draw commodities and goods created by these corporate groups into wider systems of tribute and exchange. But only by providing important services to them and assuming a major part of the resulting risks, for example, by remitting revenues and accepting inferior goods at times of dearth. States had to offer protection and patronage which, if not forthcoming, could see artisans and even peasants moving away en masse to rivals who might provide it better. Rulers also offered, as did merchant capitalists, large advances of credit to independent producers in order to contract for their services and goods. However, these advances were scarcely recoverable in the event of calamity and, as noted earlier, the contracts could be repudiated simply by return of the advance. In effect, capital had very little direct control over production (far less, say, than was achieved in Europe through systems of putting out) but carried heavier risks for failure (Washbrook 2007).

As many historians, including Roy, have noted, the Europeans on the coasts—who long ago at home had crushed most non-voluntary corporations of labour and instituted draconian master–servant laws—regularly railed against a situation where they had limited means to control quality, price, and timing of delivery. Labour relations around the European enclaves were perennially turbulent, marked by strikes, boycotts, and riots (Parthasarathi 2001). But turbulence often also marked relations between labour and particular indigenous states and merchant capitalists, who never happily forewent revenues and profits and could periodically resort to the use of force (Washbrook 1988). Yet, short of the large-scale provision of public goods and fixed private investments, which never seem to have been attempted, it is hard to see what alternatives there were to conceding labour's price.

Moreover, in the short term, that price could be low, leaving room for profit and revenue surplus, if irregularly. Labour's price was closely related to its subsistence costs which, depending on factors such as climate, could be cheap. Also, costs were constantly being offset by the internal reproductory logic of 'community' institutions themselves. Household systems of production included the (self-exploited) labour of women and children for the price of a man; caste could be used to slash the price/subsistence expectations of the 'lowly', even if it also raised the costs of employing the 'high-born'. Transport systems, such as the self-breeding, openly grazing pack-bullock caravans of the banjaras or the wind-blown *dokie*s (barges) floating up and down the coasts, could carry goods almost for nothing, providing time was not a major consideration (Washbrook 2007). Rulers and attendant merchant capitalists were able to extract surpluses and make profits from the system, if never with great certainty.

Yet need for certainty is precisely what grew across the seventeenth and eighteenth centuries, leading to deepening political pressures. With ships to fill on tight sailing schedules, the Europeans found volatility increasingly irksome and profit-threatening. As Roy himself notes, there is a case that the Europeans were drawn towards the greater use of political force, and to strengthening long-standing dreams of sovereignty, by imperatives for better control of price, quality, and time—which meant reducing the privileges of labour (Roy 2014; Parthasarathi 2001).

Moreover, certainly in the eighteenth century, European expectations were joined by those of indigenous rulers and merchant capitalists-now-turned-bankers on a much larger scale (Leonard 1979). In the wars of succession following the weakening of the Mughal imperium, rival regional states needed to tighten their grip on cash flows to reproduce their increasingly mercenary military machines; and, as merchants turned bankers to finance wars (and gain greater liens on revenues), they needed steadier flows of tribute and profit to meet ever more urgent calls for loans and expenses (Bayly 1983). Further, of course, both regional rulers and merchant/bankers were by now heavily imbricated in European-carried commerce itself— the key to specie flows.

Viewed this way, the transformation of the Indian state system in the eighteenth century, and the growth within it of European power, can be seen as an (admittedly very complex) strategy of capital. As India was increasingly drawn into the circuits of global capitalism emerging from the sixteenth century, the independence of its artisanal and farmer producers, protected by powerful corporate walls, came under threat. Unsurprisingly, the eventual victory of the English East India Company was attended—as would seem broadly agreed upon—by a series of revenue and rental offenses through the imposition of deeper monopolies over many markets (such as that for textiles) and through the de-legitimation of many forms of corporate organization (such as lineage) before the regulations of the colonial law and state (Washbrook 2004).

At the same time, however, it would be a mistake to suppose the struggle between labour and capital ever simply won, by one side or the other, and the result a straightforward realization of the universal ideals of the modern/capitalist state—where the 'individual' becomes separated from corporate protection and subjected to the 'dominance' of a general rule of property through the state. The Company and, later, Crown state were well aware of the shallowness of their own political authority and, well before the 1857 Mutiny and Civil Rebellion, of the risks that they ran by directly confronting Indian sociability en masse. Also, they came to appreciate that they, too, faced a form of the same dilemma previously faced by Indian rulers and capitalists, namely, that without the provision of public goods and private investment on a massive scale, they also had to be reliant on the goods, services, and skills generated out of the older corporations of kin, caste, and sect, and could not afford entirely to dispose of them. It was never the remit of colonial rule to 'modernize' Indian society rather than just a few strategically important parts of it.

The result was the development of a peculiar species of capitalism under the colonial dispensation, which sometimes has defied attempts to be classified as any species of capitalism at all. For example, if patterns of class formation were traced, they would suggest less a process of proletarianization than one of petty bourgeoisification. The ownership of 'small' property massively proliferated, in both land and manufacture, as efforts were made to harness household units of production to new fields of resources. India possessed an expanding frontier of land settlement, in most regions, until the end of the nineteenth century as forest margins were cut back and petty agricultural production was established (Bayly 1989b). After a brief, if chronic, period of 'de-industrialization' in the middle decades of the nineteenth century, as the full impact of Britain's Industrial

Revolution was felt, artisanal production revived and became a lead-ing motor force of the industrial economy—which it still is (Haynes 2012). Over 80 per cent of 'industrial units' in India today employ less than 10 workers (Mazumdar and Sarkar 2008). Capital drew most of its profits from the self-exploitative logic of household pro-duction and from the differentials still imposed on social reproduc-tion costs by the influence of caste. What this also meant was that class *per se* emerged less directly as the axis of social exploitation and conflict than gender, generation, and (caste) race.

Above the household, colonial (and later national) laws did not seek to fully universalize either capital or the subject/citizen. Under Company rule, a thin legal realm was constructed that gave domi-nance over social reproduction to contract, debt, and the payment of taxation. But, elsewhere, issues such as the ownership, inheritance, and privileges of property were subsumed under 'personal' laws, specific to different communities and claiming to hark back to an Indian 'custom' that the courts pretended to maintain. In effect, the universal laws of capital were confined to Europeans and the colo-nial state; 'Indian' capital lived on in a realm of pseudo-tradition (Washbrook 1981).

Later in the nineteenth century, as the Indian economy was drawn further into global capitalism and Indian actors began to take a leading role, this started to change as Ritu Birla has seen. Efforts were made from the 1880s to construct a basis of implicit national law, affecting both Indian and European capital alike. However, the contradictions of the colonial situation limited their realization. In effect, community-specific institutions—such as the 'Hindu' joint family and the religious 'charitable' trust—became embedded in the structure of the new laws (Birla 2009). Also, the obligations of household and caste continued to influence the way in which the law dealt with social obligation. With modifications, this has continued down to the present day where India still does not have a single, unified code of civil law (Roy and Swamy 2016).

The implications for the structure of Indian capital have been many—which even its latter-day emergence as a motor force in the global economy have not altered. The celebrated Tata conglomerate now presides over a US 100 billion-dollar 'tea-to-cement' empire, serving inter alia as the largest single private employer in the United

Kingdom and the arbiter of the fate of the British steel industry. However, in structure, it is still a 'family firm' whose high rate of accumulation remains protected by religiously validated tax privileges: the majority of the stock in its principal 'holding company' (Tata Sons) is owned either by family members and affines or else by a charitable trust.

Until 20-odd years ago, the distinctive, neo-traditional structures of Indian capitalism frequently led to it being written-off as 'primitive' or 'antiquated' in comparison to the supposedly 'universal-modern' structures of Anglo-American business; just as institutions such as caste were associated only with economic backwardness. Strikingly, with India now the fastest growing economy in the world and its global reach widening, such judgements are being discarded. Caste, at the top, may be seen as promoting investment in, and the acquisition of, very high skills—as much in the Brahmin-dominated IT industry today as 'early-moderns' would have said in the artisan caste-dominated handicraft industries of yesteryear. Also, the degrees of 'trust' generated in family-based, kinship-based, and caste-based community organizations may be superior to anything actually obtainable in the real world under the universal laws of capital—as, not least, the recent global financial crisis has demonstrated.

But, no less on the labour side of the issue, these same community-based forms of organization permit the offsetting of labour's full reproduction costs against continuing subsidies provided by the discriminations of gender, generation, and caste, and they underpin an 'informal' sector, unprotected by workplace laws, which now covers 90 per cent of the labour force. In India, wealth has come to be accumulated and secured in the hands of a very narrow elite, entry to which is protected by various forms of social ascription—religion, caste, and family. However, and reciprocally, labour has been increasingly stripped of its share in the social product and seen its skills and security 'casualized' as its community institutions suffer ever more intensive battering and squeezing.

If this process is what actually produces the fastest-growing capitalist economy in the contemporary world, it leaves room for a provocative thought. Perhaps Anglo-Americana ought no longer to be regarded as providing the template for understanding the global history of capitalism, where its institutions can be seen now to represent redundant forms. Rather, the real character of 'late' capitalism suggests that the future could actually lie with economies like that of India, whose past, thereby, would acquire a quite different set of historical meanings.

Bibliography

Austin, Gareth. 2014. 'Capitalism and the Colonies.' In *The Cambridge History of Capitalism II*, edited by Larry Neal and Jeffrey G. Williamson. Cambridge: Cambridge University Press.

Balachandran, Gopinath. 2003. *India and the World Economy 1850–1950*. Delhi: Oxford University Press.

Barratt Brown, Michael. 1972. *Essays on Imperialism*. Nottingham: Spokesman Books.

Bayly, Christopher Alan. 1983. *Rulers, Townsmen and Bazaars: North Indian Society in the Age of British Expansion 1770–1840*. Cambridge: Cambridge University Press.

———. 1989a. *Imperial Meridian: The British Empire and the World 1780–1830*. London: Longman.

———. 1989b. *Indian Society and the Making of the British Empire*. Cambridge: Cambridge University Press.

———. 2004. *The Birth of the Modern World 1780–1914: Global Connections and Comparisons*. Oxford: Blackwell.

Birla, Ritu. 2009. *Stages of Capital: Law, Culture and Market Governance in Late Colonial India*. Durham, NC: Duke University Press.

Cain, P.J and A.G. Hopkins. (1986) 1987a. 'Gentlemanly Capitalism and British Expansion Overseas I and II.' *Economic History Review* XXXIX(4): 501–25.

———. (1986) 1987b. 'Gentlemanly Capitalism and British Expansion Overseas I and II.' *Economic History Review* XL(1): 1–26.

Crafts, Nicholas. 1985. *British Economic Growth during the Industrial Revolution*. Oxford: Clarendon Press.

Cuenca-Estaban, Javier. 2007. 'India's Contribution to the British Balance of Payments 1757–1812.' *Explorations in Economic History* 44(1): 154–76.

David, Lance E. and Robert A. Huttenback. 2009. *Mammon and the Pursuit of Empire: The Political Economy of British Imperialism 1860–1912*. Cambridge: Cambridge University Press.

De Vries, Jan. 2008. *The Industrious Revolution: Consumer Behaviour and the Household Economy 1650 to the Present*. Cambridge: Cambridge University Press.

Frank, Andre Gunder. 1967. *Capitalism and Underdevelopment in Latin America*. New York: Monthly Review Press.

Ghosh, Shami. 2015. 'How Should We Approach the Economy of Early Modern India?' *Modern Asian Studies* 49(5): 1606–56.

Guha, Sumit. 2001. *Health and Population in India from the Earliest Times to the Present*. London: Hurst Publishers.

Habib, Irfan. 1965. *The Agrarian System of Mughal India*. Bombay: Asia Press.

———. 1982. 'Population.' In *The Cambridge Economic History of India* I, edited by Irfan Habib and Tapan Raychaudhuri. Cambridge: Cambridge University Press.

———. 1985. 'Studying a Colonial Economy—Without Perceiving Colonialism.' *Modern Asian Studies* 19 (3): 355–81.

Harley, C. Knick. 2014. 'British and European Industrialization.' In *The Cambridge History of Capitalism I*, edited by Larry Neal and Jeffrey G. Williamson. Cambridge: Cambridge University Press.

Haynes, Douglas E. 2012. *Small-Town Capitalism in Western India 1870–1960*. Cambridge: Cambridge University Press.

Leonard, Karen. 1979. 'The Great Firm Theory and the Decline of the Mughal Empire.' *Comparative Studies in Society and History* 21(2): 151–67.

Marshall, Peter. 1976. *East India Fortunes: The British in Bengal in the Eighteenth Century*. Oxford: Oxford University Press.

———.1987. *Bengal: The British Bridgehead*. Cambridge: Cambridge University Press.

Mazumdar, D. and Sarkar, S. 2008. *Globalization, Labor Markets and Inequality in India*. London and New York: Routledge

McKendrick, Neil, John Brewer, and J.H. Plumb. 1982. *The Birth of a Consumer Society*. London: Europa Press.

Neal, Larry. 2014. 'Introduction.' In *The Cambridge History of Capitalism I*, edited by Larry Neal and Jeffrey G. Williamson. Cambridge: Cambridge University Press.

North, Douglass, C. 1990. *Institutions, Institutional Change and Economic Performance*. Cambridge: Cambridge University Press.

O'Brien, Patrick Karl. 2014. 'The Formation of States and Transitions to Modern Economies.' In *The Cambridge History of Capitalism I*, edited by Larry Neal and Jeffrey G. Williamson. Cambridge: Cambridge University Press.

Parthasarathi, Prasannan. 2001. *The Transition to a Colonial Economy: Weavers, Merchants and Kings in South India 1720–1800*. Cambridge: Cambridge University Press.

————. 2011. *Why Europe Grew Rich and Asia Did Not: Global Economic Divergence 1650–1800*. Cambridge: Cambridge University Press.

Perlin, Frank. 1983. 'Proto-industrialisation and Pre-colonial South Asia.' *Past&Present* 98: 30–95.

————.1985. 'State Formation Re-considered.' *Modern Asian Studies* 19(3): 415–80.

Polanyi, Karl. 1944. *The Great Transformation*. New York: Farrar and Rinehart.

Richards, John F. 1981. 'Mughal State Finance and the Pre-modern World Economy.' *Comparative Studies in Society and History* 23(3): 285–308.

————. 1987. *The Imperial Monetary System of the Mughal Empire*. Delhi: Oxford University Press.

Roy, Tirthankar. 2013. *An Economic History of Early Modern India*. London: Routledge.

————. 2014. 'Capitalism in India in the Very Long Run.' In *The Cambridge History of Capitalism I*, edited by Larry Neal and Jeffrey G. Williamson. Cambridge: Cambridge University Press.

————. 2015. 'Economic History of Early Modern India—A Response.' *Modern Asian Studies* 49(5): 1657–66.

Roy, Tirthankar and Anand V. Swamy. 2016. *Law and the Economy in Colonial India*. Chicago: Chicago University Press.

Sen, Asok K. 1977. 'A Pre-British Economic Formation in the Eighteenth Century.' In *Perspectives in Social Science* I, edited by Barun De. Calcutta: Centre for Social Science.

Stein, Burton. 1960. 'The Economic Functions of a Medieval South Indian Temple.' *Journal of Asian Studies* 19(2): 163–76.

————. 1985. 'State Formation and Economy Re-considered.' *Modern Asian Studies* 19(3): 387–413.

Subrahmanyam, Sanjay and C.A. Bayly. 1988. 'Portfolio Capitalists and the Political Economy of Early Modern India.' *Indian Economic and Social History Review* 25(4): 401–24.

Tomlinson, B.R. 1979. *The Political Economy of the Raj*. London: Macmillan.

Wallerstein, Immanuel. 2011. *The Modern World-System I*. Berkeley: California University Press. (New Edition).

Washbrook, David. 1981. 'Law, State and Agrarian Society in Colonial India.' *Modern Asian Studies* 15(3): 649–721.

————. 1988. 'Progress and Problems.' *Modern Asian Studies* 22(1): 57–96.

————. 1997. 'From Comparative Sociology to Global History.' *Journal of the Economic and Social History of the Orient* 40(4): 410–43.

————. 2004. 'South India: The Colonial Transition 1770–1840.' *Modern Asian Studies* 38(3): 479–516.

————. 2007. India in the Early Modern World Economy.' *Journal of Global History* 2(1): 87–111.

————. 2012. 'The Indian Economy and the British Empire.' In *India and the British Empire*, edited by Douglas M. Peers and Nandini Gooptu. Oxford: Oxford University Press.

Wink, Andre.1986. *Land and Sovereignty in India: Agrarian Society and Politics under the Eighteenth-Century Maratha Svarajaya*. Cambridge: Cambridge University Press.

Wong, R. Bin. 2014. 'China before Capitalism.' In *The Cambridge History of Calitalism I*, edited by Larry Neal and Jeffrey G. Williamson. Cambridge: Cambridge University Press.

Yazdani, Kaveh. 2017. *India, Modernity and the Great Divergence: Mysore and Gujarat (17th–19th Centuries)*. Leiden: E.J. Brill.

5

Mysore's Pre-colonial Potentialities for Capitalist Development and Industrialization

Kaveh Yazdani

What were Mysore's[1] pre-colonial potentialities for capitalist development and industrialization during the reigns of the Muslim rulers Haidar 'Ali (r. 1761–82) and Tipu Sultan (r. 1782–99)? Eric Mielants (2007: 124) argued that '[w]ithout the intervention of European capitalism, the indigenous development of capitalism [in India] would have been extremely unlikely.' However, David Washbrook (2007: 109) cautions that it is far less clear why India 'should have failed to make use of industrial technologies once they had been invented elsewhere and become notionally available to it'. In this chapter, it will be discussed whether Mysore's socio-economic trajectory during the second half of the eighteenth century possessed any leeway of moving towards an industrial take-off in the absence of

[1] Kingdom/sultanate of Mysore during the reigns of Haidar 'Ali and Tipu Sultan. Its capital at the time was Srirangapatna.

colonial rule. It is suggested that the South Indian sultanate was in a transitory stage, which left open the prospects of a successful shift towards industrial capitalism.

On the one hand, the image of isolated village communities permeating Mysore needs to be qualified, as a number of eighteenth-century Indian and Mysorean villages depended on outside goods and were far from being self-sufficient (Yazdani 2017: 116–220). Rural areas were partly monetized and a two-way flow of commodities was visible in some parts of the country. Commodity production for the market, as well as an increased level of division of labour, were important features of rural crafts and agricultural production. Significantly, levels of agricultural productivity in Mysore and advanced parts of Western Europe were roughly comparable. This was the basis for Mysore's advancements in the spheres of commerce and production (Yazdani 2017: 130–64).[2]

On the other hand, capitalist social relations in both the agricultural and manufacturing sectors of Mysore appear to have been in their formative stage. It would be delusive to assume that the mode of production was already capitalist. A market for landed property, essential for capitalist relations of production, seems to have been very rudimentary (Yazdani 2017). Mysore did not experience any consumer revolution and did not have elites who praised the logic of capital accumulation. By contrast, it is likely that Tipu's policy vis-à-vis segments of the indigenous merchants, the alienation of large numbers of Hindus, Christians, and even certain Muslim groups in the wake of Tipu Sultan's establishment of an Islamic theocracy, as well as the negligible support of secular education were wide-ranging impediments to the implementation of capitalist social relations.[3]

In this chapter, the focus will lie on issues related to wage labour and capitalist relations of production, Tipu Sultan's measures of semi-modernization, and possible state-related obstacles to the emergence of capitalism. Due to the lack of space, I will neither delve into aspects of agricultural productivity, regional market integration, the

[2] For agricultural productivity in comparative perspective, see also Sivramkrishna (2009, 2015) and Pingle (2017).

[3] For matters of education, see Yazdani (2017: 279–85). For the establishment of an Islamic theocracy, see Yazdani (2017: 308–36).

degree of monetization, mechanisms of *Smithian* growth, property rights, living standards, the class structure of society, and 'human capital', nor the administration and bureaucracy. However, commerce and Mysore's mercantilist policies will be partially examined.[4]

Wage Labour and Capitalist Relations of Production

In 1800, around 17–25 per cent of the agrarian population of South India consisted of agricultural labourers. While most of them were in a state of bondage, there were also hired labourers—showing that 'wage labour' was by no means absent in pre-colonial India (Kumar 1965: 181, 191).[5] In line with Aleksandr Ivanovich Chicherov, Eugenia Vanina (2004: 103–5) confirms that, between the sixteenth and eighteenth centuries, there is abundant evidence that well-off Indian artisans such as weavers did employ 'wage labourers'. Indeed, we might assume that the more advanced parts of Mughal India and its successor states had entered an early phase of a transition period. At the same time, we do not have satisfactory figures regarding the overall number of the hired workforce. The early-nineteenth-century Scottish observer, physician, and naturalist Francis Buchanan (1762–1829)[6] not only pointed out that 'a few weavers

---

[4] For these aspects, see Yazdani (2017: Chapter 2).

[5] Habib ([1995] 2002: 197) confirms that the landless labourers 'belonged to the menial castes, compelled to serve the interests alike of peasants and of superior cultivators, and forming therefore a vast rural semi-proletariat, maintained entirely through non-economic compulsion'. For the merchants' employment of 'wage labour' in plantations, workshops, and the like in pre-colonial India, see Chicherov (1971: 186–227). For the European Companies' engagement of 'wage labour' in India, see Chicherov (1971: 227–9).

[6] Buchanan is one of the most important contemporary witnesses because he travelled through a number of South Indian places (for example, Mysore, Canara, and Malabar) between April 1800 and July 1801 in order to enquire about 'the state of agriculture, arts, commerce; the religion, manners, and customs; the history natural and civil, and antiquities, in the dominions of the Rajah of Mysore' on the authority of the East India Company. He published the results of his research in 1807, in three volumes with more than 1,500 pages.

are rich enough to be able to make cloth on their own account, and of consequence sell it to the best advantage' (Buchanan 1807, Vol. 2: 240),[7] but he also indicated that there was a noticeable amount of landless 'wage-laborers' who received payments mostly in kind, but also in cash.[8] Moreover, Chicherov (1971: 220) has argued that the country's scale of sugarcane cultivation and production of sugar 'formed the foundation for the emergence of the capitalist manufacture in sugar production', while 'the owners of the manufactures conducted intensive capitalist commodity agricultural production on leased lands; which indicates the development of new, capitalist relations in agriculture' (Chicherov 1971: 222–3). He further put forward that in Bangalore, the economic hub of Mysore, as well as in Kolar and Hoskot, 'features of developing capitalist manufacture … stand out clearly also in the manufacture of indigo dyestuff', where about 25 'wage laborers' were 'simultaneously engaged for almost two months in bringing in the harvest and boiling the solution' (Chicherov 1971: 226). However, it can be misleading to propose that agrarian manufacturing was already capitalist as pre-capitalist modes of production still prevailed. Indeed, Asok Sen (1977: 80–1) has convincingly argued that Mysore's agriculture was not capitalist because a considerable degree of economic exchange—for instance, between cultivator and artisan—was still based on transactions in kind. However, it may be held that the allusion to 'wage labourers' in agriculture and manufacturing reflects the existence of some primary elements of capitalist development, as Mysore possessed a potential class of wage labourers that could have served the factories of an early stage of industrialization.[9] In fact, the presence of migrant,

---

[7] Significantly, Pavlov (1978: 57) points out that, in Mysore, the 'weavers never cultivated the soil nor did seasonal work for rich peasants'.

[8] In the work of Buchanan, there are various allusions to farmers who hired landless 'wage laborers' for both cash and kind. See, for example, Buchanan (1807: Vol. 1, 124–5, 134, 298, 405, 415; Vol. 2, 108, 217, 315–16, 525, 562; Vol. 3, 25, 36–7, 226, 298, 398).

[9] As Marx (1982: 453) pointed out: 'The simultaneous employment of a large number of wage-labourers in the same labour process, which is a necessary condition for this change, also forms the starting-point of capitalist production.' Most recently, Vries (2013: 426) has reasserted that Britain,

seasonal, or landless 'wage labour' and commodification of parts of the produce hints at the potentialities of capitalist social relations.[10] But since wage labour as such can be traced back to antiquity, the phenomenon per se does not say much about the overall potentialities towards industrial capitalism.[11]

As to Mysore's social relations of production, Buchanan encountered a private manufacturer who employed 12 workers to produce iron and steel at Ghettipura, near Magadi. Interestingly, the total sum paid to the labourers amounted to 1,300 *fanams*,[12] whereas the net profit of the owner accounted for 1,004 fanams, thus nearly as much as the 12 'wage labourers' employed. At another forge, there were 22 labourers. The duration of iron production depended on the particular furnace

---

'because of high wages of its proletarians, their permanent availability for and dependency on the labour market and the fact that they also depended on a market for their consumption—[was] a far more likely candidate for innovation in production and for industrialization than China or any other country in the world.'

[10] As a result, Marx's (1982: 478) argument that in India, 'most of the products are destined for direct use by the community itself, and are not commodities', needs to be qualified for a number of regions of *middle modern* (1500–1800) South Asia.

[11] In antiquity, as early as the third millennium BCE, there is evidence that wages were paid and labourers were hired (for example, in Ur, Babylon, Egypt, Achaemenid Persia, Greece, and the Roman Empire). See Silver (1995: 135–40); Bayat (1994: 189–91). For wage labour during the European Middle Ages, see Epstein (1991). In the case of India, Habib (2002: 264) argues that:

> A class of wage labourers would seem to have been created by the Indian caste system in antiquity.... The class of rural labourers in India did not thus 'appear ... sporadically' with money rent (Marx) but was already in full formation, since its original creation and continuance was due not to the operation of market ('economic') forces but to social or caste ('non-economic') compulsion. Conversely, the rich peasant accumulation even when it obtained a money/commodity form, rested on dominance over a subject (not 'free') proletariat. But money relations must have strongly reinforced this original 'non-economic' dominance, through intensifying differentiation among the peasantry.

[12] In Mysore, one fanam was the equivalent of about eight pence.

at hand and often amounted to between 8 and 10 months. However, some labourers—such as those of the forge in Doray Guda where 20 workmen were employed—worked during the whole year. Four forges operated year-round and during the four months of monsoon rain, they collected 'as much sand as a furnace can smelt in the remainder of the year' (Buchanan 1807, Vol. 1: 171).[13] In some iron forges, labourers and headmen were employed for at least eight months a year. As Buchanan (1807, Vol. 1: 175) observed, one of the privately owned smelting houses burnt 'thrice a day, for about eight months with 32 days each, without any allowance for holidays'. Concerning the labour force, there were four men who collected iron sand, six charcoal makers, four labourers at the smelting house, and six labourers in the forging house (Buchanan 1807, Vol. 1: 175). However, in a number of other districts such as Madhu-giri, Chin-narayan-durga, Hagalawadi, and Devaraya-durga, labourers only worked for four to six months and survived off odd jobs for the rest of the year (they worked as peasants, vendors of firewood, and so on). One of the privately owned smelting houses employed four bellows-men,[14] three men who made charcoal, and four women and one man who collected and washed the sand. With regard to steel, we know that in 1 of the 5 forges in the districts of Chin-narayan-durga and Devaraya-durga, 13 people were employed (Buchanan 1807, Vol. 2: 16–19; Vol. 3: 361–2). According to Buchanan (1807, Vol. 2: 21), there was

a head workman, who makes the crucibles, loads them, and builds up the arch; and four reliefs of inferior workmen, each consisting of three persons, one to attend the fire, and two to work the bellows. Each set therefore, in the working season, labours only four hours in the day; except every fourth day, when they must attend double that time. They are all cultivators; and in the leisure time which they have from the furnace, they manage their fields. There is also a proprietor, who advances all the money required, and who receives payment when the steel is sold.

In this region, the profit of the iron mine's proprietor probably amounted to merely 25 per cent of the value of output. Similarly, at

[13] See also Buchanan (1807: Vol. 2, 35–7; Vol. 3, 361).
[14] During that time, these professions were practiced mostly by men.

Chica-bayli-caray, 22 workers were employed at the two furnaces: 9 charcoal-makers, 1 ore digger, 1 buffalo driver, 1 ironsmith, 6 bellows-men, and 4 hammer-men. The owner obtained about a quarter of the total output (Buchanan 1807, Vol. 2: 16–19; Vol. 3: 361–2). Therefore, Ivanovich V. Pavlov (1964: 40) has argued that 'the great difference between the share of the owner and those of the ordinary workers and the primitive division of labour are indications of new rudimentary capitalist relations, and in particular show traits of an advance towards capital'. As a matter of fact, the division of labour of some of the forges and furnaces had reached a substantial level. Buchanan (1807, Vol. 1: 175, 177; Vol. 2: 440) listed collectors of iron sand, makers of charcoal, labourers at the *smelting house* and *forging house*, including bellows-men, hammer-men, head workmen, and the like that were paid in money and obtained between 6 and 12 fanams per season.

Interestingly, Chicherov has argued that the production of coloured glassware had reached such a high division of labour that it deserved the label of a capitalist cooperation. The geologist, botanist, and physician Benjamin Heyne (1770–1819) observed that 20 men were involved in the manufacturing of glass. The team of researchers under the pen name 'Saki' go even further than Chicherov and claim that glass production had reached the stage of a capitalist manufactory (Chicherov 1971: 209; Saki 1998: 486).

It is significant to note that there were well-off weavers who could afford to employ two to five servants to work for them. According to Buchanan (1807, Vol. 1: 216–17), the 'servants live in their own houses; but although paid by the piece, they are generally in debt to their masters, and are consequently bound in the same manner as the servants of the farmers'.[15] In South India and other parts of the subcontinent, some artisans who had accumulated sufficient money even became entrepreneurs. There is no statistical data available on the number of weavers who hired servants or became entrepreneurs. Nonetheless, we know that the Pattegars, for instance, who were among the wealthiest weavers of Mysore, employed a caste of dyers

---

[15] See also Buchanan (1807: Vol. 2, 264) and Ramaswamy (1985: 84). It is not entirely clear what is meant by 'servant', but it seems that they were something between wage labourers and bonded labourers.

(the *Niligaru*) in order to dye their yellow silk with indigo. Thus, according to Saki, the 'Pattegars advanced raw material to the Niliga dyers and obtained dyed silk from them. This brought the Pattegaras into a relation of what buyers-up had with producers' (Buchanan 1807, Vol. 1: 212–13; Chicherov 1971: 223; Saki 1998, Vol. 1: 481; Vanina 2004: 138).[16] Moreover, Vijaya Ramaswamy (1985: 84) points out that the 'weavers have themselves been given the title "Chetti" in some records. The title "Chetti" affixed to the names of weavers shows they must gradually have risen to the rank of merchants'.[17] This is significant, as Karl Marx (1991: 452) argued that 'the really revolutionising way' is when the producer becomes 'a merchant and capitalist, in contrast to the agricultural natural economy and the guild-bound handicraft of medieval urban industry'.[18] In the

[16] According to Saki (1998: 522–36), increased commodity production during the eighteenth century gradually dissolved the caste structure of Mysore.

[17] A Chetti is a 'member of any of the trading castes in S. India, answering in every way to the Banyans of W. and N. India'. It could mean 'shopkeeper', but generally signified 'merchant'. See Yule and Burnell (2006: 189–90).

[18] Pavlov (1964: 38–9) was of the opinion that 'well-to-do weavers employing hired workers often served merely as middlemen between the latter and the traders. Such relations retarded the advance towards higher forms of capitalist organization of production'. On the other hand, Tapan Raychaudhuri (1983: 24) argues that:

Parsee master-carpenter building ships for European companies with the help of hired labour represented the most advanced form of a manufacturing organization found in other industries as well. Not all artisans were dependent on dadni or controlled by merchants. In mid-eighteenth century Bengal there were affluent weavers employing their own capital who sold freely on their own accounts. In mid-eighteenth century Lucknow, the number of 'apprentices' so employed by a master printer of textiles could be as high as 500. It is not clear if they worked at home or in their masters' establishments. In the Kashmir shawl industry the large workshops containing up to 300 looms were in fact the property of master craftsmen (ustads) and four-fifths of the sales proceeds, net of cost, was distributed among the workmen, the fifth being the ustad's share. Some carpenters in Bengal

particular case of eighteenth-century Mysore, the aforementioned evidence relativizes Irfan Habib's (1969: 67) assumption (quoting Bernier) that, in Mughal India, 'in general in the various crafts there were only very few independent master craftsmen of any substance'. This is of special importance, since Habib (1969: 67) reminds us that enrichment 'might in time have enabled some weavers to expand their production by no longer confining it to the household but engaging apprentices and servants. This would have been an important development, possibly representing a step in the evolution of capitalism'. In addition to that, we have some evidence that merchants controlled the producers through the so-called *dadani* system. Merchants and intermediaries in parts of East, West, and South India not only made cash but also advancements in raw materials (Yazdani forthcoming). As Buchanan (1807, Vol. 2: 239–40) observed, in Nala-rayana-pallyam, 'native merchants frequently make advances for the cloth intended for country use. These persons endeavour to keep the weavers constantly in their debt; for, so long as that is the case, they can work for no other merchant, and must give their goods at a low rate'. In another passage, he reported that, some women 'receive the cotton wool from the merchants, and spin it for hire' (Buchanan 1807, Vol. 3: 317; Sen 1977: 101; Parthasarathi 2001: 60–1). There is also evidence for the advance of coarse cloth in early-nineteenth-century Gurumkonda (Cuddapah): 'Coarse cloth is manufactured by the inhabitants for their use and for the merchants, who buy the thread and employ them on hire' (Kumar 1965: 357). Regarding advances, Buchanan (1807, Vol. 2: 264) added that 'those who once get into the debt of a native merchant are ever afterwards little better than slaves, and must work for him at a very low rate'. Thus, in the particular case of Mysore, the dadani system, at the turn of the nineteenth century, was more similar to the English putting-out system than has previously been suggested. It is not unlikely that

---

and Bihar similarly hired workers and when the latter's number was sufficiently high, the proprietor of the workshop stopped working himself. The emergence of artisans as 'capitalist-entrepreneurs'— Marx's 'truly revolutionary way' in the transition from mercantile to industrial capitalism—was thus not absent from the Indian scene.

this process had already started during the reigns of Haidar and Tipu. Significantly, the weavers of Mysore not only produced high-quality cloth in cotton and silk, but also coarse and mediocre textiles for the purpose of everyday use. These were either exported or sold at weekly markets (Buchanan 1807, Vol. 1: 40, 207–26). As Heyne (1814: 83) pointed out, a few years after Tipu's overthrow, '[a] great deal of cloth is manufactured in different parts of the country, particularly about Bengalore; but little of it is exported. In case of a great demand for the European market, it might be obtained from this place in considerable quantity'.

Tipu Sultan's Measures of Semi-modernization

In the process of implementing capitalist social relations, the state played a crucial historical role as the mercantilist and protectionist policies in England made plain (Marx 1982: 873–940).[19] The late-eighteenth-century ruler of the kingdom of Mysore, Tipu Sultan, equally took some measures that were intended to enhance productivity and stimulate economic development. As Buchanan (1807, Vol. 1: 222) noted, wealthy weavers were encouraged to invest in textile manufacturing by dint of relatively low taxes levied on weavers who possessed more than two looms. Significantly, Pavlov (1978: 143) argued that the 'arrangement under which one owner had several looms was so wide spread that it was reflected in Mysore's tax legislation.... Thus, Mysore's tax policy encouraged the enlargement of weaving workshops'. The social stratification of certain artisans

[19] Regarding mercantilism, Vries (2013: 425) points out that historically there are '*more* examples of economies that first went through an initial phase of protectionism before they opened up and successfully competed on a global market'. Furthermore,

at least until the 1830s, and in several respects even longer, [Britain] was a fiscal-military, mercantilist and imperialist state.... Taxes were very high, as well as public debt. There was an extensive bureaucracy and a government that intervened quite often in economic affairs. Expenditures for the army and navy were staggering. The country was very protectionist and not exactly democratic (Vries 2013: 433).

apparently increased, as the '*Cuttery* [weavers] are more affluent than the *Puttuegars*, and these again are more wealthy than any other kind of weavers' (Pavlov 1978: 212–13).

Tipu was eager to introduce technological innovations in the sphere of mechanical engineering. This is crucial as industrial capitalism is unthinkable without these technological advancements. Tipu's war captive James Bristow mentioned 'the arrival of thirty artists from France ... with a view to instruct Tippoo's subjects in manufactures, and aiding this Asiatic ally of France with mechanical knowledge'.[20] The Company officer Captain William Macleod also pointed out that the 'Regular Infantry are armed like European Troops with Firelocks and Bayonets made in his own Country by the assistance of French Artificers, who have taught the Mysoreans many of the European Mechanical arts.'[21] Interestingly, Tipu was well versed in mechanical devices and it was reported that he had himself constructed a condensing engine (Yazdani

[20] AN: C/2/189: Isle de France le 7 ventose au 6eme de la République française, p. 264. In a newspaper article, Bristow mentioned that there were 32 artisans, consisting of founders, glass blowers, sugar bakers, china makers, watchmakers, broad cloth weavers, armourers, a surgeon, and a doctor. FSH: AFSt/M 2 A 2: 18: 'Escape from Captivity. Narrative given by Bristow, whose escape from Tippoos, Dominions, was mentioned in a former Calcutta Paper and who is now there', *Calcutta Gazette*, 30 June 1791. However, in his book, he reduced the number to 30 foreign artisans. See James Bristow (1793: 104). See also the following sources where the number of 30–33 French artisans residing in Mysore is given: Treguilly (1992: 584–5) and Gobalakichenane (1997: 87).

[21] TNSA: Military Sundry Book, Vol. 60 A (1783–4): Extract of a Letter from Tippoo Sultaun to Meer Moyeen ud Deen Cawn, sent to the Commissioners for their information, dated 19 November 1783, received on 28 November 1783, p. 184; TNSA: Military Sundry Book, Vol. 60 A (1783–4), Extract of a letter from Bangalore, dated 28 October 1783, p. 192; TNSA: Military Sundry Book, Vol. 60 A (1783–4), Military Sundries 101: William Macleod, Of Tippo's Military Force in October 1794, Selum 26 November 1794, p. 110. According to Colley (2003: 276), over 1,300 British troops and at least 2,000 EIC *sepahi*s (sepoys) were still alive in 1784, when they were rendered to the British after the peace treaty was signed.

2014: 107, 111). It is important to note that Mysore harboured a number of sophisticated machines. In 1794, Edward Moor, who served as captain of a contingent during the Third Anglo–Mysore War, reported that a machine was discovered in Bangalore that was driven by a pair of bullocks and could bore 50 muskets and a gun or 130 musket barrels at once. Another similar engine for boring cannons also existed and both the machines appear to have been French productions (Moor 1794: 479). However, these two machines were not the only engines employed in Bangalore. British Lieutenant Roderick Mackenzie (1794: 46), for instance, saw a machine, drawn from a French encyclopaedia that was capable of producing 'different samples of carabines, but very unequal in the bore'. Bangalore's pioneering stance in terms of machinery is also corroborated by the painter Robert Home who visited Bangalore in 1791. He pointed out that Haidar and Tipu 'established here a mint, a foundry for brass cannon, a machine for boring them, another for musket barrels, which will bore a hundred and thirty at once' (Home 1794: 2). In 1800, British Lieutenant-Colonel Alexander Beatson (1759–1830) found 11 large powder magazines, 11 armouries for making and finishing small arms, 2 foundries for cannons, and 3 buildings with machineries for boring guns and muskets in Srirangapatna (Beatson 1800: 139). Buchanan further observed a machine for watering fields *(Capily)* and a machine for raising water and removing 'superfluous water from the rice-grounds' *(Chakram, Yatam)* in different parts of the country (Buchanan 1807, Vol. 1: 46, 263, 294, 329, 341, 356, 365, 367, 369, 373, 400, 405; Vol. 2: 1, 45, 254, 299, 324, 402, 461–2; Vol. 3: 43, 45, 144, 146, 154, 356). Last but not least, other mechanical devices were equally in use like oil and sugar mills (Buchanan 1807, Vol. 1: 159–61, 340–2, 228).

Tipu relentlessly searched for additional astronomers, geomancers, physicians, as well as craftsmen (for example, carpenters and ironsmiths) who were able to produce muskets, cannon-pieces, matchlocks, clocks *(gharial)*, glass, chinaware, and mirrors for the purpose of bringing them to Mysore. He looked for specialists who could locate mines of sulphur, silver, and gold. Tipu even thought that he could obtain mineral coal in the Ottoman domain and instructed his officials to bring large quantities of 'stone coal' *(sang-i angisht)* along with them from Jeddah or Muscat, despite the fact that the sultan had access to forests and Mysore was capable of producing cheap charcoal. Most significantly, Tipu ordered his embassies in Turkey and France to engage four experts who were willing to come to Mysore in order to explore the presence of coal ores (Husain 2001: 26, 32–3, 36–7, 42, 53 [3b, 16b, 6b, 7a–b, 52b, 10b, 11b, 61b]; Ali 1982: 137).[22] Therefore, Irfan Habib is of the opinion that 'Tipu was … perhaps the first Indian potentate (if not the first Indian) to apprehend the value of coal and try to obtain it' (Habib 2001: xiv; Husain 2001: 23). With regard to watches, it is significant to note that they seem to have played a practical purpose for time management among government officials. In his *Regulations*, Tipu even ordered every *'amil* (head of a district) to entertain a *sarraf* (banker) and a clock (Section 102).[23] Although we hardly know anything about Mysore's capacity of clock production, the order that every *'amil* was to entertain a clock suggests

---

[22] As Parthasarathi (2011: 11) points out, in India, 'the abundance of wood meant that there was no need to experiment with coal and the exploitation of its sizable deposits would await the nineteenth century'. This argument had already been put forward by Qaisar (1982: 81–2). However, we should also bear in mind that, in England, wood scarcity alone does not explain the application of fossil energy. Warde (2009: 9) points out that 'by the early 18th century, over half of the energy consumed in England was supplied by coal'. As Vries (2012: 639–64, 649) emphasizes, 'Britain was already experimenting with new ways of producing energy when population pressure still was quite low. Wood scarcity was often a problem because demand was so high, *not* because supply was so low.' See also Nef ([1988] 1998).

[23] IOR: H/251: Translation of Regulations of Tippoo Sultaun for the Management of his Country: directed to the Aumils and Serishtadars now in office as well as those who may hereafter be employed in the District of Raicottah subordinate to the cutcherry of Bangalore (by Francis Gladwin), dated the first of the month Ahmedy of the year Delow, in the hand writing of Hassan Moonshy, writer to Lallah Gobindroy, employed by the Dewan of the royal Cutcherry. These regulations contained 125 clauses. Henceforth: 'Regulations' (Raicottah). As Landes (1998: 49) reminds us: 'The clock provided the punctuation marks for group activity, while enabling individuals to order their works (and that of others) so as to enhance productivity. Indeed, the very notion of productivity is a by-product of the clock'.

that at least some of Tipu's administrators must have used clocks for organizational purposes.[24]

Tipu's courtier Mir Hussein 'Ali Khan Kirmani (1864: 83, 286) also indicated that scissors, penknives, clocks, and daggers were manufactured in Mysore.[25] Interestingly, we know that two master clockmakers from Paris (Mr Debay and Mr Sandor Gendre) settled in Mysore in 1788 (Yazdani 2017: 295).

Obstacles to the Emergence of Capitalism

In Mysore, there were a number of barriers in terms of the emergence of capitalism as the dominant socio-economic system. According to Asok Sen (1977: 80–1):

---

[24] Lucas confirms that: 'Clocks in the form of public church and tower clocks became fairly widespread from the fourteenth century in European towns and cities and, until the mid-eighteenth century, this was most people's experience of clocks.' Significantly, pre-colonial Indian towns and cities do not seem to have had any public clocks. However, Lucas (2005: 75) also points out that, in Europe,

> it was only in the later eighteenth and nineteenth centuries that domestic or interior clocks became at all common in middle-class and, later, working-class homes, as well as inside public rooms such as taverns or workshops. It was only at this time, it has been suggested, that using clocks as time-reckoning developed among the majority of the population. Prior to that time, clocks were simply used as time indication.

[25] Significantly, it seems that mechanical clocks had not been built during the Mughal period. See Habib (1969: 62). According to the late seventeenth-century observer Ovington (1696: 281), the reason was that Indians 'seldom continue their just Motions for any long time, by reason of the Dust that flies continually in the Air, which is apt to clog and stop the Wheels'. According to Ovington's contemporary Bowrey (1993: 195), Indians 'have invented a very good method' for reckoning time themselves, most probably referring to water clocks. With reference to Kirmani, Chicherov (1971: 188) claims that 'Hyder Ali established a karkhana which incorporated also [sic] weaving establishments employing hired weavers, who did not own means of production.' This is a false statement, as Kirmani did not mention whether the labourers used their own tools or not.

despite the provision of adequate usufructuary rights for the cultivators, of the rights of sale and transfer of lands, the farming system came to crystallize in a pattern of counter-dependence between the farmers and the state, again a pattern not appropriate to the emergence of private property free from the overriding constraints of politics and religion ... the agrarian economy yet lacked the conditions for the rise of a class that had the motive and capacity to achieve complete autonomy of wealth-making along the lines of capitalist development. The logic of private wealth-making was still not built into a prime concern for increasing the share of surplus accumulation. A system of produce-sharing and its widespread acceptance could not but act against the logic of such unhindered accumulation ... except for the sole institution of *Inamkutcodukee*,[26] almost all other means and instruments of implementing his [Tipu's] policies were laid in the efficiency of statecraft and an ever-expanding bureaucracy. Neither his traditional context, nor his own individual talent could take cognizance of the limits of those means and instruments, in the absence of autonomous social forces coming to be in accord with the economic goals of the Sultan's policies.

Furthermore, he argues that:

the mercantile economy of Tipu Sultan aimed mainly at a combination of the functions of the merchant and sovereign and did very little to ensure the liberation of the society's sphere of economic activity from the authority of the state and bureaucracy. Time and again,

---

[26] *In'am* land was rent-free land that used to be in the hands of mosques and Hindu temples. During Tipu's reign, a considerable amount of this land seems to have been confiscated either to be used productively or as a substitute for the wages of government officials.

Inamkutcodukee was rent-free land assigned to landlords or merchants who were willing to privately finance the construction or repair of tanks, wells, ramparts, forts, and the like or even provide for the expenses of populating a village. The existence of this assignment is affirmed by Buchanan (1807, Vol. 3: 453–4) who wrote that:

When a rich man undertakes at his own expense to construct a reservoir for the irrigation of land, he is allowed to hold in free estate *(Enam)* and by hereditary right, one-fourth part of the lands so watered.... The Tanks to which there is a person of this kind are notoriously kept in better repair, than those which the government supports.

economic activity was directly subordinate to political and military interests. Indeed, the whole framework of Tipu's land revenue and commercial systems ... was laid in elaborate provisions for bureaucratic control, restrictions, exclusive privileges and prohibitions. Needless to say, such policy directions would not be compatible with the long term interests of trade and industry, nor with the preparation of the society and economy for the making of an industrial revolution under the aegis of capitalism. (Sen 1977: 95)

Nonetheless, we should bear in mind that Tipu's economic policy not only increased agricultural growth, but connected the country to new markets and generated trading incentives for foreign merchants. Moreover, the diminishing liberties of indigenous merchants and the 'bureaucratic control, restrictions, exclusive privileges and prohibitions' were also intended to weaken the British and their allies. It potentially could have been a temporary policy that would have ceased with the defeat of the British. At the same time, what was crucial for the occurrence of an industrial revolution was not so much the level of circulation but the pivotal transition from mercantile to industrial capital. The state, as the principal merchant—not unlike the private economy—was also capable of moving from the sphere of circulation to production as soon as the socio-economic conditions were ripe for an industrial breakthrough. Accordingly, theoretically speaking, a categorical denial of Mysore's potentialities for a sort of industrialization is not a well-sustained hypothesis. It has been debated whether eighteenth-century India and Mysore, in particular, could have triggered an indigenous industrial revolution without colonialism. The most powerful rejection for the possibility of an autonomous process of industrialization in Mysore has been presented by Asok Sen. In his own words, the

most prominent obstacle, speaking generically, was the absence of forces and perspectives to work for the emergence of civil society and the whole complex of individualization of property and socio-economic change.... Whether in respect of agriculture, or that of trade and industry, Tipu's means of striking an advance could not go beyond the elaborate manipulations of statecraft which continued and even accentuated the stranglehold of politics and bureaucracy on the processes of appropriation and use of economic surplus. (Sen 1977: 103)

However, Sen conflated industrial capitalism with industrial revolution. Conversely, there is reason to assume that an industrial take-off can be achieved along non-capitalist lines and without the presence of strictly capitalist social relations of production.[27] In Sen (1977), we hear the echo of Irfan Habib (1969: 33) who—more than 50 years ago—argued that 'for all societies other than those of our own day, the only possible road to modern industry lay through capitalism'.[28] The analysis at hand, however, suggests that Mysore was in a transitional phase, implying that the possibilities for a more or less home-grown process of industrialization were open—all the more if the tools, machines, and innovations of the British Industrial Revolution would have become available. Indeed, an indigenous state-led process of forced industrialization could have been possible in the absence of colonial intervention, albeit later, when the socio-economic circumstances would have been ripe for such a transition. As the cases of Belgium, Germany, Japan, Russia, and China have demonstrated, a state-centred transition towards modern economic growth is feasible without the necessity of imitating the exact trajectory of the British Industrial Revolution. As a matter of fact, in countries such as Belgium and Prussia, the state played a crucial role in the industrialization process.[29] Even Sen, who has vehemently rejected that Mysore could have experienced an industrial breakthrough in the absence of British colonial rule, has admitted that Germany, Russia, and Italy attained industrial growth 'through state-sponsorship, support and control, rather than through the establishment of bourgeois social hegemony' (Sen 1977: 106). In short, Mysore's agrarian, commercial, manufacturing, military, technological, bureaucratic, and overall economic dynamism opened a window and fed the transition

[27] For a process of forced industrialization along non-capitalist lines, see Bahro (1977). Wrigley (1998: 115) even went as far as claiming that, historically, the connection between capitalism and industrialization was casual rather than causal.

[28] Sen was also influenced by Avineri (1968: 154), who argued that for Marx, capitalism was a precondition for the emergence of industrialization. Thus, he wrote that 'the industrial revolution for Marx is not the beginning of the capitalist process, but rather its culmination'.

[29] For a short overview, see Parthasarathi (2011: 248–51).

towards a possible new socio-economic order—which, in the long run, could have stimulated an indigenous industrial revolution. But due to short, as well as long-term socio-economic, techno-scientific, and institutional advantages in Western Europe and Northeast Asia, an industrial breakthrough was more likely to occur in advanced regions of eighteenth-century Britain, the Netherlands, and even France and China.

Tipu tried to restrict the personal gain of local merchants and his state monopolies undermined their commercial opportunities. He also took punitive measures against those merchants who collaborated with his enemies and posed a threat, most notably to segments of the Mappilas and Jewish traders.[30] However, despite the obvious disadvantages of independent merchants that were not under the auspices of the state, the weakening of their economic stance should

---

[30] As Buchanan (1807: Vol. 2, 420) noted: 'About fifty years ago the *Moplays* of this place were very rich, and possessed vessels that sailed to *Surat, Mocha*, Madras and Bengal; but the oppression of *Tippoo* has reduced them to great poverty.' The principal merchants of Canara told him that under Tipu 'the merchants suffered terrible oppressions, and that under his government the greater part of them were ruined' (Buchanan 1807: Vol. 3, 58). Das Gupta (1967: 107, 114) has noted that the Jewish merchant of Calicut, Isaac Surgun, was compelled to pay Rs 40,000 as a fine to Tipu in 1788 and was placed under house arrest. According to Guha (1985: 104–5), 'there is no doubt evidence to prove that during the 1770s he [Tipu] made the Jewish merchants of Calicut disgorge a large share of their wealth; but we must not forget that they had largely built their fortunes as agents of those very European Companies who the Sultan had chosen to attack.' By and large, the mercantile class of Mysore seemed less developed than in other parts of India like Gujarat and Bengal. Even Saki (1998: 450), who has emphasized the favourable conditions of merchants in late-eighteenth-century Mysore, has admitted that the

> merchant class of inland Karnataka ... was economically still a weak force....
> This weakness as a class was reflected in its ignorance of overseas markets and trade prospects, in its weak capital base, in its almost non-existent infrastructure in terms of possession of ships, almost no skilled manpower to man the sea-borne vessels and convey the merchandise, and the inability to project its state power across its frontiers in order to safeguard it from colonial piracy.

not be exaggerated. In contrast to public servants and soldiers of the Mysore army, native merchants could generally travel within the country without holding passes ('Mysorean Revenue Regulations' [1793] 1795: 31 [Section 55]). What is more, apart from the trade in state monopolies,

> they might deal freely in all others, without let or hindrance from the *Asofs* [civil governor], who, on the contrary, were directed to be aiding to them in their commercial pursuits. No other persons ... were, on any account, to be suffered to exercise the same free trade. The several *Asofs* and *Aumils* ['amils], throughout the country, were allowed to employ their own property in trade; and were, moreover, exempted from the payment of duties. (Kirkpatrick 1811: xlvi–xlvii)

In fact, we know of a few wealthy merchants during Tipu's reign. Buchanan (1807, Vol. 3: 87) reported that the 'principal merchant is *Murtur Sangaia*, a *Banijigar*, who lives at *Hara-punyahully*, but has factories in every part of the peninsula'.[31] He also mentioned a Muslim called Mousa, who was the principal merchant of Tellicherry and a man of 'immense wealth' (Buchanan 1807, Vol. 2: 420, 530, 532).

Tipu also founded new bazaars or market towns (Buchanan 1807, Vol. 1: 301). Armenian merchants were equally allowed to trade freely without having to pay duties and possessed full freedom of movement, in case they were willing to first sell their goods to the government at a 'fair price'. Tipu was especially interested in their silk stuffs and was willing to provide the merchants with a residence and labourers.[32] Tipu also held *kothi*s (trading houses) outside of Mysore in order to purchase and sell goods and commodities. The merchandise was brought to the kothis of the merchants and hire

---

[31] Buchanan did not indicate what kind of factories Sangaia was running.

[32] Kirkpatrick noted that it is not clear from which country these Armenian merchants came from. See Kirkpatrick (1811: 192, 467) and Qadir (1968: 15). Since pre-Mughal times, Armenians were trading with India and especially during the reign of Akbar, they increasingly settled down in the capital, where their first church was built in 1582. As early as 1666, Armenians lived in Madras. See Neill (2004: 384, 387).

charges were paid to them, while government officials and soldiers were in charge of supervising the trading houses. There were two kothis in each Kutch and Muscat, one at Hormuz, and one located at Jeddah (Husain 2001: 52; Kirkpatrick 1811: 192, 189xci).[33] According to Mohibbul Hasan (2005: 345), 'efforts were made to establish factories at Aden, Bushire and Basra, but without success. It was, however, the factory at Masqat, established in 1785, that was most important, because it was through this that exports from the Mysore kingdom were distributed over the Persian Gulf, and imports from the Persian Gulf were brought to Mysore.'

What is more, Tipu employed 'bankers' in those places, where his bills of exchange were accepted. Tipu himself accepted the bills and they seem to have been the main medium of payment, especially when it came to high sums (Gopal 1971: 101–2; Kirkpatrick 1811: 7, 77, 183–4, 194). From 1793 onwards, Tipu planned to expand the number of trading houses up to 30 within his own dominions and up to 17 outside his territory (all within the Indian subcontinent except for one in Muscat) (Kirkpatrick 1811: xli, xliii).[34] Colonel Wilks believed that, at the end of Tipu's rule, 'every respectable Soucar and merchant was plundered of all his visible property, and the greater numbers were absolutely ruined' (Wilks 1805: 39). Even though this statement may be exaggerated, it is likely that Tipu's policy vis-à-vis segments of the indigenous merchants was a serious setback with respect to the implementation of capitalist social relations. As long as Tipu opposed the emergence of a powerful and autonomous merchant class, Mysore would be dependent on outside support in order to modernize. However, a self-supporting and dynamic process of modernization was hardly feasible without

[33] IOR: H/472: John Duncan to the Right Honorable Richard Earl of Mornington, Surat Castle, 25.5.1800, 427. The kothis at Kutch (at Mundhi and Mundra) were established in 1789 and had a staff of 7 *daroghas* (chief officers, superintendents, or heads of a customs or excise station) and 150 sepahis. See Hasan (2005: 344).

[34] Tipu's officers were 'to be instructed to purchase and send hither all the rare and curious productions of those countries, which on arriving here, are to be sold [on our account or for our benefit]. In like manner are the rarities and commodities of this country to be sent to the aforesaid factories and there sold [on our behalf].' See also Habib (1999: xxxii).

an independent mercantile community. Since there were no other powerful social forces and hardly any notable personalities in court or the bureaucracy who seem to have shared Tipu's economic impetus and overall vision, the whole process of semi-modernization stood on shaky ground (Sen 1977: 102). The following remark by Tipu's envoys reveals the absence of a local bourgeoisie within his domain:

> We are not surprised that the king of France has rich and powerful noblemen at his court. But we are astonished that there are rich and grand merchants of the status of M. Réveillon, a trader in wallpaper. What a source of riches in France! A banian of France is worth a raja in India. M. Réveillon's well-organized manufacture is like a small province. He is its governor and his workers its inhabitants. M. le gouverneur has his palace, gardens and grove there, where he gave us a reception fit for a prince. (Lafont 2000: 175, note 75)

This stood in sharp contrast to the developments in seventeenth- and eighteenth-century Gujarat, the northwestern Indian province that harboured one of the most affluent and powerful merchant communities of its time (Yazdani 2017: Chapter 3).

***

Mysore's economic structure was based on a partly monetized and commercialized pre-industrial market economy. This is quite notable, as the entirety of Haidar's and Tipu's rule was steeped in military conflict and warfare, apart from short periods of relative peace, as for example, between 1769 and 1780 (Fullarton 1787: 62–3).[35] Although many hired workers in Mysore possessed their own tools, well-off artisans, such as weavers, employed 'wage labourers', alluding to the potentialities for the emergence of rural capitalist social relations. Significantly, not more than 45 per cent of the population of Canara—a region where urban commodity production was less developed than in other parts of the country—were pure cultivators

---

[35] For the military establishment of the sultanate of Mysore, see also Yazdani (2019b).

(Yazdani 2017: 125). Haidar and Tipu increased their commercial ties with both Indian and foreign (especially West Asian) countries— reflected in Tipu's establishment of new trading houses and his favourable treatment of foreign merchants. By dint of *Etatization*,[36] state ownership of the means of production, the reorganization of the administration (including the military establishment and centralization via the decimation of the *poligars*[37] and zamindars), the substitution of hereditary positions by state officials, the destruction of the traditional mercantile community, the monopolization of key commodities, and the establishment of a state-run bank, Haidar and particularly Tipu and the bureaucratic class he created rose to the position of the country's principal merchants (Yazdani 2017: Chapter 2, Section 2.2). With the consolidation of their power, they managed to increase public revenue, weaken the British East India Company, and stimulate the economy.[38]

Mysore possessed a vibrant textile sector for the purpose of both luxury and 'mass consumption'. State allowances and incentives (for example, tax exemptions) further enhanced the production of textiles. Commodities were generally destined for the home market. Importantly, most of the weavers did not pursue other occupations and well-off weavers could afford to hire servants, while some even succeeded in becoming merchants. The production of blankets, leather goods, sugar, and oil were also part and parcel of the manufacturing sector. There were private cooperations and manufactories, as well as state-led *karkhanas* (manufactories) for the production of glass, paper, carriages, gunpowder, ships, and metal goods such as steel wires, cutlery, boilers, coins, and tools (for example, agricultural implements, chisels, nails, scissors, horse-shoes). In state-led karkhanas, a centralized economic development programme that was partly based on coercion and force was pursued by Tipu Sultan. Iron and

[36] Etatization stands for the process of 'nationalization' of non-governmental lands, commerce, goods- and commodity-producing units, the bureaucracy, military establishment, institutions, and the like before the advent of nation states.

[37] Poligars refers to a sort of landlord or warlord with the hereditary right to collect revenues.

[38] For the increase of revenue, see Yazdani (2017: Chapter 2, Section 2.3).

steel production heavily increased during his reign and the greater share of it was used for the manufacture of weapons (for example, flintlocks, cannons, rockets, and so on). These were produced with boring machines and were either almost on par with European products (in the case of muskets and cannon) or even more advanced (in the case of rockets) (Yazdani 2017: Chapter 2, Sections 2.2.5 and 2.5).[39] While, European furnaces, techniques, and tools were more efficient, Mysore's steel was apparently superior to anything known in Europe during the early-nineteenth century. Forges were generally run by private entrepreneurs and there is evidence that some of them realized considerable profit. They paid many of their workers in cash, and in a number of cases, the degree of labour division was of substance, while rudimentary capitalist relations of production emerged. Besides boring machines, other mechanical devices like machines for watering fields, raising and removing water, and oil and sugar mills were also fabricated. Significantly, between 200 and 400 British prisoners of war and more than 30 French and other European artisans were either engaged or forced to work in the production of weapons and other commodities in late-eighteenth-century Mysore (Yazdani 2014: 106; 2019b). Indeed, the recruitment of foreign artisans helped to leapfrog certain stages of technological development. Although mainly military, it reflected both Mysore's 'privileges of backwardness' and the indigenous potentialities of capitalist development.[40] Apart from that, it is noteworthy that even mechanical watches were produced in late-eighteenth-century Mysore. Actually, clocks had to be employed by the 'amils of the

[39] For the production of rockets, see Yazdani (2017: Chapter 2, Section 2.5; Yazdani 2019b).

[40] As Trotsky (2008) explained, a 'backward country assimilates the material and intellectual conquests of the advanced countries.... The privilege of historic backwardness—and such a privilege exists—permits, or rather compels, the adoption of whatever is ready in advance of any specified date, skipping a whole series of intermediate stages.... The development of historically backward nations leads necessarily to a peculiar combination of different stages in the historic process. Their development as a whole acquires a planless, complex, combined character.... Under the whip of external necessity their backward culture is compelled to make leaps.

country (*Regulations*),[41] which suggests that they had a clear organizational purpose. At the same time, they were not produced on a large scale, indicating that the organization of production was still in a rudimentary stage of development. All this suggests that—similar to other advanced parts of eighteenth-century Western Europe and South and East Asia—Mysore too was in a transitory phase of socio-economic development, possessing both promising potentialities and significant impediments for the emergence of modern economic growth. Whereas Mysore's trajectory was certainly less capitalist than of the Netherlands, England, and Gujarat, an indigenous state-led process of forced industrialization in the absence of colonial intervention cannot be ruled out, given the sultanate's pervasive measures of centralization and semi-modernization throughout the second half of the eighteenth century.

Bibliography

Unprinted Primary Sources

Archives Nationales (AN): C/2/189.
Frankesch-Hallesche Stiftung (FSH): AFSt/M 2 A 2: 18.
India Office Records, British Library (IOR): H/251; IOR: H/472.
Tamil Nadu State Archives (TNSA): Military Sundry Book, Vol. 60 A (1783–4); Military Sundries 101.

Printed Primary and Secondary Sources

Ali, Sheikh B. 1982. *Tipu Sultan: A Study in Diplomacy and Confrontation.* Mysore: Rao and Raghavan.
Avineri, Shlomo. 1968. *The Social & Political Thought of Karl Marx.* Cambridge: Cambridge University Press.
Bahro, Rudolf. 1977. *Die Alternative: zur Kritik des real existierenden Sozialismus.* Köln: Europäische Verlagsanstalt.
Bayat, Assef. 1994. 'Historiography, Class, Iranian Workers.' In *Workers and Working Classes in the Middle East: Struggles, Histories. Historiographies,* edited by Zachary Lockman. Albany: State University of New York Press.

---

[41] IOR: H/251: Translation of Regulations of Tippoo Sultaun..., p. 253.

Beatson, Alexander. 1800. *A View of the Origin and Conduct of the War against Tippoo Sultann*. London: W. Bulmer and Co.

Bowrey, Thomas. 1993. *Geographical Account of Countries Round the Bay of Bengal: 1669–1679*, edited by R.C. Temple. New Delhi: Asian Education Services.

Bristow, James. 1793. *A Narrative of the Sufferings of James Bristow*. London: J. Murray.

Buchanan, Francis. 1807. *A Journey from Madras through the Countries of Mysore, Canara and Malabar*, 3 Vols. London: Cadell.

Chicherov, Aleksandr Ivanovich. 1971. *India—Economic Development in the 16th–18th Centuries*. Moscow: Nauka.

Colley, Linda. 2003. *Captives*. New York: Knopf.

Das Gupta, Ashin. 1967. *Malabar in Asian Trade, 1740–1800*. Cambridge: Cambridge University Press.

Epstein, Steven A. 1991. *Wage Labor and Guilds in Medieval Europe*. Chapel Hill: University of North Carolina Press.

Fullarton, William. 1787. *A View of the English Interests in India: And an Account of the Military Operations in the Southern Parts of the Peninsula, During the Campaigns of 1782, 1783, and 1784. In Two Letters; Addressed to the Right Honourable the Earl of *********, and to Lord Macartney and the Select Committee of Fort St. George. By William Fullarton of Fullarton, M.P.F.R. SS. of London and Edinburgh, and Late Commander of the Southern Army on the Coast of Coromandel*. London: T. Cadell.

Gobalakichenane, M. 1997. 'La Revolucion Française des Tamouls de Pondichery (1790–1793).' PhD dissertation, University of Nantes, France.

Gopal, Mysore Hatti. 1971. *Tipu Sultan's Mysore: An Economic Study*. Bombay: Popular Prakashan.

Guha, Nikhiles. 1985. *Pre-British State System in South India Mysore 1761–1799*. Calcutta: Ratna Prakashan.

Habib, Irfan. 1969. 'Potentialities of Capitalistic Development in the Economy of Mughal India.' *Journal of Economic History* 29(1): 32–78.

———. 1999. 'Introduction: An Essay on Haidar Ali and Tipu Sultan.' In *Confronting Colonialism: Resistance and Modernization under Haidar Ali & Tipu Sultan*, edited by Irfan Habib. New Delhi: Tulika.

———. 2001. 'Introduction.' In *State and Diplomacy under Tipu Sultan. Documents and Essays*, edited by Irfan Habib. Delhi: Tulika.

———. (1995) 2002. *Essays in Indian History: Towards a Marxist Perception*. London: Anthem Press.

Hasan, Mohibbul. 2005 [1971]. *History of Tipu Sultan*, Delhi: Aakar Books.

Heyne, Benjamin. 1814. *Tracts, Historical and Statistical on India: With Journals of Several Tours through Various Parts of the Peninsula.* London: Robert Baldwin.

Home, Robert. 1794. *Select Views in Mysore: The Country of Tippoo Sultan; From Drawings Taken on the Spot by Mr. Home; with Historical Descriptions.* London: Bowyer.

Husain, Iqbal. 2001. 'The Diplomatic Vision of Tipu Sultan: Briefs for Embassies to Turkey and France, 1785–86.' In *State and Diplomacy under Tipu Sultan. Documents and Essays,* edited by Irfan Habib. Delhi: Tulika.

Kirkpatrick, William, ed. 1811. *Select Letters of Tippoo Sultan to Various Public Functionaries.* London: Black, Parry, and Kingsbury.

Kirmani, Mir Hussein Ali Khan. 1864. *The History of the Reign of Tipu Sultan, Being a Continuation of the Neshani Hyduri.* Translated by Colonel W. Miles. London: Oriental translation fund of Great Britain and Ireland.

Kumar, Dharma. 1965. *Land and Caste in South India: Agricultural Labor in the Madras Presidency during the Nineteenth Century.* Cambridge: Cambridge University Press.

Lafont, Jean-Marie. 2000. *Indika: Essays in Indo-French Relations 1630–1976.* New Delhi: Manohar.

Landes, David S. 1998. *The Wealth and Poverty of Nations: Why Some Are So Rich and Some So Poor.* London: Little, Brown and Co.

Lucas, Gavin. 2005. *The Archaeology of Time.* London: Routledge.

Mackenzie, Roderick. 1794. *A Sketch of the War with Tipu Sultaun.* Vol. 2. Calcutta.

Marx, Karl. (1867) 1982. *Capital. A Critique of Political Economy.* Vol. 1. London: Penguin.

———. 'Capital'. (1894) 1991. *A Critique of Political Economy.* Vol. 3. London: Penguin.

Mielants, Eric. 2007. *The Origins of Capitalism and the 'Rise of the West'.* Philadelphia: Temple University Press.

Moor, Edward. 1794. *A Narrative of the Operations of Captain Little's Detachment....* London: J. Johnson.

'"The Mysorean Revenue Regulations". From the Original Persian, Under the Seal of Tippoo Sultaun, in the Possession of Colonel John Murray, Calcutta 1792.' 1793. In *British India Analyzed: The Provincial and Revenue Establishments of Tippoo Sultan...,* edited by Charles Francis Greville, Part 1. Translated by Burrish Crisp. London: R. Faulder.

Nef, John U. 1932. *The Rise of the British Coal Industry.* Vol. 3. London: Routledge.

Neill, Stephen. (1984) 2004. *A History of Christianity in India: The Beginnings to AD 1707.* Cambridge: Cambridge University Press.

Ovington, John. 1696. *A Voyage to Suratt, in the Year 1689*. London: Jacob Tonson.

Parthasarathi, Prasannan. 2001. *The Transition to a Colonial Economy: Weavers, Merchants and Kings in South India 1720–1800*. Cambridge: Cambridge University Press.

———. 2011. *Why Europe Grew Rich and Asia Did Not: Global Economic Divergence, 1600–1850*. Cambridge: Cambridge University Press.

Pavlov, Vladimir Ivanovich. 1964. *The Indian Capitalist Class: A Historical Study*. New Delhi: People's Publishing House.

———. 1978. *Historical Premises for India's Transition to Capitalism (Late 18th to Mid-19th Century)*. Moscow: Nauka.

Pingle, Gautam. 2017. 'Paddy Yields in Pre-industrial South India.' *Economic & Political Weekly* 52(16): 36–45.

Qadir, Khwaja Abdul. 1968. *Waqai-i Manazil-i Rum: Diary of a Journey to Constantinople*, edited by Mohibbul Hasan. Delhi: Asia Publishing House.

Qaisar, Ahsan Jan. 1982. *The Indian Response to European Technology and Culture (A.D. 1498–1707)*. New Delhi: Oxford University Press.

Ramaswamy, Vijaya. 1985. *Textiles and Weavers in Medieval South India*. Delhi: Oxford University Press.

Raychaudhuri, Tapan. 1983. 'The Mid-Eighteenth-Century Background.' In *Cambridge Economy History of India, Vol. 2, c.1751–c.1970*, edited by Dharma Kumar. Cambridge: Cambridge University Press.

Saki. 1998. *Making History: Karnataka's People and Their Past*. Vol. 1. Bangalore: Vimukthi Prakashana.

Sen, Asok. 1977. 'A Pre-British Economic Formation in India of the Late Eighteenth Century: Tipu Sultan's Mysore.' In *Perspectives in Social Sciences, Vol. 1: Historical Dimensions*, edited by Barun De. Calcutta: Oxford University Press.

Silver, Morris. 1995. *Economic Structures of Antiquity*. Westport: Greenwood Press.

Sivramkrishna, Sashi. 2009. 'Ascertaining Living Standards in Erstwhile Mysore, Southern India, from Francis Buchanan's Journey of 1800–01: An Empirical Contribution to the Great Divergence Debate.' *Journal of the Economic and Social History of the Orient* 52: 695–733.

———. 2015. 'Estimating Agricultural Production in Mysore and South Canara from Buchanan's Journey (1800–1801). Positioning India in the Great Divergence.' *Economic and Political Weekly* 1(16): 66–76.

Treguilly, Philippe Le. 1992. 'Les Francais en Inde au temps de la guerre d l'indépendence Americaine (1778–1788).' [The French in India at the Time of the American War of Independence (1778–1788)]. PhD dissertation, University of Paris-Sorbonne.

Trotsky, Leon. 2008 [1930]. *History of the Russian Revolution*. Chicago: Haymarket Books), pp. 4–5.

Vanina, Eugenia. 2004. *Urban Crafts and Craftsmen in Medieval India (Thirteenth–Eighteenth Centuries)*. New Delhi: Munshiram Manoharlal.

Vries, Peer. 2012. 'Challenges, (Non-)Responses, and Politics: A Review of Prasannan Parthasarathi, 'Why Europe Grew Rich and Asia Did Not: Global Economic Divergence, 1600–1850', *Journal of World History* 23 (3): 639–64.

————. 2013. *Escaping Poverty: The Origins of Modern Economic Growth*. Vienna: Vienna University Press.

Warde, Paul. 2009. 'Energy and Natural Resource Dependency in Europe, 1600–1900.' BWPI Working Paper, 77. The University of Manchester: Brooks World Poverty Institute.

Washbrook, David. 2007. 'India in the Early Modern World Economy: Modes of Production, Reproduction and Exchange.' *Journal of Global History* 2: 87–111.

Wilks, Major Mark. 1805. *Report on the Interior Administration, Resources, and Expenditure of the Government of Mysoor.*... Fort William: Order of the Governor General in Council.

Wrigley, E.A. (1988) 1998. *Continuity, Chance and Change: The Character of the Industrial Revolution in England*. Cambridge: Cambridge University Press.

Yazdani, Kaveh. 2014. 'Haidar 'Ali and Tipu Sultan—Mysore's 18th Century Rulers in Transition.' *Itinerario* 38(2): 101–20.

————. 2017. *India, Modernity and the Great Divergence: Mysore and Gujarat (17th to 19th C.)*. Leiden and Boston: Brill.

————. 2019a. 'South Asia in the Great Divergence Debate'. In *Oxford Research Encyclopedia of Asian History*, edited by David Ludden et al. Available at https://oxfordre.com/asianhistory/abstract/10.1093/acrefore/9780190277727.001.0001/acrefore-9780190277727-e-354?rskey=MLMeF0&result=12; accessed on 23 October 2019.

————. 2019b. 'Mysore at War. The Military Structure during the Reigns of Haidar Ali and Tipu Sultan.' In *A Great War in South India. German Accounts of the Mysore Wars, 1766–1799*, edited by Ravi Ahuja and Martin Christof-Füchsle. Oldenbourg: De Gruyter.

————. (in preparation). 'Dadani: Indian vs. European Forms of Organizing Economic Production', in Dilip Menon (ed.), *Tropic of Capricorn: Concepts from the Global South*.

Yule, Henry and A.C. Burnelll, eds. (1903) 2006. *Hobson-Jobson. A Glossary of Colloquial Anglo-Indian Words and Phrases*. New Delhi: Rupa & Co.

6

Capitalism's Missing Link

What Happened to Southeast Asia?

Eric Tagliacozzo

The new two-volume *Cambridge History of Capitalism* is a real achievement; it is no easy task to try to map out the genealogy and directions of the many headed beast we now call 'capitalism' in two books, however thick they may be. The effort should be lauded, and the attempt is nothing if not timely. Yet the result is (perhaps inevitably) uneven—the volumes are stronger on some parts of the world than others, on some temporal interludes than others. This is not because of the authors chosen to pen the chapters, all of whom seem to have warmed up to the task. Rather, it is because of the nature of the framework itself, as there were always going to be lacunae in the setting of any table along these lines. One large lacuna is 'the case of the missing region'—Southeast Asia. I say this not because I am a card-carrying Southeast Asianist by trade. Rather, I say this because Southeast Asia is almost wholly absent from the book. That might be okay if we were talking about the penetration of capitalism into Antarctica, though even here a case could be made, I imagine, for inclusion based on mineral rights and other topics of interest.

But for Southeast Asia, the 'miss' feels more serious, because (as I will argue), some of the buds of what we now think of as global capitalism began sprouting here. Some of the at least initially viable alternatives to capitalism in the evolution of the last 500 years also found fecund ground in this part of the world. My contribution looks at this dual history, and asks how this part of the planet might be brought more productively into the global debate of what capitalism means. There is not a huge amount of existing scholarship about Southeast Asia's place in the genesis of global capitalism. This is because the eyes of most critics have been on Manchester and Birmingham, as well as the cotton ports of the American South and other locales in thinking about how these processes got off the ground. These places were indeed important, but across the planet on the other side of the world, there were indeed changes happening that impacted this story. Tracing these energies requires languages other than the ones usually associated with the story of capitalism's rise (English, French), and delving into other traditions, many of them little known to Western academic audiences. Yet it is precisely because this region's story is so little told that its history provides fresh avenues of insight into the ongoing debate of capitalism as a global phenomenon that affects us all.

More than many places, perhaps, Southeast Asia entered the stream of global economic history in the fourteenth to eighteenth century period—the years that we traditionally point to as the foundational era of capitalism. These were the places that the contact-period voyages of Columbus, Da Gama, and Cabral were looking for when the ships left Iberia; these were the places where spices, gold dust, and other 'exotic' commodities were known to be.[1] It makes perfect sense that these regions were implicated in the story of cataclysmic changes that swept the planet in the early modern

---

[1] Southeast Asia is an imprecise designation, of course—as a term, it came into being some centuries after this 'contact period' began. But it is a useful toponym for thinking about the larger landscapes and seascapes of Monsoon Asia, east of what is today India. Southeast Asia's present-day geography includes 11 separate countries: Burma, Thailand, Laos, Cambodia, Vietnam, Malaysia, Singapore, Indonesia, Brunei, East Timor, and the Philippines.

period, as these were the primary destinations for much of the West's global exploration. Of course, this was not just a one-sided meeting. Southeast Asian societies were also undergoing transformations en masse when these exchanges began to take place. Scholars of many stripes have become more and more interested in these transvaluations, not only via external triggers like capitalism, the subject of the present volume, but also via those that seem to have had internal motors as well.[2]

This is evident not only today, but in the thoughts of some of the great interpreters of these changes, even while they were actually happening. Adam Smith, for example, writing in England in the 1770s, felt that the Indies and the Indian Ocean generally were sites of enormous energy and flux. All along these shores, he saw commerce being pushed forward by millions of eager hands, although ominous signs of developing inequalities already existed. Smith thought that this burgeoning, massive trade ultimately ensnared all nations that participated in its conduct, regardless of their geographic origins (Benton 1995; Smith 1976: 223–4). Karl Marx, thinking about this same geographical set of affairs nearly a century later, saw a different vista unfolding before his eyes. Production was now overtaking mercantilism as the organizing principle of wealth in the region, and England, not by itself, but together with other Western societies, was no longer keen on sharing the rewards of interaction.[3] 'In India', he wrote in the third volume of his master work *Capital*, 'the English applied their direct political and economic power, as masters and

[2] Much of this discussion was initiated by the University of Wisconsin historian John Smail, whose seminal ideas on 'autonomous histories' (and their possibilities) in Southeast Asia reoriented the field for decades after his writing in the 1960s. Prior to Smail, Southeast Asian history was often seen as 'from the deck of a ship', an apt metaphor for colonial continuity.

[3] In Marx's world, England was nearly unchallenged as a global actor, with a global reach and concomitant global consequences to its policies and actions. The Iberian countries had faded, Holland (now the Netherlands) was on the wane, and France had clearly lost out to the British in India by this time. Only Germany threatened this near-hegemony—but that particular storm was still very much on the historical horizon. Only later on towards the end of the nineteenth century, but particularly in the twentieth century, would the United States and Japan be added to this list.

landlords, to destroying these small (indigenous) economic communities' (Marx 1976: 451). Marx's observation easily held true for the gathering European dominion in the rest of Southeast Asia as well, whether these landscapes were English or continental in colonial origin.

In the pages that follow, I examine these changes and some of their attendant historiographies through three brief rubrics. The first of these sub-genres is temporally dependent and focuses on the evolution of territory vis-à-vis economic history in this part of the world. I argue that Western notions of territorial control took root only very slowly in Southeast Asia, and in a rather piecemeal fashion, affecting the ways that capitalism could ultimately take a hold in that region. The second rubric under study here is the nature of the commercially interested state itself, as state formation took place across the thousands of kilometres of Southeast Asia where empires were born, lived through divergent cycles of development, and then ultimately died. I argue here that the nature of state formation also changed during this era vis-à-vis economic history in interesting and, ultimately, recordable ways. Finally, the third genre I explore below has to do with the nature of the economic stimuli causing these processes (including capitalism), its various frequencies, and its provenances. I push for an idea that more of these energies were Asian and local than has previously been supposed, though several generations of scholars have told us that the West was mostly responsible for an evolution towards what we ultimately term 'modernity' in the region.

The Evolution of Territory vis-à-vis Economic History in Southeast Asia

Gareth Austin (2014: Chapter 10, 301) rightly notes in his essay 'Capitalism and the Colonies' in Volume II of *The Cambridge History of Capitalism* that 'the history of empire is longer than the history of capitalism. It is also wider'. In the period that interests us here, there were few, if any, hard and fast borders in this part of the world. In insular Southeast Asia, an upstream–downstream approach to statecraft characterized most political situations, whereby polities on both the upper and lower ends of rivers dealt with each other along these avenues of transport, economically (and also politically) across the width of the world's largest archipelago.[4] Downstream polities tended to be stronger, though were not always so, if only because they mediated the terms of economic exchange with uplanders vis-a-vis commodities, which came in from the rest of the world. Thus, items such as beeswax, animal horns, and rare and precious barks went downriver, while the manufactured goods of a global, burgeoning capitalism (such as porcelain and muskets) went upriver. On the Southeast Asian mainland in the first millennium BCE, a different political rationale developed with the mandala system. Mandala courts were centred around one great metropolis, whose authority (both political and economic) radiated outwards in ever-weakening circles until it ceased to be effective at all. The great Cambodian kingdom of Angkor was one example of this system, but Siamese Sukhotai (1238–1438 BCE) and Ayudhya (1351–1767 BCE) were also iterations of this pattern, as were a number of other centres scattered elsewhere on the mainland.[5] The amorphous zones where these circles overlapped were the closest thing that existed to our modern conception of international borders. Yet people in these regions paid commercial tribute to both powers, or to neither of them, or to one or the other, all depending on the oscillation of regional power (Bronson 1977; Wheatley 1983).

Further up in the hills of the northern parts of the Southeast Asian mainland, the mandala system was less relevant because there were comparatively few stalwart political centres that could mirror the likes

[4] The division I employ here of 'insular' and 'mainland' Southeast Asia is a largely accepted convention of scholars of the region; historical patterns often did not look the same between these two parts of this arena. I will discuss some of the differences that the two sub-regions suggest further on in this chapter, especially vis-à-vis the work of Anthony Reid and Victor Lieberman. Increasingly, there is a feeling among scholars, however, that the suggested binary has been too strong, and that certain patterns cross the land/sea divide of the region.

[5] We could also include other inland, agrarian polities to this list, including the variety of states or proto-states centered around what is today Mandalay, Sagaing, Ava, and Pagan in northern Burma (as well as still other confederations in what is today Laos, northern Thailand, and Yunnan Province in China).

of these lowland polities. Rather, a different template emerged with caravan trades dictating much of the political power of the region, as transverse, bisecting lines of commercial traffic became very important to local 'states' and proto-state polities. Much of this upland region has recently been affixed with an encapsulating name, called 'Zomia' in one signal study (Scott 2009).[6] Cotton boats transporting huge quantities of raw cotton along upland river systems in the Himalayan watershed were very important to this trade, as were mule caravans carrying gems, guns, and slaves along the upland trading routes between Laos, Siam (now Thailand), Burma (now Myanmar), and southwestern China. International capitalism grafted easily onto these thoroughfares. Political entities appeared in the hills and valleys based on who could control these trade routes and tax them, as well as on who could control highland agricultural production— mostly dry-field rice, but also increasingly opium poppies—at the same time. 'Borders' in the modern, globalized understanding of the term were essentially non-existent. Yet the idea of frontiers between these polities did nonetheless exist, as mountain villages sometimes found themselves in the uncomfortable position of being requisitioned for tax—in cash, or in kind—from several political centres at once (Tagliacozzo 2004). The most pointed analysis of this whole Byzantine highland system has been Thongchai Winichakul's classic *Siam Mapped*, which showed how, with the entrance of Europeans into this arena in the later nineteenth century, things began to change. As the British and French competed for economic resources in the hills, it became more and more important for flags to be planted into the ground to designate claims over rights in classical Marxian fashion. It also eventually became important to indigenous regimes as well, and as a result of this dialectic, a many centuries-long pattern

[6] Although James Scott has been most closely aligned with the 'Zomia concept' in the scholarly literature, Scott has generously pointed out in his writings that the first progenitor of the idea was actually Willem van Schendel, a historian/anthropologist working out of Amsterdam in the Netherlands. The Zomia thesis takes in hills that stretch across modern 'area-studies' designations of East Asia, South Asia, and Southeast Asia, essentially linking a massif of often inter-connected highlands from Assam in eastern India to portions of high-cordillera Vietnam.

for political and commercial mechanisms of managing frontier areas began to change (Thongchai 1994).[7]

The late eighteenth and early nineteenth centuries have, in fact, traditionally been many historians' choice for Southeast Asia's entrance into some sort of tenuous 'modernity' of the capitalist economic system. Yet increasingly, there is a growing feeling among scholars that during this era, the energy behind Southeast Asia's evolution still may have come primarily from internal sources. This was a time when three great indigenous dynasties were formed on the mainland—the Konbaung in Burma (1752–1885), the Chakri in Siam (1782 to the present), and the Nguyen court in Vietnam (1802–1945) (Thant 2001; Woodside 1971; Wyatt 2003). It was only after 1820 or so that Europeans started to substantially affect these energies from outside Southeast Asia. The year 1819 can be highlighted as a watershed date with the founding of the commercial entrepôt of Singapore, while the First Anglo-Burmese War (1824) and the Burney Treaty in Siam (1826), both of which extracted economic concessions from Southeast Asian kingdoms, are also important signposts for this transitional decade.[8] Indigenous polities started to formulate strategies for dealing with European intrusions during this time, as it became clearer and clearer that the latter were becoming dangerous as the decades wore on (Blusse and Gaastra 1998). Though *The Cambridge History of Capitalism* has a chapter devoted to this process, titled 'The Spread and Resistance to Global Capitalism', next to nothing appears in this space about the Southeast Asian experience in this regard (O'Rourke and Williamson 2014: Chapter 1). It is important for us to note, therefore, that local

---

[7] Thongchai's book *Siam Mapped* has been so influential here in picking apart the history of mapped space in Siam that its lessons have been applied to many other world areas, where some of the same processes were underway. His monograph has shown better than any other how indigenous and European ideas of the nature of geographic space and national imaginings came into collision over the 'long nineteenth century'.

[8] It is interesting to note that only a couple of years after Singapore's 'founding' as a British entrepôt in the region, it had become the largest port in Southeast Asia in terms of the number of ships calling and the combined tonnage of these vessels.

actors were as important in weaving the economic historical tapestry of this era as any agents or influences from without, despite decades of historiography telling us the exact opposite. This newer line of thought has written Southeast Asians back into their own history in ways that were denied to them for quite some time, an important historiographical development to be sure.

It really only seems to be in the later decades of the nineteenth century that the actual territorial tableaux of Southeast Asia began to be turned inexorably into what we might now term a 'capitalist landscape'. Donald Nonini (1992) and J.M. Gullick (1987) have shown in precise detail how this was accomplished in British Malaya, as a heavily forested isthmus was gradually cleared and then seeded with monocropping regimes, primarily rubber palms (but also other crops in different districts, like pepper, gambier, and so on). Ian Brown (1988) has elaborated on a similar state of affairs in non-colonized Siam, where Thai elites (bolstered by Chinese and then English capital) did much the same in the growing districts of the southern half of the country, orienting this new agricultural regime more and more towards the world market. In the Philippines, indigo and tobacco played much the same role, with late Spanish and eventually American capital changing the landscape over a period of decades into a giant production basket, which was explicitly oriented towards feeding world demand. This process of land accumulation, land development, and rights reassignment also impoverished Filipino peasants at the same time, very much enriching not only foreign capitalists, but eventually an elite land-owning indigenous class (Cushner 1976). But it was perhaps in Sumatra, in the growing districts of Deli and elsewhere around modern Medan, where these energies became most apparent. Here, Dutch and then all sorts of other foreign capital literally changed the landscape from one of the most untouched ecosystems in the region to an orderly, cut-and-ribboned assemblage of plantations in the matter of only a few years. In 1863, a Dutch tobacco planter began all of this in a single place, but by the mid-twentieth century, a huge, orderly machine of agricultural capitalism had been assembled with shipped-in labour (mostly from southern China, South India, and Java) alongside strict rules on gender, race, and residence among the new seeded populations. Ann Stoler ([1979] 1995a) has described this new architecture in painstaking detail, showing how this was accomplished in a space where, previously, there were much more free-flowing systems of land tenure, population movement, and inter-ethnic contact. Territory itself had been redefined and reorganized, in other words, in a systemic fashion in numerous places. Certain parts of Southeast Asia looked almost nothing like they had only a few decades ago.

Political Polities and Economic 'Modernity' in the Region

The levers of state formation are another way in which the fourteenth to eighteenth century can be looked at productively in monsoon Asia, both before and after the appearance of what we call 'capitalism' in the region. In Southeast Asia in particular, much of the historiographical heat and light examining this process has been generated by the so-called Reid/Lieberman debate. Both these towering scholars wrote a pair of books laying out their visions of the evolution of Southeast Asia in the period that is interesting to us here. Lieberman's volumes followed Reid's books, and he engages head-on with the former two volumes, measuring his own vision against that of Reid's across a number of issues. These include demographics, the imposition of royal will as a characteristic for area polities and commercial change across the region as a whole (Lieberman 2003, 2009; Reid 1988, 1993). One of Lieberman's main assertions in this historiographical grappling is that he feels that Reid's volumes—themselves very much game-changing, and worthy of a serious read by anyone interested in this part of the world—went too far in some places, and not far enough in others when it comes to what state formation means.[9]

Examined in a nutshell, Lieberman feels that Reid may have over-emphasized the importance of the outside world's influence on evolving statecraft in early modern Southeast Asia. At the same time, he feels he underemphasized a number of internal characteristics that were particularly noticeable vis-à-vis the mainland polities of the region.

---

[9] The comparative discussion between the two books is notable for its absence of high theory on state formation: this is very much a 'down in the trenches' debate, about what statecraft looked like on the ground. It would be interesting to see what the prophets of theory on state formation (such as Migdal and others) might make of this debate.

Debates on religion and Confucian doctrine, both vis-à-vis statecraft and trade, are part of this debate.[10] But the larger point is that, for Lieberman, state formation and economic practice were evolving organically on the Southeast Asian mainland in a rhythm at once its own, and in step with other societies that were also dealing with the initial tendrils of global capitalism around the same time. Where Reid saw a certain amount of unity to Southeast Asia as a whole during this era, at least vis-à-vis trade, Lieberman sees more of a division between the mainland and the island world. He instead espies continuities of the former with regions further afield on the Eurasian continent.

In fact, by the end of the time period concerning us in this book, the mainland polities of 'Burma', 'Siam', and 'Vietnam' had become strong, vital centres and exemplars, in a way, of the possibilities of maturing commercial states for this part of the world. Yet I wonder if some scholarship of recent years points to a more fluid understanding of this time outside of the dictates of state formation *per se*, as trans-local migrations, trade, and even changes in the modalities of economic power projection began to dilute the power of indigenous states. Indeed, one important aspect of the new(-ish) scholarship on this period is its attention to the notion of 'overlapping spheres'. Since the construction of most historiography on the late eighteenth and early nineteenth centuries has traditionally been drawn more or less along country lines, it seems important to heed studies that have bridged these lines, since the lines themselves didn't exist very strongly yet in historical time and space. One way that this is increasingly being done for this period is the explicit reference to arenas that do not currently conform to Southeast Asia's national political boundaries (Giersch 2001, 2006; Wyatt 1997). Increasingly, there has been an attempt to analyse landscapes that were at one time closely linked through capitalist enterprise and trade, though these same landscapes now lie under the auspices of separate independent nation states.[11]

---

[10] For more details, see Rafael (1988), Geertz (1976), Tambiah (1976), and Spiro (1992) for the Philippines, Java, Siam, and Burma, respectively, and on Confucianization in Vietnam, see Taylor (1987), Whitmore (1976), and Woodside (1982).

[11] As only one regional example, see Andaya (2008), but also see earlier steps in this direction in Bassett (1989) and Suwannathat-Pian (1988).

A second way is increasingly to take a theme—trans-regional agricultural regimes and their taxation might be one useful one—and then to use this theme to suggest continuities over geography, as some scholars have done (Brocheux 1995; Elson 1997; O'Connor 1995).[12] Giovanni Federico (2014: 50, 56–7, 63, 72), in Chapter 3 of Volume II of *The Cambridge History of Capitalism*, has a short stab at things here, for example, but although India and especially China get a mention and a bit of text (and some figures), Southeast Asia is again notably absent. Both of these approaches that I have listed earlier have the advantage of linking regional economic energies to local ones, since the structure of the normative narrative of the Southeast Asian past during this period has favoured the latter approach, until only very recently.[13]

Peter Boomgaard (2009: 55–78) has suggested that in terms of two major indices that we might well equate with state formation—rice-production levels, and also labour productivity—Southeast Asia was

[12] Examining the modalities of colonial plantation complexes across Southeast Asia is a project that still needs to be attempted by some brave soul (and preferably someone with admirable language skills in the main European linguistic traditions represented in Southeast Asian colonialism, that is, English, French, Dutch, and Spanish). British historian John Furnivall made a start towards this half a century ago, but stopped at comparisons between the British and Dutch in Southeast Asia, and especially their productive and organizational capacities in Burma and Indonesia. The time is ripe for someone to commence a serious study again along these lines, using modern techniques, to look for the fault lines of both commonality and difference between the various colonial regimes. A study such as this would go far in helping us to figure out if the region ultimately fractured along imperial lines of control, or over ecological (or other) ones, based more on the particular systems of crop growth themselves.

[13] Few regions have been as enamoured of the study of nationalism as Southeast Asia; this is the 'house' that Benedict Anderson built, and before him George Kahin, his friend, colleague, and teacher. Since the study of nationalism was so prominent at Cornell, where both of these scholars taught, trans-national approaches were less favoured for a long time by many of their students. This dynamic is even more interesting because the founding generation of Southeast Asian scholars at Cornell, such as O.W.W. Wolters, were regionalists in geist, approach, and interpretation in the decades before this.

nowhere near the levels being achieved by Western states in the nineteenth century. He argues convincingly from data that he has been able to accumulate that Java, the landscape deemed most 'productive' in these two capacities, was behind both Finland and Portugal, two 'backwaters' of Europe (both geographically and productively) in the nineteenth century. He puts this argument forward as a kind of counterweight against more hopeful appraisals of Southeast Asian 'development', which have started to litter the literature on Southeast Asian history as a whole. Yet the timeframe of Boomgaard's analysis is, to me, problematic: the nineteenth century can be split into segments, at least in the Southeast Asian case. State formation in the region looked little like it did in the beginning of the 1800s as it eventually did by the end of that same century. So, the saying 'comparisons are odious' might come into force here. This data might be more relevant if they were linked both backwards and forwards in time to other subsets of data, which try to measure these concerns both before and after capitalism really started to get a foothold in the region. For this, we have to disabuse ourselves of the notion of looking at round 'centuries' as benchmarks, be more willing, perhaps, to split these convenient temporal cachements, and attach the relevant numbers to units that make more sense. We might be better served, therefore, to state that state formation changed radically over the course of the nineteenth century in the region, rather than either before or after it. This seems to be closer to the truth of the economic evolution of Southeast Asia, and the political imbrications of colonialism (as well as the entrance of big capital), which came during these same decades.

Exogenous and Indigenous Economic Stimuli to Change

Discerning exogenous and indigenous economic stimuli are important in thinking through patterns and energies in Southeast Asia for the fourteenth to eighteenth centuries. Yet *The Cambridge History of Capitalism* seems to divest itself once more of the possibilities of the Southeast Asian example in thinking through these contradictions. In Chapter 12 of Volume I, Patrick O'Brien explicitly states that he won't deal with these connections in a contribution (rather enticingly) entitled 'The Formation of States and Transitions to Modern

Economies: England, Europe, and Asia Compared' (O'Brien 2014: 380). He then goes on, however, to tell us that there are 'analogous cases' of the 'maritime polities of Southeast Asia' with the 'political economy of European mercantilism' and its effects 'on the strategic and economic policies pursued by Ottoman, Safavid, Mughal, and Ming-Qing dynasties and elites' (O'Brien 2014: 388).[14] It might be prudent for us here, therefore, to revisit some of the linking themes that were beginning to constitute Southeast Asia as a discrete region before the age of high imperialism and its attendant capitalist acquisitions began at the end of this time period.

One of these themes is the importance of 'great families' in Southeast Asia, as the region moved from the eighteenth into the nineteenth century and into new forms of social, political, and economic organization (Day 1996). Many of these families were, in fact, local, but many of them also had Persian, Arab, and Chinese roots, among other foreign trading provenances (Tagliacozzo 2009, 2011).[15] Another useful theme is the changing role of the polity itself in these equations, not just in Siam, where the most detailed and sophisticated work has been done on this question, but elsewhere in this diffuse patchwork of emerging states as well. Conceptions of the physical shape and make-up of a 'state' changed markedly during this time, as foreign notions of 'fixedness' replaced the overlapping concentric sphere of local geographic models in parts of the region

---

[14] This is one among a number of places in the volume where one sees that Southeast Asia is clearly not deemed important enough to be 'noticed' in comparison to its larger and more productive neighbours (that is, China and India). Yet, at the time, Southeast Asia certainly was deemed to be important by colonial administrators, and gallons of imperial ink was spilt on its productive capacities, its trade, and its future possibilities.

[15] Few places evince the level of miscegenation that Southeast Asia does over the longue durée. Because Southeast Asia was generally so open to trade and had such a broad, welcoming cadence to travellers passing through, many of these voyagers (the vast majority of them men) intermarried in the ports and established families in the region. These same families then became important in many places across the 'lands beneath the winds', and the scions of these families eventually took up office (commercial and political) in a number of these most important city-state/ports scattered across the region.

over time. Pan-Southeast Asian conceptions of gender were also malleable and changing during this epoch, as new forms of expectations for both females and males came to bear with the arrival of foreigners and foreign ideologies (such as Christianity and Islam, which together converted fully half of all Southeast Asians during the early modern period) (Andaya 2006; Reid 1988; Stoler 1995b).

In fact, increasingly, scholars are arguing these days for the primacy of local engines of economic causality in explaining change (even in the face of the juggernaut of capitalism), and even change of a comparatively late date. In terms of colonial commercial influence and usurpation, most of Burma was not yet British by the third or fourth decade of the nineteenth century, for example, nor yet were any of Siam's border regions, as they would be later in the west and south. Cambodia and Laos were not yet at all controlled by the French. Vietnam was not yet under Gallic influence either, and the southern extremes of the Philippines and its trade routes south to the Malay World were only beginning to be incorporated by Spanish 'gunboat diplomacy' around this time. In Malaya, the Pangkor Engagement, and, with it, the British Forward Movement, started only in 1874, even if a few commercial ports and islands answered to the English before this (such as Singapore and Penang). The majority of the Indies' Outer Islands saw no Dutch flags until after 1873, when the initial defeat in battle at Aceh pushed Dutch colonial pride into serious empire building (Charney 2009; Edwards 2007; Evans 2002; Gullick 1987; Locher-Scholten 1994; Loos 2006; Warren 1981; Zinoman 2001). On the face of it, therefore, the early nineteenth century does seem to be too soon for the 'foreign' to have equal weight with the 'local' in the story of the evolution of any capitalist economic 'modernity' in Southeast Asia. We need to take more seriously the notion that Southeast Asians were, for the most part, masters of their own destinies before the capitalism brought by Europeans changed things irrevocably across a wide spectrum of local space at a later time.

By the middle to later decades of the nineteenth century, of course, the picture changes drastically. At that time, the kind of political encroachment that Europeans were foisting upon other parts of the planet was also happening in Southeast Asia, and there, in many sectors, it was happening en masse. Plantation peripheries were created on the Malay Peninsula and on British Borneo; in the latter locale, the British North Borneo Company was set up in 1878, its mission simply to produce as much large-scale agricultural and mining surplus as the landscape would allow, under the control of a corporate board in faraway London (Doolittle 2011). The British importation of large numbers of Indian labourers and small-scale merchants into the Burma Delta accomplished this too, turning a part of Burma that was once swampy and underutilized (and remarkably under-populated as well) into the rice bowl for the colony, and indeed—later on, at least—for much of British Asia as a whole (Adas [1974] 2011). The French stripped the jungle from parts of their Indo–China colony and seeded the land with rubber plantations instead, whose products eventually were exported to help fuel the world's embrace of automobiles, a new transportation technology which exploded in the early decades of the twentieth century (Brocheux and Hemery 2010). And the Dutch remade Sumatra and Kalimantan, the so-called *Buiten Bezittingen* or 'Outer Islands' of the Netherlands Indies, in much the same way. Where previously only Java and a few other small stretches of their evolving colony had really been controlled and utilized, economically, the growth and spread of plantations and mines controlled by private capital after 1870 literally transformed the landscape (Stoler [1979] 1995a). These were changes of a whole new order to what had been seen previously, and show us that capitalism in its truest, more mature sense came rather late to most of the region. This is in direct opposition to the normative narrative of European conquest in the region, whereby Western encroachment and development began in earnest literally right after the Portuguese arrival in 1511, the usual date put forward for the beginnings of Western involvement in the region.

***

Southeast Asia can be thought of as something of a test case for the processes of economic modernity that were sweeping the globe from the fourteenth to the end of the eighteenth centuries. One might say this, of course, for other global areas—the Americas, Africa, the Eurasian Steppe, even Oceania—but there are some very good reasons to think that the density of exchange may have been thickest here. Due to this, the resultant economic changes in many area societies, along a number of indices, give us clues as to what the widespread (and sometimes totalizing) transformations were that were attendant upon the world getting much, much smaller during a relatively short period. This is despite the fact that in *The Cambridge History of Capitalism*, Southeast Asia as a region only receives (by my count) one full paragraph and a few scattered mentions over some 1,100 pages of text (Neal 2014, Vol. II: 311). Nevertheless, borders and boundaries began the process of changing from particular local forms to newer, Western-influenced ones. States took on economic engines that were 'modern' in conception, relying in some places less on absolutism and more on the ability to concentrate and wield commercial power through bureaucracies. Crucially, the societies of Southeast Asia also made choices on how they were to be economically organized, choices which were sometimes based on models and energies from afar, but which were—more often than not—still local in inception, well up into the 'long nineteenth century'. It was really only in this century, which is mostly outside of the scope of my own writing here, that change began to spread in a truly wholesale manner in this part of the world.

Yet as with everything involving economics, there was a price for all of this change. One price was greater connection to emerging global norms—political, religious, cultural, but especially economic in nature. As mentioned previously in this chapter, fully half of the population of Southeast Asia, for example, became either Muslim or Christian during this time period, which changed many local attitudes about everything, from gender relations to politics and from sexual moralities to the nature of commercial exchange itself. Local ways of doing things, sometimes many centuries old in provenance, began to be replaced more by doing things as they were now accomplished along an arc of globally connected societies. This could be a good thing in some contexts, but often it was not so for autochthonous people. In parts of Southeast Asia, for example, merchants now needed imperial permission to be able to trade, when, before, they came and went as they pleased. Also, there was less and less by way of pastoral moral economies in Southeast Asia as time went on, as the dictates of an emerging world market—the hallmark of a maturing Capitalism, capital 'C'—drew more and more localities into its ambiguous embrace. Patron/client relations broke down, and the beginnings of capitalism in its most recognizable, contemporary guises began to appear in seedling form throughout the area that Anthony Reid called the 'lands beneath the winds'. This is a story for another book, and another timeframe, but those seeds often first began to sprout here. Due to these reasons, and the complexities of the legacies of engagement, we need to see this four-century span in the region as a problematic one at best. Many of the energies unleashed in that period are still, in fact, with us now, evolving in ways that are still manifest in our own, imperfectly shared world.

It will be a job for future researchers to determine how much the patterns in evidence in Southeast Asia may, in fact, have been shared elsewhere on the globe in discernible ways when it comes to generating the history of capitalism. For too long, these precedents have only been looked for in the West, the broad arc stretching from England's factory towns to the American South, where cotton and other products connected the Atlantic World into new circuits of relationality that had not existed before. This was indeed a new world being created, on the bones of an older world of contact and exchange, which was now receding into the distance several centuries after the Columbian exchange. Yet that exchange was never limited to the Atlantic in its total aspect, nor in its ramifications. Regions like Southeast Asia were also an important part of this story. This was so both in the incredible opportunities they brought to those who began exploring the wider world (vis-à-vis spices, and other products), and also in the ways that Southeast Asians resisted the burgeoning onslaught of capitalism after it had become the dominant paradigm of political and economic connection over the course of the nineteenth century. These linking histories of incorporation and refusal, adaptation and survival, need to be more fully fleshed out on the global scale, in landscapes that are less known than the ones where capitalism's history was originally written. When that happens, the 'true history' of the genesis of our modern world will be more fully accomplished, in a story that sees all of us as component parts of a wider whole.

Bibliography

Adas, Michael. (1974) 2011. *The Burma Delta: Economic Development and Social Change on an Asian Rice Frontier, 1852–1941*. Madison: University of Wisconsin Press.

Andaya, Barbara Watson. 2006. *The Flaming Womb: Repositioning Women in Early Modern Southeast Asia*. Honolulu: University of Hawai'i Press.

Andaya, Leonard. 2008. *Leaves from the Same Tree: Trade and Ethnicity in the Straits of Melaka*. Honolulu: University of Hawaii Press.

Austin, Gareth. 2014. 'Capitalism and the Colonies.' In *Cambridge History of Capitalism*, Vol. II, edited by Larry Neal and Jeffrey G. Williamson, pp. 301–47. Cambridge: Cambridge University Press.

Bassett, D.K. 1989. 'British Country Trade Networks in the Thai and Malay States, 1680-1770.' *Modern Asian Studies* 23(4): 625–44.

Benton, Ted. 1995. 'Adam Smith and the Limits to Growth.' In *Adam Smiths' Wealth of Nations: New Interdisciplinary Essays*, edited by Stephen Copley and Kathryn Sutherland, pp. 144–70. Manchester: Manchester University Press.

Blusse, Leonard and Femme Gaastra, eds. 1998. *On the Eighteenth Century as a Category of Asian History: Van Leur in Retrospect*. Aldershot: Ashgate Publishing.

Brocheux, Pierre. 1995. *The Mekong Delta: Ecology, Economy, and Revolution, 1860–1960*. Southeast Asia Monograph no. 12. Madison: University of Wisconsin.

Brocheux, Pierre and Hemery, Danile. 2010. *Indochina: An Ambiguous Colonization*. Berkeley: University of California Press.

Bronson, Bennet. 1977. 'Exchange at the Upstream and Downstream Ends: Notes Toward a Functional Model of the Coastal States in Southeast Asia.' In *Economic Exchange and Social Interaction in Southeast Asia: Perspectives from Prehistory, History and Ethnography*, edited by K.L Hutterer. Ann Arbor: University of Michigan.

Brown, Ian. 1988. *The Elite and the Economy in Siam, 1890–1920*. Singapore: Oxford University Press.

Charney, Michael. 2009. *A History of Modern Burma*. Cambridge: Cambridge University Press.

Cushner, Nicholas. 1976. *Landed Estates in the Colonial Philippines*. New Haven: Yale University Southeast Asian Studies.

Day, Tony, 1996. 'Ties That (Un)bind: Families and States in Premodern Southeast Asia.' *Journal of Asian Studies* 55(2): 384–409.

Doolittle, Amity. 2011. *Property and Politics in Sabah, Malaysia: Native Struggles Over Land Rights*. Seattle: University of Washington Press.

Edwards, Penny. 2007. *Cambodge: The Cultivation of a Nation, 1860–1945*. Honolulu: University of Hawai'i Press.

Elson, R.E. 1997. *The End of the Peasantry in Southeast Asia: A Social and Economic History of Peasant Livelihood, 1800–1990s*. New York: St. Martin's Press.

Evans, Grant. 2002. *A Short History of Laos: The Land in Between*. Chiang Mai: Silkworm Books.

Federico, Giovanni. 2014. 'Growth, Specialization, and Organization of World Agriculture.' In *Cambridge History of Capitalism*, Vol. II, edited by Larry Neal and Jeffrey G. Williamson, pp. 47–81. Cambridge: Cambridge University Press.

Furnivall, John S. 1956. *Colonial Policy and Practice: A Comparative Study of Burma and Netherlands India*. New York: New York University Press.

Geertz, Clifford. 1976. *The Religion of Java*. Chicago: University of Chicago Press.

Giersch, C. Patterson. 2001. '"A Motley Throng": Social Change on Southwest China's Early Modern Frontier, 1700–1880.' *Journal of Asian Studies* 60(1): 67–94.

———. 2006. *Asian Borderlands: The Transformation of Qing China's Yunnan Frontier* Cambridge: Harvard University Press.

Gullick, J.M. 1987. *Malay Society in the Late Nineteenth Century: The Beginnings of Change*. Singapore: Oxford University Press.

Huntington, Ellsworth. 1907. *The Pulse of Asia, a Journey to Central Asia Illustrating the Geographical Basis of History*. Boston: Houghton Mifflin.

Lieberman, Victor. 2003. *Strange Parallels: Southeast Asia in Global Context, 800–1830 Volume 1: Integration on the Mainland*. Cambridge: Cambridge University Press.

———. 2009. *Strange Parallels: Southeast Asia in Global Context, 800–1830 Volume 2: Mainland Mirrors: Europe, Japan, China, South Asia and the Islands*. Cambridge: Cambridge University Press.

Locher-Scholten, Elsbeth. 1994. 'Dutch Expansion in the Indonesian Archipelago Around 1900 and the Imperialism Debate.' *Journal of Southeast Asian Studies* 25(1): 91–111.

Loos, Tamara. 2006. *Subject Siam: Family, Law, and Colonial Modernity in Thailand*. Ithaca: Cornell University Press.

Marx, Karl. 1976. *Capital*, Vol. III. New York: Vintage.

Nonini, Donald. 1992. *British Colonial Rule and the Resistance of the Malay Peasantry*. Southeast Asia Monograph Series. New Haven: Yale University.

O'Brien, Patrick. 2014. 'The Formation of States and Transitions to Modern Economies: England, Europe, and Asia Compared.' In *Cambridge History of Capitalism*, Vol. I, edited by Larry Neal and Jeffrey G. Williamson, pp. 357–402. Cambridge: Cambridge University Press.

O'Connor, Richard. 1995. 'Agricultural Change and Ethnic Succession in Southeast Asian States: A Case for Regional Anthropology.' *Journal of Asian Studies* 54(4): 968–96.

O'Rourke, Kevin and Jeffrey Williamson. 2014. 'Introduction: The Spread of and Resistance to Global Capitalism.' In *Cambridge History of Capitalism*, Vol. II, edited by Larry Neal and Jeffrey G. Williamson, pp. 1–21. Cambridge: Cambridge University Press.

Rafael, Vicente. 1988. *Contracting Colonialism: Translation and Christian Conversion in Tagalog Society under Early Spanish Rule*. Ithaca: Cornell University Press.

Reid, Anthony. 1988. *Southeast Asia in the Age of Commerce: The Lands beneath the Winds*. Vol. 1. New Haven: Yale University Press.

———. 1993. *Southeast Asia in the Age of Commerce: The Lands beneath the Winds*. Vol. 2. New Haven: Yale University Press.

Scott, James. 2009. *The Art of Not Being Governed: An Anarchist History of Upland Southeast Asia*. New Haven: Yale University Press.

Smith, Adam. 1976. *An Inquiry into the Nature and Causes of the Wealth of Nations*. Vol. I. Oxford: Clarendon Press.

Spiro, Melford. 1992. *Buddhism and Society: A Great Tradition and Its Burmese Vicissitudes*. Berkeley: University of California Press.

Stoler, Ann. (1979) 1995a. *Capitalism and Confrontation on Sumatra's Plantation Belt*. Ann Arbor: University of Michigan Press.

———. 1995b. *Race and the Education of Desire: Foucault's History of Sexuality and the Colonial Order of Things*. Durham: Duke University Press.

Suwannathat-Pian, Kobkua. 1988. *Thai-Malay Relations: Traditional Intra-Regional Relations from the Seventeenth to the Early Twentieth Centuries*. Singapore: Oxford University Press.

Tagliacozzo, Eric. 2004. 'Ambiguous Commodities, Unstable Frontiers: The Case of Burma, Siam, and Imperial Britain, 1800–1900.' *Comparative Studies in Society and History* 46(2): 354–77.

———, ed. 2009. *Southeast Asia and the Middle East: Islam, Movement, and the Longue Duree*. Palo Alto: Stanford University Press.

Tagliacozzo, Eric and Chang, Wen-Chin, eds. 2011. *Chinese Circulations: Capital, Commodities and Networks in Southeast Asia*. Durham: Duke University Press.

Tambiah, Stanley. 1976. *World Conqueror and World Renouncer: A Study of Buddhism and Polity in Thailand against a Historical Background*. Cambridge: Cambridge University Press.

Taylor, Keith. 1987. 'The Literati Revival in Seventeenth-Century Vietnam.' *Journal of Southeast Asian Studies* 18(1): 1–23.

Thant, Myint-U. 2001. *The Making of Modern Burma*. New York: Cambridge University Press.

Thongchai, Winichakul. 1994. *Siam Mapped: A History of the Geo-Body of a Nation*. Honolulu: University of Hawaii Press.

Warren, James, Francis. 1981. *The Sulu Zone*. Singapore: Singapore University Press.

Wheatley, Paul. 1983. *Nagara and Commandery: Origins of the Southeast Asian urban Traditions*. Chicago: University of Chicago Press.

Whitmore, John. 1976. 'The Vietnamese Confucian Scholar's View of His Country's Early History.' In *Explorations in Early Southeast Asian History*, edited by Kenneth Hall and John Whitmore, pp. 193–201. Ann Arbor: University of Michigan SE Asian Studies

———. 1971. *Vietnam and the Chinese Model: A Comparative Study of Nguyen and Ch'ing Civil Government in the First Half of the Nineteenth Century*. Cambridge: Harvard University Press.

Woodside, Alexander. 1982. 'Conceptions of Change and of Human Responsibility for Change in Late Traditional Vietnam.' In *Moral Order and the Question of Change: Essays on Southeast Asian Thought*, edited by Alexander Woodside, pp. 104–49. New Haven: Yale University Southeast Asian Studies.

Wyatt, David. 1997. 'Southeast Asia "Inside Out", 1300-1800: A Perspective from the Interior.' *Modern Asian Studies* 31(3): 689–710.

———. 2003. *Thailand: A Short History*. New Haven: Yale University Press.

Zinoman, Peter. 2001. *The Colonial Bastille: A History of Imprisonment in Vietnam, 1862–1940*. Berkeley: University of California Press.

7

The Birth of Capitalism in Global Perspective

Henry Heller

The view of capitalist origins that still dominates scholarship is that of Robert Brenner and the political Marxists, a perspective which is not merely Eurocentric but Anglocentric (Brenner 1976: 30–75). As is well known, Brenner developed the work of Maurice Dobb ([1946] 1963) on the decline of feudalism and rise of capitalism. Dobb argued that peasant revolts and demographic decline during the late medieval crisis led to the end of feudalism. Brenner agreed with this, but further claimed that during this crisis, changes in social property relations unique to England set the stage for the subsequent development of capitalism. Having retained most of the arable land despite the crisis, the English nobles were able to impose economic rents on tenants sixteenth century onwards. It was rent that forced tenants to become progressively more efficient producers.

Among other things that tenants did to enhance profitability, one was that they deployed wage labour in increasingly efficient ways and thereby were able to accelerate the accumulation of capital. In other words, the development of relative exploitation, which itself was a dependent variable of changes in social property relations, lies at the heart of the origins of capitalism. It is this dynamic confined to England that determined and shaped the development of the market, colonialism, and slavery in the rest of the world (Brenner 1977: 25–93).

There are several points to be made in rejoinder to this view. Behind Brenner's perspective is the assumption that rational or more or less perfect and competitive markets operated already in the sixteenth century. On the contrary, I take the position that such markets were only in the course of formation and that the state played a large role in facilitating this process. At the beginning of the sixteenth century, a national market did not exist and especially not in the crucial commodities of grain and labour (Wrightson 2000: 102–4). The market was still deeply embedded in local and regional economies as suggested by Karl Polanyi (1957). Instead of understanding the market as historically evolved, Brenner has reified it into an ahistorical institution that operated in the sixteenth century as it operates in modern times. Moreover, while gains were made in relative exploitation in England sixteenth century onwards, the real breakthroughs in this regard only came in the eighteenth century during the so-called agricultural revolution (Heller 2011: 87).

The development of relative exploitation is undoubtedly an essential feature of the new capitalist system. But it is important to reassert that absolute exploitation and primitive accumulation were likewise essential and augmented the development of relative exploitation. That was true in the early phases of capitalism and is no less true today. This suggests that far from being a strictly economic process, capital accumulation relied on political and social compulsion as much as on market forces, and this paper assumes, contrary to the political Marxist view, that capitalism is not merely an economic phenomenon, but a mode of production which includes the influence of not only economics but also politics and culture.

Notable is Brenner's emphasis on the role of the landlord class as opposed to the peasants, bourgeoisie, and workers. True, his account of capitalism starts from the peasant revolts of the fourteenth century. But whereas others have stressed the victories of the peasants and the consequent differentiation of them into wage labourers and employers of labour, Brenner instead emphasizes the retention of control by English landlords and their ability to dictate economic terms to would-be capitalist farmers. This is despite the fact that the very existence of economic rents was disputed before the eighteenth century (Heller 2011: 99). Moreover, Brenner's economism ignores the role of ongoing ideological/religious struggle in the liberation of the late medieval peasantry (Harman 2008: 187). This is doubly true with respect to the Tudor and Stuart period (Durston and Eales 1996: 268–9). Marx, in his discussion of the birth of capitalism in sixteenth-century England, does speak of social property relations, stressing the relationship between agrarian farmers and rural wage earners and the new social and political importance of profit. Brenner's stress is rather on the social property relationships between landlords and their tenants and the continued force of rent (albeit capitalist rent). The ideological and ultimately political significance of the struggle between landlords and their tenants is ignored (Whittle 2000: 310; 2013). Indeed, the role of the state and of revolution in constructing markets and in the transition to capitalism is dismissed (Heller 2011: 118–27). Likewise, capitalism having appeared in the sixteenth century, it is assumed that it faced no serious opposition. The Tudors and Stuarts tended to favour it more than monarchies on the continent, but at the same time, the English state until the Revolution reflected the interests above all of the nobility and established church. The end of feudal property relations and economic monopolies as well as the power of the established church were anathema to them and their opposition represented a serious obstacle to the consolidation of capitalism. By virtue of their control of the repressive and ideological apparatus of the Tudor and Stuart governments, the monarchy represented an ongoing barrier to the consolidation of capitalism (Manning 1991, 1996, 2003). Indeed, control of the state was the keystone of early modern revolutions. But for Brenner, the bitter constitutional, class, and religious struggles of the seventeenth century have at best only a secondary significance. Capitalism conceived of in mature economic terms existed from the beginning of the sixteenth century and the class and legal struggles of the Tudor and Stuart period are of secondary significance at best. Brenner's view of the transition is not only economistic but, we conclude, is also deeply anachronistic and ahistorical.

Brenner's insistence, at least in his early work, that capitalism developed more or less exclusively in England is also quite parochial. Its beginnings cannot be understood by looking at England alone. Capitalism—from the start a single system—actually began in Italy, spread to Germany, and then to the Netherlands and France. England was the last stop in this progression (Heller 2011: 52). Many of the factors leading to the development of capitalism in England were also present in these other countries. The key difference between these countries, where the development of capitalism was arrested or limited, and England lay in the balance of power between capital, the state, and feudal power. Italy failed to consolidate a territorial state thanks to the strength of merchant capital being too great, while in Germany and France, feudalism itself proved too strong. Our study of these cases will demonstrate that, in addition to the economic conditions stressed by Brenner, two political conditions were critical to the successful development of capitalism: the existence of a territorial state and the influence of capitalist or incipiently capitalist classes over the state. The faltering of capitalism in Italy, France, and Germany sheds light on the importance of the more propitious political conditions, which obtained in Holland as well as in England. And capitalism, being a single system that developed in an uneven fashion, meant that its eventual consolidation in Holland and England came at the expense of its further development on the continent of Europe (Heller 2011: 52).

The earliest process of capitalism, that is, the expropriation of the peasantry, took place all across Western Europe. It assumed different forms and followed different speeds and paths in different countries. Sooner or later, it cleared a path to the development of capitalism. England was only the classic case of this process (Heller 2011: 75).

Capitalism certainly developed earliest in the city-states of fifteenth-century Florence, Milan, and Venice based on their highly developed agriculture and advanced commercial, manufacturing, and banking enterprises. Despite political division, the late medieval period saw the emergence of an internal market for labour and goods in the peninsula and, as a consequence, the appearance of agrarian capitalism in the fertile Po Valley. Capital there entered and transformed agricultural production and producers were transformed into wage labourers. Industrial development was likewise strongest there, especially in Lombardy. Lacking a centralized territorial state that could protect it and too dependent on feudal and absolutist power, Italian capitalism succumbed in the late sixteenth century (Heller 2011: 54–61).

Brenner simply ignores this Italian experiment. He furthermore flatly denies that capitalism developed in France. For him, the origins of capitalist accumulation lay in England alone. The notion that both feudalism and a subordinated capitalism could dialectically coexist within the absolute state is excluded by Brenner's mono-causal positivist logic, which insists that the key to capitalist development is the supposed existence of economic rents in a rational market. Indeed, in Brenner's hands, the example of France reinforces the uniqueness of English capitalism by becoming the perfect foil for the latter, experiencing the same upsurge of class struggle as England in the late middle ages with a very different outcome. In France, peasants came to control roughly 45 or 50 per cent of the land as against only 25 or 30 per cent in England. As a result of the greater share of property retained by the French peasantry, whatever tendency there was towards capitalism in sixteenth-century France was arrested. It is then the differing allocation of property and the contrasting relations of production that determined the divergent evolution of the two countries in the early modern period (Heller 2011: 71–4). In the eyes of Brenner, England is the model and norm of capitalist origins. France is the feudal *Other*. France remains the pre-eminent example of failed transition.

As the most important Marxist authority on the transition question today, Brenner's view matters a great deal. His treatment of France has provided grist for the mill of the revisionist trend in historiography, which has sought to sever the relationship between the French Revolution and the development of capitalism. Since Marx, it has been the view of Marxists that, like the English Revolution, the French Revolution was a bourgeois and capitalist revolution. Such a view was a fundamental feature of the Marxist view of history. The Brenner thesis suggested to some that given the non-capitalist evolution of France under the Ancien Régime, such a bourgeois and capitalist revolution was, to say the least, doubtful (Comninel 1987; Lafrance 2018; Miller 2018). In a curious way, Brenner's view based in Marxism dovetailed with a developing scholarly and political trend against the Marxist view of the French Revolution known as revisionism. This undeniably conservative historiographical current, ascendant since the 1980s, attacked the idea that the Revolution in France could be understood as a bourgeois and capitalist revolution (Heller 2017: 26–7).

Under French absolutism, feudal rent dominated to the point that there was no capitalist bourgeoisie according to revisionism (Heller 2017: 54–8). But in fact, the sixteenth century saw an ongoing advance of the capitalist bourgeoisie. The religious civil wars (1562–94) were undoubtedly a period of economic regression and confused conflict of all against all—the bourgeoisie divided against itself, peasants against peasants, as well as against nobles and townspeople, and, to top it all, nobles against nobles, and all sides in revolt against the state. On the other hand, there can be no doubt that class conflict between the bourgeoisie and nobles was the critical element.

The essential arena of conflict was a struggle over the land in which the peasantry was being drawn in on the side of the bourgeoisie. The response of the nobles was to abandon the peasants to violence. The nobility responded to the threat from below by carrying on a class war from above (Heller 2011: 73). But the pugnacious French bourgeoisie were prepared to challenge the nobility in a way that the German bourgeoisie did not. Far from exhausting itself in the long war, the bourgeoisie, in league with the urban plebeians and an increasingly aroused peasantry, were prepared to confront noble power more and more as the conflict unfolded. The concept of noble status itself came under ideological attack (Heller 2011: 73). In the end, the Catholic and Protestant nobles who had revolted were forced back into obedience to the king in order to protect themselves from the growing menace of the Third Estate. This was the basis on which the Bourbon Henri IV (1594–1610) was able to begin reconsolidating the monarchical state (Heller 2011: 73).

The increasing political and social assertiveness of the bourgeoisie was based on its growing economic strength. The civil wars were hideously destructive and resulted in a considerable economic and demographic regression. In the south of France, the capitalism that had developed in the first part of the sixteenth century faltered. On the other hand, things were very different in the richer grain lands of the north. The violence and heavy taxation of the civil wars may have forced many subsistence peasants off the land, but the bourgeoisie benefited from what amounted to primitive accumulation. A class of rural bourgeoisie in pursuit of profit was able to consolidate itself. The increased dependence of the expropriated peasantry on wages ensured the availability of abundant supplies of cheap labour for agricultural work. A wave of interest in agricultural improvement, new mechanical inventions, and new manufactures developed during the religious wars, which continued through the reign of Henri IV. Indeed, the Bourbon monarchy sought to support and control these initiatives through its mercantilist policies.

The seventeenth-century French state tried to contain this bourgeoisie while favouring the reconsolidation of the power of the nobility and church. That it was successful in the short run was signified by the decline of the so-called sixteenth century offensive of profit in favour of an offensive of rent. On the other hand, the rural and urban bourgeoisie that had emerged in the sixteenth century, though hard-pressed, survived and persevered in the seventeenth century. It re-emerged with new vigour in the Age of Enlightenment. Capitalism expanded prodigiously in the last century of the Ancien Régime. Pace Brenner and others, the revolution that came at the end of that century was undoubtedly not merely bourgeois, but also capitalist (Heller 2017: 54–79).

The case of German capitalism is yet more interesting because it links directly to the relationship between capitalism in Europe and its connection to the rest of the world. Italian capitalism continued to be significant until the close of the sixteenth century. Over the decades of the 1500s, however, it came to be rivalled by the emergence of another pole of capitalist development in Holland and England. But between the 1470s and the 1520s, the most dynamic focus of up-and-coming capitalism in Europe was Germany or the so-called Holy Roman Empire. Its geographical position between still-dominant Italy and the emerging Netherlands helps to explain its dynamism. But more significant was the extraordinary expansion of its mining and metallurgical industries. Especially important were the gold and silver mines of the Tyrol, Erzgebirge (Saxony/West Bohemia), and Hungary/Eastern Slovakia. Organized and controlled on a capitalist basis, these mines, which employed tens of thousands of wage workers, provided the liquid capital in the form of precious metals that was critical to the spectacular early expansion of the capitalist economy in Europe (1470–1530). Silver and gold from Central Europe also supplied virtually the only commodities Europeans could exchange for Chinese, Malay, and Indian silks, spices, and porcelains. It was the precious metals from these mines that allowed the first stage of the cycle of capitalist accumulation in German and European agriculture and manufacturing to take place. Control of precious metals or capitalist money meanwhile facilitated the opening of new trans-oceanic sea lanes, circumventing in part the Mediterranean and allowing Europeans for the first time to trade directly with Asia. When German production of silver and gold petered out after 1530, the influx of American silver and gold allowed this initial direct commercial link to expand into an enormous world market (Heller 2011: 61). It is our argument that the availability of this world money in the form of precious metals, first from Germany and then the Americas, was as indispensable to the development of capitalist accumulation as were capitalist relations of production.

Population growth and overseas expansion led to an expansion of demand for commodities in Germany from the last third of the fifteenth century. Not only did the gold and silver mining sector expand prodigiously, capitalist relations of production were established throughout this key sector with technical progress and substantial capital investment by capitalists from Nuremberg and other south German cities. Moreover, the influence of financial and merchant capital was also apparent to a greater or lesser degree in the grain and wood trade and the extensive metallurgical, wool, silk, linen, fustian, grain, salt, glass-making, and printing industries that spread across the face of Germany (Heller 2011: 66). But in Germany, a powerful feudal reaction consolidated itself as the capitalist economy and financial and merchant capital advanced. Capitalism exacerbated class conflict at every level of German society, prompting noble violence, increased feudal dues, and growing attempts to impose or re-impose serfdom on the peasantry, especially in southern and southwest Germany and the Rhineland in the late fifteenth and early sixteenth centuries. The imposition of serfdom even served as a tool by which territorial princes exerted their authority. On the other hand, though they lacked leadership and common objectives, the resistance of the common people became equally fierce, leading to the plebeian, worker, and peasant protests that characterized the period leading to the crisis of the Reformation. The further development of capitalism was also hemmed in by the imperial and feudal order. The Habsburg Emperor sought to rule a universal European state, not a unified and centralized Germany. The Emperor, as well as the territorial princes, blocked such a national political project. At the same time, serfdom and feudalism fundamentally barred the route to the development of capitalism in agriculture.

In Germany, serfdom and lordship grew stronger at the end of the fifteenth and beginning of the sixteenth century and the new economic dynamism, in fact, made possible the simultaneous strengthening of not only capitalism but also feudal reaction. The result of this volatile contradiction was the famous social and political explosion known as the German Peasants' War (1524–5), characterized by Friedrich Engels as an early bourgeois revolution (Engels 1850a: 422). As their power grew, Germany's territorial princes levied heavier taxes and servile obligations on the peasants (Heller 2011: 66). The patrician rulers of the towns were allied to the feudal lords and oppressed the rest of the urban population, including the rich and not-so-rich burghers. The burghers appear as a moderate opposition, aspiring to share in the town governments from which they were excluded and attacking the privileges and property of the clergy. Beneath them came the plebeians—ruined burghers, small-scale artisans, apprentices, day labourers, and the numerous forerunners of the lumpen proletariat, some of whom became part of a radical opposition. No better, perhaps even inferior to them, were the peasants who earlier had engaged in numerous local revolts, but who had never come together in a general national revolt.

Though Germany was politically and economically divided on the eve of the peasant revolt, the Reformation created a crisis during which revolutionary political and social ideas spread deeply and broadly in the population (Engels 1850a: 411). During this crisis, three large camps coalesced: Catholic or reactionary; Lutheran bourgeois reformist; and revolutionary. The religious conflicts of the sixteenth century were class conflicts fought out on the basis of the shibboleths of religion. This was the result of the ongoing powerful influence of the church, as a consequence of which all questions—political, juridical, social, and economic—were still posed largely in religious terms; the church was the all-embracing synthesis and the most general sanction of the existing feudal order. With roots deep in the middle ages, the heretical ideology of the burghers, to which some of the nobility also subscribed, called for the material dispossession of the wealth and privileges of the ecclesiastical order (Heller 2011: 63–4). Agreeing with such notions, peasant and plebeian radicals took things a step further by calling for political, social, and even economic equality. The propertyless, of whom there were increasingly large numbers, challenged the notion of a class-based society by espousing in utopian fashion the idea of all things in common.

The Catholic conservative camp included the imperial authorities, the ecclesiastical, and some lay princes, the richer nobles, the prelates, and urban patricians. The Lutheran camp attracted to itself all the propertied members of the opposition, including the mass of the nobility, the burghers, and even some lay princes who wished to seize the property of the church and increase their independence from the Holy Roman Empire. The peasants and plebeians constituted the radical party. The most important leader of the latter group was Thomas Münzer, who vainly advocated communism and a pantheism which, according to Engels, approached atheism (Heller 2011: 64).

While the aspirations of the radical party were doomed to fail, so too were those of the more moderate reformers. No effective alliance between elements of the nobility and the bourgeoisie of the English sort emerged. In the latter country, serfdom had largely disappeared by the end of the Middle Ages and the old nobility was virtually wiped out in the Wars of the Roses, replaced by a new nobility of bourgeois origin. In contrast, serfdom was still rampant in Germany and the nobles drew their income largely from feudal sources. Political power lay overwhelmingly at the local and regional level.

The nearest approximation to a bourgeois revolutionary programme was articulated by Wendel Hipler in the so-called Heilbronn Manifesto issued at the height of the Peasant War. Engels (1850a: 461) is careful not to claim that Hipler's programme was an expression of the bourgeoisie but rather 'what may be described as the cross-section of the nation's progressive elements, [which] anticipated *modern bourgeois society*' (Heller 2011: 63–4). While nominally written on behalf of the peasantry, the Heilbronn programme called for a standardized currency, standard weights and measures, abolition of internal customs duties, and so on, demands which were more in the interests of the townspeople than the peasantry. In order to reach out to the nobility, concessions were made that substantially approached the modern system of redemption and would have transformed feudal into bourgeois landlordship.

Engels compares the German Peasants' Revolt to the French Revolution from a political point of view. In the case of the eighteenth-century revolution in a politically unified France, the whole country was split into two clearly opposed camps. In a deeply divided sixteenth-century Germany, this was a rank impossibility. On the other hand, Engels saw the Peasants' War not simply as a German event but as an international one based on the prospects for the further development of capitalism. As he reiterated on returning to the theme many decades later, 'Reformation—Lutheran and Calvinist— is the No. 1 bourgeois revolution, the Peasant War being its critical episode ... Revolution No. 1, which was more European than the English and spread in Europe much more rapidly than the French' (Engels 1850b: 411). Indeed, the Reformation spread throughout Western and Central Europe.

The failure of this German early bourgeois revolution meant the subservience of capitalism in Germany to the forces of absolutism and feudalism until after the French Revolution. This subordination was reinforced by the growing superiority of capitalism in Holland and England, which integrated Germany into their economic orbit. Brenner and his school ignore this international European perspective on the development of capitalism in favour of a parochial Anglocentric perspective. But this essay's criticism of the political Marxist perspective puts into doubt the Eurocentric perspective on the development of capitalism itself. For Brenner's school, the non-European world is extraneous to the development of capitalism. While not questioning the fact that Europe was the centre of an emerging capitalism, it takes seriously Marx's own view that the birth of capitalism was simultaneously the product of both new relations of production and the creation of the world market. In so doing, it reviews the principal Marxist views on the significance of the development of the world market and the effects of early capitalism on the non-European world. Moving beyond discussion of these theories, it further argues that the development of capitalist world money out of the gold and silver produced in Latin America was critical to the emergence of the world market by lubricating exchange relations across the globe. More significantly, it suggests that this world money in the form of gold and silver bullion served an entirely new role by becoming indispensable in transforming the creation of value through new relations of production into an ongoing process of self-expansion, or, in other words, made possible the accumulation of capital. Hence, we contend that the origins of capitalism were perforce as much extra-European as European.

It is important to make clear in the first place that capitalist relations of production were by no means a European affair. Organized and controlled on a capitalist basis, wage labour came into existence beyond Europe during the sixteenth century. It was a striking characteristic of economic relations in the gold and silver mines of Bolivia and Mexico (Brown 2012: 47–8, 50, 64). The advanced technology used in this industry and the capital relations of production that prevailed in it, both in the Old and New World, are striking. John Tutino (2011) has furthermore demonstrated that capitalist relations of production were to be found not only in the Mexican mines, but also extended into the valley of Mexico from the conquest period. Equally significant is the role of gold and silver as veritable world money in the newly emergent capitalist world economy linking the Americas, Europe, and Asia (O'Flynn and Giraldez 2008: 359–87). The silverization of the Chinese economy, which took place in the sixteenth century, stimulated the development of an incipient or embryonic industrial capitalism in China and through the spectacular growth of Chinese exports of silks and porcelains, became the principal axis of the emerging world market (Dixin and Chengming 2000: xxvi, 90, 318, 375, 377; O'Flynn and Giraldez 2008: 359–87). The essential element in facilitating that market then was silver and gold, which began to take the form of capitalist money or money that embodied for the first time the accumulation in financial form of increasing amounts of abstract labour or value that made possible the accumulation of capital. The emergence of capitalist world money then constituted as much a founding principle of capitalism as did the widespread development of wage labour in England and Europe.

It is true, as we have noted, that as the capitalist system developed globally, it was northwest Europe–Britain, northern France, Holland, and northwest Germany that came to dominate the system. This was because wage labour became dominant in northwest Europe while less productive feudal and slave relations of production predominated elsewhere, including the New World and China. A first attempt to theorize the global development of capitalism was made by Eric Hobsbawm (1976: 159–64) using the concept of uneven development. He did so as his contribution to the celebrated debate on the transition from feudalism to capitalism back in the 1950s. In this highly original contribution informed by a dialectical view of history—a contribution which has been largely ignored—Hobsbawm put the emphasis on the role of uneven development in the evolution of capitalism throughout its history. As capitalism developed, West European advance came directly at the expense of Eastern Europe and Asia, Africa, and Latin America. The process of West European transition throughout its early history entailed turning other areas into dependent economies and colonies.

Hobsbawm's conception of the transition is a dialectical one, in which unevenness plays a central part. Gain in one place is invariably at the expense of other places, even those that were initially more developed. In this schema, the advance of Holland and England towards capitalism entails the re-feudalization of Italy and Germany and the feudalization of Poland, Hungary, and Russia and the progressive subordination of the Global South through colonialism. Eastern Europe and the Global South were turned into dependent economies and colonies. Seizing resources from advanced areas or later on from colonized regions became an intrinsic feature of West European development. In other words, the emergence of capitalism has to be understood in terms of an ongoing worldwide process of appropriation based on uneven development both within and outside Europe. Hobsbawm (1976: 164) concludes that 'the net effect of European capitalism was to divide the world ever more sharply into two sectors: the "developed" and the "under-developed" countries, in other words, the exploiting and the exploited'. From the perspective of the non-European world or rather the non-West European world, the onset of capitalism was a zero-sum game played at its expense.

Immanuel Wallerstein's (1974) world-systems theory may be regarded as an elaboration and systematization of Hobsbawm's conception. In common with Dobb and Brenner, Wallerstein acknowledged that the class struggles of the fourteenth century marked the crisis of European feudalism. But in contrast to their stress on changes in the relations of production as key to capitalist origins, Wallerstein emphasized overseas expansion which, in the first instance, was a way out of the impasse of class conflict from the perspective of the ruling class. It led towards the beginning of capitalism. The expansion of the world market is an exit from class conflict.

Marx had noted that the sixteenth century saw both the emergence of proletarian labour as well as the world market. For him, these two developments tied together dialectically marked the beginning of the capitalist epoch. But Wallerstein (1974: 37–8, 77, 127) acknowledged the importance of the proletarianization of labour only in passing, emphasizing instead the emergence of the world market or a trade-based division of labour as the starting point for accumulation. Geographically, this 'world economy' of the sixteenth century expanded to western, southern, and east central Europe and included the Mediterranean, Latin America, and the coast of West Africa (Wallerstein 1974: 68).

Wallerstein may have de-centred proletarian or wage labour, but only to place it in his more widely conceived capitalist world-system. Its three main sectors were distinguished on the basis of the forms of labour each featured, the forms favoured by ruling classes in each sector based on the economic constraints, and possibilities for profit within the emerging world market. At the core of the system in north-west Europe, wage labour became the dominant form of exploitation in agriculture and manufacture. In the semi-periphery that embraced the rest of western and central Europe, tenant farming, sharecropping, and petty commodity craft production prevailed. In the peripheral zones of East Europe, Africa, and Latin America, which produced mainly grain and sugar, serfdom and slavery or coerced cash crop labour became the rule (Wallerstein 1974: 86–7, 95, 103, 104–7, 112, 116). The existence of free or wage labour specified or defined the emerging capitalist economy, Wallerstein (1974: 127) acknowledged, as "'relations of production" that define a system are the "relations of production" of the whole system, and the system at this point in time is the European world-economy'. But free wage labour could not be found throughout the world-system, Wallerstein insisted. Free labour was the form of labour control used for skilled work in core countries. Coerced labour was used for less skilled work in peripheral areas. The combination of free and unfree labour was the essence of capitalism (Wallerstein 1974: 122). This was a radical redefinition of capitalism, motivated by Wallerstein's belief that accumulation at the centre was based not merely on the exploitation of wage workers in Europe but also on the exploitation of producers on the capitalist periphery. Wallerstein's conception of labour systems is equivalent to Althusser's notion of the capitalist social formation in which the dominant mode of production is capitalist but in which the subordinate modes of slavery and feudalism coexist.

In the core, the market became the principle means of the control of labour. But such capitalist states also tended to be strong with regard to other strong states and with respect to weaker political entities in the semi-periphery and the periphery. In the periphery, states were weak. In the latter two zones, political or physical coercion of the labour force persisted and was even intensified, as they were absorbed into the capitalist world-system (Wallerstein 1974: 308–12, 355). The development of classes was a function of, or depended on, international division of labour. In this system of uneven development and of strong states dominating and coercing weaker ones, economic surpluses tended to move from the periphery and semi-periphery towards the core. Over the long term, underdevelopment in the periphery developed in tandem with development in the core based on unequal exchange (Wallerstein 1974: 95–6, 100). The initial advantages of higher skill levels and more fixed capital reinforced by greater political power provide the core countries with a cumulative advantage over states located towards the periphery. 'Hence', concludes Wallerstein, 'the ongoing process of a world-economy tends to expand the economic and social gaps among its varying areas in the very process of its development' (Wallerstein 1974: 350). For Wallerstein, there is a single capitalist world-system, which questionably makes the Polish noble extracting labour from a serf, a French noble collecting rent from a subsistence peasant in the Auvergne, and an English noble collecting rent from a capitalist farmer in Kent equally capitalist parts of the same process. But French and Polish nobles cannot remotely be considered capitalists. Furthermore, Wallerstein's notion of strong states at the centre and weaker ones towards the periphery does not fit the historical evolution of absolutist states like the Ottoman Sultanate in its heyday.

Marx's conception of uneven global development has been further developed by David Harvey. Harvey understands the development of capitalism as proceeding through the recurrent renewal of the process of capital accumulation by means of what he terms a spatial fix. Harvey argues that one of the ways that capitalism has repeatedly attempted to overcome its crises of over-accumulation is through the abandonment of older centres of accumulation that have exhausted their profit potential towards new poles of accumulation. In the contemporary context, the movement of investment capital from the United States towards China is a perfect example (Harvey 2005: 122–3). Indeed, the interest of Harvey in the historic displacement of the centre of capitalist accumulation from one to another is obviously connected to the post–World War I displacement of the focal point of capital from London to New York and the possible future transfer of the global centre of capitalism to Asia. Such displacements provoke severe social and political turbulence in what Harvey calls a switching crisis. Giovanni Arrighi has lately attempted to show the pertinence of Harvey's conceptions of spatial fix and switching crisis to an understanding of the outbreak of signal crises and the initiation of a financial or declining phase of imperial power in the historical cycles of successive Genoese/Spanish, Dutch, British, and American political hegemonies. In each instance, it is the displacement of capital from a place where over-accumulation has led to stagnation towards a fresh centre of accumulation that provokes crisis and political and social conflict (Arrighi 2009).

It was Marx (1975, Vol. 35: 743–4) himself, of course, who had pointed out how capital had successively moved from Venice to Holland to England and finally to the United States from one pole of accumulation to the next through the mechanism of the international banking and financial system. While we have limited hard or quantitative data of such capital movements, the sequence has been more or less confirmed by Fernand Braudel (1979: 118, 202–7, 228, 252–3) and Richard Goldthwaite (2009: 135–6). It is to Harvey's credit that he has brought this geographical dimension of the historical movement of capital to the fore. Nonetheless, this spatial displacement of capital should be seen in the light of Marx's more fundamental notion of uneven development, which he considered a characteristic feature of capitalism. Throughout, it is the state and the hierarchical order of the international state system that provides the political framework for these displacements.

The theorizations of Hobsbawm, Wallerstein, Harvey, and Arrighi allow us to understand capitalism's beginnings as a global system. But they assume rightfully that Europe and the United States were at the core of the system. I do not see how that reality can be erased despite recent post-colonial attempts to provincialize Europe. After all, in my view, being in the vanguard of capitalism is no particular virtue. From a political point of view, the Left has always assumed that capitalism had a centre. Moreover, it seems to me important in a political sense to always locate the headquarters of capitalism rather than to pretend that it existed everywhere or that such a system, having no centre, really does not matter in a political sense. In order to bombard the headquarters, it is necessary to know its location. The historical significance of the imperialism of the major capitalist powers has always mattered to the rest of the world.

Nonetheless, a useful attempt to minimize a Eurocentric perspective has lately been offered by Alexander Anievas and Kerem Nişancıoğlu (2015) (see also Fabry 2018). They demonstrate the political or economic importance of non-capitalist and non-European societies to the development of capitalism. To break out of the pervasive Eurocentrism in the debate, they turn to Trotsky's theory of uneven and combined development. Trotsky (1932, Vol. 1: 2–4) argued that the capitalist mode of production transformed the general law of uneven development, which holds that societies grow at different paces, some faster and others slower, at various points in time. He maintained that capitalism's unique expansionary qualities led it to penetrate pre-capitalist modes of production, subordinating their economies and states to its laws of development. It thus produced hybrid societies, combining the world's most advanced and backward features. His paradigmatic example was, of course, Russia at the turn of the twentieth century. It had been a backward, feudal society ruled by the autocratic tsarist state. European capitalism penetrated it towards the end of the nineteenth century, producing a hybrid formation that combined advanced capitalist development with backward feudal relations (Anievas and Nscancioglu 2015: 44–50).

Anievas and Nişancıoğlu use uneven and combined development as a methodology to show how capitalism came into being through an international, inter-societal process. They demonstrate how more developed tributary modes of production in societies like China and the Ottoman Empire suffered the 'penalty of progressiveness', their more advanced economic systems and stable states stifled the development of capitalism within their societies. By contrast, the economic and geopolitical interaction between them and less-developed feudal Europe, in particular Holland and England, granted them the 'privilege of historical backwardness', as they incorporated more advanced productive forces from elsewhere (Anievas and Nişancıoğlu 2015: 104, 106, 115, 250). Moreover, under 'the whip of external necessity', Europe was forced to compete geopolitically with its more advanced rivals, a dynamic that provided the condition for the development of capitalism in Holland and England (Anievas and Nişancıoğlu 2015: 46).

Within this framework, Anievas and Nişancıoğlu radically recast the process of capitalist development as the result of the inter-societal interaction between European feudalism and the Mongol Empire, the Ottoman Empire, the conquest of the Americas, the establishment of the slave trade and plantations, and the colonization of Asia. This international version of history is perhaps their book's most significant contribution. They begin by demonstrating how the Mongol Empire spurred the development of merchant capital throughout Europe. The Pax Mongolica opened up the Silk Road, dramatically increased trade, and transferred the Empire's higher development of its productive forces to backward Europe. This encouraged the formations of cities, which had a gravitational pull on peasants to leave the countryside and become wage labourers, especially in the Italian city-states (Anievas and Nişancıoğlu 2015: 67, 71–7).

The Mongol Empire was also the source of the bubonic plague that caused the Black Death in Europe, which decisively changed the balance of class forces in England, driving lords to become capitalist farmers and peasants to become rural labourers. Thus, the Pax Mongolica forms an international precondition for the rise of

English agrarian capitalism as recounted by Brenner (Anievas and Nişancıoğlu 2015: 77–88). But Anievas and Nişancıoğlu contend that without the geopolitical competition from the Ottoman Empire, Holland and England would never have undergone the transition to capitalism. The Ottomans' more advanced tributary mode of production buttressed a more stable, unified state compared to Europe's squabbling feudal states. As a result, they were able to deploy a far larger military force against their rivals in Europe.

The most powerful state in Europe, the Habsburg Empire, had no choice but to deploy a disproportionate amount of its forces against the Ottomans. The geopolitical rivalry between the Habsburgs and the Ottomans facilitated Holland and England's capitalist development in two ways. First, it offered their merchants significant trade opportunities. Second, it provided them the geopolitical space to develop capitalism and complete their bourgeois revolutions. With the Habsburgs preoccupied, Holland managed to successfully carry through the Dutch Revolt and establish the first capitalist nation state. In England, the Habsburg's preoccupation with the Ottomans ensured their isolation from any threat and led to a relative demilitarization of the feudal lords, thereby weakening their power over the peasantry and compelling some of them, in the wake of the Black Death, to adopt capitalist agriculture (Anievas and Nişancıoğlu 2015: 91–120).

However, without the conquest of the Americas and the development of plantation slavery, Anievas and Nişancıoğlu argue, the new capitalist powers could have been strangled and certainly would not have undergone capitalist industrialization. The Ottomans were the principal reason that the European societies reoriented from the Mediterranean to the so-called New World. And once they did, the plunder of the region reinforced the differential patterns of development between the feudal absolutist powers like Spain and those of the newly capitalist Holland and England. Driven by its feudal military preoccupation of competing with the Ottomans, Spain used its horde of gold and silver to pay off loans it had taken out to pay for its military. Much of that treasure ended back in Holland and England to expand their new system.

Anievas and Nişancıoğlu also show how the colonial slave trade and the hybrid labour regime of plantation slavery, which fused capitalist pressures of production for the market with pre-capitalist relations of production, provided the raw material for industrialization—cotton, for example, being the basis for England's textile boom. The combination of these inter-societal dynamics thus made possible capitalist development in Holland, England, and eventually the rest of Europe (Anievas and Nişancıoğlu 2015: 120–73). But this was not an evolutionary process. They argue that bourgeois revolutions were necessary to establish capitalist states to defend and reproduce capitalist class rule internally against the exploited classes and internationally against both capitalist and pre-capitalist rivals (Anievas and Nişancıoğlu 2015: 174–214).

***

Let me conclude by returning to and amplifying my earlier discussion of the importance of the creation of world money for the onset of capitalism. Recognition of the importance of money to the operation of capitalism is not merely a scholarly exercise. As we know, we currently live under the rule of a globalized financialized capitalism in which money capital is at the core. This is a principal reason why Marxists today are preoccupied with Marx's theory of money (Moseley 2005). In this light, it seems to me more important than ever to try to understand theoretically and historically the role that money played in early capitalism in terms of the development of the world market, but also the beginnings of the process of capital accumulation. As we have noted, it is striking that the production of gold and silver, both in the New World and the Old, was itself a vanguard capitalist industry in the late fifteenth and sixteenth century using wage labour and seeing major investments in technological improvements. In other words, the production of money was itself a major source of the production of value. Although not a Marxist, Ian Blanchard has done pioneering work on the relationship between the growing availability of gold and silver, the development of credit markets, low interest rates, and the pace and direction of productive investment in the continent and in England in the sixteenth century. The gradual relocation of the centre of gravity of financial capital and lower interest rates from Italy, Germany, and Spain to Antwerp and London, as described by Blanchard, is particularly noteworthy. Equally important is the relationship between low interest rates and investment in agricultural improvement in the Netherlands and southern England (Blanchard 2005: 109, 112, 114–16, 105–22). Blanchard's work helps us to understand that money at this point began to assume a new role. Not only did it serve to create a world market, it began to take on the function of facilitating capitalist accumulation.

In the ancient world and in the Middle Ages, money served as a means of purchase or payment and also as a hoard. During antiquity, highly developed markets came up in the Greek and Roman period in which gold and silver served as universal equivalents for other commodities. On this basis, commercial relations on a considerable scale developed in the Mediterranean and beyond. Likewise, following the hiatus of the Dark Ages, the Middle Ages saw the redevelopment of these exchange relations that now embraced Western Europe. Precious metals were accumulated as hoards by the established church and by Italian bankers. In Florence, Venice, and Milan banking became a speciality, which increasingly facilitated international commerce and the financing of war by high and late medieval states and kingdoms. Some Italian cities like Florence and Venice were able to coin money, which achieved international acceptance as currency. Kingdoms like France and England established mints and were able to mint and circulate coins, facilitating trade within their territories.

From antiquity onwards, money was particularly important as a form of payment that allowed landowners, merchants, and tax collectors to exploit the labour of small-scale producers. Until the advent of capitalism, the hoarding of money, the use of money in exchange, and the development of credit money were the way money functioned. These functions of money would continue under capitalism. But money barely functioned as a means of accumulating capital. For that to happen, two things were necessary. In the first place, surplus value and, coincidentally, profits had to become a significant aspect of the economy. This was only possible if significant numbers of producers were forced to become wage workers and sell their labour time in such a way that excess of it could become available as surplus and profits. Secondly, an accumulation cycle had to emerge in which the production and circulation of commodities ended with the accumulation of profits in the form of capitalist money, part of which could be reinvested. The function of money that embodied surplus value for purposes of reinvestment represented an entirely novel use. Alongside the emergence of extensive development of wage labour, this change marks a quantitative leap or revolutionary change signalling the emergence of a new mode of production.

Now with the advent of new capitalist relations of production, money began to develop an entirely novel function, namely, to embody abstract labour or value. In this way, it opened the way for the accumulation of capital. This alone makes it clear that the political Marxist view that ignores the creation of the world market and puts all the stress on the emergence of capitalist relations of production, fails to take into account the role of money in the capitalist economy and, by doing so, does not deal with the emergence of accumulation as a fundamental aspect of the new mode of production. Moreover, given that the source of this new capitalist world money lay outside of Europe, the political Marxist view that the beginnings of capitalism were simply an English or European matter is untenable.

Bibliography

Anievas, Alexander and Kerem Nişancıoğlu. 2015. *How the West Came to Rule: The Geopolitical Origins of Capitalism*. London: Pluto Press.

Arrighi, Giovanni. 2004. 'Spatial and Other "Fixes" of Historical Capitalism.' *Journal of World-Systems Research* 10: 527–39. Available at http://jwsr.ucr.edu/; accessed on 9 July 2019.

Blanchard, Ian. 2005. 'International Capital Markets and Their Users, 1450–1750.' In *Early Modern Capitalism: Economic and Social Change in Europe, 1400-1800*, edited by Maarten Prak, pp. 105–23. London and New York: Routledge.

Braudel, Fernand. 1979. *Civilisation matérielle, économie et capitalisme, XVe-XVIIIe siècle*. Paris: A. Colin.

Brenner, Robert. 1976. 'Agrarian Class Structure and Economic Development in Pre-industrial Europe.' *Past & Present* 70: 30–75; republished in T.H. Aston and C.H.E. Philpin, eds. 1985. *The Brenner Debate: Agrarian Class Structure and Economic Development in Pre-Industrial Europe*, pp. 10–63. Cambridge: Cambridge University Press.

———. 1977. 'The Origins of Capitalist Development: A Critique of Neo-Smithian Marxism'. *New Left Review* 104: 25–93.

———. 1982. 'The Agrarian Roots of European Capitalism.' *Past & Present* 97: 16—113; republished in T.H. Aston and C.H.E. Philpin, eds. 1985.

The Brenner Debate: Agrarian Class Structure and Economic Development in Pre-Industrial Europe, pp. 213–327. Cambridge: Cambridge University Press.

Brown, Kendall. 2012. *A History of Mining in Latin America; From the Colonial Era to the Present*. Albuquerque: University of New Mexico Press.

Comninel, George. 1987. *Rethinking the French Revolution: Marxism and the Revisionist Challenge*. London: Verso.

Dixin, Xu and Wu Chengming. 2000. *Chinese Capitalism, 1522–1840*. Hounslow, Basingstoke, New York: St. Martin's Press.

Dobb, Maurice. (1946) 1963. *Studies in the Development of Capitalism*. New York: International Publishers; London: Routledge & Kegan Paul.

Durston, Christopher and Jacqueline Eales, eds. 1996. *The Culture of English Puritanism, 1560–1700*. New York: St. Martin's Press.

Engels, Friedrich. 1850a. 'The Peasant War in Germany'. Vol. 10, pp. 397–482, in Marx and Engels, *Collected Works*, translated by Richard Dixon. London: Lawrence & Wishart/New York: International Publishers/Moscow: Progress Books.

———. 1850b. *Peasants War 1524–5*. Moscow: Foreign Languages Publishing House.

Fabry, Adam. 2018. 'Symposium on Alexander Anievas and Kerem Nişancıoğlu's *How the West Came to Rule* (2015)'. *Historical Materialism* 26(3): 39–51.

Goldthwaite, Richard A. 2009. *The Economy of Renaissance Florence*. Baltimore: Johns Hopkins University Press.

Harman, Chris. 2008. 'An Age of Transition? Economy and Society in England in the Later Middle Ages: The Field and the Forge: Population, Production and Power in the Pre-industrial West.' *Historical Materialism* 16(1): 85–99.

Harvey, David. 2005. *The New Imperialism*. Oxford: Oxford University Press.

Heller, Henry. 2011. *The Birth of Capitalism: A Twenty-First Century Perspective*. London: Pluto Press.

———. 2017. *The French Revolution and Historical Materialism*. Leiden: Brill.

Hobsbawm, Eric. 1976. 'From Feudalism to Capitalism.' In *The Transition from Feudalism to Capitalism*, edited by Rodney Hilton, pp. 159–64. London: New Left Books.

Manning, Brian. 1991. *The English People and the English Revolution*. London: Bookmarks.

———. 1996. *Aristocrats, Plebeians and Revolution in England 1640–1660*. East Haven, CT: Pluto Books.

————. 2003. *Revolution and Counter-Revolution in England, Ireland and Scotland 1658–60*. London: Bookmarks.

Marx, Karl. 1975. *Capital*, Vol. 1. In Karl Marx and Friedrich Engels, *Collected Works*, 35 Vols, translated by Richard Dixon. London: Lawrence & Wishart; New York: International Publishers.

Miller, Stephen. 2018. 'Peasant Farming in Eighteenth- and Nineteenth-Century France and the Transition to Capitalism under Charles de Gaulle.' In *Case Studies in the Development of Capitalism*, edited by Xavier Lafrance and Charles Post, pp. 87–109. London: Palgrave MacMillan.

Lafrance, Xavier. 2018. 'The Transition to Industrial Capitalism in Nineteenth-Century France.' In *Case Studies in the Development of Capitalism*, edited by Xavier Lafrance and Charles Post, pp. 111–37. London: Palgrave MacMillan.

Moseley, Fred, ed. 2005. *Marx's Theory of Money: Modern Appraisals*. New York: Palgrave Macmillan.

O'Flynn, Dennis and Arturo Giraldez. 2008, 'Born Again: Globalization's Sixteenth Century Origins: Asian/Global Versus European Dynamics.' *Pacific Economic Review* 13(3): 359–87.

Polanyi, Karl. 1957. *The Great Transformation*. Boston: Beacon Press.

Trotsky, Leon. 1932. *History of the Russian Revolution*, translated by Max Eastman, 3 Vols. New York: Simon and Shuster.

Tutino, John. 2011. *Making a New World: Founding Capitalism in the Bajío and Spanish North America*. Durham: Duke University Press.

Whittle, Jane. 2000. *The Development of Agrarian Capitalism: Land and Labour in Norfolk, 1440–1580*. Oxford: Clarendon Press; New York: Oxford University Press.

————, ed. 2013. *Landlords and Tenants in Britain, 1440–1660: Tawney's Agrarian Problem Revisited*. Woodbridge: Boydell Press.

Wallerstein, Immanuel. 1974. *The Modern World-System*. New York: Academic Press.

Wrightson, Keith. 2000. *Earthly Necessities. Economic Lives in Early Modern Britain*. New Haven: Yale University Press.

II

CASE STUDIES IN THE HISTORIES
OF CAPITALISMS

8

One-Off Capitalism in Song China, 960–1279 CE

Kent Deng

Historical Background

It has been commonly recognized that Song China (960–1279 CE) led the world in science, technology, commerce, urbanization, as well as economic and demographic growth (Deng and Zheng 2015). Conventional wisdom points to its predecessor, the Tang dynasty (618–907 CE), as the root cause of the Song miracle.[1] However, the available historical evidence supports anything but this rosy and

[1] The issue is known as the 'Tang–Song Transition/Transformation', an idée fixe beginning in 1910 with Naito (1947: Chapter 1); also Fogel (1984: 170). For the Tang political, economic, artistic, and demographic influence, see Hartwell (1982), Esherick and Rankin (1990), Bol (1992), and Smith and von Glahn (2003). However, scholars in China see discontinuity in political and economic institutions after the Tang, see Deng (1986, 1990), Qi (2000), Lin (2005), Zhang (2006), Ge (2000: 357–60), Huang (2003), Li (2010), and Bao (2004).

ahistorical hypothesis. The truth was that there was a massive discontinuity from the Tang to the Song dynasty.

Understanding this discontinuity is key to understanding the Song growth and its one-off fate. First of all, politically speaking, at the end of the Tang rule, the empire of China was totally in ruins and dissolved into 10 kingdoms—Wu (902–37), Qianshu (907–25), Wuyue (907–78), Min (909–45), Nanhan (917–71), Jingnan (924–63), Chu (927–51), Houshu (934–65), Nantang (937–75), and Beihan (951–79). A period of warring states recurred on the East Asian mainland.

Secondly, territorially and demographically, the empire's size shrank to less than half of its peak extent during the Tang period by the time the Song empire-builder brought his territory together; the reduction of farmland accounted for 80 per cent, and that of population, 67 per cent.[2] To be precise, control over the Tang frontier regions in Central Asia, the Mongolian Steppe, and Manchuria had been lost, together with the Silk Road and the Great Wall itself. These lost regions were controlled by new countries hostile to China.

Thirdly, geopolitically, the Song northern borders were under the constant threat of invasions from nomads. Such a situation left China's east coast as the only possibility for the Songs to conduct trade (Deng 1997: Chapter 4; Gipouloux 2009: Chapters 4–5).

Last, but not the least, institutionally, the Tang and the Song systems were starkly different. The Tang Empire ran a twin-track political system. Its civil services were by and large based on a meritocracy and social mobility through schooling, imperial examinations, and regular performance assessments. But its military was based on a feudal aristocracy and foreign mercenaries. In the end, it was military feudalism that wrecked the Tang state.[3] The Song state ran a meritocracy in both the civil and military services. This explains why in the Song period, per capita, the number of imperial degree holders was the highest out of all dynasties that ever ruled China. On

---

[2] Based on the available data for 755 CE (Tang) and 976 CE (Song), see Liang (1980: 6).

[3] The problem began as early as 755 CE when Tang General An Lushan (703–57) rebelled in the north. The last military rebel was Pang Xun (?–869) in the south.

the economic front, the Tang practiced state ownership of farmland, which was leased out to farmers, known as 'equal land leasing' (*jun tian zhi*). Buying and selling farmland was illegal. Under the Song, farmland was overwhelmingly privately owned; and trade with land was common. During the Tang, the fundamental economic policy was still physiocratic. Tang foreign trade was mainly land based, characterized by the tea-horse exchange (*cha ma maoyi*), primary goods being traded on both sides. The Song period was mercantilist with foreign trade being overwhelmingly sea-oriented with exports of manufactures. Finally, even the Song culture was very different from that of the Tang. There was a rise of neo-Confucianism under the leadership of Cheng Jing (1032–1085), Cheng Yi (1033–1107), and Zhu Xi (1130–1200) at the expense of Buddhism, which had gained popularity among the Tang upper classes. In addition, the Song verse (*song ci*) worked on very different rules from the Tang poem (*tang si*). The list could go on.

Factors that Dictated Changes during the Song

Two exogenous factors that dictated changes during the Song were: (*a*) a 'Little Ice Age' in East Asia during the eleventh century and (*b*) external threat of invasions and conquests along the long and open northern land borders of the Song territory. During 1000–1120 CE, the temperature on the East Asian mainland dropped 1–2°C with unprecedented drought thereafter (Zhu 1972: 36).[4] According to Chinese sources, the occurrence of warm weather dropped 90 per cent compared to the period either immediately before or after 1000–1120 CE (Song et al. 2002: 343). The onslaught of cold weather delayed the harvest season in North China by about a month (Tuotuo [1345] 1986, Vol. 7: 5716), reduced land yield by 20 per cent north to the Yangzi River (Song et al. 2002: 187; Zhang 1988: 123–4; Zheng 1996: 39–43), and pushed China's rice-growing belt southwards by about 2–4 degree latitudes—from the Yellow River, 500-kilometres

---

[4] There was a cycle of little ice ages in the last two millennia: 1 CE, 536, 1000, 1350, 1650, 1750, 1800; see Flohn (1969: 236) and Schneider and Mass (1975). For the global temperature decline, see Loehle (2007). For drought, see Song et al. (2002: 123).

southward, all the way to the Yangzi River (Cheng 1992: 13–14; Zhao and Yin 2011: 71). In addition, the cold and dry weather destroyed the flora across North China and accelerated soil erosion, which in turn silted up the Yellow River bed and caused the river to burst its banks frequently. For example, in 1108, the city of Julu in Hebei was completely submerged by silt several metres deep (Kang 2011: 117). The Huai and Yangzi rivers also behaved erratically due to the disequilibrium caused by climate change (Song et al. 2002: 120, 176, 226–7, 261, 281, 297, 317, 340–1, 369–70). According to the Song official Ouyang Xiu (1007–72), floods in Hebei Province wiped out 50–90 per cent of crops in 13 counties (Ouyang 1986, Vol. 2: 965).

The immediate human response to this climatic change was to abandon farming in North China. In 996, the Song court official Chen Jing (948–1026) reported that 'across 30 prefectures of 1,000 *li* surrounding the capital, only 20–30 percent arable land is cultivated' (Tuotuo [1345] 1986, Vol. 7: 5711).[5] Over time, it went from bad to worse. In 1069, Hou Shuxian, an official in charge of farming, reported that 'in the capital region, over 10,000 *qing*,[6] or half the total arable land, is not farmed' (Xu [1809] 1976: 4901).[7] Nationwide, in 1067, 11 per cent of all registered farmland (4.4 million qing) was deserted (*feitian*) (Tuotuo [1345] 1986, Vol. 7: 5712). In another account, 70 per cent of farming households did not farm all their registered land and did not pay the expected taxes either (Tuotuo [1345] 1986, Vol. 7: 5712). In this context, the Song farmland declined by about half (Table 8.1).

Meanwhile, evidence indicates that land was still plentiful in the warmer Yangzi region. According to Shen Kuo (1031–95), the Song writer,[8] '[In 1074], I have witnessed in Liangzhe Province lots of idle and unregistered lands yet to be farmed in vast areas in Wenzhou, Mingzhou and Taizhou' (Xu [1809] 1976: 4905). This was a century

[5] The term 'li' was elastic. Historically, it meant consistently '300 paces long'. A modern observation makes it 500 metres. Hence, 1,000 Song li is approximately equal to 500 kilometres.

[6] One qing is equal to 100 *mu* and 1 Song qing is equal to 6 *ha*.

[7] One Song picul (*shi*) is equal to 46.2 kg.

[8] Shen ([1095] 1975) serves as the evidence of the Song scientific achievements across a wide spectrum.

Table 8.1 Fluctuations in Farmland vs Growth in Household Numbers

Year	Farmland (10^5 qing)	Index	Households (10^6)	Index
1021	52.5	100	8.7	100
1054	22.8	43	10.8	124
1065	44.0	84	12.9	148
1085	24.8	47	18.0*	207
Average	36.0		12.6	

Note: * Year 1086 figure.
Sources: Data for farmland based on Tuotuo ([1345] 1986, Vol. 7: 5712, 5716); data for households based on Liang (1980: 122–4) and Wu (2000, Vol. 3: 346–7).

after the government granted permission to farmers in the Yangzi region to self-declare ownership over unclaimed land (Xu [1809] 1976: 6333). Moreover, farmers were granted 50 per cent tax reduction for farming idle land (Xu [1809] 1976: 6070), and cultivation of rice was made completely tax-free (Tuotuo [1345] 1986, Vol. 7: 5711). Farmers seem to have emigrated to the south. As a result, North China had the lowest population growth rate among the three main regions of the country (Table 8.2).

Remarkably, emigrant farmers introduced dry farming skills to the Yangzi Valley and added one extra crop to the annual production cycle in that region (Cheng 1992: 98–100). A double cropping regime was established with (*a*) a summer crop (rice) taking 145–75 days, immediately followed by (*b*) a winter crop (wheat) taking 175

Table 8.2 Regional Population Growth, 980 CE vs 1101 CE

Zone	980	1101	Annual %
North (Yellow River)	1,680,755 (100)	3,750,266 (223)	0.67
South 1 (Yangzi River)	2,536,634 (100)	7,262,900 (286)	0.87[9]
South 2 (Pearl River)	879,117 (100)	3,677,907 (418)	1.19

Sources: Liang (1980: 164) and Wu (2000, Vol. 3: 122–35). See also Shiba (2001: 148).

[9] For an estimate at one per cent per annum, see Shiba (2001: 148).

days or more. It turned the previously sluggish agricultural season to a productive one. Call it an industrious revolution, if you will. This change was documented in 1037: 'the Lower Yangzi region nowadays has a rice crop after a wheat crop, two crops a year' (Zhu [1037] 2014, Vol. 1, 'Wuchan'). The practice was also reported by the court official Ouyang Xiu (1007–72): 'People raise debts in winter and repay their debts with their winter-wheat harvest in early summer' (cited in Hua 1982: 23). The Song government 'Green-Shoots Loan' (*qingmiao fa*) of 1069 was designed to help those whose winter wheat crop failed (Tuotuo [1345] 1986, Vol. 7: 5726). In addition, the Pearl River region was brought under rice farming despite its reputation of being infested with tropical diseases. These new developments added about 140 million *piculs* (6.5 million metric tons) of extra grain to the Song aggregate food supply (Table 8.3). Such a change qualifies as a 'mini-green revolution'.

Table 8.3 Farmland and Food Outputs across the Song Territory

	Zone	10^6 mu Farmland*	Main Grain Type	Picul/ mu
Pre-LIA	North	±180	Millet/wheat	1.0
	South (1)	±250	Rice	2.0
	South (2)	?	Rice	?
	Total piculs	±680 × 10^6		
During LIA	North	?	Millet/wheat	1.0
	South (1)	±250	Rice + winter-wheat	2.8
	South (2)	±120	Rice	1.0[10]
	Total piculs	±820 × 10^6		
	Piculs gained	±140 × 10^6		

Note: * Based on the data for 1111 CE; ? = data unavailable; LIA = the 'Little Ice Age'; 1 Song picul (shi) = 46.2 kilograms. South (1) = the Yangzi River Zone; South (2) = the Pearl River Zone.
Sources: Farmland is based on Tuotuo ([1345] 1986, Vol. 7: 5712). Land yield levels are based on Wu (2009: 115), Ge and Gu (2000: 78–9), and Qi (1986: 38–9).

[10] Due to the lack of information on yield improvement, it is safe to keep it low.

Table 8.4   Metal Outputs Seen from Government Procurements, 997–1077 CE (in *Catties*)

Year	Copper	Tin	Lead	Iron
997	4,122,000	269,000	793,000	5,748,000
1077/8	21,744,750	6,159,300	7,943,350	28,500,000
Annual %	2.1	4.0	2.9	2.0

Note: Government procurement rate was set at 30 per cent of all metal outputs. It was mandatory (Wang 2005: Chapter 3). One Song *catty* = 0.6 kg.
Sources: Ma (1307, Vol. 18: Entry 'Mining'), see also Du (1998: 44) and Wei (2011: 436).

With this green revolution, Song China escaped a Malthusian crisis. Not only that, a secure food supply fuelled the rise of non-farming sectors such as mining and manufacturing. For example, production of metals took off in a big way during the Song (Table 8.4). A conservative estimate suggests a workforce of 100,000 households to produce these metals (Qi 1987, Vol. 2: 735).

Here, copper, tin, and lead were key ingredients to meet the need for 1–5 billion bronze coins per year for the Song market activities (as in 1021–80) (Qi 1987, Vol. 2: 609). This amount of coins showed a 37-fold increase from the previous Tang level (820 CE) (Hu 2004: 236). Producing so many coins a year needed another 5–15 million working days (Qi 1987, Vol. 2: 608–9) or 14,000–42,000 full-time workers.[11]

The lion's share of demand for iron came from the need for nails and rivets in shipbuilding. During the Northern Song, a cheap way to build large seagoing ships, known as the 'clinker method',[12] was developed, which required a huge input of iron nails and rivets to

[11] Based on 300–1,000 coins per worker per day; see Qi (1987, Vol. 2: 615).

[12] The 'clinker method' allows a ship hull to be built with overlapping layers of planks by semi-skilled workers and, hence, saves labour training. Its opposite number is the 'kravell method', which is characterized by a seamless hull made of a single layer of planks done by highly skilled carpenters.

hold wooden planks together to make a hull.[13] The Northern Song's seagoing fleet had about 3,000 large cargo ships of 500–1,000 ton loading capacity each (Deng 1997: 68, 80; G. Deng 1999: 12). The Song river fleet boasted of another 3,000 ships of 200-ton displacement (Deng (1997: 62, 66, 82). Given that building a traditional ship of a medium size (a 70-tonner) required 100 m³ of wood planks and 5 metric tons of iron nails and rivets (G. Deng 1999: 29, 31), the aggregate inputs in the Song shipbuilding were in the region of 5 million m³ of planks and a quarter of million tons of nails and rivets (G. Deng 1999: 27). Moreover, 970 CE onwards, iron coins were mass-produced in the region of 400 million pieces (*wen*) a year (Yan et al. 2000: 403).[14] Other common objects made of iron included weapons, statues, musical instruments (for example, gongs and cymbals), and tools (Ebrey 1999: 144). Furthermore, iron sheets were also used to produce copper with an input–output ratio of 2.4:1, called extraction/electrowinning method (*dantong fa*).[15] Steel was produced from iron during this period, although its quantity is unknown.[16] It is in this context that Song China was dubbed as the highest iron producer per capita in the world before 1750 (Hartwell 1962).

It is documented in 1040 that it took 700 industrial households in Shaanxi to produce 100,000 catties of iron (60 metric tons) a year (Wagner 2001: 181–3). To use this labour-iron output ratio, the Song 28.5 million catties of iron would require 200,000 industrial households, excluding iron mining, coal mining, charcoal marking (hence lumbering), and transportation.[17]

[13] For iron nails and rivets for shipbuilding, see G. Deng (1999: 47–8) and Qi (1987, Vol. 2: 681–8). Note: ship nails and rivets have to be made of pure iron to avoid erosion in sea water.

[14] For the historical context, see von Glahn (1996).

[15] The annual copper output with this method once reached 380,000 catties. The iron input required could account for some one million catties. See Qi (1987, Vol. 2: 567–8).

[16] There were three documented ways to make steel with iron, see Hu (2004: 205–7).

[17] Modern chemical analysis has revealed a high sulphur content in Song iron products as the evidence for the use of coal in smelting, see Hu (2004: 191).

Another growth area was porcelain. For the first time in history, the Song artisans invented quartz-based ceramics to achieve genuine waterproof porcelain. This was a quantum leap from the earthenware of the previous Tang. The 'kaolin quartz' had to be mined from rocks, ground to fine powder, and baked for weeks at a temperature above 1200°C, which can only be achieved by using charcoal or coke. The porcelain industry is fully qualified as a heavy industry. There were 28 porcelain production centres during the Song, although the size of the workforce remains unknown (Li 2005, Vol. 3: 48–55; Qi 1987, Vol. 2: 690–700).

Other non-farming sectors included paper, textiles, salt, and beverages. Paper-making boomed in response to the demand for books for religious practise, education, and the imperial examinations to recruit civil servants.[18] Eight prefectures became specialized in the business (Zhang 2003: 206–7). Huizhou Prefecture and Xinan Prefecture alone were able to produce 1.4 and 1.5 million sheets a year, respectively (Hu 2004: 51; Needham 1954–2000, Vol. 5, pt 1: 47). A recent archaeological discovery made in Fuyang reveals a paper factory dating back to 1009 CE with a floor area of 22,000m^2. The daily pulp output is estimated to be 10 tons (Zhu [1037] 2014).

From a green revolution to mining and manufacturing, the response of the Songs to climatic change was highly rational by the standard of homo economicus. In the process, land, capital, technology, and labour were channelled to non-food sectors where returns were higher. One thing can be certain: China was moving away from its long tradition of physiocracy (or 'agricultural fundamentalism'). This change was similar to 'Lewis dualism' (Lewis 1954). (The Lewis Model refers to the hypothesis by Arthur Lewis, a British economist. It assumes that a transitional economy has two distinctive sectors, one traditional [farming] and the other modern [manufacturing]. The model suggests that the latter pays a higher wage due to its

---

[18] During the Song period, the numbers of candidates who received their imperial degrees in a year was five times that of the previous Tang and 3.4 times that of the Qing half a millennium later, see Yang (2012: 47). From 1080 to 1113, a total of 300 million characters were carved on 400,000 printing blocks in Fujian for the circulation of a Chinese translation of the *Tripitaka*; see Kang (2011: 157).

higher labour productivity. Then, based on rational choices, workers in the traditional sector join the modern sector voluntarily. After a while, this one-way movement of labour will transform the economy and render it completely modern without much difficulty.)

The second exogenous factor was the threat from nomads on the long northern borders of the Song territory. By 910 CE, all the Tang northern mega-provinces together with the Silk Road and Great Wall were lost to nomads (see Table 8.5). With the onslaught of the climatic change and decline in farming in North China, the threat of nomadic attacks and conquests loomed large: The Jurchens took over North China in 1127 CE; and the Mongols conquered South China in 1279 CE after defeating the Jurchens in North China in 1234 CE. It is entirely logical to suggest that climatic change persuaded the nomads to expand southwards.

The Song state was not entirely passive. It organized two offensive campaigns in 979 and 986 to retake 16 prefectures where the Great Wall was located from the Khitans. But both ended with humiliating defeats (Zeng 2003). Soon, a strategy of appeasement was adopted to pay tribute to the nomads for peace (Bao 2004: 5, 34, 187–209; Tsang 1997). The '1004 Chanyuan Treaty' with the Khitans specified the Song annual tribute to be 200,000 bolts of silk cloth and 100,000 *taels* of silver (3.7 metric tons). In addition, the treaty stipulated that the Song borders were to be free of defence trenches in order to allow the nomad cavalry to enter the Song territory as it wished. With a ratchet effect, the nomad demand increased to 300,000 bolts of silk and

Table 8.5   Northern Frontiers, the Tang vs the Song

Region	Tang Governorate	Song Neighbour	Modern Proximity (c. 1900)
Northwest	Anxi	Tangut Xixia	Gansu and Xinjiang
North	Anbei	Khitan Liao	Mongolia (Inner and Outer)
Northeast	Shiwei	Jurchen Jin	Manchuria

Note: The Liao Kingdom of the Khitans (916–1125), the Xixia Kingdom of the Tanguts (1038–1227), and the Jin Kingdom of the Jurchens (1115–1234).
Source: Tan (1991: 43–4, 51–2).

200,000 taels of silver (7.4 metric tons) under the new 1042 'Guannan Treaty' (Mao 2012: 166, 176). Apart from the Khitans, the Tanguts demanded another 130,000 bolts of silk, 500,000 taels of silver, and 200,000 catties of tea as their price for peace (Mao 2012: 177). In addition, nomads demanded for many luxuries available from beyond the Song territory.[19]

In 1124 CE, the Khitan Liao regime was toppled from its perch and replaced by the powerful Jin Kingdom of the Jurchens as the enemy of the Song. The Jurchens had a very different approach towards Song China. Instead of raking in annual tribute, they went for conquest. In 1126, the Jurchens forced the Songs to pay 5 million taels of gold, 50 million taels of silver, 2 million bolts of silk, and 11,000 draft animals (Mao 2012: 50, 277). In the following year, they emptied the Song Treasury, taking away another 378,000 taels of gold, 7,140,000 taels of silver, and 1,040,000 bolts of silk (Mao 2012: 50, 277). In the same year (1127), the Jurchens stormed in and annexed the northern part of the Song territory.

Nevertheless, the Songs did have total peace until 1127 and partial peace until 1279. So, the tribute worked. Paying the nomads created unprecedented financial pressure, which in turn caused the Song state to resort to many measures that were compatible with mercantilism in a bid to generate more wealth for the sake of paying the nomads' annual ransom. Now, with the rise of mining and manufacturing, what the state needed to do was to tax the new outputs of the non-farming sectors on the one hand, and to encourage exports in exchange for silver and luxuries in particular on the other.

To demonstrate this policy shift, first of all, there was an increase in liquidity (see Table 8.6). In 1041–8, the government seigniorage profit increased 24-fold (Peng 1965: 448; Tuotuo [1345] 1986, Vol. 7: 5738). The real novelty in the Song quantitative easing was the invention of paper currency, the first in the world. From 1023 to 1107, the amount of paper currency issuance increased 40 times (Qi 1987, Vol. 2: 1087).

---

[19] The Jurchens imported lychee, longan, mandarins, olives, bananas, sugar, sappan wood, rhinoceros horns, elephant tusks, and cinnabar from China; see Tuotuo (1986, Vol. 9: 7039).

Table 8.6 Money Supply during the Song Period (in 10^6)

Year	New Bronze Coins Issued	New Iron Coins Issued
976	300 (60)	—
980	500 (100)	500 (100)
1030	1,000 (200)	210 (42)
1045	3,000 (600)	430 (86)
1077	3,730 (746)	986 (197)
1080	5,060 (1012)	889 (178)
Annual %	2.8	0.6

Sources: Peng (1965: 451), Wang (1995: 750–3), and Qi (1987, Vol. 2: 609–10).

Second, a direct consequence of the increased liquidity was monetization of the Song economy to the extent that the tax-payment
structure changed in favour of cash, called *zhebian* (Zhang 1992).
Between 1021 and 1065, the cash component of the Song tax revenue swelled 226 per cent and the cash share in the total tax revenue jumped from 17.6 to 51.6 per cent (Quan 1948: 202). On
the other face of the same coin, the poll tax collected in homemade
cloth became stagnant and the land tax collected in grain declined
absolutely (Table 8.7).

In the end, the economic structure changed in favour of the non-
agricultural sector (Table 8.8).[20]

Third, there was a rise in foreign trade. As the Silk Road was firmly
controlled by nomads, the only possibility to trade with the outside
world was by sea. Such a need produced a 'linkage effect': Maritime

Table 8.7 Tax Payments in Kind

Year (CE)	Homemade Cloth (bolts)	Grain (picul)
997	2,180,000	31,707,000
1077	2,672,323	17,887,257
Annual growth %	0.2	−0.7

Source: Liang (1980: 288–9).

[20] See also Hartwell (1966) and Shiba (1970).

Table 8.8 Structural Change of the Song Economy Seen from Taxation, 997 CE vs 1077 CE

Year	Total Revenue (10^9 coins)	Agricultural Share (%)	Non-agricultural Share (%)
997	35.6	65	35
1021	57.2	48	52
1077	70.7	30	70

Sources: Ye (1991: 108). See also Bao (2001: 282, 316–19).

trade was openly encouraged for the first time by the imperial government.[21] To facilitate a maritime growth, larger and better seaworthy ships were designed and built; new sea routes were opened; new trading destinations were explored; and high profits were expected (Gong 1961; Ma 1955; Zhou [1178] 1983). At its peak, the Song fleet had 3,000 strong seagoing ships of 500–1,000 tonnes (Deng 1997: 68, 80; G. Deng 1999: 12). These were specially designed 'Fuzhou ships' (*fuchuan*) (Deng 1997: Chapter 2), equipped with the most sophisticated technology of the time, including sails, magnetic compass, and sea charts (as documented in Zhu 1119 and A. Li 1956, Vol. 54). New sea routes began to link coastal China to as far as the Arabian Peninsula (Tazi) and the East African coast (Zanj) (Zhou [1178] 1983).[22] Persians and Arabs were also invited to operate in Song ports (Zhao [1125] 1956; Zhou [1178] 1983).[23] Meanwhile, customs officials were handed down performance quotas to fulfil (K. Deng 1999: 268). Soon, the maritime duties doubled,[24] contributing 15 per cent to the total government revenue (Chen and Wu 1981: 180–2; see also Guo 1997a: 390–405).

Moreover, the government actively took part in marketeering and profiteering through monopsony and monopoly. For example,

---

[21] For a survey of studies of the Northern Song government trade policy, see Li (2007: 10–25).

[22] Reference also from Shen (1985).

[23] For nine wealthy Arabs in China, see Lin (1986: 417–19).

[24] Calculation is based on 238 per cent inflation of food prices from 1101 to 1125; see Long (1993: 159).

the Bureau for Maritime Trade (*shibo si*) was granted the power to procure maritime imports as a monopsonist and resell them to the domestic market as a monopolist. Between 1076 and 1078, an amount of frankincense, worth 1.5 billion coins, was arbitraged by the state (D. Deng 1986: 100). The arbitrage yielded 100 per cent profit (Tuotuo [1345] 1986, Vol. 7: 5751, 5752). It was also reported that the state-run spice trade produced a profit margin of over 70 per cent (G. Deng 1999: 88).

Furthermore, the arbitrage policy was extended to the domestic market for metals, silk textiles, salt, and wine. Over 100-million decilitres of wine, 400-million catties of salt, and 3,000,000 bolts of silk cloth were handled by the government on a yearly basis (Hu 2004: 353, 402; Li 2007: 466).

It becomes clear that the impact of the two exogenous factors—the climatic change and the geopolitical shift—became convergent forces to cause some fundamental changes in the Song economy: Openness replaced autarchy; mercantilism replaced physiocracy; and monetization/marketization/profiteering replaced self-sufficiency.

Nature of Capitalism in Song China

In hindsight, the double whammy of agricultural vulnerability caused by climatic change and military weakness compared to the powerful nomads turned out to be overwhelmingly favourable for radical socio-economic changes in Song China, which in turn altered China's old growth trajectory to allow the economy to move towards a market economy and capitalism.

First of all, evidence shows that it was the Song state that was chiefly responsible for internalizing the exogenous shocks and turning them positively towards unprecedented monetization, marketization, and openness. By definition, therefore, Song period growth was state-led from the beginning till the end. The role of the private sector and private entrepreneurship were but secondary.

Second, regarding mining and metallurgy, the backbone of the Song growth, the vast majority of enterprises were state owned. This was particularly true for large 'conglomerates' (*jian*) and medium 'factories' (*ye, wu*) that were established and controlled by the central and/or provincial governments (Wang 2005: Chapter 4). Such large firms hired a workforce of 10,000 workers each; and the medium ones, several thousands (Tuotuo [1345] 1986, Vol. 7: 5754–7). Evidence suggests that workers were drafted from the able-bodied adult population in more or less the military service fashion (Tuotuo [1345] 1986, Vol. 7: 5754–7).

In this context, the Song state was fully capable of drafting enough soldiers for an army of an increasing size (Tuotuo [1345] 1986, Vol. 7: 5762) (see Table 8.9).

It was common for the Song state to draft a large number of people for public projects too. For example, the government amassed 200,000 workers to build an irrigation system in Hangzhou in 973 and employed several million working days to build a dyke along the sea front against tidal waves in 1012, again in Hangzhou (Tuotuo [1345] 1986, Vol. 7: 5503–4).

Small mining and metallurgy operations, called 'pits' (*keng*) and 'furnaces' (*lu*), were often in private hands. They tended to be family businesses; but owners of pits and furnaces still needed government licenses and were obliged to sell a proportion of their outputs to the state (Tuotuo [1345] 1986, Vol. 7: 5754–7).

The government kept a firm control over other industries as well. Monopoly was imposed on both ends of production and marketing of wine. It all began with yeast rationing. The government workshops produced 2,220,000 catties of yeast per year to be sold to private breweries (Wei 2011: 356, 361). All the breweries were obliged to sell their outputs, annually 100 million *sheng*,[25] back to the government agents (Hu 2004: 353). No private marketing of wine was allowed. Revenues from the wine monopoly matched the entire trade duties of the empire (*shangshui*) (Wei 2011: 351).

Table 8.9 Increase in Number of Soldiers, 976–1048 CE

Year	Number of Soldiers	Index
976	378,000	100
1048	1,259,000	333
Annual growth (%)		1.7

[25] 100 million sheng is about 7.5 million tons.

Similarly, tea planters were obliged to sell their products to government agents. The aggregate amount of tea going through the system was 23–29 million catties (13,730–17,300 metric tons) a year, earning the government 100–300 million bronze coins (Hua 1982: 76, 109; Zhu 1984). All salt fields were state-owned. The government then issued salt permits (*yanyin*) to tax-farmers who were often wealthy merchants. In 1078, salt permits fetched a total of 23 billion coins (Li 2007: 222). Light industries such as paper-making could be privately owned but had the government as a main buyer due to the need for paper currency and the daily running of the bureaucracy, including documents and the imperial examinations. The private market for religious readings and Confucian schooling was a distant second.

Third, the main beneficiary of the Song economic growth and structural change was the state. The very fact that the Song regime survived for so long was a result of the annual ransom payment. In other words, business profits and revenues became the main source of government legitimacy.

In a nutshell, the hand of the state was visible and busy in the Song economy.

Ending of the Song Growth

The Song prosperity in manufacturing and trade was injured after the aforementioned Jurchen takeover of North China in 1127 CE. The conquerors destroyed the Song industrial centres in their controlled region, including most of the Song iron factories (X. Li 1956: 87, 744). The colonizers forced large numbers of the Chinese into slavery (Tuotuo [1344] 1986, Vol. 9: 7029–30, 7094, 7108, 7113).[26] The same labour policy was carried out by the Mongols who replaced the Jurchens in 1234 CE. The main difference was that the Mongols were vicious towards the Chinese.

Under the Mongol rule, by 1291, the population in North China dropped by half (Wu 2000, Vol. 3: 625). Among those who survived,

---

[26] About half of the Chinese were forced into slavery, see Han and Chen (1986, Vol. 2: 56). Note: Mongols implemented large-scale production slavery on China's soil for the first time since c. 100 BCE.

millions were enslaved (*quding*), including all the skilled artisans;[27] properties belonging to the Chinese were confiscated; vast land areas were enclosed as grazing land for Mongol horses.[28] Metal tools were banned, and so were martial arts (Han and Chen 1986, Vol. 1: 392; Vol. 2: 44–5). Furthermore, the Mongols increased tax burden multifold on the Chinese: The household tax increased 20 times (Han and Chen 1986, Vol. 1: 391, 429; Vol. 2: 48; also see Guo 1997b, Vol. 1: 302, 493); in some cases, the land tax was set as high as the yield level *per se* (Han and Chen 1986, Vol. 1: 391, 429; Vol. 2: 48). The Mongol paper currency led to a hyperinflation (Han and Chen 1986, Vol. 1: 427). Consequently, the price of rice increased about 40 times and salt, 30 times (Yu 2000: 712–3). The market was forced to go back to barter trade (Han and Chen 1986, Vol. 2: 92).

In addition, culturally, the Mongols made no attempt to accept the Chinese culture or language in the Mongol Yuan Court.[29] Of the 11 Yuan emperors, only 1, Emperor Chengzong (r. 1294–1307), ever made an effort to learn Chinese calligraphy, though unsuccessfully. Confucianism was replaced by Buddhism. Politically, official positions were reserved for Mongols and their trusted mercenaries of the 'coloured-eye' race (*semuren*): West Asians and Europeans (Han and Chen 1986, Vol. 1: 6, 430–1; Vol. 2: 2).[30] Economically, no Chinese

[27] Large numbers of slaves were reported to be used as gifts in Mongol diplomacy, see Han and Chen (1986, Vol. 2: 424, 430).

[28] According to the Yuan official record, the forcefully created state farmland through appropriation by the Mongol state from Chinese legal owners amounted to 17.5 million mu. About 500,000 households became serfs, see Han and Chen (1986, Vol. 1: 362, 374–5). See also Perkins (1969: 23–4, 197–9), Chinese Academy of Agricultural Sciences (1984, Vol. 2: 51–3), Zheng, Jiang, and Zhang (1984: 242–4, 254–5), Hu (2004: 589–604), and Han and Chen (1986, Vol. 1: 361–2, 375; Vol. 2: 47).

[29] Of all the known travels to the Yuan Empire by outsiders, the languages, both written and spoken, in use in the Empire were Mongolian, Persian, Turkish, Arabic, and Latin. See Han and Chen (1986, Vol. 2: 434–50).

[30] Marco Polo was allegedly appointed as a high-ranking official working for the Mongol Imperial Court because of his eye colour. It is questionable whether Marco Polo ever spoke Chinese, used chopsticks, drank tea, or saw the Great Wall. If he physically went to China, he lived, at best and,

was allowed to engage in large business or long-distance trade (Han and Chen 1986, Vol. 2: 43). In essence, the Mongol rule in China was akin to full-fledged apartheid against the majority population of the Chinese (Han and Chen 1986, Vol. 1: 9; Vol. 2: 54–5).

After 1279, the Mongol policy was carried out in South China and consequently ended what remained of the Song growth story.

***

The rise of the industrial and commercial sectors in Song China was a result of historical contingency rather than an organic growth from the pre-Song past, which was marked by the physiocracy-cum-farming that China was famous for. Even so, being a forerunner in fast growth in heavy industry and international trade in the 'medieval world', Song China managed to yield good returns from a new type of economy that bore many similarities with modern capitalism, which needs entrepreneurship, capital investment, and business profits to exist and flourish. What separates Song China from the modern West is the absence of individual entrepreneurship, and, rather, the presence of 'state entrepreneurship' à la Alexander Gerschenkron (1962).

It is a historical tragedy that Song state-led capitalism was one-off in the end. The harsh reality was that Song China was the victim of two waves of brutal invasions and conquests by northern nomads—the Jurchens and then the Mongols. Song China did not stand a chance. To be fair, though, China did not have the necessary innate conditions for a structural change and industrial/commercial growth of the Song type either before or after the Song period. Once the exogenous conditions for the Song growth and development disappeared, China went all the way back to its old growth pattern for another half a millennium from 1368 to 1911. It was not until Deng Xiaoping's reforms in the 1980s that the market economy in mainland China took off to a comparable degree, again resulting from the visible and busy hand of the state (Deng 2015: Chapter 7).

---

if at all, in a non-Chinese circle of Mongols and their cronies, see Wood (1995). In addition, there is no record on Marco Polo and his services to the Mongols from the known Yuan official documents.

Bibliography

Bao, Weimin. 2001. *Songdai Difang Caizhengshi Yanjiu* [A History of Local Finance during the Song Period]. Shanghai: Shanghai Classics Press.

————. 2004. *Songdai Zhidushi Yanjiu Bainian* [A Century-Long Study of the Song Institutions]. Beijing: Commercial Press.

Bol, Peter. 1992. *This Culture of Ours*. Stanford: Stanford University Press.

Cheng, Minsheng. 1992. *Songdai Diyu Jingji* [Regional Economy during the Song Period]. Zhengzhou: Henan University Press.

Chinese Academy of Agricultural Sciences, ed. 1984. *Zhongguo Nongxue Shi* [History of Chinese Agronomy]. Beijing: Sciences Press.

Deng, Duanben, ed. 1986. *Guangzhou Gangshi* [A History of Port Guangzhou]. Beijing: Maritime Press.

Deng, Gang. 1997. *Chinese Maritime Activities and Socio-economic Consequences, c. 2100 B.C.–1900 A.D.* New York, London and West Port: Green Wood Press.

————. 1999. *Maritime Sector, Institutions, and Sea Power of Premodern China*. London and New York: Greenwood Press.

Deng, Guangming. 1986. 'Tantan Youguan Songshi Yanjiude Jige Wenti' [Issues on Study of Song history]. *Shehui Kexue Zhanxian* (*Social Science Front*) 2: 137–44.

————. 1990. 'Songdai Wenhuade Gaodu Fazhan' [High-Level Culture in the Song Period]. *Lishi Yanjiu* 1: 64–9.

Deng, Kent. 1999. *The Chinese Premodern Economy*. London: Routledge Press.

————. 2015. *Mapping China's Growth and Development in the Long Run, 221 BC to 2020*. London: World Scientific Press and Imperial College Press.

Deng, Kent and Lucy Zheng. 2015. 'Economic Restructuring and Demographic Growth, Demystifying Growth and Development in Northern Song China, 960–1127.' *Economic History Review* 68(4): 1107–31.

Du, Wenyu. 1998. 'Tang Song Jingji Shili Bijiao Yanjiu' [A Comparison of Economic Strength between the Tang and Song Periods]. *Zhongguo Jingjishi Yanjiu* (*Research in Chinese Economic History*) 4: 37–52.

Ebrey, P.B. 1999. *The Cambridge Illustrated History of China*. Cambridge: Cambridge University Press.

Esherick, J.W. and M.B. Rankin, eds. 1990. *Chinese Local Elite and Patterns of Dominance*. Berkeley: University of California Press.

Flohn, Hermann, ed. 1969. *World Survey of Climatology. Vol. 2. General Climatology*. New York: Elsevier Science Ltd.

246   Kent Deng

Fogel, J.A. 1984. *Politics and Sinology*. Cambridge, MA: Harvard University Press.

Gaohua, Chen and Wu Tai. 1981. *Songyuan Shiqide Haiwai Maoyi* [China's Maritime Trade during the Song and Yuan Periods]. Tianjin: Tianjin People's Press.

Ge, Jinfang and Gu Rong. 2000. 'Songdai Jiangnan Diqude Liangshi Muchan Jiqi Gusuan Fangfa Bianxi' [Estimation and Evidence of Yield Level in the Lower Yangzi Region during the Song Period]. *Hubei Daxue Xuebao (Bulletin of the University of Hubei)* 3: 78–83.

Ge, Zhaoguang. 2000. *Qi Shiji Zhi Shijiu Shiji Zhongguode Zhishi* [Knowledge in China from the Seventh to the Nineteenth Centuries]. Shanghai: Fudan University Press.

Gerschenkron, Alexander. 1962. *Economic Backwardness in Historical Perspective*. Cambridge, MA: Harvard University Press.

Gipouloux, Francois. 2009. *The Asian Mediterranean: Port Cities and Trading Networks in China, Japan and Southeast Asia, 13th–21st Century*. Cheltenham: Edward Elgar.

Gong, Zhen. 1961 [first published during Ming Dynasty]. *Xiyang Fanguo Zhi* [Journeys to Foreign Countries in the Indian Ocean]. Beijing: Zhonghua Books.

Guo, Zhengzhong. 1997a. *Liansong Chengxiang Shangpin Huobi Jingji Kaolue* [The Commercial and Cash Economy of the Northern and Southern Song Periods]. Beijing: Economics and Management Press.

———. 1997b. *Zhongguo Yanye Shi* [A History of the Salt Sector in China]. Beijing: People's Press.

Han, Rulin and Chen Dezhi. 1986. *Yuanchao Shi* [History of the Yuan Dynasty]. Beijing: People's Press.

Hartwell, R.M. 1962. 'A Revolution in the Chinese Iron and Coal Industries during the Northern Sung, 960–1126 A.D.' *Journal of Asian Studies* 21(1): 153–62.

———. 1966. 'Markets, Technology, and the Structure of Enterprise in the Development of the Eleventh-Century Chinese Iron and Steel Industry.' *Journal of Economic History* 26(1): 29–58.

———. 1982. 'Demographic, Political, and Social Transformation of China, 750–1550.' *Harvard Journal of Asiatic Studies* 42(2): 365–442.

Hu, Xiaopeng. 2004. *Zhongguo Shougongye Jingji Tongshi, Song Yuan Juan* [A General Economic History of Handicraft Industry in China, the Song and Yuan Periods]. Fuzhou: Fujian People's Press.

Hua, Shan. 1982. *Songshi Lunji* [Collected Essays on Song History]. Jinan: Qilu Press.

Huang, Shaoping. 2003. *Minnan Wenhua Yanjiu* [Southern Fujian Culture]. Beijing: Central Literature Press.

Kang, Baoling. 2011. *Beisong Wenhua Zhongxin Yanjiu* [Central Gravity of Culture during the Northern Song Period]. Beijing: Guangming Daily Press.

Lewis, A.W. 1954. 'Economic Development with *Unlimited* Supplies of *Labour*.' *Manchester School* 22(2): 139–91.

Li, Ao. (1183) 1956. *Xu Zizhi Tongjian Changbian* [Enlarged Comprehensive References for State Management]. Beijing: Zhonghua Books.

Li, Hua Rui, ed. 2010. *Tangsong Biangelunde Youlai Yu Fazhan* [Origin and Development of the Notion of the Tang–Song Transition]. Tianjin: Tianjin Classics Press.

Li, Jiannong. 2005. *Zhongguo Gudai Jingjishi Gao* [A Drafted Economic History of Premodern China]. Wuhan: Wuhan University Press.

Li, Xiao. 2007. *Songchao Zhengfu Guomai Zhidu Yanjiu* [Procurement System of the Song Government]. Shanghai: Shanghai People's Press.

Li, Xinchuan. (1202) 1956. *Jianyan Yilai Xinian Yaolu* [Annuals of Important Events since 1128. Beijing: Zhonghua Books.

Liang Fangzhong, 1980. *Zhongguo Lidai Hukou Tiandi Tianfu Tongji* [Dynastic Data for China's Households, Cultivated Land and Land Taxation]. Shanghai: Shanghai People's Press.

Lin, Tianwei. 1986. *Songdai Xiangyao Maoyi Shi* [A History of Spices, Perfume and Pharmaceuticals Trade during the Song Period]. Taipei: China's Cultural University Press.

Lin, Wenxun. 2005. 'Shangpin Jingji' [Commodity Economy]. *Wenshizhe (Literature, History and Philosophy)* 1: 40–7.

Loehle, Craig. 2007. 'A 2000-Year Global Temperature Reconstruction Based on Non-Treering Proxies.' *Energy and Environment* 7–8(18): 1048–58.

Long, Denggao. 1993. 'Songdai Liangjia Fenxi' [Food Prices in the Song Period]. *Zhongguo Jingjishi Yanjiu* [Research in Chinese Economic History] 1: 151–60.

Ma, Duanlin. 1307. *Wenxian Tongkao* [Comprehensive Study of Historical Records]. Publisher unknown.

Ma, Huan. (1451) 1955. *Yingya Shenglan* [Tours to Great Sites Overseas]. Beijing: Zhonghua Books.

Mao, Zhixiang. 2012. *Songchaode Duiwai Jiaowang Geju* [External Relations of the Song Dynasty]. Yangzhou: Guangling Books.

Naito, Konan. 1947. *Chūgoku Kinsei Shi* [An Early Modern History of China]. Tokyo: Hirofumi Press.

Needham, Joseph. 1954–2000. *Science and Civilisation in China*. 7 vols. Cambridge: Cambridge University Press.

Ouyang, Xiu. 1986. *Ouyang Xiu Quanji* [The Collected Works of Ouyang Xiu]. Beijing: China Books.

Peng, Xinwei. 1965. *Zhongguo Huobi Shi* [A History of Currencies in China]. Shanghai: Shanghai People's Press.

Perkins, D.H. 1969. *Agricultural Development in China*. Edinburgh: University of Edinburgh Press.

Qi, Xia. 1986. 'Songdai Shehui Shengchanlide Fazhan Jiqizai Zhongguo Gudai Jingji Fazhan Guochengzhongde Diwei' [Productivity Increase in Song Times and Its Importance in China's Premodern Economic Growth]. *Zhongguo Jingjishi Yanjiu (Research in Chinese Economic History)* 1: 29–52.

———. 1987. *Songdai Jingjishi* (An Economic History of the Song Period). Shanghai: Shanghai People's Press.

———. 2000. 'Tangsong Zhiji Shehui Jingji' [Socio-economy during the Tang–Song Era]. *Zhongguo Jingjishi (Chinese Economic History)* 1: 95–108.

Quan, Hansheng. 1948. 'Tang Song Zhengfu Suiru Yu Hubi Jingjide Guanxi' [Relationship between Government Revenues and the Cash Economy]. In *Guoli Zhongyang Yanjiuyuan Lishi Yuyan Yanjiusuo Jikan* [Bulletin of the Institute of History and Linguistics, Academia Sinica], Vol. 20, edited by Academia Sinica. Taipei: Academia Sinica.

Schneider, S.H. and Clifford Mass. 1975. 'Volcanic Dust, Sunspots, and Temperature Trends.' *Science* 190(4216): 741–6.

Shen, Fuwei. 1985. 'Zhenghe Baochuanduide Dongfei Hangcheng' (Zheng He's Treasure Fleet and Its Voyages to the Eastern African Coast). In *Zhenghe Xia Xiyang Lunwen Ji* (Selected Works on Zheng He's Voyages in the Indian Ocean), edited by Institute of Maritime History of China, pp. 166–83. Beijing: People's Communication Press.

Shen, Kuo. (1095) 1975. *Mengxi Bitan* [Notes of Dreams]. Beijing: Relics Press.

Shiba, Yoshinobu. 1970. *Commerce and Society in Sung China*. Ann Arbor: University of Michigan Press.

———. 2001. *Songdai Jiangnan Jingjishi Yanjiu* [An Economic History of the Lower Yangzi Region during the Song Period]. Nanjing: Jiangsu People's Press.

Smith, P.J. and Richard von Glahn, eds. 2003. *The Song-Yuan-Ming Transition in Chinese History*. Cambridge, MA: Harvard University Asia Center.

Song, Zhenghai, Gao Jianguo, Sun Guanlong, and Zhang Binglun. 2002. *Zhongguo Gudai Ziran Zaiyi Dongtao Fenxi* [Dynamic Analysis of Natural Disasters in Premodern China Hefei: Anhui Education Press.

Tan, Qixiang. 1991. *Jianming Zhongguo Lishi Dituji* [Concise Maps of Chinese History]. Beijing: China's Map Press.

Tsang, Shui-lung. 1997. 'War and Peace in Northern Sung China.' PhD Dissertation, University of Arizona.

Tuotuo. (1344) 1986 'Jin Shi' [History of the Jin Dynasty]. In *Er-shi-wu Shi* [Twenty-Five Official Histories], Vol. 9. Shanghai: Shanghai Classics Press.

———. (1345) 1986. 'Song Shi' (History of the Song Dynasty). In *Er-shi-wu Shi* (Twenty-Five Official Histories), Vol. 7. Shanghai: Shanghai Classics Press.

Von Glahn, Richard. 1996. *Fountain of Fortune: Money and Monetary Policy in China, 1000–1700.* Berkeley : University of California Press.

Wagner, D.B. 2001. 'The Administration of the Iron Industry in Eleventh-Century China.' *Journal of the Economic and Social History of the Orient* 44(2): 175–97.

Wang, Lingling. 2005. *Songdai Kuangyeye Yanjiu* [Study of Mining and Metallurgy during the Song Period]. Shijiazhuang: Hebei University Press.

Wang, Shengduo. 1995. *Liangsong Caizheng Shi* [A Fiscal History of the Northern and Southern Songs]. Beijing: Zhonghua Books.

Wei, Tian-an. 2011. *Songdai Guanying Jingji Shi* [An Economic History of the State-Run Sector during the Song Period. Beijing: People's Press.

Wood, Frances. 1995. *Did Marco Polo Go to China?* London: Westview Press.

Wu, Hui. 2009. *Zhongguo Jingjishi Ruogan Wentide Jiliang Yanjiu* [Quantitative Studies of Chinese Economic History]. Fuzhou: Fujian People's Press.

Wu, Songdi. 2000. *Zhongguo Renkoushi* [Demographic History of China]. Shanghai: Fudan University Press.

Xu, Song. (1809) 1976. *Song Huiyao Jigao* [Edited Administrative Statutes of the Song Dynasty]. Taipei: Xin Wenhui Press.

Yan, Fushan, Gao Fengying, Yuan Lin, and Zhou Yanling. 2000. *Liansong Tieqian* [Iron Coins of the Song Dynasty]. Beijing: Zhonghua Books.

Yang, Ling. 2012. *Songdai Chuban Wenhua* [Printing Culture of the Song Period]. Beijing: Relics Press.

Ye, Tan. 1991. 'Songdai Gongshangye Fazhangde Lishi Tezheng' [Features of Development in Handicrafts and Commerce during the Song Period]. *Shanghai Shehui Kexueyuan Xueshu Jikan (Academic Quarterly of the Shanghai Academy of Social Sciences)* 2: 103–11.

Yu, Yaohua. 2000. *Zhongguo Jiage Shi* [A History of Prices in China]. Beijing: China's Price Press.

Zeng, Ruilong. 2003. *Jingyue Yuyan Songliao Zhanzheng Junshi Zainande Zhanlue Fenxi* [Fighting Along the Great Wall: A Strategic Analysis on the Fiasco of the Song–Lao War]. Hong Kong: Chinese University Press.

Zhang, Guogang. 2006. 'Tangsong Biange' [Changes in the Tang and Song Periods]. *Shixue Jikan* (*Study of History Monthly*) 1: 8–10.

Zhang, Jiacheng. 1988. *Qihou Yu Renlei* [Climate and Humankind]. Zhengzhou: Henan Science and Technology Press.

Zhang, Jianguang. 2003. *Tang Wudai Jiangnan Gongshangye Buju Yanjiu* [Industrial and Commercial Distribution in the Lower Yangzi Region during the Tang and Five Dynasties]. Nanjing: Phoenix Press.

Zhang, Xiwei. 1992. 'Songdai Zhebianzhi Tanxi' [Tax Payment Conversions during the Song Period]. *Zhongguoshi Yanjiu* (*Study of Chinese History*) 1: 26–33.

Zhao, Hongjun and Yin Bocheng. 2011. 'Gongyuan 11 Shijihoude Qihou Bianleng Dui Songyihou Jingji Fazhande Dongtai Yingxiang' [Dynamic Impact of Cooling Down in Climate after the Eleventh Century on Economic Development in Post-Song China]. *Shehui Kexue* (*Social Sciences*) 4: 68–78.

Zhao, Rukuo. (1125) 1956. *Zhufan Zhi* [Records of Foreign Peoples]. Beijing: Zhonghua Books.

Zheng, Xuemeng. 1996. *Zhongguo Gudai Jingji Zhongxin Nanyi He Tangsong Jiangnan Jingji Yanjiu* [Southward Shift of the Centre of Economic Gravity of China and the Tang–Song Economy]. Zhengzhou: Yuelu Books.

Zheng Xuemeng, Jiang Zhaocheng, and Zhang Wenqi. 1984. *Jianming Zhongguo Jingji Tongshi* [A Brief Panorama of Chinese Economic History]. Harbin: Heilongjiang People's Press.

Zhou, Qufei. (1178) 1983. 'Lingwai Daida' [Knowledge about South China and Beyond]. In *Wenyuange Siku Quanshu* [*The Qing Imperial Complete Collection of Books in the Wenyuan Library*], edited by Ji Jun, Vol. 347, Pt 6. Taipei: Taiwan Commercial Press.

Zhu, Changwen. (1037) 2014. *Wujun Tujing Xuji* (Illustrated Maps of the Lower Yangzi, continued). Available at http://wenxian.fanren8.com/06/05/62/2.htm; accessed on 1 January 2014.

Zhu, Kezhen. 1972. 'Woguo Jinwuqiannianlai Qihou Bianqiande Chubu Yanjiu' [Climatic Changes in China in the Past 5,000 years.] *Kaogu Xuebao* [Bulletin of Archeology] 1: 15–38.

Zhu, Yu. 1119. *Pingzhou Ketan* [Talks on Pingzhou]. Publisher unknown.

Zhu, Zhongseng. 1984. 'Songdai Chazhi Chanqu' [Tea Production Regions in Song China]. In *Songshi Yanjiu Ji* [Collected Papers on Song History], Vol. 15, pp. 291–350. Taipei: National Translation Bureau.

9

The First Capitalist Nation

The Development of Capitalism in England

Joseph E. Inikori

There has been a recent revival of interest in the history of capitalism, seen by some as the historical project most relevant to the central issues of our contemporary world (Neal and Williamson 2014).[1] The 2014 two-volume *The Cambridge History of Capitalism* best illustrates this revival of interest (Neal and Williamson 2014). At this early stage of the rapidly expanding new literature, we must endeavour to avoid loosely using terms that make scientific communication difficult, if not impossible. In tracing the historical development of capitalism, the first problem is to identify correctly the constituent elements of capitalism as a socio-economic system. The identification exercise

---

[1] As Summers (2014) puts it: 'In many respects the history of capitalism is the history most relevant to our times.' Editorial review of *The Cambridge History of Capitalism.*

must rest on clear conceptual and methodological imperatives. The leading question is, which elements enable us to capture most clearly and precisely the socio-economic and political dynamics of the capitalist system of production, so that our analysis of its long-run process of development focuses on the most central factors. We must bear in mind that the history of capitalism is not the history of everything. Tracing the history of economic growth and development is not the same thing as tracing the development of capitalism, as several chapters in *The Cambridge History of Capitalism* seem to imply.

The analytical task in tracing the long-run historical development of capitalism as a socio-economic system requires focusing the narrative on the historical development of the central elements that distinguish capitalism unambiguously from other socio-economic systems. That is the way to present a sharply focused study. The chapter addresses this problem from the start in the first section to provide a clear focus for the historical analysis of the rise of capitalism in England, the first capitalist nation in the world. This is followed in the second section by the conceptual framework that informs (in the third section) the assembling and analysis of the historical evidence showing the process and the main factors that gave rise to the establishment of a capitalist economy and society in England by the mid-nineteenth century. The conclusion is drawn up in the last section. While the local conditions and the prevailing global context within which the capitalist system of production emerges may introduce some particularities, cultural or otherwise, the chapter contends that the defining elements of capitalism remain the same and the main factors in the historical process that gave rise to them are essentially similar in their dynamics. Apart from location and some specific historical conjuncture, there is nothing uniquely English, cultural or otherwise, in the English process. The factors that mattered most in that process could, therefore, offer some insights for the study of the process in other major regions of the world.

Constituent Elements of Capitalism as a Socio-economic System

Since Karl Marx (1952; [1867] 1976) conceptualized the term, identifying the constituent elements that distinguish capitalism unambiguously from other socio-economic systems has engaged the intellectual energy of some of the best minds (Antonio and Glassman 1985; Brenner 1977; Dobb 1946, 1958; Frank 1967, 1998; Hilton 1978b; Kaye 1984; Taylor 1979; Wallerstein 1974, 1983; Weber 1958, 1978; Wood 1991). As Rodney Hilton (1978a: 145) affirmed decades ago:

> The history of capitalism was once studied by its supporters and its critics on the basis of reasonably common agreement as to what both meant by the term. 'The subject of capitalism', wrote Professor M.M. Postan, 'owes its present place in political and scientific discussion to the work of Marx and the Marxians'. Many historians substantially follow him. Mr. E. Lipson in his *Economic History of England* on the whole adopts Marx's definition of Capitalism. He agrees that its essential feature is the division of classes between propertyless wage-earners and entrepreneurs who own capital.

Since the 1960s, there has been some attempt to redefine capitalism with emphasis on elements such as attitudes, commercial relations, profits extraction, and large-scale organization of production (Frank 1967; Macfarlane 1987; Wallerstein 1974, 1983). These attempts were very much anticipated and rejected by the earlier writers, who insisted on precision and incorporation of the elements that matter most. As the eminent British economic historian R.H. Tawney (1958: 1(b)–(c); emphasis added) put it emphatically:

> Capitalism, in the sense of great individual undertakings, involving the control of large financial resources, and yielding riches to their masters as a result of speculation, money-lending, commercial enterprise, buccaneering and war, is as old as history. Capitalism, as an economic system, resting on the organization of legally free wage-earners, for the purpose of pecuniary profit, by the owner of capital or his agents, *and setting its stamp on every aspect of society*, is a modern phenomenon.

It is significant that Tawney stressed the idea of capitalism as an economic system that structures every aspect of society. Both in his *Protestant Ethic* and *Economy and Society*, Max Weber emphasized similar elements. Weber drew a clear distinction between what he called 'modern capitalism' and other socio-economic forms that have existed in all 'civilized countries' throughout history. He made this clear at the very beginning of the *Protestant Ethic*:

> The impulse to acquisition, pursuit of gain, of money, of the greatest possible amount of money, has in itself nothing to do with capitalism. This impulse exists and has existed among waiters, physicians, coachmen, artists, prostitutes, dishonest officials, soldiers, nobles, crusaders, gamblers and beggars. One may say that it has been common to all sorts and conditions of men at all times and in all countries of the earth, wherever the objective possibility of it is or has been given. *It should be taught in the kindergarten of cultural history that this naïve idea of capitalism must be given up once and for all.* (Weber 1958: 17; emphasis added)

For Weber, the employment of legally free labour as the numerically dominant form of the labour process is what distinguishes capitalism from all other socio-economic systems. Without 'the rational capitalistic organization of (formally) free labour', he argued, 'what is generally called commercialization, the exchanges, etc ... would have nothing like the same significance, above all for the social structure and all the specific problems' of the capitalist world (Weber 1958: 21–2). Weber's emphasis on free wage labour (separated from the means of production) as the defining element of capitalism is brought out more clearly in his *Economy and Society*:

> The relative independence of the artisan, the producer under the putting out system, the free seigneurial peasant, the travelling associate in a *commenda* relationship, the knight and vassal rested on their ownership of tools, supplies, finances and weapons with which they fulfilled their economic, political and military functions and maintained themselves. In contrast, the hierarchical dependence of the wage worker, the administrative and technical employee, the assistant in the academic institute *as well as* that of the civil servant and the soldier is due to the fact that in their case the means indispensable for the enterprise and for making a living are in the hands of the entrepreneur or the political ruler.... This all-important economic fact: the 'separation' of the worker from the material means of production, destruction, administration, academic research, and finance in general is the common basis of the modern state, in its political,

cultural and military sphere, and of the private capitalist economy. (Weber 1958: 1394)[2]

Weber (1958: 23–4) could not be clearer about what he thought should be the main focus of the history of capitalism: 'In a universal history of culture the central problem for us is not, in the last analysis, even from a purely economic view-point, the development of capitalistic activity as such, differing in different cultures only in form. ... It is rather the origin of this sober bourgeois capitalism with its rational organization of free labour.'

It is clear enough from the literature on capitalism that attempts from the 1960s to redefine notwithstanding, most students of the subject, Marxists and non-Marxists, specify the relationship between free wage earners and the owners of capital or their agents as the defining element that distinguishes capitalism unmistakably from all other forms of socio-economic organization.[3] As Ernesto Laclau

---

[2] The application of this conception of capitalism, with the relation of free wage earners to capital as the distinguishing element, enabled Palestinian economist Tony Cliff (a Trotskyist) to study the Soviet economy, which evolved from Stalinism, and its East European extensions as a variant of capitalism—*bureaucratic state capitalism*, in which the means of production (capital) is owned by the state and the state bureaucracy relates to free wage earners, who own no capital, the same way the bureaucracy in private corporations relates to free wage earners owning no capital in private enterprise economies. A telling difference is the monopoly exercised by the state as the sole capitalist employer, eliminating the competition among capitalists on the labour market in a private enterprise economy. This heightens the class struggle between the working class and their capitalist employer, the state bureaucracy. This analysis led Tony Cliff to the conclusion, in 1947, that 'the class struggle in Stalinist Russia must inevitably express itself in a gigantic spontaneous outbursts [*sic*] of millions' in a proletarian revolution. See Callinicos (1991: 19–20) and Cliff (1948, 1988).

[3] Some of the well-known studies of capitalism in Africa adopting the Marxian conception include Iliffe (1983), Cooper (2014) and Hill (1970); a collection of essays on the development of capitalist agriculture in Latin America also adopted the Marxian conception (Duncan and Rutledge 1977). It should be noted that in his last major work, *ReOrient*, Gunder Frank abandoned his conception of capitalism based on market exchange, which led him to date its creation to 1492. He affirmed that the

(1971: 25) put it in his critique of Gunder Frank, 'the fundamental economic relation of capitalism is constituted by the free labourer's sale of his labour-power, whose necessary precondition is the loss by the direct producer of ownership of the means of production'. This conception of capitalism captures the dynamics of the capitalist system far more precisely and accurately than all others. As I expressed it elsewhere:

> The form of combination of labour power and capital, which is compelled by the employment of free wage labour, facilitates the appropriation of surplus value by the owner of capital through the payment of wages that are less than the value produced by labour. This form of appropriation is subtle, relative to all other forms; it takes place without the glaring view and consciousness of the labourer and it does not entail the use of non-market and non-economic force. But because both wage labour and capital move freely on the market, there is a strict minimum level beyond which labour wage cannot fall. In consequence, the owner of capital is compelled to engage in an eternal effort to raise labour productivity, on which alone the magnitude of his appropriated surplus and survival depend in the long run. These are the central dynamics of capitalism that distinguish it unambiguously from all other systems of production. And they are fully and precisely captured only by the conception of capitalism centred on free wage labour. (Inikori 2001: 10)

Capitalism conceived this way allows us to investigate its development over time with a sharp focus, because we know exactly what we are looking for: the market conditions which produced over long-time periods the mass of workers separated from their means of production and entrepreneurs who accumulated those means of production, together with the social and political repercussions that followed. No other conception of capitalism as a socio-economic system offers similar precision. A case in point is the most recent conception in *The Cambridge History of Capitalism*: 'Capitalism, therefore, can be defined usefully as a complex and adaptive economic system operating within broader social, political, and cultural

---

establishment of capitalism dates from the nineteenth century, following 'the industrial revolution in Europe' (Frank 1998: xix).

systems that are essentially supportive' (Neal 2014: 4).[4] Since this definition does not identify the constituent elements of capitalism with clarity and measurable precision, it is difficult to conduct a sharply focused long-run study of the rise of capitalism as a socio-economic system, particularly as causes and effects are confusingly mixed up. For example, the culture of capitalism did not produce capitalism; historically, it was the other way around. Similarly, with the insights of institutional economics,[5] we know that the political power structure of mature capitalist societies did not predate capitalism; it was the ultimate outcome of the long-run development process that established the capitalist system of production.[6]

As already hinted, the growing new literature on the history of capitalism is contributing considerably to our knowledge of the process that gave rise to capitalism and the contribution of some key factors, such as slavery in the Americas, to the process (Baptist 2014; Brandon 2015; Piketty 2014; Schermerhorn 2015). But, a manifest tendency of not being rigorously grounded on the long-established conceptual historiography of the subject often makes it difficult to distinguish between process and outcome; sometimes, both are labelled capitalism. We are beginning to understand better the immense contribution of slavery in the Americas to the historical process that produced capitalism. But slave plantations and other production organizations based on slave labour are not, by definition, capitalist enterprises. There is also the argument that the conception of capitalism going back to Karl Marx and Max Weber does not adequately capture the dynamics of capitalism in the twenty-first century, because workers now have pension and the informal sector (self-employed, low

---

[4] Larry Neal (2014: 2) talks about 'many varieties of capitalism', to which four elements are common: 'private property rights; contracts enforceable by third parties; markets with responsive prices; and supportive governments'.

[5] In particular, see North (1990). North's discussion of the historical evolution of interest groups with relative bargaining power sets the stage for analysing how the establishment of the defining elements of capitalism structures state power and determines the main direction of state policy.

[6] These points have nothing to do with base-superstructure model. It is simply a matter of realistic historical sequence of causation.

labour productivity sector) has become very large in many economies. This argument misses the current reality by a wide margin. Reality requires quantitative measurement. The vast majority of the actively employed population in today's mature capitalist economies earn the greater part of their personal incomes from wages and salaries.[7] What is more, pensions, like unemployment payments, are another form of wages and salaries. The fact that job creation (jobs paying wages and salaries) is the dominant theme in the politics of all mature capitalist societies of today testifies unambiguously to the fact that no conception of capitalism captures the socio-economic and political dynamics of the capitalist system as precisely and accurately as the one that goes back to Karl Marx and Max Weber. Irregularity of employment has been the central socio-economic and political problem of capitalism since the nineteenth century.

Conceptual Framework

W. Arthur Lewis's (1954) model of 'economic development with unlimited supplies of labour' can be reformulated to provide a helpful conceptual framework for our narrative. Lewis's model economy has two sectors: a tiny capitalist sector and an immense subsistence sector comprising peasant cultivators working on their own land. The subsistence peasant sector is where the unlimited supplies of labour are located. Lewis's theoretical task is to conceptualize the market conditions that will induce the vast majority of the subsistence peasant producers to move into the capitalist sector as wage workers. It should be noted that Arthur Lewis was not explicitly concerned with the development of capitalism per se; his concern was economic development in general. Understandably, he did not define his terms, capitalist economy and subsistence economy. However, his use of the term 'capitalist' is consistent with our conception of capitalism elaborated earlier. After contemplating the possibility of capitalists 'hiring out their capital to peasants', he wrote: 'More usually, however, the use of capital is controlled by capitalists, who hire the services of

---

[7] This basic fact is the main source of the problem of the social distribution of income that Karl Marx wrote about elaborately, recently revisited by Piketty (2014: 1–27).

labour. The classical analysis was therefore conducted on the assumption that capital was used for hiring people' (Lewis 1954: 124–5).[8] Thus, Lewis's model economy will transition from non-capitalist to a capitalist economy after the capitalist sector has absorbed the bulk of the actively employed population.

The main mechanism for the transfer of labour from the subsistence to the capitalist sector in Lewis's model economy is wages. If real wages in the capitalist sector offer consumption levels sufficiently higher than those in the subsistence sector, labour will move from the latter to the capitalist sector:

> The wage which the expanding capitalist sector has to pay is determined by what people can earn outside that sector. The classical economists used to think of the wage as being determined by what is required for subsistence consumption, and this may be the right solution in some cases. However, in economies where the majority of the people are peasant farmers, working on their own land, we have a more objective index, for the minimum at which labour can be had is now set by the average product of the farmer; men will not leave the family farm to seek employment if the wage is worth less than they would be able to consume if they remained at home. (Lewis 1954: 126–7)

It is not clear in the Lewis model economy where the expanding capitalist sector is located, in agriculture or in manufacturing or both. It appears Lewis thought more about manufacturing, but that is not particularly important. What is important is that the Lewis model does not say explicitly what factors are behind the expansion of the capitalist sector, with the wages that compel the movement of labour from the subsistence sector, particularly, since the model economy is a closed economy (unconnected to other economies, especially, not involved in trade with other economies), and it is not a bureaucratic state capitalism like Stalin's Russia. We reformulate the model economy, making

---

[8] Our definition of subsistence production is different from that of Lewis (1954: 124–5): 'The subsistence sector is by difference all that part of the economy which is not using reproducible capital'. An economy in which the bulk of the output is consumed directly by the producers' households, without sale in the market, is a subsistence economy by our definition.

it an open economy, engaged actively in international/intercontinental trade. Population–land ratios and their changes over time are dynamic elements in the reformulated model; so, too, are market opportunities for the production of manufactures and natural resource–based commodities for export. The supplies of labour are not necessarily unlimited initially. Unlike Lewis's (1954: 122) contention that 'there is no evidence that the birth rate ever rises with economic development', our reformulated model accommodates the possibility of birth rate increases being one of the dynamic elements.

The Emergence of Capitalism in England

The establishment of a capitalist economy in England was preceded by a long-drawn-out process of commercialization of socio-economic life in the country. The available evidence suggests that the market sector of the Domesday economy (1086) could not have been more than 25 per cent of England's GDP (Britnell and Campbell 1995).[9] Between 1086 and 1600, the dominant labour relations changed from a combination of subsistence production (production mainly for the immediate consumption of the producers, with very little market exchange) and tributary labour (including slaves and serfs producing mainly to provision their lords and their subordinates) to self-employed labour (producing mainly for market exchange) (Inikori 2002: 28–33; Postan 1954). The ending of slavery in England left serfdom as the dominant labour relation. By the mid-fifteenth century, serfdom also ended, setting the stage for the intensification of the commercializing process. Contrary to the Marxian schema, in which capitalism followed the ending of serfdom, it took more than three centuries after the ending of serfdom for a capitalist economy to be established in England. What followed the demise of serfdom was the development of production mainly for market exchange by self-employed labour (organized in families) freed from the burden of serfdom. By the seventeenth century, the English economy was fully commercialized, but not yet capitalist.

[9] See other essays in the volume, in particular, Snooks (1995: 27–54); Mayhew (1995: 55–77); Campbell (1995: 132–93); Also see Inikori (2002: 24–33).

Estimates based on Henry VIII's tax subsidy of 1525 show that out of a total population of roughly 2.4 million in England at the time, there were 600,000 free wage workers and their dependents and 1.65 million peasant 'family farmers' (Levine 1984: 88, 112). Estimates for 1688 show there were 227,440 self-employed families in the agricultural sector and 284,997 wage-earning families in all sectors of England's economy (Lindert 1980: 685–712), meaning that family farmers (the celebrated yeoman farmers) still outnumbered wage-earning families in English agriculture in the late seventeenth century. G.E. Mingay pointed out the timeline and the market conditions for the capitalist transformation of English agriculture in his argument that the transformation of copyholders and freeholders into wage labourers occurred largely after 1660, caused mainly by more than a hundred years of low and fluctuating agricultural prices that hit the small cultivators disproportionately hard (Allen 1992: 1–21; Mingay 1968: 29). Consistent with our model, this means that prolonged low agricultural prices made wage incomes in the capitalist sector more attractive to self-employed small cultivators. David Levine (1984: 112) followed the same timeline when he stated that the family farmers were displaced as the numerically dominant producers in English agriculture in the mid-eighteenth century by tenant farmers employing wage labour.

The growth of large farms employing wage labour was very much aided by the growth of manufacturing and commerce, which increased non-agricultural employment. Family farmers in England had adopted a homeostatic demographic practice to maintain the equilibrium between family size and the family land through delayed marriage, young men and women waiting until the family land came to their possession before marrying and raising their own families (Levine 1977, 1984: 87–127; 1985: 168–203; Wrigley 1983; Wrigley and Schofield 1981). The growth of manufacturing and commerce gave rise to expanding non-agricultural employment, which provided non-agricultural incomes for young men and women to marry early and raise families, thereby reducing the age at first marriage for women, and at the same time reducing the number of women remaining unmarried for life. The resulting increase in birth rate was the main source of population growth in England from the mid-eighteenth century to the mid-nineteenth (Wrigley 1983).

It follows from the demographic evidence that industrialization in England in the eighteenth and nineteenth centuries largely created its own labour through the demographic response of peasant and proletarian families (families dependent mainly on wages) to the demand for industrial labour. As David Levine has demonstrated, expropriated peasants (peasants who lost their lands) contributed less than 50 per cent of the increased number of proletarians in England from 2.5 million in 1700 to 14 million in 1850 and 16.5 million in 1871, the rest coming from population growth among peasant families and the proletarian families themselves, as they both responded to employment opportunities in the expanding non-agricultural sectors, particularly industrial employment (Levine 1984: 104–15; 1985: 170–1). All this is confirmed by the regional distribution of manufacturing and population growth in England, as shown in Tables 9.1A, 9.1B, and 9.2. [10]

Taking the distribution of adult males (20 years and above) as representative of the main features of the labour employed in the economy, the data in these tables allow us to view the main characteristics of the English economy at the beginning of the fourth decade of the nineteenth century. Overall, it is clear that legally free wage earners were now the numerically dominant labour in the economy. Of the total 2,759,083 adult males employed in the national economy, 1,558,563 (56.5 per cent) were wage/salary employees. Of the 980,750 employed in agriculture, 744,407 (75.9 per cent) were wage earners, 141,460 (14.4 per cent) employers (including owner cultivators and tenants), and 94,883 (9.7 per cent) self-employed (owner cultivators and tenants). Factory workers (314,106) constituted only 24.6 per cent of the 1,278,283 employed in manufacturing and handicraft and retail trades; the remaining 964,177 (75.4 per cent) were in the latter category. By our conception of capitalism, the national economy had become capitalist by 1831. So, too, were agriculture and the major components of the service sector (import and export, shipping, internal transportation, finance, education, government), which employed, in all certainty, the 500,050 wage earners unassigned by the census enumerators to the listed sectors

[10] These tables appeared earlier in Inikori (2015: Tables 9.2, 9.3, and 9.4, 247, 249, 250).

Table 9.1A England's Counties' Economies in Comparative Perspective, 1831 Census

	Lancashire	Yorkshire (West Riding)	Essex	Suffolk	Norfolk	England
			Selected Counties in England			
Area (acres)	1,117,260	1,629,890	979,000	918,769	1,292,300	31,770,615
Population	1,336,854	976,359	317,597	296,317	390,054	13,091,005
Males 20 Years Plus:	313,097	231,666	79,023	71,376	93,498	3,199,984
(a) Employed in manufacture or in making manufacturing machinery	97,517	74,669	871	676	4,740	314,106
(b) Employed in retail trade or in handicraft as masters or workmen	86,079	60,109	18,953	18,167	26,543	964,177
Occupiers employing labourers	6,658	7,096	4,561	4,526	5,229	141,460
Occupiers not employing labourers	9,714	10,636	888	1,121	2,718	94,883
Labourers employed in agriculture	20,949	24,502	38,234	33,040	37,466	744,407
Labourers employed in labour not agricultural	60,546	33,685	6,727	5,336	6,577	500,050

Note: Essex, Norfolk, and Suffolk make up England's southeast region known as East Anglia, being compared in this table with the part of northern England comprising Lancashire and the West Riding of Yorkshire. Although the enumerators intended the term 'manufacture' to apply only to factory manufacturing, some proto-industrial production may have been included, as they noted that separating manufacture from handicraft was difficult.

Source: 1831 Census, enumeration abstract, II, *Parliamentary Papers*, 1833, XXXVI, pp. 832–3.

Table 9.1B England's Counties' Economies in Comparative Perspective, 1831 Census

	Selected Counties in England					
	Stafford	Nottingham	Warwick	Kent	Surrey	Middlesex
Area (acres)	736,290	525,800	567,930	972,240	474,480	179,590
Population	410,512	225,327	336,610	479,155	486,334	1,358,330
Males 20 Years Plus:	101,632	56,582	83,239	115,655	119,565	358,521
(a) Employed in manufacture or in making manufacturing machinery	26,755	14,260	11,375	476	2,065	11,064
(b) Employed in retail rade or in handicraft as masters or workers	24,766	14,683	32,579	34,257	44,139	163,220
Occupiers employing labourers	3,781	2,643	2,838	4,361	1,873	1,050
Occupiers not employing labourers	3,649	2,414	1,142	2,152	727	490
Labourers employed in agriculture	16,812	11,799	15,644	36,113	16,761	11,376
Labourers employed in labour not agricultural	22,690	5,628	10,358	15,245	24,878	79,735

Note: Kent, Surrey, and Middlesex are the home counties (counties adjacent to the capital city, London). Stafford, Warwick, and Nottingham are Midland counties.

Source: *1831 Census*, enumeration abstract, II, *Parliamentary Papers*, 1833, XXXVI, pp. 832–3.

Table 9.2 Area and Population of Selected English Counties, 1600–1831 (in thousands)

County	Area (Acres)	Population				
		1600	1700	1750	1801	1831
Lancashire	1,117.3	183.7	232.5	317.2	703.1	1,336.9
West Riding (Yorkshire)	1,629.9	199.7	242.0	323.5	590.5	976.4
Essex (East Anglia)	979.0	156.6	164.7	188.5	237.9	317.6
Suffolk (East Anglia)	918.8	139.9	159.2	166.7	223.9	296.3
Norfolk (East Anglia)	1,292.3	173.1	230.9	233.6	285.4	390.1
Stafford	736.3	78.4	114.9	150.8	254.7	410.5
Nottingham	525.8	79.0	92.2	88.4	146.6	225.3
Warwick	567.9	66.2	87.4	132.5	215.9	336.6
Kent	972.2	153.4	160.7	183.7	322.5	479.2
Surrey	474.5	85.8	124.3	151.0	279.9	486.3
Middlesex	179.6	283.3	522.4	584.6	852.9	1,358.3
England	31,770.6	4,161.8	5,210.6	5,921.9	8,671.4	13,091.0

Note: Essex, Norfolk, and Suffolk make up England's southeast region, known as East Anglia. Kent, Surrey, and Middlesex are the home counties (counties adjacent to the capital city, London). Stafford and Warwick are West Midland counties and Nottingham is one of the East Midland counties.

Sources: Population figures for 1600, 1700, 1750, and 1801 are from Wrigley (2009: Table 3, 721). The population figures for 1831 and the area figures are from *1831 Census*, enumeration abstract, II, *Parliamentary Papers*, 1833, XXXVI, 832–3.

(Table 9.1A). But, as Table 9.1A shows, the industrial sector was still dominated numerically by self-employed handicraft producers. The national economy, therefore, was yet to achieve industrial capitalism.

But there were county economies that had already achieved industrial capitalism (with more people employed in factory production than in handicraft and retail trades) at the time of the 1831 census. Of the total 260,514 adult males employed in Lancashire's economy in 1831: 179,014 (68.7 per cent) were wage/salary employees; 56.1

per cent of those in agriculture were wage earners; and factory workers (97,517) constituted 53.1 per cent of those in manufacturing, retail trade, and handicraft (183,596). The comparable figures for the West Riding of Yorkshire are: wage/salary employees, 63.1 per cent of the total (210,697); wage earners, 58 per cent of those in agriculture (42,234); and factory workers, 55.4 per cent of those in manufacturing and handicraft and retail trades (134,778). For the West Midlands county of Stafford (Table 9.1B): 67.3 per cent of the total (98,453) were wage/salary employees; 69.4 per cent of those in agriculture were wage earners; and factory workers, 51.9 per cent of those in manufacturing and handicraft and retail trades. In all the remaining English counties, wage/salary employees constituted less than 50 per cent of those in manufacturing and handicraft and retail trades. Lancashire can be called the first industrial capitalist economy in the world, with 31.05 per cent of all factory employment in England at the time; followed by the West Riding of Yorkshire, and the West Midlands county of Stafford a distant third. The two contiguous northwest regions, Lancashire and the West Riding of Yorkshire, together had approximately 55 per cent of England's total factory employment in 1831; adding Stafford, these three regions had about 63 per cent of the national total. In contrast, factory employment in the three counties of East Anglia (Essex, Suffolk, Norfolk), with a total area of 3.2 million acres, just slightly less than that of the three former regions combined (3.5 million acres), was only 2 per cent of the national total. Though capitalist by 1831, the economy of East Anglia (southeast England) was far from that of industrial capitalism, with handicraft production and retail trades overwhelmingly dominant. So, too, were the economies of the other southern counties.

The regional distribution of capitalist industry points strongly to the main causal factors in the process of capitalist development in England over the long period of this study. From 1086 to 1650, population growth and the wool trade (raw wool production for export, followed by woollen textile production for export and for the domestic market, and raw wool production for both markets) were the main operating factors (Inikori 2002: 24–33). East Anglia was a major beneficiary of the developments of this period (centred on trade with continental Europe) at a time when Lancashire and the West Riding of Yorkshire were among the most backward counties in England. The development of agrarian capitalism in East Anglia occurred during this period, stimulated by raw wool exports and proto-industrial production of woollen textiles. Population growth and raw wool production raised the value of land to the advantage of rearers of large sheep (a land-intensive agricultural production) and reduced the earnings of self-employed, small landholders; while proto-industrial, woollen textile production (a labour-intensive economic activity) and commerce offered wage employment, with incomes higher than those from small family farms.

From 1650 to 1850, there was a dramatic geographical change in the markets for English manufactures, particularly woollen textiles. For several centuries, northwest Europe (Germany, Holland, Flanders, and France) and northern Europe (Norway, Denmark, Iceland, Greenland, and the Baltic) were the main export markets for English woollen textiles. From the second half of the seventeenth century, English producers lost much of those markets as local production expanded in those regions, sometimes under mercantilist policies. From 1699/1701 to 1772/1774, English woollen cloth export to northwest Europe and northern Europe declined absolutely by 37.4 per cent and 38.9 per cent, respectively. For the whole period, 1701–1806, the export of English woollen cloth to northwest Europe and northern Europe decreased absolutely from £1,544,000 to £1,002,000.[11]

While English woollen cloth exports to northwest and northern Europe decreased absolutely, exports to Atlantic markets (West Africa, the Americas, Portugal, and Spain) grew phenomenally. Exports to the Americas and western Africa increased from £185,000 a year in 1699–1701 to £1,148,000 in 1772–4; in 1804–6, £3,413,000; and £5,177,000 in 1854–6. Exports to the Americas and western Africa moved from 6.1 per cent of English woollen exports in 1699–1701 to 50.2 per cent in 1804–6, moving down to 40.7 per cent in 1854–6 (Inikori 2002: Table 9.1, 414). Exports to Portugal and Spain, which were part of the Atlantic markets for all practical purposes,[12] also

[11] All figures computed from Davis (1962, 1979).

[12] Portuguese and Spanish export and import trade with their European partners in the eighteenth century depended largely on their American colonies. The imports (a large percentage of which was re-exported to the

grew during the period, particularly during the Brazilian gold export boom of the first six decades of the eighteenth century. The evidence is strong that for much of the eighteenth and early nineteenth century, Atlantic markets (including Portugal and Spain) could not have absorbed less than 60 per cent of total English woollen exports (Inikori 2015: 243–4).

The expanding Atlantic markets were captured largely by producers in the West Riding of Yorkshire. The older export-producing regions in the south, particularly East Anglia and the West Country, were outcompeted. Consequently, much of the growth in total English woollen exports in the eighteenth century (from £3.0 million in 1701 to £6.8 million in 1806) was concentrated in the West Riding, no less than 72 per cent of whose total output was exported in 1772 (Inikori 2015: 244). Its capture of rapidly expanding export markets led to growing concentration of the woollen textile industry in the West Riding, increasing from 20 per cent of the national total in 1695 to 60 per cent in 1800 (Inikori 2015: 243–5).

Similar to woollen textiles in the West Riding, cotton textile production for export to Atlantic markets was central to the transformation of Lancashire from virtually the most backward of England's counties for centuries to the first capitalist industrial society in the world. Lancashire, like the West Riding, took advantage of its low wages, arising from poor agricultural resources, and the early development of Liverpool as a leading English port in British trade with Africa and the Americas to capture the Atlantic export markets for English cottons (Farnie 1979; Wadsworth and Mann 1931; Walton 1987, 1989). For this reason, the industry concentrated increasingly in Lancashire. In 1787, the county had close to one-half of the capital value of all cotton mills in Great Britain; in 1820, 165,000 (68.8 per cent) of the 240,000 handloom weavers in Britain were in the county (Inkster 1991: 65, fn. 17, 320; Timmins 1993: 25, 26, 37, 39).[13] The great

---

colonies) were paid for largely with re-exports of colonial goods. See Inikori (2002: 203–8, 413–15, 420).

[13] As of 1820, handloom weaving was still overwhelmingly dominant in weaving in Britain. Scotland had 47,000 out of the 240,000 (19.6 per cent) handloom weavers. In 1820, handloom weavers constituted 25 per cent of the total labour force in Lancashire.

concentration of cotton textiles production in Lancashire meant that the industry's explosive growth between 1760 and 1851—total British gross output increased from £0.6 million in 1760 to £5.4 million in 1784–6 (annual average), £11.1 million in 1798–1800, £30 million in 1815–17, and £48.6 million in 1851 (Deane and Cole 1962: Tables 42 and 43, 185, 187)—was equally concentrated in the county.

Like the West Riding, the bulk of Lancashire's total output was exported. Initially, the exports went, almost entirely, to western Africa and the Americas. Between 1700 and 1774, western Africa and the Americas absorbed between 79.6 per cent and 94 per cent of total British cotton textile exports; in 1784–1806, it was between 52 .3 per cent and 69.2 per cent (Inikori 2002: Table 9.9, 448). When exports to Portugal and Spain are included, the share of Atlantic markets increases further, especially in 1784–1806.

The rapid growth of industrial production and commerce in Lancashire and the West Riding gave rise to the growth of employment, which in turn induced rapid population growth in both regions. They had the highest birth rates among all England's counties between 1750 and 1831. Table 9.2 shows the geographical area and population of selected English counties in selected years from 1600 to 1831. From the figures in the table, the population of England increased by 42.3 per cent in 1600–1750, 46.4 per cent in 1750–1801, and 51.0 per cent in 1801–31. Comparable figures for the three counties of East Anglia together for the same periods are 25.4 per cent, 26.9 per cent, and 34.4 per cent, respectively; for the West Riding, they are 62.0 per cent, 82.5 per cent, and 65 .4 per cent, respectively; for Lancashire, they are 72 per cent, 121.7 per cent, and 90.1 per cent, respectively. It is clear from these figures that the population of East Anglia stagnated over the period, being considerably below the national growth rate. On the other hand, the growth rates for the West Riding and Lancashire were far above the national rate, and several times East Anglia's rate. It is significant that in 1750, the counties of East Anglia had a combined population of 588,800 and Lancashire had 317,200; in 1831, the comparable figures are 1,004,000 and 1,336,900, respectively.

The explosive growth of population in Lancashire and the West Riding occurred at the same time that their wages were rising in association with the growing demand for labour in industries experiencing expansion of production for Atlantic markets. Lancashire and the West Riding moved from being among the lowest wage counties in 1767–70 to being among the three highest wage counties (Inikori 2002: 65). Thus, the domestic market in both regions also experienced considerable expansion during the period. It was this combined expansion of export markets and the regional domestic markets that created market conditions for the growth of the factory system and the development and diffusion of new technologies in Lancashire and the West Riding. Factory employment in the West Riding woollen textile industry was 50.3 per cent of England's total in 1835; it was 65.1 per cent in 1850 (Gregory 1982: Table 2.11, 61). Lancashire overwhelmingly dominated the mechanization of cotton weaving from the 1830s: 56.5 per cent of power looms employed in cotton weaving in Great Britain in 1835 were in Lancashire; in 1850, the proportion was 70.9 per cent (Timmins 1993: Table 1.1, 20). This is why Lancashire and the West Riding dominated wage/salary employment in manufacturing in England in the first half of the nineteenth century. The growth of the factory system and technological innovation greatly reduced manufacturing cost per unit of output and rendered self-employed, small-scale handicraft production uncompetitive. This made wage income more attractive than income from handicraft self-employment, turning handloom weavers and other small-scale, self-employed producers into factory wage/salary workers.

As mentioned earlier, the other English county which developed industrial capitalism between the mid-seventeenth and mid-nineteenth century was the West Midlands county of Stafford that dominated the iron industry in England in the late eighteenth and early nineteenth century. Like the major counties producing iron and ironware in the West Midlands (Warwickshire, Shropshire, Staffordshire, and Worcestershire), Stafford sold its products largely in Atlantic markets, which, together, offered large and fast-growing markets that made the West Midlands the location for the major inventions and technological innovations in the iron industry (Inikori 2002: 67–71). The relatively high-wage jobs created drew workers to manufacturing in factories and also induced population growth similar to Lancashire and the West Riding, albeit to a much lesser extent, as the tables show.

***

As the first capitalist nation in the world, the development of capitalism in England was a long-drawn-out process—the ending of tributary labour (slavery and serfdom); the growth of production for market exchange by family labour, freed from the burden of feudalism, and the diminution of non-market production (subsistence production), leading to the growth and geographical expansion of the market economy; the development of market conditions that led to the loss of ownership of the means of production by the vast majority of legally free producers and their concentration in a few hands, inducing, as a matter of economic choice (as opposed to extra-economic coercion), the mass of legally free producers to sell their labour power to holders of the means of production, the ultimate outcome of the process. All these developments had their socio-political repercussions—the build-up of competing interest groups with conflicting interests and institutions over time. This chapter has focused on the economic process, following the careful identification of the constituent elements that distinguish capitalism unambiguously from all other socio-economic systems and the conceptual framework that informs the collection and analysis of the pertinent historical evidence.

The main question addressed in the chapter is the historical origins of the market conditions that produced a mass of wage/salary workers as the numerically dominant form of the labour process in England by the mid-nineteenth century. Population growth and international/intercontinental trade, operating and interacting, were the central factors in the process. The wool trade to northwest and northern Europe interacted with population growth to lead the process in the centuries preceding 1660. Thereafter, the dynamic centre of the process shifted decisively to the Atlantic world. British military domination of the Atlantic ensured the domination of Atlantic trade, shipping, and finance by British entrepreneurs from the mid-seventeenth to the mid-nineteenth century. The Industrial Revolution, with its factory and mechanized system of manufacturing, was largely the product of this development. In its initial regions of origin, the Industrial Revolution made self-employed handicraft production less economically rewarding than wage/salary employment in the factories. It is not for nothing that England's regions (Lancashire, the West Riding, and to a lesser extent the West Midlands, particularly Stafford), which dominated the Atlantic markets, were the first to achieve industrial capitalism, as the evidence presented has shown. The southern English counties that had benefited from the early trade with continental Europe (especially the three counties of East Anglia), and were far ahead of the Midlands and northern counties by 1660, fell significantly behind thereafter, because they lost much of their European markets (often due to mercantilist policies in those markets) and were relatively less competitive in the Atlantic markets. Like England's national economy as a whole, they had become capitalist, by definition, in the fourth decade of the nineteenth century, but had not yet achieved industrial capitalism.

Based on the economically, socially, and politically more pertinent conception of capitalism and the conceptual framework we have applied, we contend that there is nothing uniquely English, culturally or otherwise, in the process we have traced and analysed, possible differences in historical conjuncture and the like notwithstanding. We believe, therefore, that insights from the English process would be helpful in the study of capitalist development elsewhere. Let it be said, again, that we must resist the temptation of turning the history of capitalism into the unfocused history of everything.

Bibliography

Allen, Robert C. 1992. *Enclosure and the Yeoman: The Agricultural Development of the South Midlands, 1450–1850.* Oxford: Clarendon Press.

Antonio, Robert J. and Ronald M. Glassman, eds. 1985. *A Weber–Marx Dialogue.* Lawrence, Kansas: University Press of Kansas.

Baptist, Edward E. 2014. *The Half Has Never Been Told: Slavery and The Making of American Capitalism.* New York: Basic Books.

Brandon, Pepijn. 2015. *War, Capital, and the Dutch State (1588–1795).* Leiden: Brill.

Brenner, Robert. 1977. 'The Origins of Capitalist Development: A Critique of Neo-Smithian Marxism.' *New Left Review* 104: 25–92.

Britnell, Richard H. and Bruce M.S. Campbell, eds. 1995. *A Commercialising Economy: England 1086 to c.1300.* Manchester: Manchester University Press.

Callinicos, Alex. 1991. *The Revenge of History: Marxism and the East European Revolutions*. University Park, PA: The Pennsylvania State University Press.

Campbell, Bruce M.S. 1995. 'Measuring the Commercialisation of Seigneurial Agriculture, c.1300.' In *A Commercialising Economy*, edited by Richard H. Britnell and Bruce M.S. Campbell, pp. 132–93. Manchester: Manchester University Press.

Cliff, Tony. 1948. 'The Nature of Stalinist Russia.' *Revolutionary Communist Party Internal Bulletin* (June).

———. 1988. *State Capitalism in Russia*. London: Bookmarks Press.

Cooper, Frederick. 2014. *Africa in the World: Capitalism, Empire, Nation-State*. Cambridge, MA: Harvard University Press.

Davis, Ralph. 1962. 'English Foreign Trade, 1700–1774.' *Economic History Review* (2nd series) 15(2): 285–303.

———. 1979. *The Industrial Revolution and British Overseas Trade*. Leicester: Leicester University Press.

Deane, Phyllis and W.A. Cole. 1962. *British Economic Growth, 1688–1959: Trends and Structure*. Cambridge: Cambridge University Press.

Dobb, Maurice. 1946. *Studies in the Development of Capitalism*. London: Routledge and Kegan Paul.

———. 1958. *Capitalism: Yesterday and Today*. London: Lawrence and Wishart.

Duncan, Kenneth and Ian Rutledge, eds. 1977. *Land and Labour in Latin America: Essays on the Development of Agrarian Capitalism in the Nineteenth and Twentieth Centuries*, edited in collaboration with Colin Harding. Cambridge: Cambridge University Press.

Farnie, D.A. 1979. *The English Cotton Industry and the World Market, 1815–1896*. Oxford: Clarendon Press.

Frank, Andre Gunder. 1967. *Capitalism and Underdevelopment in Latin America*. New York: Monthly Review Press.

———. 1998. *ReOrient: Global Economy in the Asian Age*. Berkeley: University of California Press.

Gregory, Derek. 1982. *Regional Transformation and Industrial Revolution: A Geography of the Yorkshire Woollen Industry*. Minneapolis: University of Minnesota Press.

Hill, Polly. 1970. *Studies in Rural Capitalism in West Africa*. Cambridge: Cambridge University Press.

Hilton, Rodney. 1978a. 'Capitalism: What's in a Name?' In *The Transition from Feudalism to Capitalism*, edited by Rodney Hilton. London: Verso.

————, ed. 1978b. *The Transition from Feudalism to Capitalism*. London: Verso.

Iliffe, John. 1983. *The Emergence of African Capitalism*. Minneapolis: University of Minnesota Press.

Inikori, Joseph E. 2001. 'Slavery and the Rise of Capitalism.' In *Slavery, Freedom and Gender: The Dynamics of Caribbean Society*, edited by Brian L. Moore, B.W. Higman, Carl Campbell, and Patrick Bryan. Barbados, Jamaica, Trinidad and Tobago: University of the West Indies Press.

————. 2002. *Africans and the Industrial Revolution in England: A Study in International Trade and Economic Development*. Cambridge: Cambridge University Press.

————. 2015. 'The Industrial Revolution in Atlantic Perspective: County History and National History.' In *The Legacy of Eric Williams: Caribbean Scholar and Statesman,* edited by Colin A. Palmer. Jamaica, Barbados, Trinidad and Tobago: The University of the West Indies Press.

Inkster, Ian. 1991. *Science and Technology in History: An Approach to Industrial Development*. New Brunswick, NJ: Rutgers University Press.

Kaye, Harvey J. 1984. *The British Marxist Historians*. Cambridge, England: Polity Press.

Laclau, Ernesto. 1971. 'Feudalism and Capitalism in Latin America.' *New Left Review* 67: 19–38.

Levine, David. 1977. *Family Formation in an Age of Nascent Capitalism*. New York: Academic Press.

————. 1984. 'Production, Reproduction, and the Proletarian Family in England, 1500–1851.' In *Proletarianization and Family History*, edited by David Levine. Orlando: Academic Press.

————. 1985. 'Industrialization and the Proletarian Family in England.' *Past & Present* 107: 168–203.

Lewis, W. Arthur. 1954. 'Economic Development with Unlimited Supplies of Labour.' *Manchester School of Economic and Social Studies* 22: 139–91; reprinted in Deepak Lal, ed. 1992. *Development Economics*. Vol. I. Aldershot, Hants, England: Edward Elgar.

Lindert, Peter H. 1980. 'English Occupations, 1670–1811.' *Journal of Economic History* 40(4): 685–712.

Macfarlane, Alan. 1987. *The Culture of Capitalism*. Oxford: Basil Blackwell.

Marx, Karl. 1952. *Wage Labour and Capital,* translated from the German edition of 1891, prefaced and edited by Frederick Engels. Moscow: Progress Publishers.

Marx, Karl. (1867) 1976. *Capital: A Critique of Political Economy*. Vol. 1. Translated by Ben Fowkes, with Introduction by Ernest Mandel. New York: Penguin Books and New Left Review.

Mayhew, Nicholas. 1995. 'Modelling Medieval Monetization.' In *A Commercialising Economy*, edited by Richard H. Britnell and Bruce M.S. Campbell, pp. 55–77. Manchester: Manchester University Press.

Mingay, G.E. 1968. *Enclosure and the Small Farmer in the Age of the Industrial Revolution*. London: Macmillan.

Neal, Larry and Jeffrey G. Williamson, eds. 2014. *The Cambridge History of Capitalism*. 2 Vols. Cambridge: Cambridge University Press.

North, Douglass C. 1990. *Institutions, Institutional Change and Economic Performance*. Cambridge: Cambridge University Press.

Piketty, Thomas. 2014. *Capital in the Twenty-First Century*, translated by Arthur Goldhammer. Cambridge, MA: The Belknap Press of Harvard University Press.

Postan, M.M. 1954. *The Famulus: The Estate Labourer in the XIIth and XIIIth Centuries*, Economic History Review, Suppl. 2.

Schermerhorn, Calvin. 2015. *The Business of Slavery and the Rise of American Capitalism, 1815–1860*. New Haven: Yale University Press.

Snooks, Graeme Donald. 1995. 'The Dynamic Role of the Market in the Anglo-Norman Economy and Beyond, 1086–1300.' In *A Commercialising Economy*, edited by Richard H. Britnell and Bruce M.S. Campbell, pp. 27–54. Manchester: Manchester University Press.

Summers, Lawrence H. 2014. 'Editorial Review', edited by Larry Neal and Jeffrey G. Williamson. *The Cambridge History of Capitalism*, 2 Vols. Cambridge: Cambridge University Press.

Tawney, R.H. 1958. Foreword. In Max Weber, *Protestant Ethic and the Spirit of Capitalism*, translated by Talcott Parsons. New York: Charles Scribner's Sons.

Taylor, John G. 1979. *From Modernization to Modes of Production: A Critique of the Sociologies of Development and Underdevelopment*. London: Macmillan.

Timmins, Geoffrey. 1993. *The Last Shift: The Decline of Handloom Weaving in Nineteenth-Century Lancashire*. Manchester: Manchester University Press.

Wadsworth, A.P. and J. de L. Mann. 1931. *The Cotton Trade and Industrial Lancashire*. Manchester: Manchester University Press.

Wallerstein, Immanuel. 1974. *The Modern World-System: Capitalist Agriculture and the Origins of the European World Economy in the Sixteenth Century*. Vol. I. New York: Academic Press.

———. 1983. *Historical Capitalism*. London: Verso.

Walton, John K. 1987. *Lancashire: A Social History, 1558–1939*. Manchester: Manchester University Press.

Walton, John K. 1989. 'Proto-industrialisation and the First Industrial Revolution: The Case of Lancashire.' In *Regions and Industries: A*

Perspective on the Industrial Revolution in Britain, edited by Pat Hudson. Cambridge: Cambridge University Press.

Weber, Max. 1958. *The Protestant Ethic and the Spirit of Capitalism.* New York: Charles Scribner's Sons.

————. 1978. *Economy and Society: An Outline of Interpretive Sociology,* edited by G. Roth and C. Wittich. Vol. 2. Berkeley: University of California Press.

Wood, Ellen Meiksins. 1991. *The Pristine Culture of Capitalism: A Historical Essay on Old Regimes and Modern States.* London: Verso.

Wrigley, E.A. 1983. 'The Growth of Population in Eighteenth-Century England: A Conundrum Resolved. *Past & Present* 98(1): 121–50.

————. 2009. 'Rickman Revisited: The Population Growth Rates of English Counties in the Early Modern Period.' *Economic History Review* 62(3): 711–35.

Wrigley, E.A. and R.S. Schofield. 1981. *The Population History of England, 1541–1871: A Reconstruction.* Cambridge, MA: Harvard University Press.

10

The Thin Line between Economic Dynamism and Social Stability

Regulation and Deregulation in Japan
(Twelfth to Nineteenth Century)

Masaki Nakabayashi

What is capitalism? Moreover, how can we discuss the formation of capitalism productively? A possible way is to treat capitalism as a system of efficient product and factor markets, with market participants responding to the relative prices between markets (Neal 2014: 4). However, some of these traits date back to ancient civilizations such as the Roman and Chinese empires. The long history of some elements of capitalism begs the question of exactly when a sustainable capitalist regime came into existence. Neal and Williamson (2014) have addressed this question by examining various historical paths of early modern Western and Eastern economies.

One of the most influential views that *The Cambridge History of Capitalism* and other 'institutionalist' works have put forward is a sustained focus on the rise of the fiscal state. In many economies, commodity markets emerged and had integrated at an early stage. The integrated product market is admittedly a fundamental premise for the rise of capitalism; it has always existed in every growing economy throughout global history. Factor markets, namely, financial and labour markets, are the necessary next stage in the emergence of capitalism. In most advanced economies, the state played an essential role in building its financial markets in both early modern and modern times as it sought to finance a costly mode of modernized warfare through bond flotation. A reliable market that attracted investments was one of the driving forces of the rising British Empire. This national financial market invested in large businesses as well. Other imperialist states followed suit. In this sense, the rise of a fiscal state was a vital stepping stone for the rise of British capitalism and those of other advanced economies (O'Brien 2014).

In addition to the creation and expansion of the financial market, another challenge of pre-modern and early modern societies was the coexistence of the other two free factor markets, that is, labour and land markets. Although most advanced economies achieved liberalization of the goods market in their early stages of development, the liberalization of the labour market was much more delayed and only gradual. Note that in the United States, white indentured labourers were only emancipated in 1865 along with black slaves. In 1900, the United States finally rendered indenture illegal. The United Kingdom too continued to admit some forms of coercive contracts until the end of the nineteenth century. While the land markets were liberalized since the Glorious Revolution of 1688 (Bogart 2011), the labour markets had been coercive during most of the modernization process in the United Kingdom. This was the case in the United States as well (Steinfeld 1991, 2001).

In modern capitalist economies, free financial, labour, land, and product markets are connected through firms. Provided that the corporate sector produces enough added value by procuring inputs from the financial and labour markets and providing products to the downstream/consumption markets, the free financial, labour, land, and product markets remain stable. The United Kingdom and the United States achieved this phase around the end of the nineteenth century.

In Japan, deregulation with the objective of gaining perfectly free financial, labour, and product markets was completed by the Meiji Restoration, after the imperial court and the western lords defeated the shogunate and the eastern lords in 1868. The reform was achieved through the enactment of the Constitution of the Empire of Japan in 1890, the Civil Code in 1898, and the Commercial Code in 1899. Modern capitalist firms arising from the establishment of the Tokyo Stock Exchange and the Osaka Stock Exchange in 1878 were critical catalytic agents.

However, this does not mean that deregulated markets of finance, labour, and products had not existed before the Meiji Restoration. Since the fourteenth century, the Japanese administration had tried to strike a balance between the dynamics of factor and product markets and the stability of society. The early modern Edo (now Tokyo) shogunate from 1600 to 1868 was based on stability, while the medieval Muromachi shogunate pursued the liberalization of land and financial markets. In this chapter, we reflect upon Japanese economic history since the Muromachi shogunate, which replaced the Kamakura shogunate and established free factor markets in medieval times. After officially introducing free markets in the fourteenth century, for centuries to come, the administration had difficulties in taming free markets; in particular, those of finance and labour and, thus, attempted to strike a balance between the dynamics of growth and the stability of society. These efforts made way for the emergence of a modern state that fully realized the transition to a modern capitalist economy in the late nineteenth century.

The issue, however, is not only about the past. Balancing growth and stability has always been a critical problem for advanced economies, even after they fully liberalized financial and labour markets around the end of the nineteenth century. A great swing towards regulation was widely observed in the 1930s, responding to the Great Depression. We have experienced a swing in the other direction since the 1980s. Now we are facing a swing towards tighter regulations again after the global financial crisis of 2008. The efforts made by three shogunates in Japan since the twelfth century are still useful lessons today and need to be taken into account to be able to tame modern capitalism and avoid endangering social stability.

Let us now review the growth trend in the periods with which we are concerned. Since the Maddison Project is contested and not sufficiently reliable, we cite the latest estimates. Figure 10.1 shows the estimates of Japan's per capita gross domestic product (GDP) in comparison with those of China and European economies. During the reign of the Kamakura shogunate, between 1185 and 1333, the Chinese economy under the Song and Mongol dynasties enjoyed the last phase of its economic superiority. It had lasted for about 2,000 years, and its per capita GDP was almost twice as high as that of Japan. However, Japan's per capita output picked up in the fifteenth century and productivity growth accelerated

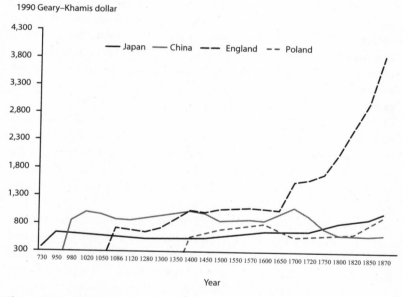

Figure 10.1   Per Capita Real Gross Domestic Product, 730–1870 CE

Notes: The estimated values are presented in Table 10.1A. Years between estimated point years are completed by linear trends in the figure.

Sources: Japan, China, England, Netherlands, Italy, and Spain: Bassino et al. (2019). Portugal: Palma and Reis (2019). Germany: Palma and Reis (2019) and Malinowski and Zanden (2017). Poland: Malinowski and Zanden (2017).

in the eighteenth century under the reign of the Edo shogunate, between 1600 and 1868. Japan surpassed China in the eighteenth century and caught up with peripheral Western regions in Central and Eastern Europe by the mid-nineteenth century. More specifically, the per capita GDP of Japan in the nineteenth century caught up with that of Portugal, surpassed that of Poland, and approached Germany's economic performance, though Britain's ascendancy was unsurpassed (Figure 10.1 and Table 10.1A). Japan caught up with the United Kingdom in per capita GDP by purchasing power parity in the 1970s, but the long march of becoming one of the leading advanced economies that was able to compete with empires such as the United Kingdom only began in the late 1880s after the Meiji Restoration.

Therefore, we should not undervalue the progress that was made in the realm of modernization after the Meiji Restoration, if we want to understand contemporary Japan. However, if we do not limit our scope to G7 economies and include the second layer such as Portugal and Poland in the global history of capitalism, we must be focused on the institutional arrangement of the Edo shogunate, which overtook the second layer under its reign.

The rest of the chapter is organized as follows. The first section reviews the structure of the manorial system in medieval Japan, the emergence of free markets, and how the first shogunate, the Kamakura shogunate, dealt with them. The next section describes how the second shogunate, the Muromachi shogunate, officially admitted the contribution of the financial sector but struggled to reconcile it with social stability as the indebtedness of cultivators rose. The third section analyses the policies of the third shogunate, the Edo shogunate. Given the lessons from the previous shogunate, the Edo shogunate strictly regulated the land market and the financial market. While it banned coercive labour and slavery, it also provided strong incentives to its subjects to stay on the farmland they owned instead of moving to find an urban job. In short, in principle it liberalized financial, land, labour, and product markets but also deliberately regulated the financial and labour markets to balance economic growth and social stability.

The Kamakura Shogunate, 1185–1333

The Financial Sector in the Manorial System

The manorial system, which had been formed by the tenth century, was the institutional framework of governance and land distribution in Japan until the fifteenth century. The land was technically defined by the Taiho Imperial Legal Code (*Taiho Ritsuryo*) of 701 as owned by the emperor/empress. It provided disincentives for reclamation and maintenance of farmland and resulted in stagnation. In 743 CE, the imperial court enacted the Act of Perpetual Private Ownership of Newly Reclaimed Land. The act prompted large temples and local rulers to reclaim land. A parcel of newly reclaimed land was transformed into private property by being chartered by the imperial court as a 'manor'. Large temples directly requested authorization to build manors on these lands. Local rulers, whose social class was low, first donated lands to the nobles in the capital of Kyoto and then the nobles obtained a 'Charter of Manor', which made the nobles manorial lords. Then the manorial lords appointed local rulers who had originally reclaimed the land as the agents of the manor (Nishitani, Hayashima, and Nakabayashi 2017).

A charter of the manor was technically a delegation of administrative and judicial services that had been initially provided by the imperial court. The charter of a manor granted the position of manorial lords, whose status was mostly obtained by temples and nobles. The manorial lords were in charge of judicial services and the assignment of subordinate tasks to enforce the delegated administrative and judicial duties. They were entitled to an individually fixed income from the manor. The tasks and fixed incomes were replicated in subordinate layers. In the case of large manorial lords, branch officers were assigned who oversaw local managers and were also entitled to an individually fixed income. Local managers were in charge of the collection of rent and tax from landlord farmers and were also responsible for maintaining peace and order. Manorial lords often entrusted the former task to financiers, and the latter to samurais, which literally means 'servers'. Landlord farmers were responsible for arranging contracts with subcontracting cultivators, collecting rent and tax from them, and investing in drainage channels (Nishitani, Hayashima, and Nakabayashi 2017; Nishitani and Nakabyashi 2017).

The Kamakura Shogunate

The appointment of samurais thus depended on the discretion of manorial lords. To remove their vulnerability, in 1185 CE, the samurais established their administration in Kamakura, a city in eastern Japan. The administration urged the imperial court to acknowledge that the vassal samurais of the Kamakura administration were to be appointed to officers of manors—not by manorial lords but by the Kamakura administration. In effect, the appointment of samurais to officers of manors came to be enforced by the Kamakura administration, not by manorial lords who owned the manors. The manor to which a samurai was assigned as an officer was considered as the samurai's benefice. The imperial court formally authorized the Kamakura administration as a shogunate in 1192.

Samurais increasingly relied on financiers both for the financial management of their benefice territories, as well as for loans which were secured by income from their benefice territories. The monetized economy expanded and Chinese coins were imported on a massive scale and circulated as a means of currency. This tendency further accelerated the exposure of the samurai economy to the commercial and financial sectors (Honda 2017). The rising indebtedness of vassal samurais was a concern for the shogunate because the financial vulnerability of vassal samurais implied their fragility with respect to procurement of swords, armour, horses, and general logistics.

The First 'Ordinance for Virtuous Governance' of 1297

Concerned about the deepening debt, the Kamakura shogunate promulgated the first 'Ordinance for Virtuous Governance (*Tokusei Rei*)' in 1297, which ordered writing off outstanding debt or antecedent debt within the past 20 years and banned samurais from securing their debt by their benefice. Though the act was first enthusiastically appreciated by the samurais, they soon experienced difficulties in borrowing funds, and the ban on securing funds by dint of benefice was repealed the next year.

Under the reign of the Kamakura shogunate, both samurais and farmers increased their exposure to the financial sector. However, along with this first ordinance for virtuous governance, the legislation of the Kamakura shogunate, in general, regulated the financial and commercial sectors (Watanuki 2017).

The Muromachi Shogunate, 1336–1573

The Muromachi Shogunate

A revolt by the Godaigo Emperor and the leading vassal samurais, Takauji Ashikaga and Yoshisada Nitta, successfully toppled the Kamakura shogunate in 1333. However, the restoration of imperial governance disappointed the samurai class, and hence Ashikaga established the second shogunate in Kyoto in 1336. The second shogunate was called the Muromachi shogunate, named after the place of the head office of the shogunate, and also called the Ashikaga shogunate. In 1338, the new emperor installed by Ashikaga appointed him shogun.

In a significant development concerning market-enhancing policies, the Muromachi shogunate admitted the role of the finance sector as an essential one for sustainable economic growth and declared that it would protect the sector by the first legislation, the Kenmu Code (*Kenmu Shikimoku*) of 1336. Furthermore, in the reign of the eighth shogun Yoshimochi Ashikaga (1394–1423), the shogunate extended the purview of civil cases dealt with by the shogunate court (Hayashima 2017; Nishitani, Hayashima, and Nakabayashi 2017).

The Free Markets of Finance, Land, and Coerced Labour

The legal protection of the financial and land markets further deepened the farmer's reliance on these sectors. Moreover, coerced labour of either indefinite or definite terms was legal, and claims of ownership over humans were legally protected. Thus, free markets of finance and labour coexisted and were backed by the free market of coerced labour. When subcontracting farmers borrowed money for fertilizers in springtime, they secured the debt through the expected output in the fall. If the output failed to meet expectations, they were allowed to sell their family members or themselves either as slaves or indentured labourers. In a modern capitalist economy, under the principle of free labour, lenders face limited liability constraint, since a claim cannot be enforced through enslavement. This constraint did not exist in medieval Japan, as in many other pre-modern societies.

Growth or Stability?

The severe debt of farmers resulted in a higher inequality of wealth. When inequality was perceived as having gone beyond the socially accepted threshold, people revolted, demanding the writing off of debts under the provisions of the 'Ordinance for Virtuous Governance'. Responding to a major riot in 1441, the Muromachi shogunate had promulgated its first ordinance for virtuous governance. Since then, the shogunate promulgated several ordinances for virtuous governance, and individual lords extended these to their manors to fend off riots. Thus, the free market of coerced labour and periodical ordinances to write off the debts complemented the free financial and land markets in the early age. Pursuing both growth and social stability, the Muromachi shogunate legally protected the financial and land markets to achieve the former and sometimes promulgated the ordinance for virtuous governance to realize the latter (Nishitani and Nakabayashi 2017).

The Edo Shogunate, 1600–1868

Property Right Protection and Free Labour

Japan's per capita GDP finally overcame its centuries-long stagnancy and picked up in the late fifteenth century (Figure 10.1). There were technical and institutional conditions that stimulated the rise.

Firstly, techniques of paddy cultivation suitable to the natural environment of Japan had finally evolved. In the geo-climatic context of the Japanese archipelago and mountainous islands, labour-intensive and skill-intensive as well as land-saving techniques were most appropriate. Such techniques for rice cropping were established around the fifteenth century. Boosting and sustaining the fertility of paddy fields through better fertilizers and deeper cultivation and farming without years of fallowing became common (Nishitani 2017).

Secondly, institutional advancements accompanied technical progress. The enhancement of labour and skill intensity required greater efforts from cultivators. The contracts enforced by manorial lords typically stipulated that the revenues of landlord farmers, samurais, and nobles were to be based on a fixed quantity and the residual was to belong to contracted cultivators. Therefore, peasants and farmers came to have a higher incentive to increase annual output as productivity became more responsive to their efforts. Furthermore, this change enticed them to stay in a specific place instead of seeking a better contract every year. Thus, cultivators started to settle in a specific place as peasants, they formed a village with landlord farmers, and the village concluded a contract with the lord who ruled it for land tax payments. A typical setting was that the lord respected the autonomy of the village as long as the contracted land tax was paid. After the Muromachi shogunate collapsed, lords ruled independently over their territories. The village contractor system between the lords and villages prevailed between the fifteenth and sixteenth centuries (Inaba 2010; Nishitani 2017; Nishitani and Nakabayashi 2017).

The age of warfare after the collapse of the Muromachi shogunate ended through reunification under the administration of Hideyoshi Toyotomi. The administration attempted to introduce formal procedures to protect property rights. Through cadastral surveillance, peasant families were identified and registered as owners of a parcel of the farmland that they cultivated, and the administration protected property rights as long as the registered peasant family paid land tax. The policy of the Toyotomi administration was primarily based on the authorization of existing practices in advanced regions such as Kyoto and Osaka.

In 1600, Ieyasu Tokugawa defeated Toyotomi and established his shogunate in Edo, renamed Tokyo in 1868. In 1603, the imperial court formally appointed Ieyasu Tokugawa as shogun. The shogunate inherited the property protection policy from the Toyotomi administration, and within the domain that the shogunate ruled directly, the formalization of peasant families' property rights were completed in the large-scale cadastral survey of the 1670s. Through the cadastral survey, every single parcel of farmland was registered in the *Book of Cadastral Survey (Kenchi Cho)*, including the name of the owner who was responsible for payment of the land tax from the parcel. Two copies of the *Book of Cadastral Survey* were created: the mayor of the village held one of them and the other one was held by the office of the governor who was responsible for the region. Registration at the *Book of Cadastral Survey* satisfied the requirement for ameliorating property rights, based on public notification directed against any intruder, as the shogunate court indeed protected property rights. To put it differently, as long as the name of the owner was registered with a parcel of farmland, the shogunate court protected his family's ownership of the parcel against any other claimant. The reform created a huge mass of small-property owners (Mandai and Nakabayashi 2018; Nakabayashi and Moriguchi 2017).

In backward regions where improvement of the agricultural productivity was delayed, the exclusive property rights of peasant families were not necessarily established (Brown 1993: 39–112). A property right that consisted of the residual control and residual claim imposed the risk of production on the property right holder. Since the utility of the risk-averse property-right holder decreased when risks were high, he needed to be compensated to sustain the same utility level and avoid possible abandonment of cultivation (Hart 1988). If the productivity was high and farmers were more resilient vis-à-vis production risks, the former effect would dominate the latter such that exclusive property right protection led to an increase in the land tax revenue due to the ensuing growth. However, in a backward region, the latter effect might prevail. In that case, the exclusive property-right protection implied a decrease in the land tax revenue, and, hence, it was not optimal for the lord.

Granting ownership to peasants formed a point of divergence between Japan and the West, especially between the United Kingdom and Japan. In Britain, ex-feudal lords were transformed into modern property owners of the benefice they ruled. In Japan, the shogunate and lords were absorbed into the administration and peasants were guaranteed property rights of the parcel they cultivated. Furthermore, the Toyotomi administration and the Edo shogunate banned trade in humans. Not only slavery but also indentured labour and resalable indenture contracts were prohibited, which also contrasts with the West (Nakabayashi and Moriguchi 2017).

Meanwhile, to attract merchants to their domains, lords in the sixteenth century implemented a free-entry policy and curtailed the ordinance for virtuous governance, which forced financiers to write off their debts. In practice, the lords refused to authorize guilds that had enjoyed a regional monopoly and had been in charge of the governance of commerce in medieval times. The lords instead provided judicial services in their domains. In the age of warfare in the fifteenth and sixteenth centuries, with manorial lords declining and perishing, lords who emerged from the samurai class exerted exclusive enforcement power within their domains. The Edo shogunate successfully implemented the Toyotomi administration's policy. Free entry in product markets and the provision of judicial services became the principle of governance (Nakabayashi and Moriguchi 2017; Nishitani, Hayashima, and Nakabayashi 2017).

While Chinese copper coins continued to circulate in the late fifteenth century, lords also actively minted their own copper coins. The Edo shogunate declared its exclusive right to issue currency and began to mint gold and silver coins from 1601 and copper coins from 1633. After shogunate coins overwhelmingly circulated all over Japan, in 1670, the shogunate finally banned all coins except those of the shogunate itself, which served as the only currency that was legally permitted. The shogunate coins became a currency that, for the first time in Japanese history, was independent of that of the Chinese empire (Honda 2017). While the shogunate itself never issued paper notes, probably to maintain the confidence of the people in the shogunate currency, it allowed lords to issue paper notes that were convertible into shogunate coins and were to circulate only within their domains. These measures were taken to ease deflationary pressure on local economies in the wake of the shogunate's conservative monetary policy.

Regulation of the Financial, Land, and Labour Markets

In the seventeenth century, under the reign of the Edo shogunate, the principle of free product, financial, land, and labour markets was established. Although early modern Japan was a federation in which each lord assumed sovereignty for domestic affairs, most lords sooner or later followed the shogunate's policies and legislation.

However, this did not imply a return to the laissez-faire ('financial capitalism') of medieval times. The Edo shogunate seriously regarded social stability to be of utmost importance. More specifically, property rights protection in the financial market was to reconcile social stability in such a way that the shogunate would not need to implement the ordinance for virtuous governance, which was the last resort of the Muromachi shogunate to regain social stability. To achieve this goal, the shogunate imposed different regulations on the markets.

Regarding the product market, the central principle remained free entry. As the market economy grew, the shogunate court became busier, and in the early eighteenth century, the shogunate authorized merchant associations in major business sectors, granted them a regional monopoly, and delegated them the governance of trade. Although the authorization of guilds and the delegation of governance on their behalf was a setback, the central principle was considered to be free entry. A structural reform led by a minister, Tadakuni Mizuno, in the 1840s lowered barriers to become a member of a guild in order to increase competition in the product market.

For the financial and land markets, the shogunate implemented different regulations in urban and rural regions. In the cities, the financial and land markets were entirely free, and the shogunate court provided legal enforcement of contracts when a claim was filed. The public financial market was free too. In Osaka, the shogunate licensed the Dojima Rice Exchange. The lords' budget relied on land tax paid in kind that mostly consisted of rice and was paid in the fall. To meet short-term needs, the shogunate allowed lords to issue short-term bills backed by rice tax. The maturity of bills was three months, and the face value was denominated in quantities of rice. Lords issued bills by auctions to financiers first, and the financiers sold the bills to the secondary market, the Dojima Rice Exchange. The shogunate court strictly protected the claim of the rice bill holders and allowed for free trade (Takatsuki 2008; Takatsuki and Kamihigashi forthcoming).

The protection of financial claims by rice bill holders entailed some technical challenges. Early modern Japan was a federation. As the central government, the shogunate was in charge of diplomacy and the national security. But it also exercised sovereignty over domestic affairs in domains under direct rule, which included major cities such as Osaka, Edo, and Kyoto. Also, the shogunate court assumed jurisdiction over cases whose parties belonged to different domains. Meanwhile, lords exercised the sovereignty over domestic affairs in their own domains. Furthermore, the embassies of lords in Edo were permitted extraterritoriality, and this was equally applied to the warehouses of lords in Osaka. The shogunate itself never issued rice bills, and only lords issued rice bills in Osaka, a shogunate city. If an issuing lord defaulted, the relevant parties consisted of an official of the lord in charge of bill flotation and a financier in Osaka, a shogunate subject. Since the parties belonged to different domains, the case was to be handled by the shogunate governor of Osaka. Nonetheless, extraterritoriality hindered the governor's ability to inspect the warehouse in Osaka and to decide how much rice was stored. Therefore, the shogunate governor worked with financiers in Osaka to motivate lords to fulfill their financial obligations, using both the shogunate law enforcement and the reputation mechanism in the market that affected the future feasibility of bill flotation (Takatsuki 2008; Takatsuki and Kamihigashi forthcoming).

Based on this legal framework, a sophisticated security market was formed. Futures, as well as spots, were traded in the Dojima exchange, and the futures market was the world's oldest futures market of commodity-denominated securities (Takatsuki 2008; Takatsuki and Kamihigashi forthcoming).

Meanwhile, the financial and farmland markets in rural regions were heavily regulated. In 1643, the shogunate enacted a ban on the 'perpetual' sale and purchase of farmland. Under the shogunate administrative and judicial system, the court of the first instance, the lowest court, was the village office of the mayor, who was chosen among farmers of the village. Samurais were appointed as governors and governors' officials. Thus, if both parties were residents of the same village, and neither party filed a complaint in the governor's court, trade was permissible. However, trade beyond village borders was not protected by the shogunate court. This legislation aimed to prevent the owners of farms from losing their property and becoming landless tenant farmers. Also, farmers raised funds for fertilizers and other needs, typically, through loans pledged by a parcel of farmland they owned. Pledged loans enabled lower interest rates, and hence they were necessary for agricultural growth. However, once a farmer failed to perform a financial obligation, and the pledged parcel was foreclosed, he became a landless tenant farmer. The shogunate first restricted foreclosure in the mid-seventeenth century (Mandai and Nakabayashi 2017, 2018).

Labour markets were also indirectly regulated. Under the shogunate reign, any Japanese subject was a free subject. However, his/her right to be protected by the law was guaranteed only if his/her name was registered at the *Residence Registration Book* (*Ninbetsu Aratame Cho*), in which a stem family was a unit. For instance, if a young man wanted to move to a city to work in the service sector instead of farming, his movement had to be approved by the household head, usually the father, and had to be registered at *Ninbetsu Aratame Cho* of an employer or a staffing company in the city of destination. Therefore, if a boy ran away from his family, without approval from his father, just because he disliked farming, he lost the protection of the law (Saito and Sato 2012). This administrative regulation attempted to discourage the youth from leaving the agricultural sector.

However, the real effect is not evident. The restriction of movement through residential registration was abandoned after the Meiji Restoration, and it meant the removal of any restriction on movement. If the restriction under the shogunate had considerably distorted the allocation of the workforce between the primary, secondary, and tertiary sectors, the removal of the restriction after the Meiji Restoration led to improvements in labour productivity through the reallocation of the workforce between different sectors. However, the latest estimate considers the improvement in labour productivity due to the reallocation of labour after the Meiji Restoration to have been rather modest (Fukao and Settsu 2017). Urbanization rapidly increased in the seventeenth and eighteenth centuries, and surplus labour seems to have been legally relocated to the urban service sector, that is, with the consent of the head of household. (Saito and Takashima 2017).

Gradual Relaxation of Regulation in the Early Eighteenth Century

Thus, effective regulation of factor markets occurred in financial and land markets. The shogunate was puzzled over how to attain a better regulation that could reconcile growth with social stability. If the regulations were tightened, the market would price in the regulatory change and hence farmers would face higher interest rates of agricultural finance than in unregulated or less regulated markets, and agricultural growth would be hindered. If regulations were too loose, recurrent financial booms and busts would destabilize the real economy and, after repeated financial crises, the wealth inequality might surpass the socially acceptable threshold, which instigated riots of indebted farmers demanding orders to force financiers to write off their outstanding debts.

After banning the trade of farmland in 1643, the shogunate during the reign of Tsunayoshi Tokugawa introduced a legislation in 1666 to protect land-collateral loans by the shogunate court in order to avoid choking the financing of agriculture. Meanwhile, the shogunate attempted to check an increase in foreclosures due to the failure of repayment of land-collateral loans and finally banned them in 1687. However, this ban naturally squeezed agricultural finance, and, in 1695, the shogunate relegalized foreclosures due to land-collateral loans, provided that the obligations of the borrower, written in a contract, satisfied the unambiguous conditions stipulated by the shogunate order (Mandai and Nakabayashi 2017, 2018).

However, during the reign of Yoshimune Tokugawa, one of the idealistic shoguns, the shogunate banned the foreclosure of farmland in 1722 again. The ban disrupted the financial market and hence was repealed in 1723. While repealing the ban, the shogunate further detailed the rights and obligations of borrowers and stipulated a grace period after the claimant filed a case of default at the shogunate by an act in 1723. Following 1723, additional legislation to protect the right of borrowers and also the right of tenant farmers were enacted through 1741. In the two following decades, shogunate legislation formally legalized foreclosure of land-collateral loans through carefully clarifying the right of borrowers and also of tenants. In order not to choke the agricultural finance and to sustain growth, land-collateral loans were fully legalized, but still, the shogunate attempted to protect independent owner peasants by granting them fully described rights. Further, to address the reality of an increase in failing farmers who lost ownership due to land-collateral loans, the shogunate solidified the right of tenant farmers (Mandai and Nakabayashi 2017, 2018).

In some regions, the custom of restricting foreclosure remained, by allowing the ex-owner to redeem property rights if he paid back the debt even after the duration of the loan contract (Shirakawabe 2012). However, after the Meiji Registration, the legislation that legalized land-collateral loans was implemented all over Japan by the state.

***

Among other factors, capitalism is a system of resource allocation based on free product and factor markets. Some or many of the subsystems have a long history in any advanced economy under consideration. In other words, for a long time, the real challenge to advanced economies has not been the establishment of a capitalist regime but reconciling the dynamism of the capitalist regime with social stability and hence with sustainability, often threatened by an increase in financial volatility and wealth inequality. Advanced economies, including Japan, after the Second World War, have pursued this aim by a combination of redistribution of income and the regulation of free product and factor markets. While Nordic countries have emphasized the former, continental Europe and Japan have implemented the latter.

The path followed by early modern Japan solely relied on the regulation of land and financial markets, in particular. In the wake of laissez-faire financial and land markets, recurrent financial volatility, an increase in wealth inequality, and the social instability of the fifteenth century, the Edo shogunate decided to regulate the farmland and land-collateral loan markets. It aimed to contain financial volatility and to prevent an increase in wealth inequality while maintaining the principle of free product and factor markets. The outcome indicates the effectiveness of the policy. Saito (2015) estimated that, in the mid-nineteenth century, the relative income of the samurai, merchant, and farmer classes amounted to 1.2:1.1:1.0. On average, the ruling samurai class earned just 20 per cent more than the farmer class. This number does not take into account inequality within the same class and, therefore, does not capture inequality within society as a whole. Then, based on Moriguchi and Saez (2008), Milanovic, Lindert, and Williamson (2010) showed that the income inequality of late-nineteenth-century Japan was higher than that of contemporary Japan and Germany, but lower than that of the contemporary United States and the United Kingdom.

Rise in inequality and mass impoverishment were some of the consequences accompanying the growth of British capitalism. The 'primitive accumulation of capital' that Marx (1867 [1988]) discussed, that is, among others, separation of the workforce from the means of production in the United Kingdom (Marx 1867 [1988]: 741–91), dates back to the ownership structure before industrialization. In the United Kingdom, the crown granted property rights to the landed aristocracy and yeomen and not to the peasantry. Peasants were already separated from the farmland they cultivated. The modernization of agriculture that preceded the Industrial Revolution (Crafts 1985) was assisted by the ownership structure that accelerated the process of proletarianization, since tenants had little rights over the land they cultivated. The precarity of agricultural labour turned out to be an advantage during the Industrial Revolution. Proletarianization was thus a way towards achieving a capitalist economy in the United Kingdom, as Marx (1867) emphasized. However, as Austin and Sugihara (2013: 6–7) argue, this development was not necessarily a typical one.

Japan tended towards this trajectory in medieval times when inequality rose, and cultivators' claims were as vulnerable as those of their British counterparts. However, in early modern times, the shogunate chose to stabilize the peasant economy by allocating property rights to the peasantry and by regulating the market of farmland. As a result, the peasant economy remained the core mechanism of resource allocation until the late nineteenth century (Saito 2000, 2009).

In particular, the division of labour and the increase in the shares of the secondary and tertiary sectors were driven by the workforce allocation within the peasant family. For most peasant families throughout early modern times, the primary occupation remained farming. At the same time, they allocated the workforce of family members in slack seasons, often in both winter and summer, to side jobs. Typical ones included hand-weaving for females or working at a sake brewery in winter in the case of males. Alternatively, as they owned farmland, their sons and daughters went to the city to work in the service sector, usually as servants, signing contracts that lasted several years. Afterwards, they came back home, got married, and inherited the farmland and agricultural occupations (Saito 2013; Sugihara 2013: 24–7).

One of the significant rewards accruing from the strict protection of property rights to the shogunate was a high taxation rate for an early modern state. In the seventeenth century, when the shogunate introduced the property right protection system, land tax reached 30 per cent of total output that included all the primary, secondary, and tertiary sectors. Since then, the land tax was barely raised and hence, along with productivity improvements, the land tax ratio over the total output decreased to about 15–17 per cent in the nineteenth century (Imamura and Nakabayashi 2017; Koyama, Moriguchi, and Sng 2018; Nakabayashi 2012; Sng and Moriguchi 2014).

In the late eighteenth century, the tax on output product in the United Kingdom amounted to 12 per cent and has increased ever since (Daunton 2012: 112); however, that of Spain was 10 per cent in the seventeenth century (Comín Comín and Yun-Casalilla 2012: 244), that of China was 8 per cent in the mid-nineteenth century (Deng 2012: 342), and that of the Ottoman empire was less than 4 per cent until the mid-eighteenth century and 8 per cent in the mid-nineteenth century (Pamuk 2012: 321).

While the state capacity of the United Kingdom surpassed that of Japan in the eighteenth century and went far beyond, those of Southern Europe, the Ottoman empire, and China were far smaller than that of shogunate Japan. The state capacity enabled the shogunate to build a modern navy in 1855 with support from the Netherlands after the US Navy forced the shogunate to open the nation by concluding the Convention of Kanagawa in 1854.

In 1862, a gunboat of the shogunate navy visited the Bonin Islands, 1,000 km south of Edo, where Americans, British, and Hawaiians had already settled, and peacefully persuaded the American leader to admit that the islands belonged to the Japanese territory. The strategically critical section of the Western Pacific, containing the island Iwojima, was added to Japan's territories. The annexation was the first gunboat diplomacy of modern Japan. After the Bonin Islands were occupied by the US Marines in 1945, they were only returned to Japan in 1968 (Chapman 2011).

Even after the Meiji Restoration, the state continued to rely on the land tax inherited from the shogunate. On the eve of Japan's first war with China in modern times, still, 60 per cent of the state revenue came from the land tax (Nakabayashi 2012: 388–9). The revenue predominantly financed the civil and military modernization efforts made by the state after the Meiji Restoration. The shogunate protected peasants' property rights, and peasants agreed to pay high land taxes as a service in return, and this financed Japan's emergence as a modern capitalist power, after the country was opened up by force by the USA in the late nineteenth century.

The modern financial system was built on the legacy of the shogunate. The shogunate established the national currency in 1670, and the new imperial state declared the unit of the currency to be changed from the shogunate ryo to the modern yen. As for bank notes, the imperial government first introduced the US national bank system in 1872, and local banks registered as national banks issuing bank notes. The system was acceptable to the Japanese because local lords had issued paper notes with the permission of the shogunate before the Meiji Restoration. The Bank of Japan, established in 1882, replaced national banks as the only issuing bank. In 1878, the Tokyo Stock Exchange and the Osaka Stock Exchange were established, following the Belgian system. Subsequently, as early as the 1880s, Japan experienced its first stock boom, and it achieved a rapid growth of investments in the modern sector. Although the trade procedure in a security market is composed of technical details, the experience at the Dojima Rice Exchange allowed experts to get used to them quickly.

The combination of protected property rights and a regulated farmland market was conducive to social stability in early modern Japan while sustaining the growth in productivity. However, a regulation to some extent distorts resource allocation, and the resulting inefficiency in resource allocation is the cost of regulating a market. Under the shogunate, the stable and regulated market economy allowed Japan to achieve living standards comparable to those of Portugal and Poland. Without deregulation fostered by the Meiji Restoration, Japan would not have emerged as one of the seven major industrial economies.

Meanwhile, deregulation after the Meiji Restoration did not entirely remove the inherent traits of the early modern institutions. While the government deregulated farmland and the labour market in the 1870s, it also promulgated the Civil Code of 1896 and 1898, modelled on German and especially French law. More extensively than in common law countries, the family law in civil law countries stipulates the responsibility of the family to support family members (Twigg and Grand 1998). Japan's family law had already stipulated risk sharing within the household from the time of the shogunate regime, and this feature survived Westernization after the Meiji Restoration by adopting French and, to a lesser degree, German law. Arguably, this emphasis on family security in major civil law countries, such as Japan, Germany, France, and Italy, led to far larger welfare states, replacing the extensive family security, after the First World War and particularly after the Second World War (Nakabayashi 2019). The diversity of modern capitalism is also an outcome of the distinct emphasis on family security before modernization between Japan and civil law countries on the one hand, and common law countries on the other.

Appendix

Table 10.1A Per Capita Gross Domestic Product of Japan, China, and Europe, 730–1870 CE

1990 Geary–Khamis dollar

Year	Japan	China	England/Great Britain	Netherlands	Italy	Spain	Portugal	Germany	Poland
730	376								
950	635								
980		853							
1020		1,006							
1050	583	967							
1086		878	723						
1120		863							
1280	529		651			897			
1300			724		1,466	889			
1350			745	674	1,327	957			
1400		1,032	1,045	958	1,570	822			
1450	545	990	1,011	1,102	1,657	827			562
1500		858	1,068	1,141	1,408	826		1,146	702
1550							836		

1570		885	1,096	1,372	1,325	919			810
1600	667	865	1,077	1,825	1,224	876	790	806	
1650		1,103	1,055	1,671	1,372	838	830	948	
1700	675	950	1,563	1,849	1,344	817	987	939	569
1720			1,605	1,751	1,564	850			
1750		727	1,710	1,877	1,446	845	1,371	1,050	
1800	828	614	2,080	1,974	1,327	893	916	986	
1820									634
1850	903	600	2,997	2,397	1,306	1,144	923	1,428	
1870	1,011	618	3,856	2,849	1,470	1,486		1,692	946

Sources: Japan, China, England, Netherlands, Italy and Spain: Bassino et al (2019). Portugal: Palma and Reis (2019). Germany: Palma and Reis (2019). Poland: Malinowski and Zanden (2017) and Malinowski and Zanden (2017).

Bibliography

Austin, Gareth and Kaoru Sugihara. 2013. 'Introduction', *Labour-Intensive Industrialisation in Global History*, edited by Gareth Austin and Kaoru Sugihara, pp. 1–19. Abingdon: Routledge.

Bassino, Jean-Pascal, Stephen Broadberry, Kyoji Fukao, Bishnupriya Gupta, and Masanori Takashima. 2019. 'Japan and the Great Divergence, 730–1874'. *Explorations in Economic History* 72: 1–22.

Bogart, Dan. 2011. 'Did the Glorious Revolution Contribute to the Transport Revolution? Evidence from Investment in Roads and Rivers.' *Economic History Review* 64(4): 1073–112.

Broadberry, Stephen. 'When and How Did the Great Divergence Begin?'. Presented at the Fifth Asian Historical Economics Conference, Seoul National University, September 2–3, 2016.

Brown, Philip C. 1993. *Central Authority and Local Autonomy in the Formation of Early Modern Japan: The Case of Kaga Domain*. Stanford: Stanford University Press.

Chapman, David. 2011. 'Different Faces, Different Spaces: Identifying the Islanders of Ogasawara'. *Social Science Japan Journal* 14(2): 189–212.

Comín Comín, Francis, and Bartolomé Yun-Casalilla. 2012. 'Spain: From Composite Monarchy to Nation-State, 1492–1914. An Exceptional Case?' In *The Rise of Fiscal States: A Global History, 1500–1914*, edited by Bartolomé Yun-Casalilla and Patrick K. O'Brien with Francisco Comín Comín, pp. 39–66. Cambridge: Cambridge University Press.

Crafts, Nicholas F. 1985. *British Economic Growth during the Industrial Revolution*. Oxford: Clarendon Press.

Daunton, Martin. 2012. 'The Politics of British Taxation, from the Glorious Revolution to the Great War.' In *The Rise of Fiscal States: A Global History, 1500–1914*, edited by Bartolomé Yun-Casalilla and Patrick K. O'Brien with Francisco Comín Comín, pp. 111–42. Cambridge: Cambridge University Press.

Deng, Kent G. 2012. 'The Continuation and Efficiency of the Chinese Fiscal State, 700 BC–AD 1911.' In *The Rise of Fiscal States: A Global History, 1500–1914*, edited by Bartolomé Yun-Casalilla and Patrick K. O'Brien with Francisco Comín Comín, 335–52. Cambridge: Cambridge University Press.

Fukao, Kyoji, Osamu Saito, Masanori Takashima, and Kiyoshi Kida. 2017. 'Seisan, bukka, shotoku no suitei' [Estimates of Output, Prices, and Income]. In *Iwanami Koza Nihon Keizai no Rekishi Dai 1 Kan, Chusei: 11 Seiki kara 16 Seiki Kohan* [Iwanami Series on the History of the Japanese Economy, Volume 1, Medieval Times: From the Eleventh

Century to the Late Sixteenth Century], edited by Masaki Nakabayashi, pp. 289–94. Tokyo: Iwanami Shoten.

Fukao, Kyoji, Osamu Saito, Masanori Takashima, and Naoki Imamura. 2017. 'Seisan, bukka, shotoku no suitei' [Estimates of Output, Prices, and Income]. In *Iwanami Koza Nihon Keizai no Rekishi Dai 2 Kan, Kinsei: 16 Seiki Matsu kara 19 Seiki Zenhan* [Iwanami Series on the History of the Japanese Economy, Volume 2, Early Modern times: From the End of the Sixteenth Century to the Early Nineteenth Century], edited by Masaki Nakabayashi, pp. 283–300. Tokyo: Iwanami Shoten.

Fukao, Kyoji and Tokihiko Settsu. 2017. 'Seicho to makuro keizai' [Growth and the Macroeconomy]. In *Iwanami Koza Nihon Keizai no Rekishi Dai 3 Kan, Kindai 1: 19 Seiki Kohan kara Dai Ichiji Sekai Taisen Mae (1913)* [Iwanami Series on the History of the Japanese Economy, Volume 3, Modern Times 1: From the Late Nineteenth Century to the Eve of the First World War], edited by Naofumi Nakamura and Masaki Nakabayashi, pp. 2–22. Tokyo: Iwanami Shoten.

Hart, Oliver. 1988. 'Incomplete Contracts and the Theory of the Firm.' *Journal of Law, Economics & Organization* 4(1): 119–40.

Hayashima, Daisuke. 2017. 'Chusei no kinyu' [Medieval Finance]. In *Iwanami Koza Nihon Keizai no Rekishi Dai 1 Kan, Chusei: 11 Seiki kara 16 Seiki Kohan* [Iwanami Series on the History of the Japanese Economy, Volume 1, Medieval Times: From the Eleventh Century to the Late Sixteenth Century], edited by Masaki Nakabayashi, pp. 116–45. Tokyo: Iwanami Shoten.

Honda, Hiroyuki. 2017. 'Chusei kahei: Toraisen no jidai' [Medieval Money: The Age of Imported Coins]. In *Iwanami Koza Nihon Keizai no Rekishi Dai 1 Kan, Chusei: 11 Seiki kara 16 Seiki Kohan* [Iwanami Series on the History of the Japanese Economy, Volume 1, Medieval Times: From the Eleventh Century to the Late Sixteenth Century], edited by Masaki Nakabayashi, pp. 92–116. Tokyo: Iwanami Shoten.

Imamura, Naoki and Masaki Nakabayashi. 2017. 'Shotoku to shisan no bunpai' [Distribution of Income and Wealth]. In *Iwanami Koza Nihon Keizai no Rekishi Dai 2 Kan, Kinsei: 16 Seiki Matsu kara 19 Seiki Zenhan* [Iwanami Series on the History of the Japanese Economy, Volume 2, Early Modern Times: From the End of the Sixteenth Century to the Early Nineteenth Century], edited by Masaki Nakabayashi, pp. 33–49, 57–60. Tokyo: Iwanami Shoten.

Inaba, Tsuguharu. 2010. 'Community Vitality in Medieval Japan.' In *War and State Building in Medieval Japan*, edited by John A. Ferejohn and Frances McCall Rosenbluth, pp. 71–90. Stanford: Stanford University Press.

Koyama, Mark, Chiaki Moriguchi, and Tuan-Hwee Sng. 2018. 'Geopolitics and Asia's Little Divergence: State Building in China and Japan after 1850.' *Journal of Economic Behavior & Organization* 155: 178–204.

Malinowski, Mikołaj and Jan Luiten van Zanden. 2017. 'Income and Its Distribution in Preindustrial Poland'. *Cliometrica* 11(3): 375–404.

Mandai, Yu and Masaki Nakabayashi. 2017. 'Kinsei no tochi hosei to jinushi keiei' [Land Law and Landlordism in the Early Modern Times]. In *Iwanami Koza Nihon Keizai no Rekishi Dai 2 Kan, Kinsei: 16 Seiki Matsu kara 19 Seiki Zenhan* [Iwanami Series on the History of the Japanese Economy, Volume 2, Early Modern Times: From the End of the Sixteenth Century to the Early Nineteenth Century], edited by Masaki Nakabayashi, pp. 150–76. Tokyo: Iwanami Shoten.

———. 2018. 'Stabilize the Peasant Economy: Governance of Foreclosure by the Shogunate.' *Journal of Policy Modeling* 40(2): 305–27. Available at https://doi.org/10.1016/j.jpolmod.2018.01.007.

Marx, Karl. (1867) 1988. *Das Kapital: Kritik der politischen Ökonomie* [Capital. A Critique of Political Economy], *Bd. 1*. Berlin: Dietz Verlag.

Milanovic, Branko, Peter H. Lindert, and Jeffrey G. Williamson. 2011. 'Pre-industrial Inequality.' *Economic Journal* 121(551): 255–72.

Moriguchi, Chiaki and Emanuel Saez. 2008. 'The Evolution of Income Concentration in Japan, 1886–2005.' *Review of Economics and Statistics* 90(4): 713–34.

Nakabayashi, Masaki. 2012. 'The Rise of a Japanese Fiscal State.' In *The Rise of Fiscal States: A Global History, 1500–1914*, edited by Batrolomé Yun-Casalilla and Patrik K. O'Brien with Francisco Comín Comín, pp. 327–409. Cambridge: Cambridge University Press.

———. 2019. 'From the Family Security to the Welfare State: Path Dependency of the Social Security on the Difference in Legal Origins.' *Economic Modelling* 82: 280–93. Available at https://doi.org/10.1016/j.econmod.2019.01.011.

Nakabayashi, Masaki and Chiaki Moriguchi. 2017. 'Seifu no yakuwari' [Role of the Government]. In *Iwanami Koza Nihon Keizai no Rekishi Dai 2 Kan, Kinsei: 16 Seiki Matsu kara 19 Seiki Zenhan* [Iwanami Series on the History of the Japanese Economy, Volume 2, Early Modern Times: From the End of the Sixteenth Century to the Early Nineteenth Century], edited by Masaki Nakabayashi, pp. 22–33. Tokyo: Iwanami Shoten.

Neal, Larry. 2014. 'Introduction', *The Cambridge History of Capitalism, Volume 1, The Rise of Ancient Origins to 1848*, edited by Larry Neal and Jeffrey G. Williamson, pp. 1–23. Cambridge: Cambridge University Press.

Neal, Larry and Jeffrey G. Williamson, eds. 2014. *The Cambridge History of Capitalism, Volume 1, The Rise of Ancient Origins to 1848*. Cambridge: Cambridge University Press.

Nishitani, Masahiro. 2017. 'Chusei no nogyo kozo' [Structure of the Medieval Agriculture]. In *Iwanami Koza Nihon Keizai no Rekishi Dai 1 Kan, Chusei: 11 Seiki kara 16 Seiki Kohan* [Iwanami Series on the History of the Japanese Economy, Volume 1, Medieval Times: From the Eleventh Century to the Late Sixteenth Century], edited by Masaki Nakabayashi, pp. 148–77. Tokyo: Iwanami Shoten.

Nishitani, Masahiro, Daisuke Hayashima, and Masaki Nakabayashi. 2017. 'Seifu no yakuwari' [Role of the Government]. In *Iwanami Koza Nihon Keizai no Rekishi Dai 1 Kan, Chusei 11: Seiki kara 16 Seiki Kohan* [Iwanami Series on the History of the Japanese Economy, Volume 1, Medieval Times: From the Eleventh Century to the Late Sixteenth Century], edited by Masaki Nakabayashi, pp. 23–33. Tokyo: Iwanami Shoten.

Nishitani, Masahiro and Masaki Nakabayashi. 2017. 'Shotoku to shisan no bunpai' [Distribution the Income and Wealth]. In *Iwanami Koza Nihon Keizai no Rekishi Dai 1 Kan, Chusei: 11 Seiki kara 16 Seiki Kohan* [Iwanami Series on the History of the Japanese Economy, Volume 1, Medieval Times: From the Eleventh Century to the Late Sixteenth Century), edited by Masaki Nakabayashi, pp. 33–49. Tokyo: Iwanami Shoten.

O'Brien, Patrick Karl. 2014. 'The Formation of States and Transitions to Modern Economies: England, Europe, and Asia Compared.' In *The Cambridge History of Capitalism, Volume 1, The Rise of Capitalism: From Ancient Origins to 1848*, edited by Larry Neal and Jeffrey G. Williamson, pp. 357–402. Cambridge: Cambridge University Press.

Palma, Nuno and Jaime Reis. 2019. 'From Convergence to Divergence: Portuguese Economic Growth, 1527–1850'. *Journal of Economic History* 79(2): 477–506.

Pamuk, Şevket. 2012. 'The Evolution of Fiscal Institutions in the Ottoman Empire, 1500–1914.' In *The Rise of Fiscal States: A Global History, 1500–1914*, edited by Bartolomé Yun-Casalilla and Patrick K. O'Brien with Francisco Comín Comín, pp. 304–31. Cambridge: Cambridge University Press.

Saito, Osamu. 2000. 'Marriage, Family Labour and the Stem Family Household: Traditional Japan in a Comparative Perspective.' *Continuity and Change* 15(1): 17–45.

———. 2009. 'Land, Labour and Market Forces in Tokugawa Japan.' *Continuity and Change* 24(1): 169–96.

———. 2013. 'Proto-industrialization and Labour-Intensive Industrialization: Reflections on Smithian Growth and the Role of Skill Intensity.'

In *Labour-Intensive Industrialization in Global History*, edited by Gareth Austin and Kaoru Sugihara, pp. 85–106. Abingdon: Routledge.

———. 2015. 'Growth and Inequality in the Great and Little Divergence Debate: A Japanese Perspective.' *Economic History Review* 68(2): 399–419.

Saito, Osamu, and Masahiro Sato. 2012. 'Japan's Civil Registration Systems Before and after the Meiji Restoration.' In *Registration and Recognition: Documenting the Person in World History*, edited by Keith Breckenridge and Simon Szreter, pp. 113–35. Oxford: Oxford University Press.

Saito, Osamu, and Masanori Takashima. 2017. 'Jinko to toshika, ido to shugyo' [Population and Urbanization, Movement and Employment]. In *Iwanami Koza Nihon Keizai no Rekishi Dai 2 Kan, Kinsei: 16 Seiki Matsu kara 19 Seiki Zenhan* [Iwanami Series on the History of the Japanese Economy, Volume 2, Early Modern Times: From the End of the Sixteenth Century to the Early Nineteenth Century], edited by Masaki Nakabayashi, pp. 61–104. Tokyo: Iwanami Shoten.

Shirakawabe, Tatsuho. 2012. *Kinsei Shicchi Ukemodoshi Kanko no Kenkyu: Nihon Kinsei no Hyakushoteki Shoji to Higashi Ajia Shono Shakai* [Study on the Custom of Redemption of Pledged Farmland in the Early Modern Times: Farmers' Land-Holding in Early Modern Japan and the East Asian Peasant Society]. Tokyo: Hanawa Shobo.

Sng, Tuan-Hwee and Chiaki Moriguchi. 2014. 'Asia's Little Divergence: State Capacity in China and Japan before 1850.' *Journal of Economic Growth* 19: 439–70.

Steinfeld, Robert J. 1991. *The Invention of Free Labor: The Employment Relation in English and American Law and Culture, 1350–1870*. Chapel Hill: The University of North Carolina Press.

———. 2001. *Coercion, Contract, and Free Labor in the Nineteenth Century*. Cambridge: Cambridge University Press.

Sugihara, Kaoru. 2013. 'Labour-Intensive Industrialization in Global History: An Interpretation of East Asian Experiences.' In *Labour-Intensive Industrialization in Global History*, edited by Gareth Austin and Kaoru Sugihara, pp. 20–64. Abingdon: Routledge.

Takashima, Masanori, Kyoji Fukai, and Masahiro Nishitani. 2017. 'Seicho to makuro keizai' [Growth and the Macroeconomy]. In *Iwanami Koza Nihon Keizai no Rekishi Dai 1 Kan, Chusei: 11 Seiki kara 16 Seiki Kohan* [Iwanami Series on the History of the Japanese Economy, Volume 1, Medieval Times: From the Eleventh Century to the Late Sixteenth Century], edited by Masaki Nakabayashi, pp. 2–23. Tokyo: Iwanami Shoten.

Takatsuki, Yasuo. 2008. 'The Formation of an Efficient Market in Tokugawa Japan'. Institute of Social Science, The University of Tokyo, Discussion

Paper Series F–143. Available at https://jww.iss.u-tokyo.ac.jp/publishments/dp/dpf/pdf/f-143.pdf.

———. 2012. *Kinsei Kome Shijo no Keisei to Tenkai: Bakufu Shiho to Dojima Kome Kaisho no Hatten* [Formation and Expansion of Early Modern Rice Markets: The Shogunate Judiciary and the Development of the Dojima Rice Exchange]. Nagoya: Nagoya University Press.

Takatsuki, Yasuo and Takashi Kamihigashi. forthcoming. *Microstructure of the First Organized Futures Market: The Dojima Security Exchange from 1730 to 1869*. Singapore: Springer.

Twigg, Julia and Alain Grand. 1998. 'Contrasting Legal Conceptions of Family Obligation and Financial Reciprocity in the Support of Older People: France and England'. *Ageing and Society* 18(2): 131–46.

Watanuki, Tomoko. 2017. 'Chusei no koeki' [Medieval Trades. *Iwanami Koza Nihon Keizai no Rekishi Dai 1 Kan, Chusei: 11 Seiki kara 16 Seiki Kohan* [Iwanami Series on the History of the Japanese Economy, Volume 1, Medieval Times: From the Eleventh Century to the Late Sixteenth Century], edited by Masaki Nakabayashi, pp. 259–87. Tokyo: Iwanami Shoten.

11

The View from Early Modern China

Capitalism and the Jingdezhen Ceramics Industry

Anne Gerritsen

The heyday of Jingdezhen as a porcelain centre was in the Ming and the Qing. But our research has shown that because of the high degree of specialisation there was little sign of capitalist relations of production.

—Fang Xing (1926–2014) in *Chinese Capitalism* (2000: 421).

The porcelain production centre of Jingdezhen (southern China) produced fine ceramics both for the emperor and his court and for the market by employing large numbers of skilled and unskilled, waged and unwaged labour. Conventionally, the imperial kilns of the Ming (1368–1644) and Qing (1644–1911) dynasties have been held up as examples of exploitative systems that prevented the development of capitalism. This chapter explores evidence from the sixteenth-century Chinese centre of ceramics manufacture to suggest the presence of a form of capitalism in early modern China. Overall, the chapter reveals sophisticated labour management policies, waged labour, and production for global markets, pointing to a capitalist environment.

In 1985, two senior economic historians, Wu Chengming and Xu Dixin, edited and published the first of three volumes on the history of the Chinese economy, based on extensive research that had been carried out over several decades after the founding of the People's Republic of China in 1949 (Xu and Wu 1985). A selection of this research subsequently appeared in 2000 in English under the title *Chinese Capitalism, 1522–1840* (Wu and Xu 2000). This volume was explicitly Marxist in its approach; the aim of the authors was to identify 'capitalist' relations of production, where local and regional production centres were integrated into national and international economies, and commercial capital was invested in local producers to develop large-scale industrial capitalism, with a labour force that was free to sell their own labour, but without any commodities or other property to sell.[1] Wu Chengming and his co-authors were keen to reveal the emergence of an embryonic form of capitalism in China between the start of the reign of the Jiajing Emperor in 1522 and the signing of the Treaty of Nanjing (also known as the first Unequal Treaty) in 1840, and pointed to the imperialist forces that arrived in China with the outbreak of the Opium War as the most significant explanation for its halting performance in the nineteenth century. The authors of the volume pointed out that the emergence of capitalism took place significantly later than in England and discussed the reasons for the longevity of the feudal economy, but overall, they conclude that this early form of capitalism 'created conditions for the further development of capitalism' (Fang et al. 2000: 424).

One of the chapters in *Chinese Capitalism* dealt with what its author Fang Zhuofen and his colleagues called 'the porcelain industry of Jingdezhen'. This famous porcelain production centre in southern China boasted the finest white clays, hundreds of kilns, and a vast supply of skilled workers. Annually, the kiln complex of Jingdezhen manufactured hundreds of thousands of pieces of the finest wares for

---

[1] See Bramall and Nolan (2000: xv).

the emperor and his court in the so-called 'imperial kilns', and much larger quantities than that for local, regional, and ultimately global trade in the privately owned kilns. Fang Zhuofen and colleagues saw the imperial kilns of the Ming and Qing dynasties as evidence of an exploitative system that prevented the development of capitalism. 'The existence of the imperial porcelain factory was inevitably a stumbling block to the development of the private porcelain industry and the emergence of capitalist relations' (Fang et al. 2000: 313). The authors felt that the nature of the relationship between the imperial and private kilns worked as 'a form of feudal obligation imposed upon the producers' (Fang et al. 2000: 313). They admitted that 'in the Ming–Qing period private production in Jingdezhen increased considerably', but ultimately, they and Fang Xing, author of the concluding chapter of *Chinese Capitalism*, came to the view that there was little evidence of the 'capitalist relations of production in Jingdezhen' (Fang et al. 2000: 313). The specialization Fang Xing identified was thought to have scattered and fragmented the units of production, and thereby hindered the development of full-blown capitalism (Fang et al. 2000: 317).

In some ways, the assessment of Jingdezhen in *Chinese Capitalism* is echoed in R. Bin Wong's study of China in volume 1 of *The Cambridge History of Capitalism* (Wong 2014: 125–64). Like Wu Chengming and his colleagues, Bin Wong does not see full-blown capitalism in China before 1900. In his study of the Chinese economy, Wong identifies three of Larry Neal's four criteria for capitalism (private property rights, enforceable contracts, and price-setting markets), but notes the absence of a supportive government (Neal 2014: 2). Assuming on that basis that there was no capitalism in China before 1900, Wong proceeds to explore the ways in which there *was* economic growth, even if it did not lead to the forms of industrialization we see in Europe.

The question this raises is, of course, one of definition. Should we define capitalism in strict accordance with the characteristics of capitalist economic development as it occurred in European history, including the trajectory that Marx and Engels identified? Or might it be possible to define capitalism in such a way that the concept can encompass the divergent paths we might encounter in extra-European historical development? In this chapter, I explore evidence from the sixteenth-century Chinese centre of ceramics manufacture to suggest the presence of a form of capitalism in early modern China. At the very least, this evidence exhorts us to consider different chronologies and geographies than the ones that form the starting point for Neal and Williamson. I begin with a brief background of the production system in Jingdezhen, and then turn to some specific issues in the central government's management of labour force, and return to some questions about capitalism towards the end of the chapter.

Jingdezhen's Ceramics Production Centre in Historical Perspective

The manufacture of porcelain (that is, vessels made from kaolinized, feldspathic clay, glazed and fired at a temperature above 1200°C) has a long history in China, dating back to at least the third century CE. Over the centuries, kiln sites located in different parts of the Chinese Empire produced a wide range of porcelains, determined by variations in the quality of the clays, kiln technology, type of fuels for firing the wares, and preferences for colours, shapes, and designs. During the Tang dynasty (618–907), for example, one of the most prominent ceramics production sites was in Changsha, in Hunan, where potters made a wide variety of dishes, bowls, and pots, with painted decorations under a greyish-green glaze. We have an inkling of the size of the production from the wreck of a single Arab dhow that went down near Belitung, now Indonesia, on its way back from China with a cargo consisting of 70,000 pieces of Changsha wares (Krahl 2010: 209–11). By the Song dynasty (960–1279), tastes and technologies had changed again: the preference, certainly at the imperial court, was for ceramics in simple shapes, covered with smooth, monochrome glazes, made to the highest technological and aesthetic standards. Song dynasty wares appeared in various thicknesses, and in shades of greens and blues, with splashes of purple and creamy white. Over time, however, the most desirable porcelains were white porcelains, potted so thinly that they were nearly see-through.

Thirteenth century onwards, a kiln site, located at Jingdezhen in Fuliang county in the north of what is now Jiangxi province, rose to prominence. Here, the potters could make the whitest, thinnest porcelains. Superb resources, in particular the very white local clays that could be fired to extremely high temperatures, explain this rise, as do the experiments with decorations using the cobalt-blue pigments that merchants from the Muslim world brought into the Chinese empire and, as we will see below, the ability to organize production in such a way that it could be scaled up without loss of efficiency. The blue-and-white porcelain of Jingdezhen proved to be a tremendously popular commodity that was considered desirable throughout the Chinese Empire and beyond.

By the sixteenth century, kilns located in and around the Fuliang town of Jingdezhen formed the biggest ceramics-producing kiln site of the Ming dynasty, a position it continued to hold throughout the Qing dynasty and into the twentieth century, although in recent years, the title of 'porcelain capital of China' has been taken over by Chaozhou in Guangdong (Gillette 2015, 2016). Ceramic goods manufactured in Jingdezhen were transported in all directions: northwards, especially to the imperial capital in Beijing, but throughout the Empire; eastwards to Central Asia, the Islamic worlds, and overland to Europe; westwards to Korea and Japan, the Philippines and from there to the Americas; and southwards to the coastal regions of southern China, its ports, and from there by sea route to Southeast and South Asia, the Indian Ocean, and, seventeenth century onwards, to Europe and beyond.

This composite ceramics production site simply known as 'Jingdezhen' has a long and complex history; for the purposes of this chapter, I will focus only on a small part of that history, namely the characteristics of production in the last quarter of the sixteenth century. My reasons for this selection are twofold: we have extensive documentation about the management of the imperial kilns in Jingdezhen dating to the late sixteenth century (Shi 2013; Wang 1597); and although the Portuguese had started to order porcelains as per their specifications from Jingdezhen for the Portuguese market, the sixteenth century still lay before the massive increase in production for export that started with the arrival of the Dutch East India Company (called Verenigde Oostindische Compagnie or VOC) in the early decades of the seventeenth century.[2] This means we can make our claims about

---

[2] For a good overview of the global flows of porcelain made in Jingdezhen, see Finlay (2010). See also Dillon (1992).

the Chinese economy on the basis of Chinese development, not merely in response to overseas demand. A few general characteristics of the organization of production will be highlighted before I explore some of the specifics concerning labour in the ceramics manufactures of late-sixteenth-century Jingdezhen in the chapter.

Production for the Imperial Court

An important consumer of porcelain, the imperial court in Beijing made regular requests for large quantities of porcelain, to be manufactured in Jingdezhen in specific sizes, shapes, quantities, and designs, selected for suitable quality by the representatives of the imperial court based in the Fuliang county yamen (that is, the headquarters of the imperial supervision over the manufactories), and delivered to the capital by a combination of river and canal (Kerr and Wood 2004: 188; see also Wang 2010). This regular delivery of vast quantities of porcelain pieces is sometimes referred to as tribute payment, but perhaps it makes more sense to see this as a form of taxation (Fang et al. 2000: 313). Estimates suggest that the annual demand for porcelain for the imperial court during the Ming dynasty amounted to at most 100,000 pieces, although famously, in 1433, the imperial household issued an order for 433,500 pieces (Fang et al. 2000: 313; see also Pierson 2013: 9–10). This demand for tribute (or taxation) imposed upon those responsible for the running of the kilns in Jingdezhen might serve as one example of the enforceable contracting practices that Neal (2014: 2) describes in his 'Introduction', and Wong (2014: 138) discusses especially in relation to commercial transactions with foreigners. Normally, goods designated as 'imperial wares' were fired in kilns referred to as 'official kilns' (*guanyao*), which were strictly regulated, for example, in terms of the number of items that could be fired at any one time (to preserve quality). At those times, when imperial demand outstripped the production potential of the guanyao, vessels were requisitioned from the many other kilns in the area known as *minyao*, variously translated as popular kilns or folk kilns.

The practice of the imperial court to demand ceramic wares from the manufactories has often, but erroneously, been described as a monopoly of the state (see, for example, Wang 1998: 86). While it is undoubtedly true that the imperial court imposed harsh demands upon the workers in Jingdezhen, it is by no means the case that the imperial court was the only recipient of the goods produced in the kilns or that they imposed exclusive control over the entire production. The vast majority of the kilns in Jingdezhen fell outside of the purview of the imperial production processes. The minyao produced goods that were distributed to consumers throughout the region, and further afield throughout the Empire and to markets beyond the realm of the Chinese Empire. Actual annual production figures that combine guanyao and minyao are hard to obtain, because we do not have any records that account for all of Jingdezhen's production. What we do have is estimates of kiln capacity, ranging from 200 to 1000 pieces in *mantou* or bun-shaped kilns to tens of thousands of pieces fired in one session in the so-called *longyao* or dragon kilns that measured over 55 m in length and 9 m in width (Fang et al. 2000: 309). Firing a dragon kiln was seasonal (nothing happened in the cold and humid winter months), and took several days of preparation, including tasks like packing the wares inside, bricking up the entrances, and stoking the fires to temperature; several days of carefully managed firing; followed by a slow process of cooling, opening, and unpacking the kiln; and transporting and storing the goods in nearby warehouses. Even so, there were several such kilns in the area (some sources talk of hundreds of kilns), and these are likely to have been fired at least 5–10 times a year. Even without knowing the exact figure of late-sixteenth-century production output, we can call this mass production on a (proto-) industrial scale.

For the later period (that is, seventeenth century onwards), we also have estimates of imported porcelains: The Dutch imported 3 million pieces of porcelain in the first half of the seventeenth century alone (Batchelor 2006: 96).[3] Analysis of firewood consumption in the Jingdezhen region has led scholars to estimate a total annual output of 40 million pieces per year for the mid-seventeenth century, and about 60 million pieces per year for the mid-eighteenth. In that light, they argue, the total production for the imperial court amounted to less than 1 per cent of the overall output of Jingdezhen's kilns.[4]

---

[3] Batchelor's figure includes Chinese and Japanese imported porcelain. Batchelor's figures are based on Volker (1954).

[4] These figures have been pulled together in Moll-Murata (2013: 231).

Nonetheless, the connection with the imperial court is important, in part because of the administrative records we have for the guanyao production, in contrast to non-existent records for the minyao, and in part because of the circulation of skills, innovations, and new technologies that was facilitated through the manufacture of goods to the specifications issues by the imperial court.

The Issue of Labour

The production of such vast quantities of porcelain for the imperial court was heavily dependent on labour, just as large-scale projects such as the construction and maintenance of the imperial capital or the ongoing maintenance of the canal that connected the grain-producing south to the administrative centre in the north of the Empire were. The workforce that made the production of porcelain possible was largely recruited from the counties that surrounded Jingdezhen. From the start of the Ming dynasty, households that were formally listed in the population records as artisan households had an annual obligation to supply workers to Jingdezhen, and their labour served as a tax obligation. Sixteenth century onwards, however, these labour obligations had largely been converted to silver payments. We do not have any exact records for the actual size of the workforce or for the proportion of workers that were conscripted (that is, providing labour to pay off their tax obligations) and those that were free to sell their labour in the market (without any other means of production at their disposal). We do know, however, that a large number of the workers received a wage in return for their labour, paid in copper or silver, depending on the type of labour and their level of skill.

Famously, the workers in Jingdezhen produced their wares in a series of workshops, each performing strictly separated tasks. From digging, preparing, mixing, and kneading the clay; shaping the objects; applying decorations; blending and stirring the glazes to maintaining the kiln temperature and measuring the appropriate quantities of packing materials—each of the tasks were performed by separate groups of workers. Mass production of porcelain in Jingdezhen was only possible because of this assembly-line style of production, although Jingdezhen was not an exclusive site for this style of ceramics production, nor was it an innovation only implemented to deal with increasing demand from beyond the empire. Divisions of labour have been identified in ceramics production throughout China. However, only in Jingdezhen was this system as highly developed and implemented on such a large scale, and only in Jingdezhen were labourers and skilled craftspeople employed on such a vast scale.[5] And as we will see next, in Jingdezhen, vast numbers of workers were paid for their labour.

It may already be clear from this brief introduction that this production complex has features compatible with Neal and Williamson's definition of capitalism. Private property rights were in operation, as the wares produced in minyao were sold by merchants and generated profits for the investors; enforceable contracts governed both production quotas and those labouring in the kilns; and goods were produced here in response to demand from the local, regional, and ultimately global market. The question of 'supportive government' is more difficult to assess and, to my mind, needs to be tied much more closely to the issue of labour management. The centrality of labour, especially waged labour, in the rise of capitalism, is clear, but what constitutes a 'supportive' economic system is less clearly defined. Neal merely describes a 'thoroughgoing market system' where 'political, cultural and social groups', including consumers and producers, respond to the price signals generated within that market. The labour market, too, would be expected to operate within 'broader social, political and cultural systems that are essentially supportive' that facilitate responsiveness to price signals (Neal 2014: 4). In what follows, I will explore some of the issues arising from the vast need for skilled and unskilled labour in the ceramics manufactures of Jingdezhen.

The Jingdezhen Labour Market and the Different Types of Labour

From the start of the Ming dynasty in 1368, labour required in the kiln complexes was drawn from a locally based battalion (Wang

---

[5] Archaeological excavations of Tang-dynasty kiln sites show a division of labour based on potters' skills. See Kerr and Wood (2004: 429).

1597: 7.6b). Battalions, initially established in frontier areas where the incoming Ming regime sought to establish authority, were military organizations that provided both farm labour and military duties. After the establishment of the Ming Empire, the battalions continued to provide labour, which was divided between military duties (30 per cent) and farm (or other) work (70 per cent).[6] The majority of the people serving in battalions, thus, were available for other duties, including work in the ceramic industry. These were not waged workers; they performed their labour as part of their battalion duties, and the battalion was responsible for their subsistence.[7]

The labour force in Jingdezhen was made up of different types of workers: those who had been conscripted from the local battalions as well as those who had to perform labour service, or corvée labour, as part of their household taxes (Lee 1980). Corvée labourers had to work one shift once every three years, and regardless of their place of residence, they normally had to perform this labour service at the imperial capital. The corvée workers in the kiln, however, would have received dispensation from the usual duty of travelling to the capital, because the location of the imperial kilns was determined by the location of the natural resources, especially the clay.[8] Further supplementary kiln workers were also recruited, but the required level of skills was difficult to find. Those in charge of managing the kilns and responsible for the output complained that there were only few workers with the right level of skill. The painting of decorations on the porcelain bodies, for example, required refined skills and expertise that to a large extent determined the overall quality of the finished piece (Wang 1597: 7.21a).

[6] The decree establishing military units like the battalion dates from 1364, four years before the establishment of the Ming dynasty. Each province had guards of 5,000 men, made up of 5 battalions of a 1,000 men each.

[7] In Wang (1597), the cost of subsistence for workers payable by the battalion is listed as amounting to a total of 33 *liang* and 6 *qian*. It is obviously not appropriate to refer to this payment as a wage, as it was merely intended to cover the costs of keeping the worker alive.

[8] A number of other manufactures were also like this, including the weapon manufacturers in Suzhou and the textile producers of the Yangzi delta.

Several terms were in circulation to refer to the organization of such supplementary kiln workers drafted in; they were referred to as offering 'organized service' (*bianyi*) or 'hired service' (*guyi*), or as 'duty craftsmen' (*shangbanjiang*). The kind of work these additional craftsmen provided is described as follows: 'The workplace selects both untrained (*baitu*) and highly skilled (*gaoshou*) workers for firing porcelain, to provide the work for which the various artisans have not been hired, such as beating cobalt (*qiaoqing*), fluffing up cotton fibre (*danhua*), or mounting paintings (*biaobei*). ... The work done by hired labour and by government artisans is the same' (Wang 1597: 7.21a). By the middle of the Ming dynasty, many families with the hereditary status of 'artisan' were in a position to commute their labour service by means of a set payment and, in many parts of the empire, workers serving out their obligatory service were rare. But as Robert Lee (1980) has shown, in Jingdezhen, the practice of conscripted labour service continued to exist well beyond the Mid-Ming period and was still in evidence in the late sixteenth century. The option of paying off one's labour duties was certainly also in place and, in Jingdezhen, it was possible for those with hereditary artisan status either to make cash payments in lieu of their service or to hire someone else to provide the same service in their place.

The shift from performing corvée labour duties to making payments in lieu of service should be understood in the context of what is known as the silverization of the late Ming economy. From around 1500, the Chinese economy had grown significantly, in part through political stability and population growth, and in part through the production of goods like textiles, ceramics, and tea, which were exported in exchange for silver. The influx of Spanish silver, brought to China's south coast by Spanish and Portuguese merchants, made it possible for silver to be used in many, if not most, of the financial transactions in Ming China. When the Ming government decreed that all tax payments, including all corvée labour duties, also had to be paid in a single, silver payment, the so-called Single-Whip policy, the silverization of the economy grew substantially. It is around this time that China came to be seen as a silver sink of the global economy (Flynn and Giráldez 2010; Frank 1998). Arguably, it is precisely in this very significant transition from conscript or corvée labour to hired labour, or wage labour, that we see the emergence of capitalism, especially in the handicraft industries of the late Ming period (Hsu 1988: 139). The point, however, is not just that the option of hiring waged labour existed, but that the option of hiring wage labour existed as part of a complex labour market, within a political context that was 'supportive' of this complex, market-led labour management system.

In most of the workshops, several workers were supervised by a leader (*tou*, literally head). The large kilns that fired vast numbers of goods at a high temperature had a higher worker to leader ratio; 29 workers were supervised by 4 leaders (7.25:1), while the enamel-firing muffle kilns, which operated at a much lower temperature and fired fewer but more precious items, had a lower worker to leader ratio (5:1). The ratio of worker to leader also depended on the required level of skill. The workshop where they prepared the basic glaze that coated most items (*nishui zuo*) and the iron works (*tie zuo*), where they made many of the iron tools required within the workshops and the nails and hooks used for securing the wadding and wrapping of the porcelains before they were transported, both low-level skill workshops, had an even higher worker to leader ratio (10:1). On the opposite end of the spectrum, in the calligraphy workshop, the ratio was 1:1; every single worker was supervised by a head. The kind of work that was done by large numbers of workers supervised by small numbers of heads also included the auxiliary workshops, where they made the saggars (the protective cases in which fine porcelains were fired, known in English as saggars or saggers, and in Chinese as *xiabo*) to separate the porcelain goods in the kilns. Ropes, barrels, and bamboo items were other goods made in auxiliary workshops that filled the numerous workshops in and around Jingdezhen. Workshops with low worker to head ratios included the ones in which objects were created using special decorative techniques and those that employed precious materials such as lacquer. The workshops dedicated to the making of porcelain bodies of standard shapes, such as plates, dishes, and bowls of various sizes, and the decorative workshops that did not require unusual techniques all worked at a ratio of 5:1 (Wang 1597: 7.22b–23a).

In general, then, the administration of the mid-sixteenth-century imperial kilns had to deal with the challenge of securing a workforce that was both reliable and skilled. Some of the workforce was allocated to the kilns because of the long-standing hereditary status of the family. The problem there was that these were rotating shifts, and a constant pattern of change in personnel is never compatible with the development and preservation of a skilled workforce. The separation of the process into clearly defined separate tasks, the allocation of leaders to small groups of workers, and the specification of the exact tasks to be performed can, I think, all be seen as sophisticated ways of managing this specific problem of a constantly changing workforce.

The Issue of Skill in the Workforce

> If clay and glazing materials are of a fine quality, and the workers (*gongfu*) have refined skills (*jingxi*), then you need not have any concern over coarseness or contamination [of the wares]. (Wang 1597: 7.18b)

> So long as the technical skills and artistry of the craftsmen employed are both refined and based on extensive experience (*jiyi jingshu*), then they will have no difficulty in achieving success in firing pots, and they can make anything from the largest vessels to saggars. If you have workers that are only just good enough, then the biggest vessels they can make are winecups. (Wang 1597: 7.23b)

The production of porcelain in Jingdezhen was separated into distinct tasks and divided over separate, specialized workers. This way of working has been considered a key innovation in manufacturing in Jingdezhen. The implications of this division of labour are significant. Complex tasks that require a high level of skill depend on a workforce with training and expertise, while smaller and singular tasks can be completed by workers with less experience. After the initial development of the production site, which would include gaining access to the necessary resources such as stone and clay, and the establishment of suitable working methods, including the purification and refinement techniques and preparation of the pigments—all of which required high levels of knowledge and expertise, the ongoing production of porcelain could be completed with largely unskilled labour. Most of the labour tasks consisted of the acquisition and transport of raw resources, including vast quantities of firewood, and tasks like digging, chopping, pulverization, refinement, and washing of those resources. Carrying the natural resources and the bodies of porcelain in their various stages to and from different parts of the production complex also required a great deal of labour. This work was strenuous and demanding, but it was largely not dependent on specific training processes. The production of the saggars could not be done by untrained workers, but the clay did not need to be carefully purified and shapes could be rough, and so long as they could withstand the heat inside the kilns, saggars could be made by workers with a low level of training. Shaping of clay bodies could be done by workers with varied levels of skill: the potter throwing the larger pieces, including bowls, cups, and plates, was different from the potter who only worked on the smaller pieces (that is, less than one foot in diameter) (Tichane 1983: 144).

Throwing was only one of the ways in which vessels were formed; they were also made by using moulds, which was especially useful when numerous items of identical size and shape had to be produced. More unusual shapes, that is, square or polygonal, fluted or ribbed, gourd-shaped or even animal or human shaped, were created by forming individually cut pieces in the required shape, and connecting these with slip (that is, the same material used for the body of the vessel, but mixed with water to make it more mouldable). While the task of forming the required shape would have been performed by a skilled worker, the multitude of tasks that prepared the ground for this one worker could be completed by unskilled workers: making thin slabs, cutting these into pieces, preparing the slip, holding the pot, washing the pot down, moving it, drying it—all such tasks could be learnt on the job, and supervised by a worker with only a marginally higher level of skill than the unskilled workers. No worker was working in isolation, and no worker would have failed to acquire at least some of the skills of the tasks in his or her immediate surroundings. This last observation is important for two reasons. First, when new workers entered a particular workspace devoted to a single task, acquiring the necessary skills could be done within a short amount of time. Second, physical proximity to workers performing the same task allowed workers to imitate and transmit this knowledge in turn to others.

The importance of the size of ceramic bowls in learning to make pots will be a familiar issue for anyone who has ever tried their hand at throwing pots: the bigger the size, the higher the required skill. A beginner can only make small items; making anything big requires more experience and skill. The risk with workers with low pottery skills was not only a slow and resource-intensive production process, but the failure of pots in the firing process. Much better, then, to supplement the less-skilled workers with additional recruits with higher-level skills (*dian zhaomu gaoshou*), so none of the pots turned out a disaster (*shu qi bu kuyu*) (Wang 1597: 7.24a). In that sense, the labour requirement for Jingdezhen was perhaps unusual. Much of the required labour could be done by inexperienced or unskilled workers, and for this work, large numbers of migrant workers flooded the city during times of firing. They then all had to disappear again, of course, as soon as firing came to an end, because there was only work related to firing and nothing else. The owners of the kilns and the managers of the production processes benefited, while the workers suffered the consequences of the particularities of these methods of ceramics production.

Employment in Guanyao vs Minyao

From the middle of the Ming period, there were two parallel systems. On the one hand, there was the imperial kiln system (guanyao), overseen by the imperial household at the capital and driven by the need to procure large quantities of high-quality ceramics for use by the emperor and his court in Beijing. On the other hand, there were large numbers of private kilns (minyao) scattered across the region, where ceramics were made for trade, both domestically and for export. Local records list nearly 60 kilns that were classified as imperial kilns, and a further 20 that were private establishments (Kerr and Wood 2004: 197). The differences between these two types of kilns included not only their intended consumers, but also the size and shape of the kilns. Both burnt about the same quantity of firewood in a single firing, but the imperial kilns only fired around 300 pieces at once, while the private kilns increased their output by placing more than 1,000 vessels inside each fired kiln (Wang 1597: 7.17a). The unit price of the vessels fired in the imperial kiln was, thus, much higher. In the imperial kilns, pieces with only one type of glaze were fired at the same time, and they were placed away from the flames, separated by a row of empty saggars. In the private kilns, some of the coarser wares were placed in the very front and back, while the best pieces were fired in the middle of the kiln. The private kilns produced higher quantities of goods, sometimes of significantly lower quality than the imperial kiln products.

The two systems had their own employment practices. This is how it is described in the gazetteer, that is, in the state-produced document concerned with the running of the guanyao:

> The way of working at the imperial and private kilns is not the same. In the imperial workshops, workers tend to work in a perfunctory manner. In the private enterprises, they work extremely hard to safeguard their jobs, and that can make the difference between success and ruination [of the kiln]. Nowadays, in preparation for a kiln firing, those employed by the imperial kilns can make arrangements [for firing supplementary goods] with the private kilns, while at the private kilns, this is not an option. The workers at the imperial kilns are only accustomed to working within their own system, and they are dependent on their ability to sell [the goods they manufacture] at high prices. But the private kilns are all the more likely to run into difficulties because of insufficiencies [in manufactured goods and/or in resources]. (Wang 1597: 7.17b)

What is described here was a policy referred to as 'guan da min shao', literally 'imperially thrown, privately fired', a system rendered by Kerr and Wood (2004: 200) as 'official partnership with private kilns', which they see as 'a means of broadening the base of procurement of porcelain for the court'. When the production quotas for the imperial goods were too high to manage for the imperial kilns, then the ordinary wares for daily use in the palace could be fired at those private kilns that were deemed to produce wares of high enough quality (Lee 1980; Yip 1992; Yuan 1978: 45–54). The competition between the two types of kiln organizations seems to have led to a mutual dependence that was relatively productive. For the imperial kilns, it meant a greater likelihood of responding to the sometimes excessive demands of the Ming administration; for the private kilns, the collaboration with the imperial kilns offered expanded opportunities. The official kilns did not pay market prices for the commissioned items, however, leading to an exploitative situation, as Fang Zhuofen and others have pointed out (Fang et al. 2000: 312).

The description of the workers as 'working in a perfunctory manner' is fascinating and needs some unpacking. What we are hearing is, of course, an age-old defence of capitalist practice: when workers perform repetitive tasks without private incentive, they do not work as hard as they do when their job is on the line or when there is a profit to be made. Other statements underscore this attitude:

> [Workers with inherited status] keep registering their name with the authorities, and occupy [the same position] over and over again, while following their old [ways of doing things] without an open-minded attitude. And when the kilns do not hire other labourers but only hire workers [with inherited artisan status] who just perform their duties and cannot earn any [extra] money, because they are completing their required labour service, so in practice, this does not resolve [the problems of motivation in the workforce in the imperial kiln]. (Wang 1597: 7.21b)

This official documentation, intended for the effective management of the imperial kilns, points to what one can surely only describe as deeply embedded capitalist practices.

The household registration was, in principle, unchangeable. Families with artisan registration had to supply a certain number of workers to perform specific tasks, such as working in the Jingdezhen kilns. One could, as we saw, either make a set payment in lieu of this labour service or could hire someone else to perform the required labour duty in their place. However, the attempt to hire someone to replace the work normally done by someone with inherited artisan status could also give rise to problems: 'Those who lack the resources to make a straightforward payment in place of their labour duty [sometimes] hire a labourer to take on the required duties in their place. However, in the end they [that is, the registered artisans] [often] are not able to pay [these workers for their service]' (Wang 1597: 7.21b).

Labour, then, is flexible, transferable, and those who try to make a living and cope with the demands of this potentially exploitative system are forced to participate in its exploitative practices.

***

This discussion of the various issues arising in the management of the porcelain-producing labour force in sixteenth-century Jingdezhen reveals numerous problems at the micro level. From the perspective of those in charge of the imperial kilns, there were, firstly, issues that broadly fall under the category of accountability for the workforce: who is working, what is the (inherited registration) status of the workers, who is responsible for record keeping, and how should their labour be compensated? Secondly, there was a perception of issues broadly related to productivity: what was the output of the workforce, how did this output match the production quotas imposed by the imperial court, and how could the productivity of the workforce be maintained? Thirdly, there were issues related to skill and quality control, and finally, what were the working conditions in Jingdezhen? To varying degrees, these micro-level issues only concerned those who were in charge of labour in the porcelain-production city of Jingdezhen, but clearly, this socio-economic formation contained capitalist elements, which had far-reaching consequences for the workforce.

One could widen the perspective by connecting these micro-level problems to the major changes in the global economy in the latter half of the sixteenth century, most notably the global circulation of silver. It was the influx and circulation of Spanish silver within China that transformed the systems of taxation and the labour registration in late Ming China. By combining a macro-level approach, showing the global circulation of silver, with the micro-level analysis of the labour force, we perhaps see these transformations in a different light. The transition from payments in kind and hereditary corvée labour commitments in the early Ming period to tax and corvée payments made in silver in the late Ming period and the emergence of private kilns working to fulfil both imperial quota and the growing overseas demands for porcelain had a significant impact on accountability, productivity, quality, and working conditions in Jingdezhen.

This discussion of labour management practices in the late sixteenth century in Jingdezhen only reveals a very small part of the complex history of ceramics manufacture, let alone of the entire socio-economic history of early modern China. To draw significant conclusions, one would have to explore many more aspects of the industry, consider these characteristics over the many centuries of production in Jingdezhen, and compare these observations to similarly expansive discussions of the silk and cotton industries, to name but a few similarly expansive areas of economic growth in late imperial China. However, if we situate this discussion of sophisticated labour management policies with its waged labour force and its global markets in the wider context of the late Ming period, then it seems perhaps less surprising that the late Ming period is described as capitalist. Urban centres were flourishing, commercial production of manufactured goods was highly diversified and specialized, consumers were always discerning and fashion conscious, and a flourishing cultural scene catered for sophisticated readers, theatre-goers, and scholarly connoisseurs. Intellectual foment led to new developments in philosophy and religion, which provided moral justification for expressions of the self and recognition of the individual as a source of authority. Seen in that context, the emergence of a waged labour force that worked hard to produce the fine ceramics that urban residents used to display their individual discernment and taste should perhaps not be surprising and merits our attention.

Bibliography

Batchelor, R. 2006. 'On the Movement of Porcelains: Rethinking the Birth of Consumer Society as Interactions of Exchange Networks, 1600–1750.' In *Consuming Cultures, Global Perspectives: Historical Trajectories, Transnational Exchanges*, edited by J. Brewer and F. Trentmann, pp. 95–121. Oxford: Berg.

Bramall, C. and P. Nolan. 2000. 'Introduction: Embryonic Capitalism in East Asia.' In *Chinese Capitalism, 1522–1840*, edited by Wu Chengming and Xu Dixin, pp. xiii–xl. Basingstoke and New York: Macmillan.

Dillon, M. 1992. 'Transport and Marketing in the Development of the Jingdezhen Porcelain Industry during the Ming and Qing Dynasties'. *Journal of the Social and Economic History of the Orient* 35(3): 278–90.

Fang, Xing. 2000. 'The Role of Embryonic Capitalism in China'. In *Chinese Capitalism, 1522–1840*, edited by Wu Chengming and Xu Dixin, pp. 402–29. Basingstoke and New York: Macmillan.

Fang, Zhuofen, Hu Tiewen, Jian Rui, and Fang Xing. 2000. 'The Porcelain Industry of Jingdezhen'. In *Chinese Capitalism, 1522–1840*, edited by

Wu Chengming and Xu Dixin, pp. 308–26. Basingstoke and New York: Macmillan.

Finlay, R. 2010. *The Pilgrim Art: Cultures of Porcelain in World History*. Berkeley: University of California Press.

Flynn, D.O. and A. Giráldez. 2010. *China and the Birth of Globalization in the 16th Century*. Farnham: Ashgate.

Frank, A.G. 1998. *ReOrient: Global Economy in the Asian Age*. Berkeley: University of California Press.

Gillette, M. 2015. 'Globalization and Deindustrialization in China's (Former) Porcelain Capital.' In *East Asia in the World: An Introduction*, edited by Anne Prescott, pp. 219–42. Abingdon: Routledge.

———. 2016. *China's Porcelain Capital: The Rise, Fall and Reinvention of Ceramics in Jingdezhen*. London: Bloomsbury.

Hsu, Wen-Chin. 1988. 'Social and Economic Factors in the Chinese Porcelain Industry in Jingdezhen during the Late Ming and Early Qing Period, Ca. 1620–1683.' *Journal of the Royal Asiatic Society (New Series)* 120(1): 135–59.

Kerr, R. and N. Wood. 2004. *Ceramic Technology*. Science and Civilisation in China, Vol. 5: Chemistry and Chemical Technology, Part XII. Cambridge: Cambridge University Press.

Krahl, R. 2010. 'Tang Blue-and-White'. In *Shipwrecked: Tang Treasures and Monsoon Winds*, edited by R. Krahl, J. Guy, and J. Raby, pp. 209–11. Washington, DC: Arthur M. Sackler Gallery, Smithsonian Institution.

Lee, R. 1980. 'The Artisans of Ching-Tê-Chên in Late Imperial China.' MA thesis, University of British Columbia, Canada.

Moll-Murata, C. 2013. 'Guilds and Apprenticeship in China and Europe: The Jingdezhen and European Ceramics Industries.' In *Technology, Skills and the Pre-modern Economy in the East and the West*, edited by M. Prak and J.L. van Zanden, pp. 225–57. Leiden: Brill.

Neal, L. 2014. 'Introduction', *The Rise of Capitalism: From Ancient Origins to 1848*, edited by in L. Neal and J.G. Williamson, pp. 1–23. Cambridge: Cambridge University Press.

Pierson, S. 2013. *From Object to Concept: Global Consumption and the Transformation of Ming Porcelain*. Hong Kong University Press.

Shi Youming 施由明. 2013. 'Lun Jiajing yu Wanli Jiangxi sheng dazhi de zhixue jiazhi 論嘉靖与万歷《江西省大志》的史学價值' ['On the Historical Value of the Jiajing and Wanli Editions of the Jiangxi Provincial Gazetteer']. *Zhongguo difangzhi* 4: 32–36.

Tichane, R. 1983. *Ching-Te-Chen: Views of a Porcelain City*. Painted Post, New York: New York State Institute for Glaze Research.

Volker, T. 1954. *Porcelain and the Dutch East India Company, as Recorded in the Dagh-Registers of Batavia Castle, Those of Hirado and Deshima and Other Contemporary Papers 1602–1682*. Leiden: Brill.

Wang, Fei-ling. 1998. *Institutions and Institutional Change in China: Premodernity and Modernization*. New York, NY: St Martin's Press.

Wang Guangyao 王光尧. 2010. *Mingdai gongting taoci shi* 明代宫廷陶瓷史 [*Porcelain for the Imperial Court of the Ming Dynasty*]. Beijing: Zijincheng chubanshe.

Wang Zongmu. 王宗沐, ed. 1597. *Jiangxi sheng dazhi* 江西省大志 [*Gazetteer of Jiangxi Province*]. Nanjing: Nanjing tushuguan guben shanben congkan.

Wong, R. Bin. 2014. 'China before Capitalism.' In *The Rise of Capitalism: From Ancient Origins to 1848*, edited by L. Neal and J.G. Williamson, pp. 125–64. Cambridge: Cambridge University Press.

Wu Chengming, and Xu Dixin, eds. (1985) 2000. *Chinese Capitalism, 1522–1840*. Translated from Chinese by C.A. Curwen. Basingstoke and New York: Macmillan.

Xu Dixin 许涤新, and Wu Chengming 吴承明. 1985. *Zhongguo zibenzhuyi fazhan shi* 中国资本主义發展史 [*History of Capitalist Development in China*]. 3 vols. Beijing: Shehui kexue wenxian chubanshe.

Yip, Hon Ming. 1992. 'The Kuan-Ta-Min-Shao System and Ching-Te-Chen's Porcelain Industry.' In *Zhongguo Jinshi Shehui Wenhua Shi Lunwen Ji* [*Papers on Society and Culture of Early Modern China*]. Taipei: Institute of History and Philology, Academia Sinica.

Yuan, Tsing. 1978. 'The Porcelain Industry and Ching-Te-Chen, 1550–1700'. *Ming Studies* 1: 45–54.

12

Artisans, Guilds, and Capitalist Development in Cairo, 1600–1800

Nelly Hanna

The present study on production in Egypt from the sixteenth to the eighteenth century considers that the developments of the modern world had multiple sources and that they had their origins in different parts of the world outside Europe. Capitalism likewise developed in many regions over a long period. The study argues that two trends had an impact on artisans, guilds and production: the first one is the widening of international markets for certain local goods and the process of commercialization that accompanied it. There was a considerable demand in the world market for certain goods produced in Egypt, namely cloth, leather, and oil. Artisans coped with this expansion, in this period prior to the introduction of machinery, by the expansion of workshops and by more efficient management techniques.

The second trend is growing political presence in the guilds and the process and management of production, with members of the military class penetrating the guild structure, a process that expanded in the eighteenth century and culminated in the state-run industries of Muhammad Ali (1805–48).

Challenging Eurocentric Approaches

This chapter is an attempt to shed light on the ways in which we can understand the development of capitalism in a region outside Europe during the period 1600–1800.

It has a number of objectives. First, the economic history of the period between 1600 and 1800 has often been studied in relation to the Great Discoveries and to the emergence of commercial capitalism, conditions which ultimately led to the 'rise of the West'. European trading companies emerged and the new trading circuits allowed them to spread into the regions that later became associated with the Third World. Consumer demand for goods increased tremendously, resulting in a much greater bulk of exchange of merchandise and an extensive flow of money. This resulted in great commercial wealth and a growing process of commercialization (Hanna 2011a).

These transformations and their consequences are usually written from a European point of view. Regions outside Europe were considered as the 'rest of the world' or as regions which were 'outside history' until they came into contact with Europe. At that point, they became recipients of the spread of European capitalism (North and Thomas 1973).

Second, studies of capitalism were, as a result, based on the European or, more often, the nineteenth-century English experience. Its sources were taken to be based on the European experience, the trading companies of the sixteenth century, Protestantism, and so on. Its development in Europe was taken to be the standard model, sometimes described as set and well-defined features (Neal and Williamson 2014). Yet the features that characterized the English economy in the nineteenth century were unlikely to be found in other regions outside Europe.

The history of capitalism, moreover, has been studied within the framework of a diffusionist approach; that is, it had one source, in

Europe, and from there it was diffused to the rest of the world. Such diffusionist approaches are apparent in a number of interpretations, such as the Asiatic mode of production, the modernization approach, and the world-systems core periphery model. In all of these, Europe was viewed as being the centre of the world; its patterns and practices were diffused to the rest of the world (Blaut 1993). Placing the 'rest of the world' within such Eurocentric models has not advanced our knowledge about the economic history of regions outside Europe. The result is that the economic history of many of them is not well explored. We know little about the economic history of important regions like the Mughal and the Ottoman empires prior to the nineteenth century, although progress has been recently made in studies about India and Southeast Asia, where the production of textiles has received more attention than many other regions (in the Ottoman world for instance) (Mukund 1999; Reid 1990).

As an attempt to find an alternative to the top-down diffusionist approach to the history of capitalism, this chapter considers some of the developments of the period from another angle: notably from a non-European region, in this case Egypt, during the two centuries that preceded European penetration and prior to the hegemony of European capitalism. Like many other parts of the world which eventually became part of what is called the 'Third World', the period prior to European penetration was for long considered to be one of decline, a trend only reversed with the penetration of European influence.

This approach is broadly in keeping with the views of Samir Amin, one of the first scholars who argued that the developments of the modern world did not all necessarily originate in Europe; he considered that capitalism had a long period of incubation lasting several centuries, an incubation that took place in different regions of the world like Africa and Eurasia (Amin 2011: 1–7).

The present chapter also implicitly questions the idea that the 'rise of Europe' necessarily led to the decline of the non-European world. It considers that the expansion of trade between 1600 and 1800 and the process of commercialization of society and economy that accompanied it were a world phenomenon, and they had numerous and complex consequences in different regions of the world. The consequences it had depended on a combination of a world trend with local conditions and local historical trajectories, and they differed from place to place. The early stages, which the present study focuses on, differed from later ones, when capitalism became closely linked to colonialism.

The subject of the chapter considers one of these. Specifically, it explores one particular aspect, namely, that of guilds and craft production, to examine the social and economic consequences of this trade in Egypt between the seventeenth and eighteenth centuries (Hanna 2011a: 104–27). This method allows us to examine some of the specific repercussions on one particular region of a trend that had an impact on many other parts of the world. In other words, the changes that are considered in this chapter were the result of the interaction of world conditions with local conditions rather than simply imports from Europe. These changes suggest the beginnings of a capitalist trend emerging from within (rather than coming from Europe) and from below (guilds and craft production, not only trade) that was to have an impact on the developments of the nineteenth century. This model can therefore be useful to study other non-European regions prior to the penetration of European capitalism.

Trade: A Worldwide Phenomenon 1600–1800

The present chapter traces the way in which two trends had an impact on artisans, guilds, and production: the first one is the widening of international markets for certain local goods and the process of commercialization that accompanied it; the second trend is growing political presence in the guilds and the process of production.

Trade: The Obvious Impact

The impact of this trade on merchants is obvious. Merchants had important networks by which they could channel the coffee they brought in from Yemen to many parts of the world, as coffee became a fashionable drink everywhere. In the eighteenth century, they channelled spices and Indian textiles, which had also become very fashionable in many parts of the world. Merchants thus made large fortunes, as we know from their inheritance records (Raymond 1973). Since it was so lucrative, this trade also attracted members of the *Mamluk* ruling class. By the eighteenth century, they had come to control many of the financial resources of Egypt, such as the land tax and the customs taxes. They also became involved in international trade. Many of them owned ships and, at their death, left merchandise for large sums of money. Their commercial activities allowed them to amass great fortunes and to purchase urban property, ships, tax farms, and luxury items like jewels, expensive clothes, and palaces.

Trade: The Less Obvious Impact

If the impact of the intense trading conditions is evident among those who traded in international goods, it is less so among the producers of some of the goods that were exchanged, that is, the artisans and the craftsmen who made these products. One trend in the dominant historiography during the 1600–1800 period has tended to down-play the role of these craftsmen in the history of capitalism, limiting its focus on the activities of merchants and of trading companies as agents of change. Important as these may be, this does not negate a role for production and for craftsmen as agents of change. Another historiographic trend is the world-systems model, as elaborated by Immanuel Wallerstein. Here, craftsmen were the passive recipients of the detrimental conditions imposed by the spread of European capitalism in regions outside Europe, a spread which deprived them of the raw material they needed for their work. Moreover, they had to face severe competition from goods that came from the core areas of capitalism (Wallerstein 1976: 229–33). The result was detrimental to craftsmen and to production, as they became englobed in a capitalist system in which their role was subordinated to the needs of the core. This model was applied to conditions in sixteenth-century America. They have little or no bearing on conditions in many other parts of the world, and the model cannot be usefully applied in countries like Egypt or India for the period 1600–1800.[1]

In fact, the empirical data available regarding Egypt—and other regions like India—shows an entirely different picture from that of

---

[1] Nor does the idea of an 'external arena' elaborated by Wallerstein (1976: 300–48) have significant bearing on the regions I am referring to.

the world-systems model: notably that there was an expansion in the production of local goods, in particular those that had an international market. Even though the bulk of the merchants' fortunes came from the trade in coffee, they also traded in some locally produced goods made by craftsmen. Certain goods produced in Egypt, like sugar, cloth, sal ammoniac, leather, among other goods, were shipped to various destinations.

Some of the Local Items Produced in Egypt with Large Markets Abroad

Cloth

Sources regarding Egypt, such as the *Description de l'Egypte* and the consular archives of Marseilles, all show that there was a considerable demand in the world market for cloth produced in Egypt. As indicated in André Raymond's book, *Artisans et Commercants*, which made ample use of these sources, cloth was exported to the holy cities of Mecca and Medina in the Red Sea; to the various Ottoman and European ports along the Mediterranean; to North Africa and Sub-Saharan Africa; and to its main European trading partner, France (Raymond 1973: 130–1, 180–91).

The eighteenth century, in particular, seems to have witnessed an extensive growth of cloth exports, reaching destinations in four continents (Hanna 2014: 77–9). Two reasons can explain this expansion: first the growth of consumerism. In many capitals, there was a huge demand for cloth with Indian-style designs, including in Europe (Hanna 2014: 77–9). Second, the textiles from Egypt that were shipped to Marseilles were then distributed from there to the colonies. Cloth was sent to the Caribbean to clothe the slave population, and cloth from the Levant was extensively used by European merchants in West Africa to purchase slaves. These were two relatively new destinations where presumably a high level of consumption was in demand. This can, in part, explain the increase of textiles sent from Egypt to Marseilles. Although figures are rare to find, those published by Edhem Eldem show that between 1700 and 1789 (the year of the French Revolution), cloth exports from Egypt to Marseilles more than tripled in value (Eldem 2006: 283–335, 327).

Another Major Export Item: Leather

There were other locally produced goods for which there was a market abroad. Among the important ones were leather and hides (Raymond 1973: 643–4); these being exported along the Mediterranean ports, to France, Italy, Syria, and via the Red Sea to the Hijaz. Sahar Hanafi's study of commercial relations between Egypt and Bilad al-Sham shows that there was an expansion in the shipping of various kinds of hides to the Syrian ports of Tripoli, Lazaqia, Ramla, and Accre, with an estimation of 10,000 leather hides being sent in 1721 (Hanafi 2002: 174–5). The figures available regarding the export of hides to Marseilles again show a considerable increase between the beginning and the end of the century (Eldem 2006: 333). The data in the sources in Cairo indicate that the producers and sellers of leather and hides became very wealthy and there was severe competition on who could control the slaughterhouses where these hides could be obtained.

Oil: Another Key Product

To a lesser extent, flaxseed oil was used for lighting lamps and for food, as it was cheaper in comparison to the other types of oil. It was an essential ingredient in certain crafts and industries, including that of leather (Hanna 2011a: 116–17). Linseed oil was in demand abroad and mainly sent to the Red Sea, since it was used for lighting lamps in the holy cities of Mecca and Medina, and to Mediterranean ports. In addition, certain quantities were sent on a yearly basis to Istanbul, as part of the state's requirements.

The study of the methods used to reach this level of production and trade suggests an emerging capitalist development. It is, therefore, important to consider how this can change some of the dominant paradigms on the history of capitalism.

Traditional Crafts Responding to Increased Demand

Craft production, prior to the modern period, is usually associated with a 'traditional economy'. Craftsmen undertook their production in small workshops possibly employing two or three people. When the product was finished, the artisans sold it to their clients. Artisans and craftsmen, thus, were responsible for the production and sale of the goods that they made. This implied that the scale of production was small. This situation also gave them a degree of autonomy. At the same time, this system posed problems with regard to the potential expansion of the volume of production.

When faced with growing demand, some of these structures had to undergo change. In fact, this demand in international markets had significant consequences for the craftsmen that produced these goods and for their guilds, consequences that did not affect other producers of simple everyday goods that had a limited local distribution.

The Problems That Craftsmen Faced

With the rise in demand for their products, craftsmen were faced with two matters. On the one hand, there was the issue of how to increase production in order to cover demand. Such an increase must have been considerable, given the fact that local textiles made in Egypt were shipped to Jedda in the Red Sea, to Goa in Sub-Saharan Africa, to the markets of Damascus, Istanbul, Marseilles, Genoa, and to the Caribbean, to cite some of the destinations. Shipments to such distant destinations implied a certain volume of cloth that had to be produced in order to feed these markets. Yet, these goods were produced by artisans and craftsmen who, under pre-industrial conditions, did not possess high-level technology, and consequently, the issue of expansion in production posed a problem, namely how to expand production under the restrictive conditions of craftsmen.

Various kinds of solutions had to be found for artisans to cope with the demands of the merchants who exported their product. Thus, artisans had to find ways to expand their production while, at the same time, they had to cope with the traditional restrictions imposed on them by their guilds and by state demands on what they produced.

Restrictions by Guilds and the State

Although guilds and craftsmen had a lot of leeway in the production and sale of the goods produced, they were, in fact, not entirely free to carry out their work as they wished. They were expected to abide by various rules either set up by their guild or by the state. These varied from guild to guild. A guild could limit a potential expansion in the volume of goods produced if it was considered to be contrary to the idea of equitable conditions between craftsmen. For the same reason, a guild could place restrictions on the spaces artisans could use to sell or expose their goods so as to ensure that there was no unfair competition. In some cases, the guild head could be responsible for distributing raw material to the members of the guild in a more or less equitable way. Such practices did not conform to a market economy.

Moreover, the state also had a say in certain aspects of craft production. In Egypt, as in many other parts of the Ottoman Empire, the central administration could issue orders that affected artisans. There was an obligation to send a number of locally produced goods regularly to Istanbul on an annual basis. These could not be sold in the market until the required amount had been shipped to the capital. The central authorities in Istanbul required Egypt to send sugar, which was known for its high quality, to the imperial household; cords (*fitil*) and oakum (*mashaq*) were destined for the Imperial Navy (Shaw 1962: 278; Uthman 2008: 21). The producers of leather (*jalladin*) had to provide the sacks to pack sugar, gunpowder (*barud*), and coins sent as tribute to Istanbul every year; only once that was done could leather makers sell their goods in the market.[2] In addition to the annual requirements, there were occasional orders of luxury goods and certain commodities specifically commissioned for the sultan's palace, such as the rugs, some of which were intended for the imperial court and for the mosques of Istanbul.[3] In other words, a certain part of the trade between Cairo and Istanbul was directed by state needs rather than by market forces.

Encroachment by Powerful Persons

Guilds and guild members involved in the production of goods that had a large market abroad had to face another problem of a

[2] Court of Bulaq, Register 56, Case 140, dated 1679, p. 54.
[3] Court of Qisma Arabiya 37, Case 3, dated 1642, p. 1.

different nature. Their products aroused the interest of merchants who could make a lucrative business from selling them to foreign traders. Consequently, merchants tried by various means to have a say in the process of production, either by collaborating with individual artisans and making them work for them or by having a say in the guilds. When trade in local goods intensified, in the eighteenth century, guilds were faced with attempts by outsiders to the craft to encroach on them, whether they were merchants or members of the Mamluk ruling class.

Strategies to Meet Market Demand

During this period and especially in the eighteenth century, as a result of this intense commerce, certain structural changes emerged among craftsmen and their guilds, especially among those who produced goods for which there was an increase in world demand. These include textiles, leather and hides, and flaxseed oil (Hanna 2011a: 71).[4]

In order to cope with the growing market, there were several initiatives that were undertaken, which may not have conformed to the law or the spirit of the guild. The examination of court records of the period shows that in the course of the two centuries, one can observe two developments with regard to textile production: first, the creation of new guilds and second, the appearance of larger workshops (Yi 2004: 125–7).

New Guilds in Response to Market Demand

The creation of new textile guilds seems to be directly related to the rise of certain types of cloth in world fashion. These were responding to the demand in Indian-style cotton, which became fashionable in many capitals of the world, in Istanbul, Amsterdam, Paris, and so on. Several new guilds appear in the eighteenth century specially to decorate cloth with Indian-style designs (Hanna 2014: 81–5). For example, in 1709, there is a reference to a guild that specialized in dyeing Indian cotton and to a guild that specialized in the styles of

---

[4] Court of Bulaq, Register 51, Case 518, p. 238.

India and Diyarbakr, Turkey. In 1780, the *basmajiya* or printers on cotton cloth specialized in Indian designs. Finally, a guild of dyers was formed in Cairo, that specialized in taking old shawls imported from India and re-dyeing them so as to make them look new (at a much lower cost than new shawls) (Hanna 2014: 81–5).

Larger Workshops

Traditionally, textile workers worked in small workshops with four or five looms. Another indication of growth is that larger workshops seem to have appeared, a trend that Mehmet Genc also noted as taking place in Anatolia in the eighteenth century and for which evidence exists for Egypt. Recent research on this subject by Husam Abdul-Muti shows that some textile workshops towards the latter part of the eighteenth century tended to be relatively large. He cites the examples of a merchant called *khawaja* Muhammad bin Isa bin Abu Bakr al-Jamali al-Maghribi, whose textile workshop had 17 looms, and was thus a small enterprise with a relatively high number of workers, whereas the ordinary workshop usually possessed 2–3 looms; the workshop for silk textiles with 21 looms that Khawaja Mahmud Muharram, a merchant, founded as a waqf in the second half of the eighteenth century; and that of Emir Abdul-Rahman Katkhuda in the Azhar area with 17 looms (Abdul-Muti 2008: 181).

More Efficient Management Techniques

Another way to increase production so as to meet growing demand was through new forms of management. This, again, is most apparent in the production of cloth and more specifically of cloth that was in high demand. One of the most fashionable textiles that was in demand worldwide in the eighteenth century was printed cotton with Indian designs. In the different cities of the Ottoman Empire, as well as in Europe, makers of this type of cloth emerged. There were numerous attempts to imitate the Indian designs in order to limit imports from India and to expand production in order to meet consumer demand. One model is provided in relation to the production of printed cloth, one of the most fashionable and much demanded textiles. In 1780, the basmajiya in accordance with its guild head, decided to work in one specific location; the profits of the sale were to be divided according to set portions among the members. These payments were not equal, with some of the printers getting more pay than others, perhaps because they did more work or possibly because they had more experience. The guild head, who acted as supervisor to the conditions of the agreement, had a higher portion of profit than others.

There are multiple ways in which this arrangement is relevant. Two important features worked in favour of the ordinary printers. The first was that the agreement was put down on paper and was confirmed by a qadi, meaning that it was given a legal dimension. This was presumably a protection for those involved. An arrangement which placed the artisan within a specified location, and which instituted a kind of group work, under supervision by the guild head, implied more efficiency in the production of printed cloth. It is a form of rational organization of the process of production, presumably aimed to produce more and, thus, to answer higher levels of demand.

But it nevertheless also implied a partial loss of autonomy of the artisan. Artisans were no longer solely responsible for the production or sale of their product. In terms of the profit made, one could place it in a hybrid system, where it was neither a wage nor a price determined by the artisan, but a set portion of the profit, determined by the guild. The guild head made a larger profit than any of the guild members, but there was collaboration, in the sense that his profit was known in advance, which limited his chances of unusual gain at the expense of others (Hanna 2011a: 128–31). This is not so important in terms of the number of people affected by this, except insofar as it was an embryonic stage of a longer-term process.

There were other forms of re-organization or management of production that had the potential to be more efficient. One method was to group together guilds that produced different phases of one single product or that used the same raw material for their work. There are a number of examples, suggesting it could be part of a trend. For instance, a set of four textile guilds, all of them producing decorations for garments, those who made tassels in the local style (*aqqadin baladi*); those who made hussles in the Turkish style (*aqqadin fil-rumi*); those who embroidered on cloth (*habbakin*);

and those who made or sewed buttons (*azrariya*), chose one single shaykh to lead all four of the guilds.[5] The objective was presumably to facilitate the production of readymade clothes. Having one, rather than four, guild head could therefore be a way of rationalizing the production of these items and of coordinating between the different stages that a finished garment could go through. Likewise, we find a similar pattern in other sets of guilds: the guilds of butchers (*qassabin*), shoemakers (*adamiyin*), and tanners (*madabighiya*) chose one guild head to be in charge of all three guilds, from the tanners' guild; the head's orders were to be followed by the members of the three guilds. Here, the issue of handling and distributing raw materials, the hides of the slaughtered animals that would be tanned and then manufactured into shoes, would be a major consideration for all concerned.[6] A final illustration of this trend is in the four guilds that manufactured different kinds of shoes and footwear to choose a single guild head.[7]

These groupings of guilds, in addition to the efficiency they might bring to rationalization of distribution of raw material and of production, may also have been seen as a form of protection against encroachments, a subject we will now turn to.

The Political Forces

The second problem that artisans had to confront was to keep their independence in the face of attempts to encroach upon them.

For a long time, artisans struggled to remain independent. For various reasons, the textile guilds, around 12–15 in number, seem to have managed to resist the encroachment of guild heads on their members for a fairly longer time compared to the guilds of leather makers or oil pressers. One possible reason may be that textiles were produced in many guilds so it was not easy to control them. Another possible reason is that they managed to re-organize their work and restructure their guilds. This was done in several ways. One way was

[5] Court of Bab Ali 214, Case 209, dated 1731, p. 96.
[6] Court of Bab Ali 96, Case 2417, dated 1614, p. 374.
[7] Court of Bab Ali 125, Case 216, dated 1647, p. 73.

by the formation of a fund that was run along business lines and helped to consolidate the guild. This was done in the form of a pious foundation (waqf) of copper utensils that could be rented out against a certain sum of money; these were partly re-invested in the fund by the purchase of new utensils and partly used for other purposes in favour of guild members. These enterprises became common among textile guilds towards the end of the seventeenth and eighteenth centuries (Hanna 2011b: 165–89). There was, in other words, money that could be made by the guilds.

What we can discern are those aspects of guild life that became influenced by the commercialization resulting from trade, a commercialization which could influence the way that work was organized, and the relationship of guild heads to guild members.

These Tensions Give Rise to New Forms

Seen from a broader perspective, what this meant was the existence of tensions between two opposing forces. One of these was the process of commercialization that was making itself felt in various levels of society, as possibilities for making money expanded and as more people could get into the money-making circles (Hanna 2011a: 161–86). One of the manifestations of commercialization was the way that merchants dealt with guilds. Merchants had their own guilds, somewhat loosely organized when compared to crafts guilds. But when it came to dealing with crafts guilds that produced the goods they needed for their trading activities, their primary objective was to maximize their profits, to push for increased production, and possibly to channel products to fit what was in most demand in the market. In other words, the guild was a tool to maximize profit.

The second was the political forces manifested in persons with status and money, merchants and emirs, who were neither related to the craft nor had much or any knowledge of it, but who, for purposes of gain, tried to have a say or to have a measure of control over the producers and their guild, because this meant more profit from their commercial activities.

The tensions between these two forces were only resolved with the industrial policy of Muhammad Ali, who, in the early 1820s, through a set of decisions, undertook to create a state capitalism. By this, the state came to control agricultural production from the source (plantation of raw material); factories where workers (or at least some of them) were paid wages; and trade of the finished goods in the international market.

Seen from yet another angle, these conditions can be placed in an even broader perspective. They were manifested in the existence of a mixed economy that included elements of a 'traditional' economy of crafts and a command economy that has been associated with the Ottoman Empire, a commercial economy associated with merchants.

From this mixed economy, the conditions of the period and the tensions that emerged were giving rise to a capitalist economy, in which the period was experiencing some of the manifestations associated with it.

The Manifestations

Crafts were caught between two opposing forces: one, having to produce more as the market expanded, while, two, trying to keep powerful outsiders at bay, at a time (late seventeenth century onwards) when local grandees were starting to control major financial resources in Egypt. In other words, the period witnessed a growing tension between market forces and political forces.[8] The manifestations of these tensions were apparent in the relationship between artisans, guild heads, merchants, and emirs. One consequence of these tensions was the emergence of artisan entrepreneurs, often in the person of guild heads who combined craft, commercial activity, and control of tax farms.

These entrepreneurs, presumably usually with the help of those in power, not only consolidated their position within the guild but also became involved in commercial activities. Such control of the guild head over guild members may have had various objectives: for instance, to channel the production of the craftsmen so as to ensure that the guild head would appropriate a portion or else to channel

---

[8] The secondary literature has covered the eighteenth-century rise of mamluk emirs to power well. See Crecelius (1982) and Raymond (1973).

the type and level of work they produced in order to conform to the market.

The Guild Head as Businessman

Traditionally, guilds were headed by a person in the craft, who knew how a product was made, who could have a say in the quality of the finished product in case of a complaint. The guild head also had a certain responsibility for the well-being of the guild members. Certain guilds had funds to pay for members in need or to help them pay their taxes. The period between the end of the seventeenth and eighteenth centuries witnessed a shift in the relationship between guild heads and guild members. The heads of the guilds of leather makers and the heads of the guild of pressers of linseed oil became small entrepreneurs. This entrepreneurship is evident in their large-scale purchases of raw material. Repeatedly, the head of the leather makers paid the persons in charge of the slaughterhouse enormous sums of money to obtain the hides of cows, sheep, bulls; while that of the oil pressers purchased linseed in large quantities from rural areas. Guild heads, like the Jalfi family of oil pressers or the member of the Ibn Uthman family of leather makers, through various deals, controlled large amounts of this raw material by numerous purchases of hides from slaughter houses in different parts of the country (Hanna 2011a: 129). The objectives of such purchases were multiple. The example of Ahmad al-Jalfi (d. 1707) who was a presser of linseed oil and head of the guild of oil pressers is indicative. He presumably resold part of these purchases in the market, possibly to other oil pressers, which allowed him to make a profit. Moreover, as an entrepreneur, he came to own several oil presses himself, which he managed by placing family members and colleagues to run them on a daily basis. They formed partnerships and were able to invest large sums of money in the oil presses (Hanna 2011a: 116). The accumulation of profit from these crafts and commercial activities brought enough profit for this guild head to make investments in urban property, including commercial buildings that provided an additional income. By the time he died in 1707, he had become a merchant of wealth dealing in various goods and commodities and leaving an inheritance that ran into the millions. Thus, certain crafts could be a motor behind social mobility.

He was not the only one to climb the social ladder from craft to trade. Other guild heads who succeeded him followed this same pattern.[9] Heads of the leather guild became rich enough to become tax farmers, an activity usually associated with the ruling class economy.[10]

Merchants and Guilds

Changes became perceptible, especially in the eighteenth century, when persons unrelated to the craft, often merchants and occasionally members of the Mamluk ruling class (many of whom had major investments in international trade) penetrated the system. There could be various reasons for this. On the one hand, for merchants, positions like these could help them to direct production one way or another, with a view to serve their commercial interests. On the other hand, the focus on these goods could be a substitute at times when the coffee trade was in crisis. It appears that the profits of the Red Sea trade were decreasing during the last three or four decades of the eighteenth century. One of the consequences was that merchants and their partners, the members of the Mamluk ruling class who were also closely involved in the commercial activities of the Red Sea, were shifting their interest towards trade in local cloth and local leather.

Thus, our sources provide us with examples of merchant entrepreneurs with interests in the production of merchandise that can be shipped to foreign destinations. In the town of Mahalla, a major textile-producing town, Husam Abdul-Muti noted a very large workshop in which the owner had employed weavers, tassel makers, and tailors, in other words, the necessary hands to produce ready-made garments, all under his supervision. The owner was a merchant who would distribute the product. Occasionally, such entrepreneurial structures were headed by an artisan, as is indicated in Nasir Uthman's study on eighteenth-century Rashid. Here, a weaver was the organizer of production, as the weaver owned a yarn workshop, a

---

[9] Court of Bulaq, Register 60, Case 2417, dated 1699, p. 734.
[10] Court of Bulaq, Register 51, Case 505, dated 1668, p. 231.

weaving one, and a dyeing one. The weaver could thus supervise and control the stages of production. By and large, however, it was the merchants who were getting the upper hand on some of the products that had important markets (Hanna 2014: 90–1).

One by one, they started to dominate the textile guilds at the exclusion of persons from the craft itself, just like guild heads were excluded, traditionally: In 1728, the head of the guild of silk makers (*haririyin*) was a merchant. In 1734, the head of the guild of cotton cloth (*qattanin*) was a merchant. In 1737, a merchant was appointed guild head of the makers of woollen cloth (*sawwafin*). And around mid-eighteenth century, members of the Mamluk ruling class started appearing as guild heads in some textile guilds, such as guild of cloth makers (*qazzazin*); and shortly after, the head of the guild of weavers (*taifa al-hayyakin*) was an emir, Emir Ismail Odabasha Mustahfazan, in a move that was evidently undertaken with a certain amount of political pressure.[11]

A Few Commonalities between Different Guilds

Guilds did not all follow the same trajectory, and the changes that they underwent were neither uniform nor homogeneous in their details. Yet, on a broader level, their developments shared common features that point towards the early phases of an emerging capitalism. Three features point towards this emergence and they are mentioned as follows.

Commercialization

In a general way, the seventeenth and eighteenth centuries witnessed an expansion in money relations, including in institutions (like guilds) that were not essentially money-making institutions. In all the guilds that were studied, elements of commercialization, evident in one way or another, were penetrating guilds. Some guilds had activities that were run in a business-like manner. Other guilds had guild heads who used their position as a way of making money. Still

---

[11]   Court of Zahid, Register 693, Case 371, dated 1148/ 1735, p. 171.

other guilds re-organized their work structures for the purpose of producing more.

Political Presence in the Economy

One of the factors that helped further capitalism was its link to power structures. The merchants or emirs who became guild heads, who knew nothing about the craft that they headed, likewise used their position primarily to further commercial interests, rather than to advance the craft, and as a way of getting personal profits. In other words, the guild was part of their commercial enterprise. In either case, these changes brought a shift in the relationship between guild heads and guild members. The result was more hierarchy and more control from the top, as political power gained more control over the economy with the loss of autonomy that normally accompanies it (Amin 2011: 6).

The various stages in the growth of power structures in guilds have been elaborated earlier in the chapter: from the power of the guild head to the presence of merchants as guild heads, occasionally of emirs in that position, until these were replaced by the state during the reign of Muhammad Ali.

Loss of Autonomy by Craftsmen

Loss of autonomy came in degrees. There was a wide spectrum between the independent craftsman who worked in his workshop, owned his tools, produced and sold his own goods and the wage earners who did not own their tools and who produced for entrepreneurs who made profits off the finished product that they sold. Wage earners who worked in a factory, for instance, had little or no control over the way they did their work or over the sale of the products they made.

Thus, the two models of work are far apart, but between them were many shades; there were also many variations between different guilds and craftsmen. It is these that we can focus on. Seen from the angle of the craftsmen, such changes of the seventeenth and eighteenth centuries had their place on a part of this wide spectrum. Ultimately, many of these trends led to a degree of loss of autonomy of the craftsman. In short, the impact of the expanding trade shaped not only the size of the workplace and the number of guilds but also the social relation of production.

***

Significant as some of these changes were, they represented a relatively small fraction of overall production and an even smaller one of the economy. A limited number of guilds had led the way to new developments. Most of the artisans and guilds that produced everyday goods, whether they were making needles, knives, mirrors, or pipes, may not have felt the consequences of the changes that were taking place. The guilds and guild members studied here, although few in number, were nevertheless central in terms of the innovations they brought into the picture and that were ultimately linked to subsequent developments. The distance between the state project of industrial production instituted by Muhammad Ali (1805–48) was a few steps ahead. The guilds focused on goods that yielded a high value in international markets (cloth for instance); their work organization had new forms of supervision; there was reduced independence of the craftsman or artisan; these were some of the emerging features that were subsequently taken up in the factories established in the 1820s. Thus, the organization of artisans and guilds of the seventeenth and eighteenth centuries ultimately left its mark on the state capitalism instituted by Muhammad Ali at the start of the nineteenth century (Batou 1991: 401–28; Ghazaleh 2002: 124–38).

Bibliography

Court Registers of Cairo

Dar al-Wathaʾiq al-Qawmiya:
Bab Ali registers nos. 96; 125; 214
Bulaq, registers 51; 56; 60.
Qisma Arabiya register 37
Zahid register 693

Printed Sources

Abdul-Muti, Husam. 2008. ʿAl-Aʾila wal Tharwa: al-Buyut al-Tujariya al-Maghribiya fi Misr al-Uthmaniyaʾ ['Family and Fortune: Maghribi

Merchant Houses in Ottoman Egypt']. In *Silsila Tarikh al-Misriyin*. Cairo: Al-Hay'a al-Misriya al-Amma lil-Kitab.

Amin, Samir. 2011. *Global History: A View from the South*. Cape Town: Pambazuka Press.

Batou, Jean. 1991. 'L'Egypte de Muhammad-'Ali: Pouvoir Politique et Developpement Economique.' *Annales, Histoire, Sciences Sociales* 46: 401–28.

Blaut, James Morris. 1993. *The Colonizer's Model of the World: Geographic Diffusionism and Eurocentric History*. London: Guilford Press.

Crecelius, Daniel. 1982. *The Roots of Modern Egypt: A Study of the Regimes of Ali Bey al-Kabir and Muhammad Bey Abu al-Dhahab, 1760–1775*. Minneapolis: Bibliotheca Islamica.

Eldem, Edhem. 2006. 'Capitulations and Western Trade.' In *The Cambridge History of Turkey, 1603–1839*, Vol. 3, edited by Suraiya Faroqhi, pp. 283–335. Cambridge: Cambridge University Press.

Ghazaleh, Pascale. 2002. 'Manufacturing Myths: Al-Khurunfish, A Case Study.' In *Money, Land and Trade, An Economic History of the Muslim Mediterranean*, edited by Nelly Hanna, pp. 124–38. London: IB Tauris.

Hanafi, Sahar. 2002. 'Al-Ilaqat al-tujariya bayn Misr wa Bilad al-Sham al-Kubra fil qarn al thamin ashar' ['Commercial Relations between Egypt and Bilad al-Sham in the Eighteenth Century']. In *Silsilat Tarikh al-Misriyin*. Cairo: Al Haya al Misriya al Amma lil Kitab.

Hanna, Nelly. 2011a. *Artisan Entrepreneurs in Cairo and Early Modern Capitalism, 1600–1800*. Syracuse: Syracuse University Press.

————. 2011b. 'Guild Waqf: Between Religious Law and Common Law.' In *Held in Trust*, edited by Pascale Ghazaleh, pp. 165–89. Cairo: American University in Cairo Press.

————. 2014. *Ottoman Egypt and the Emergence of the Modern World*. Cairo: American University in Cairo Press.

Mukund, Kanakalatha. 1999. *The Trading World of the Tamil Merchant: The Evolution of Merchant Capitalism in the Coromandel*. Hyderabad: Orient Longman.

Neal, Larry and Jeffrey G. Williamson, eds. 2014. *The Cambridge History of Capitalism, Volume 1: The Rise of Capitalism: From Ancient Origins to 1848*, pp. 2–3. Cambridge: Cambridge University Press.

North, Douglass C. and Robert Paul Thomas. 1973. *The Rise of the West: A New Economic History*. Cambridge: Cambridge University Press.

Raymond, Andre. 1973. *Artisans et commercants au Caire au XVIIIe siècle*. Damascus: IFEAD.

Reid, Anthony. 1990. *Southeast Asia in the Age of Commerce, 1440–1680*. New Haven: Yale University Press.

Shaw, Stanford. 1962. *The Financial and Administrative Organization and Development of Ottoman Egypt, 1517–1798*. Princeton, NJ: Princeton University Press.

Uthman, Naser. 2008. 'La production de textile a Rosette au XVIIIe siècle' ['Textile Production in the Mediterranean (15th–19th Centuries)']. *Les textiles en Mediterrannee (XVe-XIXe siècle)* 29: 25–36.

Wallerstein, Immanuel. 1976. *The Modern World-System: Capitalist Agriculture and the Origins of the European World-Economy in the Sixteenth Century*. New York: Academic Press.

Yi, Eunjeong. 2004. *Guild Dynamics in Seventeenth-century Istanbul, Fluidity and Leverage*. Leiden: Brill.

13

Iranian Capitalism

Exceptionalism and Delayed Development

Rudi Matthee[1]

Since this book addresses capitalism, it seems appropriate to start the present chapter with the characterization of capitalism as stated in a recent authoritative volume on the subject—*The Cambridge History of Capitalism*. Capitalism, co-editor Larry Neal states in his 'Introduction', presupposes private property rights, enforceable contracts, markets with responsive prices, and a supportive government (Neal 2014, Vol. 1: 2).

Yet, capitalism cannot simply be defined as such, Howard Buck contends in a review of the same work. These four criteria do not add up to a definition of capitalism; they say nothing about outcomes; they are points of departure, only offer minimal

[1] I would like to thank Kaveh Yazdani and Dael Norwood for their comments and suggestions on an earlier draft of this chapter.

preconditions from which capitalism might or might not arise and develop. Additional conditions are required for that to happen: a certain development in agriculture freeing up labour for manufacturing purposes; nation states attaining a certain bureaucratic level of institutionalization that facilitates the flow of money and the exchange of goods, investment, and debt; the emergence of large firms holding enough capital and controlling market share (Buck 2015). Perhaps the most important element is the availability of capital, the 'purpose of which is to generate new, productive, wealth—capital, through investment (whereas in older times wealth chiefly served the purpose of display to enhance the authority of monarchs and elites)' (Marks 2016: 56).

Applying both sets of criteria—involving the preconditions and the actual emergence of capitalism as a revolutionary force—one must conclude that early modern Iran does not qualify as capitalist or even proto-capitalist. Until the early twentieth century and the development of its oil industry, no capital-intensive industry involving a substantial wage labour force emerged in Iran; and until the land reform launched by Mohammad Reza Shah in the 1960s broke the back of feudalism, land and owning it remained the measure of privilege and wealth in the country. According to one estimate, in the early twentieth century, modern industry in Iran probably provided no more than 850 jobs (Floor 2009: 22). And as late as 1940, only 28 out of a total of 382 factories employed more than 500 workers (Madani 1986: 14). What existed by way of economic development at that time amounted to 'primitive accumulation', in Marx's words, necessary for the formation of capitalism but in and of itself, not tantamount to it.

All this is true of the adjacent and comparable lands in the early modern period, the Ottoman Empire and India under Mughal rule. Yet this has not prevented modern scholars from claiming the existence of (proto-) capitalist features in the latter two societies. They have done so either by focusing on the receptivity to and role in capitalism on the part of religious 'minorities', by presenting signs of extensive trade or robust profit-seeking entrepreneurship as somehow 'capitalist' and by pointing to activist and centralizing rulers or by interpreting evidence of the cessation of economic expansion as a sign of 'deindustrialization', potential 'take-off' snatched away by the colonial intrusion by (typically) the British. Either way, they mostly make a case for 'merchant capitalism', with an emphasis on trade and production.[2]

This chapter considers the land in between these two territories—Iran, a country that, being more isolated from (colonial) Europe, its gaze, its political and economic intrusion, and its history-writing than either, has received little attention with regard to the topic at hand (Vali 1993: 6–7). I analyse how and why elements of capitalism beyond the existence of 'merchant capitalism' did or did not manifest themselves in early modern Iran, the period encompassing the reign of the Safavid dynasty and, more appositely, that of the nineteenth-century Qajar rulers. The Safavids established political control over Iran in 1501 and lasted until 1722, when a small band of insurgent Afghans from the margins who were nominally their subjects swept them away. The Qajars controlled Iran in the period between the 1790s and 1921, when a coup eliminated the house, replacing it, four years later, with the short-lived Pahlavi dynasty.

What follows is a discussion about long-term connections between the economy and society, state and culture in Iran in the last few centuries. My approach follows what Adelman (2015) calls an 'internalist' perspective in that it operates from the notion that industrial capitalism arose in Europe and, over time, spread around the world, in the process encountering obstacles that it did or did not manage to overcome. Yet some attention will be given to external elements, such as, for example, the tremendous nineteenth-century growth in opium production and the famine this helped cause, with Adelman's argument that such developments do not invalidate or contradict looking at internal forces as the operative ones. I also take a neo-Weberian approach to the issue, which means that my focus will be on institutions, primarily the state—encompassing the court and the bureaucracy—and its role as a force that either facilitated or hampered economic development. I will try to avoid the implicit historicist notion that early modern Iran, too, showed clear signs of

---

[2] For the Indian case, see Roy (2014) and Pamuk (2014, Vol. 1: 165). For a critique of Roy's work, see Gosh (2015). For the Ottoman case, see Pamuk (2014). Yazdani (2017) detects a proto-industrial energy in Gujarat and especially in late eighteenth-century Mysore under Tipu Sultan.

embryonic capitalism and that, barring environmental constraints and colonial deviousness, the country would have joined the ranks of the industrialized countries much earlier than it did, a notion that so often suffuses discussions of any given form of modernity or modernization with regard to the non-Western world.[3] This approach is rarely insightful and frequently apologetic. It often does little more than show that a given period witnessed a spurt of economic growth, and it is often tinged with barely masked (nationalist) defensiveness. Just as little productive, for that matter, and thus to be avoided as well, is the notion of Western 'triumphalism', which often serves as both the premise and the outcome of this type of analysis. Teleology, the idea that the emergence of capitalism in Iran in a 'European' manner was inevitable simply because, over time, the practice spread globally, is to be rejected too. That said, nothing in an honest assessment of the adaptive indigenization of a concept that inarguably originated in Europe is fundamentally going to disrupt the 'master narrative', that is, elide the preponderant role that at least the northwestern edge of the European continent continues to play as a benchmark in the development of industrial capitalism. While this should obviate the use of the term 'failure' (to develop capitalism), it also makes some reference to 'absences' (of 'capitalist' preconditions or features) or 'obstacles' (to the formation of capitalism) all but unavoidable.[4]

Conditions in the Safavid Period

Peer Vries, a key participant in the so-called Great Divergence Debate, follows a recent trend in the resurgent attention paid to the question of the preconditions for economic growth and development and the rise of capitalism in the early modern world by putting special emphasis on a 'supportive government' and its role in the emergence and development of capitalism in Western Europe and, more particularly, in Britain. Taking issue with the traditional

---

[3] The need to look comparatively at '*connections* between economy, society, state, and culture in sorting out explanatory factors' and to engage in a long-term analysis while doing so is emphasized by Kocka (2016: 93).

[4] For a foundational, Marxist-inspired essay that begins and ends with 'obstacles' (to the formation of a bourgeoisie in Iran), see Ashraf (1969).

Anglo-Saxon-inflected interpretation of the rise of capitalism as being rooted in a weak state and its laissez-faire approach to economic matters, he argues that not free enterprise, Adam Smith's 'invisible hand', but the interventionist state was principally responsible for the rise of capitalism, beginning with merchant capitalism. Whereas the early modern English state became strong and fiscally active, the Chinese state was and remained weak. Poorly funded, it wielded but weak 'infrastructural' power over the lands that it presumably controlled (Vries 2015: 56–7).[5]

I follow Vries's argument in my assessment of the nature of Iran's early modern economic development, mainly because I agree that an economic system as complex as a capitalist one could not conceivably have emerged without the kind of resources that only state support would be able to harness.

Incidentally, Safavid Iran had a 'supportive' government under Shah 'Abbas I (r. 1587–629), who is universally hailed as the most forceful and forward-looking ruler of the dynasty, indeed one of the most energetic Iranian rulers of all time. A supportive government, in turn, would not have been able to accomplish much without (private) entrepreneurial energy. The Safavid period evinces plenty such energy. Iran under the Safavids indeed was the field of operation of two groups that, in principle, might have evolved into incubators of capitalism: the Armenian merchants of New Julfa and the representatives of the English and Dutch maritime companies, the East India Company (EIC) and the Verenigde Oostindische Compagnie (VOC).

Shah 'Abbas I's track record suggests that successful premodern imperial states operated on the basis of a fragile balance between economic interventionism and an (often involuntary) lack thereof. Put another way, 'Abbas's way of governing indeed was as interventionist as any premodern or early modern society would have enabled a state to be, given inherent limits on the state's ability to 'penetrate' society, to wield 'infrastructural' power, in the terminology of Michael Mann

[5] Vries's views of what constitutes state support have been challenged by those who focus on state intervention taking the form of colonial conquest and expropriation. For examples of the state pursuing power and profit through 'war capitalism', see Beckert (2014) and Brandon (2015).

([1986] 1995). The most energetic of all Safavid rulers reorganized a tribally structured, unruly, and unreliable army and brought it under a modicum of royal control, equipping it with new arms and elevating it to a fighting force able to withstand the Ottomans. The shah chose Isfahan as his new capital and turned this centrally located city into an imperial nexus by providing it with a new political, religious, and commercial centre. He made significant improvements in his country's infrastructure by building a multitude of caravanserais and by providing road security with an ingenuous system that made regional governors financially responsible for any theft or robbery perpetrated in their domain. 'Abbas, moreover, showed an abiding curiosity in the technical achievements of European nations, commissioning a printing press on at least two occasions as well as requesting cannon and other armaments from his allies in Christian lands (Anonymous [1930] 2012: 305; Richard 1990). And he solicited merchants, domestic ones—the Armenians of New Julfa, who were accorded trading rights and privileges, including a monopoly on the export of silk—as well as foreign ones, most notably the EIC and the VOC, who were allowed to operate in his realm conducting trade at reduced toll and tax rates (for the Armenians, see Aslanian 2011). Not coincidentally, given their far-flung contacts, the Armenian New Julfa community was the first to import and operate an active printing press in Iran (Richard 1980: 483–4).

Shah 'Abbas I's approach to trade entailed a rather open economic system that left ample room for outside forces to participate in commercial life. Indeed, in its relative openness, his approach (and that of his successors) was markedly different from that of contemporary Western European states with their tendency to privilege domestic merchants and to make it difficult or even impossible for non-national ones to disembark in their ports and operate on their soil. At a time when the French state restricted the access of Armenian merchants to its ports, Shah 'Abbas I welcomed the EIC and VOC to his shores—with conditional and circumscribed rights and privileges—in part to act as a political and military counterweight to the overbearing Portuguese and in part because they fitted into his expansive commercial and political agenda, which included depriving the Ottomans of income by stimulating Iran's oceanic trade.

If this lack of 'protectionism' was a weak link in a chain that otherwise might have led to sustained 'development', more structural impediments to such a process existed as well in Iran. First of all, like early modern India, Safavid Iran was not an integrated 'national' economy but rather consisted of a multitude of oasis cities and their hinterlands, each of which constituted a regional economy, a fact that in itself gave the central government a weak hand. Far from being despotic and removed from society, as Homa Katouzian's (2003) 'aridisolatic' society model has it, the Safavid (and Qajar) state was a mixed enterprise, arbitrary in its immediate actions, but limited rather than absolutist in its ability to exercise real power, including economic power.[6]

Iran's harsh physical geography did not help either. Much of the Iranian plateau consists of vast deserts and formidable mountain ranges. That, combined with the virtual absence of navigable waterways, until modern times made the transportation of goods exceedingly difficult and costly, to the point where only the conveyance of high value-to-weight commodities was cost-effective. There was a lack of easily exploitable mineral deposits and little timber on the mostly treeless plateau, which was home to a small and scattered population, many of whom lived subsistence lives as peasants or pastoralists. Unlike India with its Gangetic Plain or Egypt with its Nile Valley, Iran was a country of limited rain-fed agricultural output and an equally limited export portfolio, making for a structural balance of payment deficit. This became critical especially in the period after Shah 'Abbas I, when Safavid state officials, confronted with growing currency shortages, became increasingly anxious about the outflow of precious metal from the country. Shah 'Abbas II's grand vizier, Mohammad Beg (in office 1656–61), facing a ballooning fiscal deficit, issued several bans on the outflow of specie and bullion. Such restrictive measures only grew in frequency and intensity under his successors (see Matthee, Floor, and Clawson 2013: Chapters 3 and 4).

Also, just as mercantilism in Europe did not obviate protectionism and certainly was not tantamount to free trade, so Shah 'Abbas I's

---

[6] Katouzian's model is a (barely acknowledged) variant on Karl Wittfogel's hydraulic society.

'mercantilism' represented a fiscal regime that was above all designed to pad the royal coffers. Shah 'Abbas's policies certainly included *elements* of mercantilism in the way he protected a specific group of merchants, exempting them from taxes and tolls, granting them the monopoly over silk exports, and allowing them freedom of worship and protection from harassment. But favouring the Julfan Armenians did not mean shielding them from royal arbitrariness and coercion. Indeed, the very establishment of the Julfan Armenian court merchant community in 1604–5 resulted in an act of violence in the form of forced resettlement. And the Julfan merchants remained a 'service gentry', beholden to the court rather than being free political and economic agents. Finally, if 'Abbas's economic policy bears some resemblance to the mercantilism of contemporary European states, its practice was not underpinned by public debate, least of all in print form. In sum, a 'strong state', though arguably necessary for the development of capitalism, was not as such conducive to its rise.

Like several forceful non-Western rulers after him, Shah 'Abbas I actively promoted trade and manufacturing, and thus may be seen as 'transitional' in a process towards 'proto-industrialization'. Yet like Peter the Great in Russia, Tipu Sultan in Mysore, India, and Muhammad 'Ali in Egypt, he also operated in an environment that was barely conducive to sustained development. In the decades following his death in 1629, Iran underwent an unmistakable retrenchment from the active diplomatic and commercial engagement with the world that he had initiated. We may call 1639, the year in which Shah 'Abbas's grandson and successor, Shah Safi (r. 1629–42) concluded a lasting peace agreement with the Ottomans, Iran's arch-enemies, a crucial moment in this process. This decision obviated maintaining close ties with European nations as potential allies against the Ottomans and thus limited Iran's interaction with the ultimate source of most technological and military innovation. More specifically, it lessened the urgency for the Safavids to keep up with military technology in the way that the Ottomans and Tipu Sultan were forced to.

The most consequential 'impediment' to the development of capitalism in Iran, finally, was a set of cultural values and practices that early modern Iran shared with most of the world and that only contemporary Western Europe was in the process of challenging and undermining at the time. In an interpretation as self-aggrandizing as it seemed self-evident, Europe's leap to industrial modernity used to be hailed as a miraculously unique achievement. A generation ago, this orthodoxy began to be challenged by scholars who advanced a revisionist interpretation of the same leap by denying its uniqueness with the argument that China and India had their own breakthroughs and that, to the extent that Europe eventually pulled ahead, its 'take-off' was contingent, mostly due to an abundance of critical natural resources or just luck. Such levelling was bound to provoke a reaction, and it did. Harking back to an earlier strand of argumentation that focused on efficient institutions as singular to the European case, various scholars in the last decade have reaffirmed the uniqueness of the European example and ascribed the singular breakthrough it represents to 'interactively generated differences' in which institutions are embedded in cultural beliefs and practices centring on applied science and 'useful knowledge'. Joel Mokyr, the most eloquent protagonist of this view, attributes Europe's 'take-off' to technological creativity and innovation embedded in an approach to life and nature not found anywhere else. While early modern (Western) Europe was no stranger to superstition, he argues, it developed a mode of thinking that enabled its secular elite to challenge and defeat obscurantism. Nor were the agents of state and religion in the West any less wary of heterodox ideas than rulers and clerics in other cultures. But Europe's dynastic divisions and competitive state structures made it difficult for any given regime to stifle ideas, which easily crossed borders to find shelter from persecution in neighbouring lands. Mokyr identifies a deep-seated validation of (manual) labour and technology in combination with an urge to harness the physical environment to human material needs. Enlightenment thinking was marked by a forward-looking belief in history, by the idea of history as development. This belief included the notion that the past is not necessarily better or wiser than the present let alone the future, and that progress is possible as well as desirable. The Republic of Letters and the competitive market of ideas it represented enabled theoretical knowledge to become applied knowledge. All this led to a concrete agenda of policy measures and institutional change, a combination of a supportive state, a belief in economic growth, and a growing cult of experimentation and empiricism in a cumulative process aiming at social progress (Mokyr 2017: 14, 19–20, 248, 254).[7]

Safavid Iran does not present a dichotomous 'absence' here. The country was distant from Europe but it was by no means an intellectual backwater. Seventeenth-century Isfahan was home to a number of brilliant philosophers and jurists who married neo-Platonic ideas to a long-standing mystical strand in Islamic thought. This so-called illuminationist School of Isfahan, represented by Mullah Sadra (1572–1640) (see Rizvi 2007), engaged in forms of epistemological inquiry that, with some qualifications, merit the label 'Renaissance' (Pourjavady and Schmidtke 2015). European visitors and residents, including well-educated missionaries, were impressed with the interest Iranians showed in mathematics, medicine, and astrology, and the level of sophistication they displayed in such fields (Windler 2018: 229–30). Nor was such creative energy confined to the capital. The southern city of Shiraz was an important cultural and intellectual centre throughout the Safavid period and it retained that reputation into the eighteenth century (Anzali 2017: 117–20; Brentjes 2004: 408–11). The Italian gentleman-scholar Pietro Della Valle found Lar, also in southern Iran, to be a freewheeling intellectual hub, commercially connected to India and filled with cosmopolitan literati, philosophers, mathematicians, and astronomers, Jewish as well as Muslim, some of them Sunni, 'men of great spirit and genius', as he called them (Gurney 1986: 111).

Such intellectual endeavour was far from being just nomocentric, hewing to religious orthodoxy and legal literalism. As was true in Ming China, scholarship in Safavid Iran was not 'inherently antipathetic to scientific study or resistant to new ideas' (De Bary 1975: 205, quoted in Mokyr 2017: 323). That there was ample room for doubt and disputation in intellectual circles is clear from the frequent debates that Iranian high officials and literati held with their European guests, diplomats, and missionaries on matters such as the nature of God and the veracity of the Trinity. Iranians were receptive to foreign influence to a remarkable degree in other ways as well. Consider the assimilation of European painting styles in

---

[7] For an analysis along the same line using historical sociology, see Anievas and Nişancioğlu (2017).

the late Safavid period. Just as they had adopted East Asian artistic techniques and themes following the thirteenth-century Mongol invasion by adapting a foreign style to their own traditions, so they proved susceptible to outside impulses four centuries later—with, arguably the same remarkable, albeit more limited results. Most modern scholars have seen in the outcome—the hybrid, so-called *farangi-sazi*, Europeanizing, style of painting—the effect of Iran's encounter with the output of a small number of Dutch painters who worked for the royal court in the early seventeenth century (Habibi 2017).

Yet any truly transformative effect of all this engagement ran up against practical as well as epistemological obstacles. Well into the nineteenth century, Iran, like the region at large, remained a manuscript rather than a print culture, preventing any rapid distribution of ideas. Lar's intellectual ferment, under pressure from a fervently Shi'i state and unsupported by the benefits of a mail system and the print revolution, faded with the passing of the Safavids (Safavid Iran did have a mail system, operated by *chapars*, mounted couriers, but it was only used to relay government orders and messages). Iranian culture also had its share of what Mokyr calls the association of the sphere of production and physical work with low-prestige culture and inferior social standing, causing elites to be mainly concerned with philosophy, poetry, history, and such leisure activities as hunting and music (Mokyr 2017: 120). Whereas the Enlightenment in Europe was deeply empiricist, the equivalent movement in Iran was and remained speculative and metaphysical in orientation. The Safavids, finally, were not averse to the idea of 'useful knowledge'. But such knowledge had to fit into their cultural universe to be assimilable. This included astronomical implements, needed for the correct computation of the constellation of the stars for prayer and royal conduct, and obviously useful military technology and engineering in general. But other seemingly clear-cut technological 'improvements' did not, as is evidenced by the inability of print culture to gain public acceptance at the time. Shah 'Abbas I, shown the principle of movable type, demonstrated an interest in acquiring a printing press (Anonymous [1930] 2012: 233, 305). But if such a press arrived, it was not until the shah's death in 1629, and it never produced any books. The printing presses owned by the Christian missionaries of Isfahan and the

New Julfan Armenian community, respectively, did generate books, yet never broke out of their confessional mould—the Armenian press was only equipped with Armenian type—and fell into disuse decades before the dynasty collapsed (Floor 1990). Logistical problems and a lack of shared purposefulness between the state and private enterprise throttled various initiatives involving technology. None of the Safavid envoys sent to Europe in the seventeenth century seemed especially curious about its culture or the manifestations of the modern world, much less in their origins and context (Matthee 2013: 22). Shah 'Abbas II (r. 1642–66) was told about the mechanized minting process that had recently been introduced in Europe. He seems to have admired the quality and efficiency of the output, but evinced no interest in acquiring this technology for his own use (Tavernier 1676, Vol. 1: 493–4). His successor, Shah Soleyman (r. 1666–94), presented with a European astronomical device constructed according to Copernican heliocentric cosmology, showed no curiosity about the contraption's technical attributes but only enquired if it was made of pure gold. A bronze mechanical clock made in Nuremberg elicited just as little interest on the part of the monarch (Kaempfer 2018: 45). And the latest models of Copernican astronomical devices that were part of the rich gifts Louis XIV sent to Iran in 1683 were spurned as 'African monsters' by the court astrologers, to be relegated to the royal warehouse (Kaempfer 2001: Letters 22 April 1684 and 1 October 1685, 168, 227–8). In sum, it is hard not to agree with Parviz Mohebbi (1996: 215–16), who offers many examples of technical know-how in Safavid Iran yet argues that a lack of encouragement of artisans and entrepreneurs on the part of a state that was keen to attract specialists but showed no interest in luring engineers and machinery to Iran accounts for the conspicuous lack of interest in applied science.

Not all initiative and experimentation dissolved after 1629 or 1639, to be sure. Nor did curiosity about the outside world vanish under 'Abbas I's successors. Mohammad Beg showed great enthusiasm for technological experimentation and a keen interest in promoting the domestic manufacture of armaments. Determined to enhance royal revenue, he also sought to unlock some of Iran's natural resources. He thus encouraged the reopening of coal mines as well as the exploration of gold and silver deposits so as to secure a domestic supply of coinage, and even hired a French mineralogist to help him in these efforts (Matthee 1991: 26–7; Richard 1995, Vol. 2: 226–9). Yet such efforts remained personal and private in origin and motivation. Shah 'Abbas's successors did not build an edifice on his 'foundations', the way, say, Catherine II did following Tsar Peter I.

Nor was the long term favourable to change. Arbitrariness and oppression increased over time. Shah 'Abbas's successors began to overtax the country's most productive merchants—or alternatively, were too weak to prevent rapacious local administrators and provincial governors from fiscally abusing merchants and artisans. One form of 'taxation' that was applied with increasing frequency was forcing merchants, domestic as well as foreign ones, either to contribute directly to the upkeep of the military or to offer loans to the state (Matthee 2000: 261). Such 'loans' were rarely, if ever, repaid. This enabled the regime to spend more than it earned without the assistance of a national bank, an institution increasingly embraced by contemporary European courts eager to collect money to wage war. The shah was also wont to confiscate the movable wealth and real estate of high state functionaries upon their dismissal and death, in a practice that was replicated on the provincial level by local magistrates vis-à-vis residents of means (Chardin 1810–11, Vol. 5: 285, Vol. 7: 405–6, Vol. 9: 209–10; Sanson 1694: 134–5).[8] Such policies did little to foster societal trust and naturally invited members of the commercial and political elite to conceal their assets and profits. Financial problems coupled with a growing focus on religious identification, meanwhile, increased pressure on Iran's non-Shi'i inhabitants, including the New Julfan Armenians. The latter community saw its taxes go up while its members were prodded to convert, causing several of the wealthiest families to pack up and decamp to the city-states of Italy and Petrine Russia, where they were welcomed and, in the case of Venice and Rome, even received citizenship.

Between the Safavids and the Qajars

The fall of the Safavids in 1722 had a dramatic effect on developments in Iran. Isfahan, the country's premier political and commercial nexus, saw its population plummet from approximately

---

[8] For the practice in provinces, see Fryer (1909–15, Vol. 3: 25).

300,000 to 30,000 after being seized and ravaged by a small band of insurgent Afghan tribesmen. Their brief rule was followed by nearly a century of decentralization and instability. Roads became chronically insecure, and parts of the country, now run by ephemeral warlords, descended into political chaos, forcing society's productive elements to scurry for cover. Some of Iran's Armenians, including members of the community of New Julfa, almost welcomed the Afghan invaders as liberators. Yet their collaboration did not shield them from the fiscal oppression to which everyone else was subjected as well. The long-term result of these developments was a continued flight of New Julfa's wealthy entrepreneurs to Russia, Italy, and India. The suburb's terminal decline would end with its near collapse during the violent and oppressive reign of Nader Shah (1736–47).

The European companies, the VOC and the EIC, meanwhile, hardly fared any better. Their business in Bandar 'Abbas, in Isfahan, and in Kerman, where they dealt in fine goats' wool, suffered grievously as a result of the Afghan onslaught. They, too, came under increasing fiscal strain, forced as they were to offer 'loans' to the state—first to the Safavids, then to the Afghans, and finally to Nader Shah. In the 1750s, despairing of any prospects of profit, they finally gave up, abandoned their remaining factories on the Persian Gulf coast, and left the country.

Most importantly, the turmoil that followed the fall of the Safavids disconnected Iran from the currents of world history, its innovations, and its technological developments, to a far greater degree than the Ottoman Empire and the Indian Subcontinent. At a time when international trade increasingly meant maritime trade, Iran suffered in particular for being virtually landlocked. Iran's most productive and most densely populated regions were located in the north, farthest from direct access to the wider world. The most fertile regions, the Caspian provinces of Gilan and Mazandaran, were remote from other parts of the country since they were separated from the plateau by the formidable Alborz range. The Russians dominated the shipping lanes of the Caspian Sea. Iran's only maritime outlet to the world, the Persian Gulf, was far away from the country's productive centres and hardly an ideal outlet. The distance to Europe was enormous, and until the advent of steam, the rhythm of the monsoon regulated navigation, forcing ships coming from and going to the West to call at Indian ports first. The Gulf littoral itself, an arid region with a scorching climate barely suited for human habitation, lacked viable ports, hubs that, like Bombay (now Mumbai) or Singapore, over time might have developed into cosmopolitan centres of innovation and experimentation. Bandar 'Abbas and, as of the late eighteenth century, Bushehr were little more than 'caravan termini' (Floor 2016: xxi). All this contributed to Iran's relative isolation from the world's main commercial and technological currents, especially, in the second half of the eighteenth century, a period of tremendous technological and political change and innovation in Western Europe.

Developments in the Qajar Period

Otto Blau, a German diplomat who, in 1857, visited Iran to investigate the country's commercial potential and subsequently wrote a very informative work on the topic, summed up Iran's predicament at the time. He drew attention to the manufacture of fine wool, mostly carpets and shawls, for which Iran was famous. He noted, though, that these were no longer known for either their former quality or durability and elegance, adding that real Kashmir shawls had always seemed superior to those made in Kerman (Blau 1858: 103). He claimed that multiple manufactured products, having diminished in quality, were either being overtaken by European products or were now only exported to adjacent countries, Russia, Turkey, and Central Asia. This was true of woven silks, brocades—as it was for colours, which had lost out to European artificial ones—cotton block prints (*qalamkari* or *kalamkari*), metal arms, swords, and firearms, which he called awkwardly made. The same was true of glassware, where the Iranians had not kept up with new technology (Blau 1858: 107–17). Iran, a British trade report from 1842 concluded, in exchange for its imports from Europe had nothing to offer 'us'—European markets—other than silk.[9]

Blau enumerated five reasons why, in his opinion, other countries had long surpassed Iran in manufacturing capacity. He began

[9] 'Report on the Silk Trade of Ghilan', 5 May 1842, in Issawi (1971: 234).

by singling out the lack of political stability and order, the result of a century of political turmoil and tribal unrest. The second reason for the malaise was the lack of capital and credit, a function of the insecurity of private property, which prevented any accumulation of capital and the emergence of a system of public credit. The third impediment, in Blau's eyes, was a lack of iron and coal deposits and the scarcity of timber. The fourth was that despite the love of novelty and the curiosity exhibited by Iranians, they showed themselves unable to turn this into something practical. And five, he noted a lack of available labour in a country where many people were still nomadic or semi-nomadic. Blau (1856: 99–101) concluded that, with few exceptions, Iranian industry remained local and small-scale while still operating at the artisanal level.

Blau's sobering assessment is consonant with what other sources tells us about Iran's economic and political conditions at the time. A century after being depleted by Nader Shah's extortionate tax regime, the New Julfan colony was a mere shadow of its former self, the number of its inhabitants having dwindled to an estimated 350. Even though the population of Isfahan at large by that time had crept back up to perhaps 75,000, large parts of its famous bazaar were still unoccupied. [10] The Qajar dynasty that had come to power at the turn of the century was initially barely in control of a sparsely populated country where individual cities and regions continued to have their own weight, measurement, and currency standards. It was also poor. One mid-century observer insisted that the central government was so impecunious that it did not have the means to pay its own administrators (Binning 1857, Vol. 2: 301, 315–16). Many rural parts still operated at subsistence level, using barter or, at best, locally struck copper coin to exchange goods and services. Twice, in 1860–1 and 1872–3, the country suffered terrible epidemics followed by famines that took hundreds of thousands of lives. [11]

The political foundations of the new state remained weak, too, not least because the Qajars wielded little authority for lack of any

[10] Col Abbott, 'Notes on Various Cities and Countries of Southern Persia, 1849–50', NA, FO 60/165, fols 23–5, 100.

[11] For the 1860–1 famine, see Kazemi (2017). The terrible famine of 1870–1 is analysed by Shoko Okazaki (1986).

credible claim to religious legitimacy. Overseeing a quasi-feudal, tribally underpinned elite composed of greedy landlords, corrupt politicians, and racketeering ulama, the Qajars were traditional in their venal governing style. Whereas in western Europe, 'the amount of gifts or services asked by government from its people tended to decrease' in the course of the eighteenth century (Vries 2015: 93), in Iran, periodic and occasional gift-giving remained essential to obtain and retain positions, and well into the twentieth century, offices continued to be sold to the highest bidder. The shah also continued the Safavid practice of routinely appropriating the assets of state functionaries.[12] Little wonder that foreign investors called reform in this area a sine qua non if the country wished to attract capital (Galbraith 1989: 20). The Qajars, in sum, presided over anything but an 'embedded' state marked by institutional representation and thus were poorly equipped to gain financial strength and resilience by way of having its people accept high taxes.[13]

Renewed contact with the outside world, meanwhile, proved to be a mixed blessing. In the early nineteenth century, Iran 'reconnected' with the larger world, but it did so in conditions of growing dependency. The country quickly fell under the political and economic influence of its two most powerful neighbours, Russia and Britain, the first intruding from the north and the second operating out of India. Both spearheaded new maritime routes. The best example is that of the link via Ottoman Trabzon on the Black Sea, inaugurated in 1830 and further facilitated by the opening of a direct maritime connection between Trabzon and Liverpool in 1847 (Issawi 1970). Shortly thereafter, an alternative route developed via Russia-controlled Georgia. As of the 1860s, the Russians began to divert the Trabzon trade to Tiflis via the port of Poti, lowering the customs dues to be paid by foreign merchants. But in the 1880s, Russian industrialists, wary of foreign competition, put pressure on their government, forcing it to reimpose the dues. This was a serious blow to Iran's export channel via the north. The beneficiary of these

[12] For examples under Naser al-Din Shah, see Shahnavaz (2005: 17–18).
[13] For this paradoxical correlation between embedded states, see Vries (2015: 228–9).

developments was the British-controlled Persian Gulf trade, which, assisted by the opening of the Suez Canal in 1869, ended up taking on the bulk of what had formerly passed between Tabriz and Trabzon (Entner 1956: 70).

This encroachment had a devastating effect on Iranian commerce and manufacturing. Especially detrimental were the preferential tariffs enforced on Iran by Russia in 1828 and by Britain in 1841. Russia in the late nineteenth century subsidized its south-bound export goods to the point where its tea, kerosene, and woollens were cheaper in Iran than at home (Entner 1956: 70). The advantage this gave to foreign entrepreneurs drove Iranian goods out of the market and reduced many Iranian merchants and manufacturers to bankruptcy or forced them to become agents of European firms. The textile industry was especially hard hit. In Yazd, the manufacturing of silk and cotton textiles markedly declined.[14] The number of looms in Kerman dwindled, and the number of cotton-weaving workshops in Kashan and Isfahan plummeted, in some cases by 90 per cent, in the course of the 1830s and 1840s (Floor 2003: 8–9; Issawi 1971: 267–8).

It is not as if the Qajar government remained passive in the face of this foreign onslaught. It was just not Fath 'Ali Shah but the reformist crown prince 'Abbas Mirza who rose to the challenge. Most early Qajar reforms were linked to Azerbaijan, the province he administered. This includes the introduction of Iran's first printing press and the attendant advent of moveable printing, followed by lithograph printing—which initially primarily put out religious and literary texts.[15] The first Iranian students sent to Europe in 1811 and 1815 to acquire practical skills, left from Tabriz as well. Even after 'Abbas Mirza's premature death in 1838, Azerbaijan remained the country's most advanced province, mainly because of its proximity to Russia-controlled Armenia and Georgia, which made great strides towards modernization in the mid-nineteenth century.

---

[14] Col Abbott, 'Notes on Various Cities and Countries of Southern Persia, 1849–50', NA, FO 60/16541.

[15] The first newspaper dates from 1837 but was government-owned and controlled, as were other publications until the late nineteenth century. A privately run critical press only came into being in the early 1900s. See Marzolph and Pistor-Hatam (2002).

The reign of Mohammad Shah (1834–48) saw some half-hearted attempts at redress, but these mainly took the form of self-sufficiency projects masquerading as import substitution, mainly in textiles. Until 1837, the Qajar regime sought to keep European companies out of the country. In that year, protests erupted against the establishment of foreign, predominantly Greek, merchant houses in Tabriz. But Mohammad Shah, who had once resisted European intrusion but by his own admission had failed to establish a native industry that could compete with foreign imports, gave in, reckoning that by allowing foreigners to engage in trade he would at least garner customs dues (Issawi 1971: 112).

The 1840s and beyond witnessed some (proposed) political reform, in part in emulation of the Tanzimat reforms in the neighbouring Ottoman Empire. This included attempts to regulate business practices, designed to prevent fraudulent bankruptcies, the curbing of the practice of *bast* (asylum), taking refuge in religious sanctuaries in order to evade the law, and governmental efforts to oversee commercial affairs (Floor 1977: 62–4). The mid-1850s also saw a stillborn, Austrian-led attempt at the creation of a national bank.[16]

Effective reform ran up against the inertia of prevailing structures, vested interests, and active resistance by those who had an economic stake in the existing system, such as rent seekers like landowners, or those who were ideologically averse to change, which included the majority of clerics. In 1850, British Consul Major Abbott claimed that 'hitherto no encouragement has been shown to native industry in Persia, or to the development of the mineral and agricultural wealth of the country'.[17] This was shortly to change with the first attempt at the creation of import-substituting factories. The driving force behind this initiative was Naser al-Din Shah's first grand vizier, the energetic Mirza Taqi Khan Farahani, better known as Amir Kabir. But the project was poorly planned and Amir Kabir's premature death—who in 1852 was killed at the orders of a suspicious shah—aborted it altogether. Subsequent initiatives fared little better. The aforementioned cotton-spinning factory was built

---

[16] Dickson, Gulhak, to Alison, London, 3 July 1865, NA, FO 248/218.

[17] Abbott, 'Report on the Commerce of South Persia,' fol. 38, NA, FO 60/165.

in the middle of the desert, far from water and fuel supply, and coal had to be brought to the site on camel back. The reason for the factory's location is said to have been its proximity to the royal hunting grounds, which means that the facility primarily served as a spectacle, *tamasha*, entertainment for the monarch. Equally unpropitious was the location of a paper mill at a site without the availability of sufficient water power (Polak 1865, Vol. 2: 53, 184; Schneider 1990: 138–9).

In the mid-1860s, Naser al-Din Shah enacted some more reforms, reorganizing his administration by creating separate departments. In 1879, he appointed another reformist chief minister, Moshir al-Dowla, tasking him with all kinds of improvements, including the encouragement of handicrafts and trade, the exploration of mineral resources, and the building of roads and bridges (Greenfield 1904: 19–20). In 1884, the same ruler convened a consultative body of the country's leading merchants. From this emerged an Assembly of Iranian Merchants, which drafted a document of intent containing, among other objectives, financial security, and the creation of notary offices for the registration of property, the creation of a small Iranian bank protecting the interests of local merchants, and preventing the importation of 'useless' foreign manufactures (Mahdavi 1990: 92–4).

All along, transport remained the country's Achilles heel, even as the proliferation of railroads, the introduction of steam navigation, and the opening of the Suez Canal vastly increased speed and commercial accessibility in Eurasia at large. The paucity of roads especially showed up Iran's traditionally tenuous connection with the sea. The problem of infrastructure is vividly illustrated in the importation of machinery. In contrast to India and the Ottoman Empire, where importing industrial equipment meant having it shipped from a European port to Bombay (now Mumbai) or Istanbul, any machinery destined for Iran had to be hauled overland, hundreds of miles, *after* reaching the country's harbours.[18]

---

[18] A good example is the heavy minting machine imported from France and transported via Russia in the 1860s that was left abandoned on the shores of the Caspian Sea, having sunk in the sands for being too heavy to be carried onwards. See Matthee (1995). The construction of a cotton-spinning factory in the same period faced similar problems. The equipment had

Here, too, some improvements were undertaken. Road construction began in earnest in 1861, when Naser al-Din Shah engaged an Austrian engineer named Albert Joseph Gasteiger to build a road between the royal palace in Tehran to the royal summer residence in Soltanabad (modern Arak). In 1864, Gasteiger was tasked to rebuild Shah 'Abbas's famous causeway along the Caspian Sea, now in serious disrepair. A decade later, the Austrian engineer led the construction of part of the road between Kangavar and the border with Iraq—mostly to facilitate a royal journey to the Shi'i holy shrines of Mesopotamia. He was finally commissioned to construct a link between Tehran and the Caspian Sea via Amol and Barforush. The completion of that last project ran into chicaneries by provincial governors and had to wait until 1899, when the Russians finished the job (Praxmarer 2013: 60–78; Wigham 1903: 393–405). Gasteiger was also the first to study the feasibility of constructing railroads in Iran (Praxmarer 2013: 97–8). Various European speculators presented proposals for rail as of the 1870s. They all failed. The high risk involved, the lack of funding, and Russian obstructionism doomed the various initiatives, so that at the turn of the twentieth century, Iran was devoid of railroads beyond five miles of suburban track between Tehran and the shrine of Shah 'Abdol 'Azim (Galbraith 1989). Even more important than railroads was the telegraph. Here, too, Gasteiger was a pioneer. In 1864, the shah asked him to help build the line between Tehran and Isfahan and towards Shiraz. He worked on it long enough to experience the many obstacles involved, including the obstructionist practices of the local population who were in the habit of stealing the poles (Praxmarer 2013: 67–75).[19]

Some scholars attribute Iran's uneven development in this period in equal measure to Qajar mismanagement and Russian and British political machinations. They point to rent-seeking elites and Iran's backward infrastructure, but also argue that the two outside powers,

---

to be hauled from the Caspian Sea across the rain-soaked, heavily forested province of Mazandaran, at enormous cost, which included the loss of 50 lives. See Polak (1865, Vol. 2: 53–4).

[19] For more information on the building of the telegraph, see Rubin (1999).

by making the country dependent on them, prevented it from developing economically (see, for example, Amirahmadi 2012). There is no question that the policies of Russia and Great Britain gave their own merchants and entrepreneurs a critical advantage vis-à-vis Iranian merchants and manufacturers. Yet their economic initiatives were mostly private in nature. At no point did the British government put its full weight behind ventures, in part not to antagonize the Russians, but more so because the 'City' (of London) showed great reluctance to invest in Iran without formal guarantees, deeming it a country of high risk and low return (Ross 2009: 391). As for the Russians, they too engaged with Iran as private entrepreneurs and, to the extent that the state was involved, trade with Iran was an instrument of political considerations rather than just a matter of economic strategy (Entner 1956: 62).

However, the effects of the foreign presence and intrusion were not all negative. Russian and British influence did little to foster a print culture similar to what was rapidly developed, along with literacy rates, in Western Europe at the time. But the opening of Iran's markets by foreign powers, whether done by way of enforced low toll and tax rates or in collaboration with Iran's ruling classes, arguably *created* as many opportunities for growth as it stifled domestic entrepreneurship.

A good example of opportunities created by Iran's growing entanglement with the world is the increase in the production of tobacco, cotton, and opium as new market-driven cash crops in the 1860s. The development was clearly part of Iran's integration into the 'international capitalist framework', whereby local labour was exploited to produce commodities for world markets. Yet the same development had a positive effect on the country's balance of trade, and it provided opportunities for domestic entrepreneurs. Lured by the prospect of better profits than could be made on cereals, taking advantage of recent improvements in cultivation and processing techniques, and utilizing newly created regular steam-driven shipping facilities between Iran and India, these began to invest massively in the production for export of the high-quality opium yielded by Iran's soil and climate. Opium especially became such a lucrative business that it turned into a means of payment, corrupting the business climate. The boom in opium production also upended traditional agricultural patterns, contributing to a shortage of cereals and the ensuing famine of 1870–1. Most importantly, in the absence of land and labour reform, the opium bonanza mostly benefited large landowners and merchants (Walcher 2008: 19). In other words, a frequent conflation in the scholarly literature notwithstanding, being drawn into an international capitalist framework did not automatically entail capitalist development in Iran. As Vries reminds us, economic growth is not the same as capitalism, even if in practice the two usually go together (Vries 2013: 24).

Carpet weaving is the best example of a traditional craft that saw tremendous growth in output as well as employment as a result of foreign-led private enterprise. For all their later fame, Persian carpets had never been an important Iranian export product. Demand surged following the 1851 Crystal Palace Exhibition in London as well as the revival of the decorative arts in Britain. Europe's growing interest in handmade carpets in the 1860s led a German carpet consortium to explore expansion in Iran. The result was the creation of a series of village looms where carpets were made according to German tastes and shapes, with aniline dyes. The centre of this proto-capitalist enterprise became Soltanabad, modern Arak (Helfgott 1994: 210–14). Further development occurred after the originally Swiss Ziegler Company of Manchester purchased the German enterprise in the early 1880s. Originally engaged in the business of exporting Manchester cotton goods to West Asia, Ziegler & Co. first set up shop in the Black Sea port of Trabzon in 1856, at that time the main commercial outlet for Iranian products. Faced with increasing European demand leading to a depletion of available carpets in Iran, and unable to count on an unreliable putting-out system, the company in the early 1870s decided to branch out to Iran by sending a representative to Soltanabad to organize and develop a modern carpet production. One reason for entering the Iranian market was an age-old problem: a lack of Iranian export products. The company was paid for its cotton piece-goods in Iranian silver, which it converted into Russian gold coins. These were then sent to Russia to be converted into sterling and transferred to London via the British banking system, pointing to the difficulties resulting from the absence of a proper banking system in Iran until the 1880s—when the first bank, the Imperial Bank of Persia, came into being, under British auspices

(Wynn 2008: 59). This type of transaction was evidently complicated and cumbersome. Conditions worsened when Iranian silver
underwent a tremendous depreciation as of the 1870s, causing the
kran to devaluate dramatically. The Iranian government, faced with
a rapidly declining stock of silver, reacted by banning silver exports.
This necessitated an intensified focus on the export of goods, leading
to a surge in the export of carpets, opium, tobacco, and cotton.

Ziegler & Co. did not enter the Iranian rug market just to
reinvest profits from the sale of cottons in Iran. In addition to carpets, they imported a variety of products—sugar, copper, cottons,
candles—and exported opium, pistachios, kilims, Kerman shawls,
and Yazd brocades. The company created an entire infrastructure in
and around the rapidly expanding town of Soltanabad, providing
healthcare and constructing a network of regional roads (Helfgott
1994: 215–24). Ziegler & Co. next opened branches in various other
Iranian cities. The result was an increase in looms from 40 in c. 1870
to 1,200 in c. 1880 in Soltanabad, and c. 5,000 in the surrounding
area, a decade later (Floor 2003: 10–11). The value of exports via
Tabriz increased from 28,000 *tumans* in 1874 to 500,000 tumans at
turn of the twentieth century (Wynn 2008: 60).

A final example of a proto-capitalist initiative, this time with official Qajar state support, occurred in the Caspian provinces. In the
1880s, the mining potential of the region caught the eye of Hajji
Mohammad Hasan, aka Amin al-Zarb, Iran's foremost entrepreneur
at the time. Amin al-Zarb, who was also in charge of Iran's mints,
was very impressed with Western technology and brought the idea
to the attention of the shah. He next received a royal concession
for the development of a mine and a smelting plant near Amol in
Mazandaran, as well as the right to exploit mineral resources, except
for gold, and land in the surrounding area. He engaged French mining engineers for these various projects. But he soon gave up, realizing
that given the enormous transportation costs, the iron produced in
his plant would never be profitable. Under royal pressure, he resumed
the project after conceiving of a connection to Mahmudabad on the
coast in the form of a 12-mile horse-drawn railway. He also received
a concession to build a road from Amol to Tehran. He next went to
Belgium to engage engineers and to purchase railroad equipment
from Cockerill & Co. of Liège.

The project got underway in 1887–8 but soon faced major problems. Local villagers, incited by a chieftain who intended to purchase the land through which the railroad would run, attacked and beat the foreign workers. The confrontation between foreign employees and Iranians also involved purchase of substandard material, theft of equipment, and intrigue against the foreign employees and attempts to make them leave so locals could take over (Olson 1980). The project thus interrupted, the tracks were left to wither. One more attempt to revive it, with participation of Russian entrepreneurs, was unsuccessful, in part because of the death of Amin al-Zarb in 1898 and in part because the Russian Mercury Steamship Company refused to have its vessels call at Mahmudabad. According to unconfirmed reports, the abandoned tracks were subsequently destroyed at the order of the Tehran government for fear that they might facilitate an attack by Russia on the capital (Kazembeyki 2003: 74–5).

***

Various structural, geographical and economic conditions impeded the development of indigenous, self-sustaining economic growth and technological development, and thus, the arrival of industrial capitalism on the Iranian plateau. Among these, a harsh physical environment marked by low rainfall, the difficulty of exploiting metal deposits, and the precarious access to blue water must count as the underlying ones. The result, low productivity and a scantiness of export commodities, would bedevil Iran throughout the early modern period and really until the discovery and exploitation of oil in the early twentieth century.

Human ingenuity might have helped overcome these impediments. Pre-twentieth-century Iran evinces an abundance of entrepreneurial energy and intellectual curiosity. But these traits were circumscribed in scope and effect. Science remained speculative rather than applied, limiting the development of 'useful' knowledge and the manipulation of nature for the benefit of human material well-being.

Behind it all stood a state that was at once invasive and uninvolved. Most recent studies about the development of capitalism in world history focus on the power of the state in either facilitating or hampering economic development. Traditional notions about the Middle Eastern state as a Leviathan notwithstanding, the early modern Iranian state was neither particularly strong in its 'infrastructural' capacity, nor 'benevolent and quite efficient', to use a term controversially applied to the contemporary Chinese state (Wong 1997).[20] The Safavids were mostly interested in maintaining internal stability, in contrast to early modern European states such as England, France, and Holland, which stimulated growth by engaging in relentless competition. With the partial exception of the reign of Shah 'Abbas I, early modern Iran saw little *systemic, sustained, and self-reinforcing* state support for commercial and artisanal activity and expansion. If anything, Shah 'Abbas's successors 'disengaged', both from their domestic realm, by giving up on their ambulant and surveilling lifestyle, and from their neighbours, most notably by way of ceasing to fight them (Marks 2016: 98). Matters worsened with the fall of the Safavids. Political chaos engulfed Iran for the duration of the eighteenth century, just as the overland trade to Europe declined and international trade increasingly became maritime trade, leading to the country's virtual disengagement from the world, its commercial currents, and its many technological breakthroughs.

Little changed in Iran's state structure with the advent of the Qajars, who were thoroughly traditional rulers who kept selling offices to the highest bidder and who followed ill-advised policies trying to overcome the effects of systemic budget deficits. Reforms, such as they were, continued to be spasmodic, individually driven rather than sustained by long-term planning, and initiated by forward-looking officials—men who lacked the ruler's unqualified support and whose death or demotion through intrigue would inevitably doom the initiative—rather than by the shah.

Iran's growing dependence on Russia and Britain, politically as well as economically, on balance had a negative effect as well, in that these powers imposed an economic regime on Iran that favoured their own merchants. Their mutually exclusive interests, moreover, effectively contributed to the country's continued infrastructural backwardness. Yet it would be a mistake to just blame foreigners for the further

---

[20] For a critique, see Vries (2015: 22, 138–63).

delay in Iran's economic development. For all the stifling effect of their political manipulation, they did help private entrepreneurs make investments, as is exemplified in the foreign-led growth of the carpet industry. It is tempting to dismiss this type of 'development' as a form of exploitation and 'dependency' that little benefitted Iran or even caused the country's economy and living standards to decline. In reality, the late nineteenth century seems to have been marked by overall growth amid the persistence of widespread deprivation and misery.[21]

By the century's end, Iran had a telegraph system, some metalled roads, and a few fledgling industries. Yet, comparatively little had been accomplished, either by private enterprise or by way of government-sponsored projects. As H.W. Maclean, reporting on the country's industry and manufacturing, observed in 1904, 'Industrial and manufacturing enterprises in Persia have rarely met with success, the number of such undertakings of any magnitude which have survived more than a year or two is small' (quoted in Schneider 1990: 141). Only the onset of the oil economy followed by Reza Shah's modernizing regime in the early twentieth century would provide the impetus for the development of modern capitalism.

Bibliography

NA. National Archives, London.

Col Abbott. FO 60/165. 'Notes on Various Cities and Countries of Southern Persia', 1849–50, NA, fols 23–5, 100.

———. FO 60/165. 'Report on the Commerce of South Persia', NA, fol. 38.

FO 248/218. Dickson, Gulhak, to Alison, London, 3 July 1865.

Adelman, Jeremy. 2015. 'What Caused Capitalism? Assessing the Roles of the West and the Rest.' *Foreign Affairs* 94(3): 136–44.

Amirahmadi, Hooshang. 2012. *The Political Economy of Iran under the Qajars*. London: I.B. Tauris.

---

[21] For the opening up of the Karun River, see Shahnavaz (2005), who sees this as having little benefitted Iran. For the debate on the state of Iran's economy, see Gilbar (1976, 1986) and Floor (2003: 15–23).

Anievas, Alexander and Kerem Nişancioğlu. 2017. 'How Did the West Usurp the Rest? Origins of the Great Divergence over the Longue Durée.' *Comparative Studies in History and Society* 59(1): 34–67.

Anonymous, ed. (1930) 2012. *A Chronicle of the Carmelites of Persia. The Safavids and the Papal Mission of the 17th and 18th Centuries.* 2 Vols. Paginated as one. London: Spottiswood; repr. I.B. Tauris.

Anzali, Ata. 2017. *Mysticism in Iran. The Safavid Roots of a Modern Concept.* Columbia: University of South Carolina Press.

Ashraf, Ahmad. 1969. 'Historical Obstacles to the Formation of a Bourgeoisie in Iran.' *Iranian Studies* 2(2–3): 54–79.

Aslanian, Sebouh David. 2011. *From the Indian Ocean to the Mediterranean. The Global Networks of Armenian Merchants from New Julfa.* Berkeley: University of California Press.

Beckert, Sven. 2014. *Empire and Cotton: A Global History.* New York: Knopf.

Binning, Robert B.M. 1857. *A Journal of Two Years' Travel in Persia.* 2 Vols. London: W.H. Allen and Company.

Blau, Ernst Otto F.H. 1858. *Commercielle Zustände Persiens [Commercial Conditions in Persia].* Berlin: Königliche geheime Oberhofbuchdruckerei.

Brandon, Pepijn. 2015. *War, Capital, and the Dutch State (1588–1795).* Leiden: Brill.

Brentjes, Sonja. 2004. 'Early Modern Western European Travellers in the Middle East and Their Reports about the Sciences.' In *Sciences, techniques et instruments dans le monde iranien (Xe-XIXe siècle) [Science, Techniques and Instruments in the Iranian World, 10th–19th Centuries]*, edited by N. Pourjavady and Ž. Vesel, pp. 379–420. Tehran.

Buck, Howard. 2015. 'Review of Neil and Willliamson (eds). *The Cambridge History of Capitalism*, Vol. 1.' *Economic History Review* 68(3): 1083–4.

Chardin, Jean. 1810–11. *Voyages du chevalier Chardin, en Perse, et autres lieux de l'Orient [Travels of the Chevalier Chardin, in Persia and Other Parts of the Orient]*, edited by Louis Langlès. 10 Vols and map. Paris: Le Normant.

De Bary, W. Theodore. 1975. 'Neo-Confucian Cultivation and the Seventeenth-Century Enlightenment', In W. Theodore De Bary, ed., *The Unfolding of Neo-Confucianism*, pp. 141–206. New York: Columbia University Press.

Entner, Marvin L. 1956. *Russo-Persian Commercial Relations, 1828–1914.* Gainesville, FL: University of Florida Press.

Floor, Willem. 1977. 'Bankruptcy in Qajar Iran.' *Zeitschrift der Deutschen Morgenländischen Gesellschaft* 127(1): 62–4.

———. 1990. 'ČĀP.' *Encyclopaedia Iranica* 4: 760–4.

————. 2003. *Agriculture in Qajar Iran.* Washington, DC: Mage Publishers.

————. 2009. *Labor & Industry in Iran 1850–1941.* Washington, DC: Mage Publishers.

————. 2016. *Bushehr. City, Society & Trade 1797–1947.* Washington, DC: Mage Publishers.

Fryer, John. A. 1909–15 [1967]. *A New Account of East India and Persia, Being 9 Years' Travels, 1672–1681,* edited by W. Crooke. 3 Vols. London: Hakluyt; repr. 1967 Millwood: NY: Kraus Reprint.

Galbraith, John S. 1989. 'British Policy on Railways in Persia, 1870–1900.' *Middle Eastern Studies* 25(4): 480–505.

Gilbar, Gad. 1976. 'Demographic Developments in Late Qajar Persia, 1870–1906.' *Asian and African Studies* 11(2): 125–56.

————. 1986. 'The Opening Up of the Qajar Iran. Some Economic and Social Aspects.' *Bulletin of the School of Oriental and African Studies* 49(1): 76–89.

Gosh, Shami. 2015. 'How Should We Approach the Economy of Early Modern India?' *Modern Asian Studies* 49(5): 1606–56.

Greenfield, James. 1904. *Die Verfassung des persischen Staates [The Constitution of the Persian State].* Berlin: Verlag von Franz Vahlen.

Gurney, John. 1986. 'Pietro della Valle. The Limits of Perception.' *Bulletin of the School of Oriental and African Studies* 49(1): 112–15.

Habibi, Negar. 2017. *'Ali Qoli Jebādār et l'Occidentalisme Safavide. Une étude sur les peintures dites farangi sāzi, leurs milieux et commanditaires sous Shāh Soleymān (1666–1694) ['Ali Qoli Jebādār and Safavid Occidentalism. A Study on So-Called Farangi-sāzi Paintings, Milieu and Patronage].* Leiden: Brill.

Helfgott, Leonard M. 1994. *Ties That Bind. A Social History of the Iranian Carpet.* Washington and London: Smithsonian Press.

Issawi, Charles. 1970. 'The Tabriz–Trabzon Trade, 1830–1900: Rise and Decline of a Route.' *International Journal of Middle East Studies* 1(1): 18–27.

————, ed. 1971. *The Economic History of Iran 1800–1914.* Chicago: University of Chicago Press.

Kaempfer, Engelbert. 2001. *Briefe, 1683–1715 [Letters, 1683–1715],* edited by Detlef Haberland. Munich: Iudicium Verlag.

————. 2018. *Exotic Attractions in Persia, 1684–1688: Travels & Observations.* Translated and edited by Willem Floor and Colette Ouahes. Washington, DC: Mage Publishers.

Katouzian, Homa. 2003. 'The Aridisolatic Society: A Model of Long-Term Social and Political Development in Iran.' In *Iranian History and Politics. The Dialectics of State and Society,* pp. 61–76. London and New York: Routledge.

Kazembeyki, Mohammad Ali. 2003. *Society, Politics and Economics in Māzandarān, Iran, 1848–1914*. London: Curzon.

Kazemi, Ranin. 2017. 'The Black Winter of 1860–61: War, Famine, and the Political Ecology of Disasters in Qajar Iran.' *Comparative Studies in South Asia, Africa and the Middle East* 37(1): 24–48.

Kocka, Jürgen. 2016. *Capitalism. A Short History*. Princeton: Princeton University Press.

Neal, Larry. 2014. 'Introduction.' In *The Cambridge History of Capitalism*, edited by L. Neil and J.G. Williamson. 2 Vols. Cambridge: Cambridge University Press.

Madani, S. Djalal. 1986. *Iranische Politik und Drittes Reich [Iranian Policies and the Third Reich]*. Frankfurt a/M, Bern, New York: Peter Lang.

Mahdavi, Shireen. 1999. *For God, Mammon and Country. A Nineteenth-Century Persian Merchant*. Boulder, CO: Westview Press.

Mann, Michael. (1986) 1995. *The Social Origins of Power*, Vol. I, *A History of Power from the Beginning to A.D. 1760*. Cambridge: Cambridge University Press.

Marks, Steven G. 2016. *The Information Nexus. Global Capitalism from the Renaissance to the Present*. Cambridge: Cambridge University Press.

Marzolph, Ulrich and Anja Pistor-Hatam. 2002. 'Zur frühen Druckgeschichte in Iran (1817 bis ca. 1900) [On the Early History of Printing in Iran, from 1817 until c. 1900].' In *Sprachen des nahen Ostens und die Druckrevolution/Middle Eastern Languages and the Print Revolution*, edited by Eva Hanebutt-Benz, Dagmar Glass, and Geoffrey Roper, pp. 249–72. Werthofen: WVA-Verlag.

Matthee, Rudi. 1991. 'The Career of Mohammad Beg. Grand Vizier of Shah 'Abbas II (r. 1642–1666).' *Iranian Studies* 24: 17–36.

———. 1995. 'Changing the Mintmaster. The Introduction of Mechanized Minting in Qajar Iran.' *Itinerario: European Journal of Overseas History* 19: 109–29.

———. 2000. 'Merchants in Safavid Iran: Participants and Perceptions.' *Journal of Early Modern History* 4(3–4): 233–68.

———. 2013. 'Iran's Relations with Europe in the Safavid Period: Diplomats, Missionaries, Merchants and Travel.' In *The Fascination of Persia: Persian-European Dialogue in Seventeenth-Century Art & Contemporary Art of Teheran*, edited by Axel Langer. Zurich: Scheidegger and Spiess.

Matthee, Rudi, Willem Floor, and Patrick Clawson. 2013. *The Monetary History of Iran, from the Safavids to the Qajars*. London: I.B. Tauris.

Mohebbi, Parviz. 1996. *Techniques et ressources en Iran du 7e au 19e siècle [Techniques and Resources in Iran from the 7th to the 19th Century]*. Tehran: Institut français de recherche en Iran.

Mokyr, Joel. 2017. *A Culture of Growth. The Origins of the Modern Economy*. Princeton: Princeton University Press.

Okazaki, Shoko. 1986. 'The Great Persian Famine of 1870–71.' *Bulletin of the School of Oriental and African Studies* 49(1): 183–92.

Olson, William J. 1980. 'The Mazandaran Development Project and Haji Mohammad Hasan: A Study in Persian Entrepreneurship, 1884–1898.' In *Toward a Modern Iran: Studies in Thought, Politics and Society*, edited by Elie Kedourie and Sylvia Haim, pp. 38–55. London: Frank Cass.

Pamuk, Şevket. 2014. 'Economic Development in the Middle East, 700–1800.' In *The Cambridge History of Capitalism*, Vol. 1, edited by Larry Neil and J.G. Willliamson, pp. 193–224. Cambridge: Cambridge University Press.

Polak, Jakob Eduard. 1865. *Persien. Das Land und seine Bewohner* [*Persia. The Country and Its Inhabitants*]. 2 Vols. Leipzig: F. A. Brockhaus.

Pourjavady, Reza, and Schmidtke, Sabine. 2015. 'An Eastern Renaissance? Greek Philosophy under the Safavids (16th to 18th Centuries).' *Intellectual History of the Islamicate World* 3(1–2): 248–90.

Praxmarer, Hieronymus. 2013. *Albert Gasteiger Khan (1823–1890)* [*Albert Gasteiger Khan (1823–1890). Travel Reports from Persia to Tirol*]. *Reisebriefe aus Persien nach Tirol*. Innsbruck: Universitätsverlag Wagner.

Richard, Francis. 1980. 'Un témoignage sur les débuts de l'imprimérie de Nor Jula.' *Revue des Etudes Arméniennes* [*A Witness to the Beginnings of Printing in New Julfa*], n.s. 14: 483–4.

———. 1990. 'Capuchins in Persia.' *Encyclopaedia Iranica* 4: 786–88. London and New York: Routlege and Kegan Paul.

———, ed. 1995. *Raphaël du Mans missionnaire en Perse au XVIIe siècle* [*Raphaël du Mans Missionary in Persia in the 17th Century*]. 2 Vols. Paris: L'Harmattan.

Rizvi, Sajjad. 2007. *Mulla Sadra Shirazi: His Life and Works and the Sources for Safavid Philosophy*. Oxford: Oxford University Press.

Ross, C.N.B. 2009. 'Lord Curzon and E.G. Browne Confront the 'Persian Question.' *The Historical Journal* 52(2): 385–411.

Roy, Tirthankar. 2013. *An Economic History of Early Modern India*. Cambridge: Cambridge University Press.

———. 2014. 'Capitalism in Indian in the Very Long Run.' In *The Cambridge History of Capitalism*, Vol. 1, edited by L. Neil and J.G. Willliamson, p. 165. Cambridge: Cambridge University Press.

Rubin, Michael. 1999. 'The Formation of Modern Iran: Telegraph, Imperialism and Society.' PhD dissertation, Yale University.

Sanson, N. 1694. *Voyage ou relation de l'estat présent du royaume de Perse* [*Voyage or Account of the Current State of the Kingdom of Persia*]. Paris: La veuve de Jacques Langlois et Jacques Langlois.

Schneider, Manfred. 1990. *Beiträge zur Wirtschaftsstruktur und Wirtschaftsentwicklung Persiens 1850–1900* [*Contributions to the Economic Structure and Economic Development of Persia, 1850–1900*]. Stuttgart: Franz Steiner.

Shahnavaz, Shahbaz. 2005. *Britain and the Opening Up of South-West Persia 1880–1914. A Study in Imperialism and Economic Independence.* Abington, Oxon and New York: Routledge.

Tavernier, Jean-Baptiste. 1676. *Les six voyages de Jean-Baptiste Tavernier en Turquie en Perse, et aux Indes* [*The Six Voyages of Jean-Baptiste Tavernier in Turkey, Persia and India*]. 2 Vols. Paris: 1676.

Vali, Abbas. 1993. *Pre-capitalist Iran. A Theoretical History.* London and New York: I.B. Tauris.

Vries, Peer. 2013. *Escaping Poverty: The Origins of Modern Economic Growth.* Vienna: Österreichische Akademie der Wissenschaften.

———. 2015. *State, Economy and the Great Divergence. Great Britain and China, 1680s–1850s.* London and New York: Bloomsbury Academic.

Walcher, Heidi A. 2008. *In the Shadow of the King. Zill al-Sultan and Isfahan under the Qajars.* London and New York: I.B. Tauris.

Wigham, H. J. 1903. *The Persian Problem. An Examination of the Rival Positions of Russia and Great Britain in Persia with some Account of the Persian Gulf and the Baghdad Railway.* New York: Scribner's.

Windler, Christian. 2018. *Missionare in Persien. Kulturelle Diversität und Normenkonkurrenz im globalen Katholizismus (17.–18. Jahrhundert)* [*Missionaries in Persia. Cultural Diversity and Norm Competition in Global Catholicsm (17–18th Century)*]. Cologne, Weimar, Vienna: Böhlau Verlag.

Wong, Bin. 1997. *China Transformed and the Limits of European Experience.* Ithaca and London: Cornell University Press.

Wynn, Antony. 2008. *Three Camels to Smyrna. Times of War and Peace in turkey, Persia, India, Afghanistan & Nepal 1907–1986. The Story of the Oriental Carpet Manufacturers Company.* London: Estate of the Late Bryan Meredith Huffner.

Yazdani, Kaveh. 2017. *India, Modernity and the Great Divergence. Mysore and Gujarat (17th to 19th C.).* Leiden: Brill.

Editors and Contributors

Editors

Dilip M. Menon is the Mellon Chair of Indian Studies and the director of the Centre for Indian Studies in Africa at the University of Witwatersrand, Johannesburg, South Africa. He pursued his education in Delhi, Oxford, and Cambridge, and received his PhD from the University of Cambridge. He has taught at the University of Cambridge, UK; the University of Yale, USA; the University of Delhi, India; and the University of the Witwatersrand. His research is centred on the social and intellectual history of modern India and, more recently, on the epistemologies and histories of the Global South. His published works include *Caste Nationalism and Communism in South India* (1994), *Saraswativijayam* (2002), *The Blindness of Insight: Essays on Caste in Modern India* (2006), and an edited volume, *Cultural History of Modern India* (2007). His interests include films, literature, and jazz.

Kaveh Yazdani is the author of *India, Modernity and the Great Divergence: Mysore and Gujarat* (2017). He received his PhD in social sciences (summa cum laude) from the University of Osnabrück, Germany, in 2014. He was granted the Prince Dr Sabbar Farman-Farmaian fellowship at the International Institute of Social History in Amsterdam in 2015 and received the title of Mellon Postdoctoral Research Fellow at the Centre for Indian Studies in Africa, the University of the Witwatersrand, Johannesburg in 2015–17, where he now holds the position of a research associate. He was a visiting residential fellow at the Warwick Institute of Advanced Study, United Kingdom, in 2017 and received the Newton International

Fellowship by the British Academy in 2018–20 (declined). He is currently working as a lecturer in economic history at the University of Bielefeld, Germany. His publications and forthcoming projects raise questions about modernity, capitalist development, the 'Great Divergence' debate, as well as the socio-economic, labour and intellectual history of South and West Asia and Europe (seventeenth to twentieth centuries).

Contributors

Kent Deng is professor of economic history at the London School of Economics, UK, and fellow of the Royal Historical Society. He joined The London School of Economics in 1995 from Victoria University of Wellington, New Zealand, where he was a senior lecturer. His research covers both premodern and modern China in a range of fields, including farming, commerce, education, governance, and foreign relations. He is the author of *Mapping China's Growth and Development in the Long Run* (2015) and *China's Political Economy in Modern Times: Changes and Economic Consequences 1800–2000* (2011). He has also co-authored *State Failure and Distorted Urbanisation in Post-Mao's China, 1993–2012* (2018).

Dennis O. Flynn is professor emeritus of economics at University of the Pacific, Stockton, California, USA (1979–2014), and director at Pacific World History Institute (2000–present). His PhD dissertation was titled *The Spanish Price Revolution and the Monetary Approach to the Balance of Payments* (1977) and linked accepted international monetary theory with silver history. He also co-created a basic economic model with Kerry Doherty in the mid-1980s.

Anne Gerritsen is professor at the Department of History and director at Global History and Culture Centre at the University of Warwick, UK. She is the Chair of Asian Art since 2018 and was the Kikkoman Chair for Asia–Europe Exchange since 2013 at Leiden University, the Netherlands. She has earned her PhD from Harvard University, USA. Her book on the local and global history of ceramics manufactures in Jingdezhen is titled *The City of Blue and White: Chinese Porcelain and the Early Modern World* (2020). She has co-edited several volumes on global material culture and the history of gift-giving with Giorgio Riello and Zoltan Biedermann, and on micro-spatial histories of labour with Christian de Vito. More recently, she has been working on the global circulation of medical commodities, specifically rhubarb, and holds a seed-grant from the Wellcome Trust, London, UK, to develop a research network on this subject.

Nelly Hanna is Distinguished University Professor and Chair of the Department of Arab and Islamic Civilizations at the American University, Cairo, Egypt. She has been a visiting professor and guest lecturer at the École des Hautes Études en Sciences Sociales (EHESS), Paris, France, in 1998; at Harvard University, USA, in 2001; and at Waseda University, Tokyo, Japan, in 2008–9. Her scholarly interest has been on Ottoman Egypt (1500–1800). Her work is focused to a large extent on the social groups outside the establishment, such as artisans, traders, and merchants, with a special emphasis on the economy and its impact on culture and society. She has published in English, French, and Arabic.

Henry Heller is professor of history at the University of Manitoba, Winnipeg, Canada. His recent publications include *A Marxist History of Capitalism* (2018), 'Class and Class Struggle' (*The Oxford Handbook of Karl Marx*, 2018), and *The Capitalist University: The Transformations of Higher Education in the United States Since 1945* (2016).

Joseph E. Inikori is professor of history at the University of Rochester, New York, USA. He is also a fellow of the Nigerian Academy of Letters. He was previously chairman of the Department of History, Ahmadu Bello University, Zaria, Nigeria. One of the pioneers of Atlantic World history, he has published extensively on Atlantic World economic history. His most recent book in the field, *Africans and the Industrial Revolution in England: A Study in International Trade and Economic Development* (2002), won the 2003 American Historical Association's Leo Gershoy Award for 'the most outstanding work in English on any aspect of the field of seventeenth- and eighteenth-century western European history' and the 2003 African Studies Association's Herskovits Award.

Leonardo Marques is professor of history of the colonial Americas at the Universidade Federal Fluminense, Niterói, Brazil. He is the author of *The United States and the Transatlantic Slave Trade to the Americas, 1776–1867* (2016) and *Por Aí e por Muito Longe: dívidas migrações e os libertos de 1888* [Near and Far Away: Debts, Migrations, and the Freedmen of 1888] (2009). His work has also appeared in eminent journals such as *Journal of Latin American Studies*, *Journal of the Early Republic*, and *Afro-Ásia*. His current research explores the connections between gold mining in Brazil and the slave trade in West Africa during the eighteenth century.

Rudi Matthee is the John and Dorothy Munroe Distinguished Professor of Middle Eastern history at the University of Delaware, USA. He currently serves as the co-editor of *Der Islam* and as a consulting editor for the *Encyclopaedia Iranica*. He is also currently president of the Persian Heritage Foundation, Fresno, California, USA. He works on the political and socio-economic history of early modern Iran and its connections with the wider world. He is the author of four prize-winning scholarly books, most recently *The Monetary History of Iran* (2013 [co-authored]), and the co-editor of five other books. He is the former president of the Association for the Study of Persianate Societies (2002–5 and 2008–11).

Masaki Nakabayashi is professor of economics at the Institute of Social Sciences, the University of Tokyo, Japan. He has earned his PhD in history from the University of Tokyo. He taught at the Department of Economics, Chiba University, Japan, from 1999 to 2002 and the Graduate School of Economics, Osaka University, Japan, from 2002 to 2008 as an associate professor of economic history. He joined the Institute of Social Sciences at the University of Tokyo in 2008 as an associate professor of economics. There, he teaches at the Graduate School of Economics, which is jointly organized by the Faculty of Economics and the Institute of Social Science. His research interests include the economic history of Japan, institutional and organizational economics, Comparative Institutional Analysis, and development economics, adopting descriptive, empirical, and theoretical approaches. His teaching experience as a visiting instructor includes places such as Keio

University, Japan; Free University of Berlin, Germany; and EHESS, Paris, France.

Alessandro Stanziani is professor of global history at École des hautes études en sciences sociales (EHES), Paris, France, and research director at Centre national de la recherche scientifique, Paris, France. He is also the current director at the Institute of Global Studies, Université Paris Sciences et Lettres, Paris, France. His main fields of interest include global history, labour history, Russian history (sixteenth to twentieth centuries), labour and the Indian Ocean (eighteenth to nineteenth centuries), economic, business, and labour history in Europe, particularly in France and Britain (eighteenth and early twentieth centuries), and food history (eighteenth to twentieth centuries).

He has also edited and co-edited eight books, and some of his publications include *L'économie en révolution. Le cas russe, 1870–1930* (1998), *Histoire de la qualité alimentaire, 18e–20e siècles* (2005), *Rules of Exchange: French Capitalism in Comparative Perspective, 18th–20th Centuries* (2012), *Seamen, Immigrants and Convicts in the Indian Ocean, 18th–Early 20th Centuries* (2014), and *Eurocentrism and the Politics of Global History* (2018).

Eric Tagliacozzo is professor of history at Cornell University, USA, where he teaches primarily Southeast Asian history. He is also director at the Comparative Muslim Societies Program (CMS) as well as of the Cornell Modern Indonesia Project (CMIP) at Cornell University, New York, USA, and the co-editor of the journal *INDONESIA*. He is the author of *Secret Trades, Porous Borders: Smuggling and States along a Southeast Asian Frontier, 1865–1915* (2005), which won the Harry Benda Prize from the Association of Asian Studies in 2007. He has also authored *The Longest Journey: Southeast Asians and the Pilgrimage to Mecca* (2013), and has edited or co-edited 10 other books on a variety of trans-regional Asian historical topics.

David Washbrook is a fellow of Trinity College, Cambridge, UK, and an emeritus fellow of St Antony's College, Oxford, UK. He has taught at the Universities of Cambridge, Oxford, Warwick, UK, as well as at the University of Pennsylvania and Harvard University,

USA. His main research interests lie in social and economic history and in southern India between the eighteenth and twenty-first centuries, on which has published extensively. His co-edited volumes include the *Routledge Handbook of the South Asian Diaspora* (2013) (with Joya Chatterji) and *Religious Cultures in Early Modern India: New Perspectives* (2012) (with Rosalind O'Hanlon).

Index

comparative Eurasian standards,
134
development of Europe and,
139–40
'dualism' thesis, 132
ecological issues, 135
eighteenth century, 144–5
fastest-growing capitalist
economy, 147–8
hidden nature of private trade,
140
impact of Industrial Revolution,
145–6
'interior' economy, 135
and Marxism, 142
mobility and exchange, 135–6
modern economic growth,
132–3, 137–8, 140
multilateral trades, 141–2
neo-traditional structures, 147
nineteenth century, 145–6
pre-colonial situation, 142–4
pre-modern history, 133–4
private rights, 137
property right, 136
rise of Mughal consumption,
133
seventeenth century textile
industry, 140–1
state system, transformation of,
144–5
industrial capitalism, 3, 10, 18, 27,
59, 135, 162, 212, 270, 307
industrial capitalist, 266
Industrial Revolution, 2, 3, 15, 22,
23, 168, 271
and New World rubber for
gaskets, 39
plantation experts immersed
in, 87
slave-produced cotton and, 88

Inikori, Joseph E., 22, 85
international capitalism, 20
Iranian capitalism, 349–75
'caravan termini', 363
carpet weaving, 371–2
consequential 'impediment' to,
356–7
and mercantilism in Europe,
355–6
overview, 349–52
Qajar period, developments in,
363–73
reign of Mohammad Shah, 367
road construction (1861), 369
Safavid period, conditions in,
352–61
Safavid and Qajar periods,
between, 361–3
Ziegler & Co., 372
Italian capitalism, 207

Japan
Dojima Rice Exchange, 296
Meiji Restoration, 295–6
Japan, capitalism in, 23–4
Edo Shogunate (1600–1868),
285–93
Kamakura Shogunate (1185–
1333), 282–4
Meiji Restoration, 23–4, 279,
281
middle modern, 23–4
Muromachi Shogunate
(1336–1573), 284–5
overview, 277–81
Pax Tokugawa, 49–50
per capita gross domestic
product (GDP), 280–1
regulation and deregulation in,
277–97
silver mining, 48–9